Lecture Notes in Artificial Intelligence 13132

Subseries of Lecture Notes in Computer Science

More information about this subseries at https://link.springer.com/bookseries/1244

Rachid Alami · Joydeep Biswas · Maya Cakmak ·
Oliver Obst (Eds.)

RoboCup 2021: Robot World Cup XXIV

 Springer

Editors
Rachid Alami ⓘ
LAAS-CNRS/ANITI
Toulouse, France

Joydeep Biswas ⓘ
The University of Texas at Austin
Austin, TX, USA

Maya Cakmak ⓘ
University of Washington
Seattle, WA, USA

Oliver Obst ⓘ
Western Sydney University
Penrith, NSW, Australia

ISSN 0302-9743   ISSN 1611-3349 (electronic)
Lecture Notes in Artificial Intelligence
ISBN 978-3-030-98681-0   ISBN 978-3-030-98682-7 (eBook)
https://doi.org/10.1007/978-3-030-98682-7

LNCS Sublibrary: SL7 – Artificial Intelligence

This Springer imprint is published by the registered company Springer Nature Switzerland AG
The registered company address is: Gewerbestrasse 11, 6330 Cham, Switzerland

Preface

RoboCup 2021 was held under unprecedented circumstances – the COVID-19 pandemic resulted in the cancellation of RoboCup 2020, and precipitated the decision to move RoboCup 2021 to an online event. Despite the many challenges, the RoboCup community came together to create an online event to great success – leagues adopted creative solutions to hold competitions in extensive simulation environments, remote hardware challenges took place via video-conferencing, and through it all succeeded in bringing together the community for a week of competitions, discussions, and presentations.

As a challenging multidisciplinary endeavor, RoboCup has the opportunity to highlight advances in robotics research that translate to better, faster, safer, more capable robots - and competition wins. This book presents the science behind the advances in robotics, including the key innovations that led the winning teams to their success, and the outcomes of research inspired by challenges across the different leagues at RoboCup.

The RoboCup 2021 symposium received a total of 42 regular research paper submissions. The submissions were reviewed by the Program Committee of 51 members, producing three reviews per paper. The committee carefully weighed the merits and limitations of each paper, and accepted 19 papers for inclusion in the symposium, for an overall acceptance rate of 45%. Each accepted paper was accompanied by a virtual poster presentation and a pre-recorded talk. In addition to the regular research papers, the symposium proceedings includes 10 invited champions papers from the winners of the RoboCup 2021 competitions. The champions papers were reviewed by at least two members of the Trustees or Executive Members of the RoboCup Federation.

Among the 19 accepted regular research papers, five papers were nominated as best paper award finalists. The awards committee evaluated the finalists based on the paper as well as their associated posters and presentations, and selected one best paper: Emanuele Antonioni, Vincenzo Suriani, Filippo Solimando, Domenico Daniele Bloisi, and Daniele Nardi — "Learning from the Crowd: Improving the Decision Making Process in Robot Soccer using the Audience Noise". The best paper award finalists included:

- Philip Reichenberg and Thomas Röfer — "Step Adjustment for a Robust Humanoid Walk"
- Moritz Zappel, Simon Bultmann, and Sven Behnke — "6D Object Pose Estimation using Keypoints and Part Affinity Fields"
- Arash Amini, Hafez Farazi, and Sven Behnke — "Real-time Pose Estimation for Multi-Humanoid Robots"
- Jan Blumenkamp, Andreas Baude, and Tim Laue — "Closing the Reality Gap with Unsupervised Sim-to-Real Image Translation"

The RoboCup 2021 symposium was delighted to host three keynote speakers:

- Dieter Fox (Nvidia Research and University of Washington): "Toward Robust Manipulation in Complex Environments"

- Jean-Paul Laumond (Centre national de la recherche scientifique, CNRS): "Robotics: The Science of Motion"
- Stefanie Tellex (Brown University): "Towards Complex Language in Partially Observed Environments"

We were saddened by the news of Jean-Paul Laumond's death in December 2021, a big loss for the robotics community. He was a pioneer in humanoid robotics and motion planning, and approached robotics from a variety of disciplines including graph theory, algorithmic geometry, control theory, and neuroscience.

We thank the members of the Program Committee and the additional reviewers for their time and expertise to help uphold the high standards of the symposium technical program, as well as the members of the awards committee for their work in selecting the best paper award. This event would not have been possible without the tireless efforts of the Organizing Committee, including the team from Underline for providing the online platform for the event. We thank the enthusiastic support and participation of RoboCuppers across the world, and the technical and organizing committees of every league. Finally, we thank Peter Stone, the RoboCup 2021 General Chair, and the Co-chairs, Luca Iocchi, Flavio Tonidandel, and Changjiu Zhou. The symposium organizers greatly enjoyed working together to help make the event a success.

February 2022

Rachid Alami
Joydeep Biswas
Maya Cakmak
Oliver Obst

Organization

Program Co-chairs

Rachid Alami — LAAS-CNRS, France
Joydeep Biswas — The University of Texas at Austin, USA
Maya Cakmak — University of Washington, USA
Oliver Obst — Western Sydney University, Australia

Program Committee

Thomas Gabel — Frankfurt University of Applied Sciences, Germany
Arnoud Visser — University of Amsterdam, The Netherlands
Farshid Faraji — Bonab Islamic Azad University, Iran
Rudi Villing — Maynooth University, Ireland
Asadollah Norouzi — Singapore Polytechnic, Singapore
Gerald Steinbauer — Graz University of Technology, Austria
A. Fernando Ribeiro — University of Minho, Portugal
Paul G. Plöger — Bonn-Rhein-Sieg University of Applied Science, Germany
Justin Hart — The University of Texas at Austin, USA
Ubbo Visser — University of Miami, USA
Ulrich Karras — RoboCup Germany Regional Committee, Germany
Luis Paulo Reis — APPIA University of Porto, Portugal
Sören Schwertfeger — ShanghaiTech University, China
Esther Colombini — Unicamp, Brazil
Daniele Nardi — Sapienza University of Rome, Italy
Ansgar Bredenfeld — Dr. Bredenfeld UG, Germany
Frieder Stolzenburg — Harz University of Applied Sciences, Germany
Nuno Lau — University of Aveiro, Portugal
Marco A. C. Simões — Universidade do Estado da Bahia, Brazil
Tetsuya Kimura — Nagaoka University of Technology, Japan
Reinaldo A. C. Bianchi — Centro Universitario da FEI, Brazil
Hiroyuki Okada — Tamagawa University, Japan
Hidehisa Akiyama — Okayama University of Science, Japan
Sven Behnke — University of Bonn, Germany
Katie Genter — The University of Texas at Austin, USA

Mauricio Matamoros	Universität Koblenz-Landau, Germany
Alexander Ferrein	FH Aachen University of Applied Sciences, Germany
Luca Iocchi	Sapienza University of Rome, Italy
Timothy Wiley	RMIT University, Australia
Yasutake Takahashi	University of Fukui, Japan
Flavio Tonidandel	Centro Universitario da FEI, Brazil
Aaron Wong	4Tel Pty Ltd., Australia
Pedro U. Lima	Instituto Superior Técnico, Universidade de Lisboa, Portugal
Peter Stone	The University of Texas at Austin and Sony AI, USA
Reinhard Gerndt	Ostfalia University of Applied Sciences, Germany
Raymond Sheh	Curtin University, Australia
Dirk Holz	Google, USA
Tomoharu Nakashima	Osaka Prefecture University, Japan
Klaus Dorer	Hochschule Offenburg, Germany
Masaru Shimizu	Chukyo University, Japan
Sebastian Marian	Elrond Network, USA
Vlad Estivill-Castro	Universitat Pompeu Fabra, Spain
Oskar von Stryk	TU Darmstadt, Germany

Additional Reviewers

Jarrett Holtz	Luis Contreras
Vincenzo Suriani	Yoshiaki Mizuchi
Sophie Siebert	Emanuele Antonioni
Stuart Fitzpatrick	Rahul Dass
Siri Padmanabhan Poti	Jan Quenzel
Domenico Bloisi	Sadegh Rabiee
Hafez Farazi	Simon Bultmann

Contents

Invited Champion Track Papers

Regular Research Papers

Ball Path Prediction for Humanoid Robots: Combination of k-NN Regression and Autoregression Methods

Yasaman Mirmohammad[1], Shayan Khorsandi[2],
Mohammad Navid Shahsavari[1], Behnam Yazdankhoo[3],
and Soroush Sadeghnejad[1(✉)]

[1] Bio-Inspired System Design Lab, Biomedical Engineering Department,
Amirkabir University of Technology (Tehran Polytechnic),
No. 424, Hafez Avenue, P. O. Box 15875-4413, Tehran, Iran
s.sadeghnejad@aut.ac.ir
[2] School of Computer Engineering, Iran University of Science and Technology,
Tehran, Iran
[3] School of Mechanical Engineering, College of Engineering,
University of Tehran, Tehran, Iran

Abstract. In this paper, we propose a method for predicting the path of the ball on the soccer field for the humanoid robots. A cost-function-based k-nearest neighbor regression method is first proposed to account for the part of the prediction which is based on previously observed data. Next, the autoregression method is utilized in order to carry out the prediction based on the current ball path. Finally, these two methods are combined to form the final prediction model. Moreover, two different schemes are introduced based upon the proposed model: fixed and adaptive schemes. In fixed scheme, the prediction is made once during the initial steps of the motion and is used throughout the whole ball movement. However, in adaptive scheme, autoregression method coefficients are updated in fixed predefined steps during the motion. This is beneficial to robustify the prediction against an externally applied disturbance on the ball path. Our proposed method is tested by simulation and practical implementation and the results demonstrate a high precision rate.

Keywords: Ball path prediction · Humanoid robots · Autoregression · K-nearest neighbor regression

1 Introduction

Object path prediction is a well-known and important task from both research and industrial point of view. Various scientific papers have considered path prediction in recent years which reflects the significance of this task in a broad

Y. Mirmohammad, S. Khorsandi and M. N. Shahsavari—Authors contributed equally to this work.

R. Alami et al. (Eds.): RoboCup 2021, LNAI 13132, pp. 3–14, 2022.
https://doi.org/10.1007/978-3-030-98682-7_1

sort of applications. The important point is, however, that various mathematical approaches have been adopted in each of these related works. For instance, flight path prediction is investigated in [1] which is based on applying a stochastic model named Hidden Markov Model (HMM). Ship route prediction is another application proposed in [2] in which a k-nearest neighbor classifier is applied as a model for predicting routes in the waterways. Ma *et al.* used a Long Short-Term Memory (LSTM)-based method for agent predictions in an analysis regarding traffic, so that the autonomous vehicle can make appropriate navigation decisions to control traffic [3]. More specifically, path prediction of a thrown body has become important in human-behavioral-based tasks in robotics, which is also reflected in different RoboCup competitions such as soccer, basketball, and other sports [4–6]. Therefore, crucial tasks which can be influenced by path prediction are shooting and passing in soccer-playing humanoids [7–10], or ping-pong/tennis-playing humanoids such as [11–14] in which a Kalman filter based estimation method is used to predict the status of the ball. Throwing-and-catching is another robotic task which has been considered in recent years, for instance [15] utilizes a feedforward neural network model for estimating the position based on the intentions of the human partner during the preparatory motion. Also tracking is one of the crucial tasks for many robot-based applications which could benefit from prediction, as [16] addressed the predictive tracking issue. Reinforcement Learning-based approaches concerning the qualitative velocity of the ball while interception can be found in [17] To mention broader examples, [18] forms a multi-Robot system in which we will face a task assignment problem for a large number of tasks and soccer-playing robots. Under these circumstances, task allocation and path planning for reaching an optimum point become necessary. Ball Path prediction can also help motion planning algorithms such as [19] in order for humanoids to generate optimal motions during a soccer match, for instance. Some tasks may inherently show a time series behavior, where the next position of the object is mainly a function of the previous positions. Several numerical approaches can be applied in this regard, such as neural networks [20–22]. Implementation of the time series approach can be viewed in [23] which proposed a deep learning approach to estimation and prediction by a bidirectional LSTM, and [24] which presented a time-delay neural network (TDNN) based approach for the path prediction of a thrown body. Other methods such as k-nearest neighbor have also been applied to path prediction problem, for instance [25] and [26] represented a nearest neighbor regression method in which the predicted trajectory is a linear combination of selected trajectories.

In our previous paper [27] we analyzed and compared different methods of ball path prediction for humanoid robots. In this work, with specific concentration on soccer player humanoid robots, we aim at predicting the ball path on a soccer field. One of the major drawbacks of the previous works is that they rely on merely either current position data or the previously gathered dataset. To address this problem, in this paper we combine k-nearest neighbor regression (hereinafter, offline) and autoregression (hereinafter, online) methods in order to account for both current path and previously learned paths. In fact, a weighted average of online and offline methods is used in this work to form the final prediction model of the ball path. This model is then divided into two schemes: fixed and adaptive. In fixed prediction scheme, after some initial steps which are reserved for the required calculations, the ball path is predicted only once and that prediction is considered valid throughout the whole ball motion. In adaptive scheme, however, the online method is updated in predefined intervals during the prediction which, in turn, updates the remaining points of the prediction thereafter. The adaptive scheme will be particularly fruitful for prediction when the ball path is suddenly changed during the motion, an issue which has not been addressed in the related works. Therefore, our contributions include: Firstly, combining k-nearest neighbor regression and autoregression methods in order to achieve more accuracy in prediction. And secondly, proposing an adaptive prediction scheme in order to robustify the prediction against external disturbances.

This paper is organized as follows. In Sect. 2, different parts of the proposed path prediction method, along with the final model, are theoretically explained. The results obtained from simulation and experimental tests are then described in Sect. 3. And finally, Sect. 4 is dedicated to conclusions and suggestions for future contribution.

2   Prediction Method

2.1   Overall Approach

Prediction of the ball path is investigated from two different perspectives in this work. On the one hand, the robot should be able to carry out the prediction task by means of learning from the previously observed paths (offline approach). On the other hand, the current motion itself could be conceived of as a time series prediction problem without regard to path dataset (online approach). These two aspects of the prediction will be discussed in the following sections and will be finally integrated to result in the ultimate prediction approach.

2.2   Offline Portion

The offline portion is responsible for taking into account the learning part of the prediction. To this end, here we adopt the k-nearest neighbor (k-NN) regression method utilized in [22] and then in [23], in both of which k is set to 2. Input of the predictor is reference measurement of the current path $C(1 : m) = \{P_c(1), P_c(2), ..., P_c(m)\}$ where m is number of frames until now and P denotes the position in the cartesian space. The database includes N paths $S_1, S_2, ..., S_N$ where each path $S_i(1 : n) = \{P_i(1), P_i(2), ..., P_i(n)\}$ and $n > m$ is the total number of frames. The model predicts the path $C(f : n) = \{P_c(f), P_c(f + 1), ..., P_c(n)\}$ where $f = m + 1$. In order to calculate this path, two guiding paths $A(1 : n) = \{P_a(1), P_a(2), ..., P_a(n)\}$ and

$B(1 : n) = \{P_b(1), P_b(2), ..., P_b(n)\}$ are taken from the database which the measured points of $C(1 : m)$ lie higher than corresponding points of path $B(1 : m)$ and lower than corresponding points of path $A(1 : m)$.

In this work, two factors are used in order to select $A(1 : m)$ and $B(1 : m)$: distance and motion slope. The distance is defined as a summation of euclidean distances between the corresponding points of the paths.

$$D(A, C) := \sum_{i=1}^{m}(A(i) - C(i)) \tag{1}$$

However, unlike [24], in which initial velocities were chosen as another factor for selecting path A and B, here we introduce the motion slope factor which is defined as the difference between the slope of path $A(s : m)$ and path $C(s : m)$ where $1 \leq s < m$. The slope of path $A(s : m)$ is defined by

$$M_A(s : m) := \frac{y_A(m) - y_A(s)}{x_A(m) - x_A(s)} \tag{2}$$

and $M_C(s : m)$ is calculated in a similar manner. The motion slope between path $A(s : m)$ and $C(s : m)$ is then computed by

$$M(A, C) := M_A(s : m) - M_C(s : m) \tag{3}$$

In order to select the proper $A(1 : m)$, a cost-function-based approach similar to what has been proposed in the literature for k-NN or kernel regression is adopted here [28]. For this aim, we design a cost function which best fulfills our requirements by linearly combining the two previously introduced factors (namely: distance and the motion slope) as follows

$$J_A := \rho \frac{|D(A, C)|}{|D_{max}(A, C)|} + \frac{|M(A, C)|}{|M_{max}(A, C)|} \tag{4}$$

where $\rho > 0$ determines the relative impact of the two factors in the cost function, and subscript max denotes the maximum value. J_A is then computed for all the candidate paths for $A(1 : n)$ and the one with the minimum cost function is selected as the final $A(1 : n)$. Equations (1) to (4) are used in an exactly similar manner for selecting the path $B(1 : n)$. Finally, the predicted path $C_{off}(f : n)$ is calculated as a linear combination of $B(f : n)$ and $A(f : n)$

$$C_{off}(f : n) = wA(f : n) + (1 - w)B(f : n) \tag{5}$$

where $0 \leq w \leq 1$. In [24], w is considered as 0.5, but here is computed by following expression.

$$w = \frac{D(B, C)}{D(A, C) + D(B, C)} \tag{6}$$

2.3   Online Portion

The online portion is regarded as the time series part of the prediction. In other words, the current path is utilized for predicting the future positions of itself. To this end, the autoregression method is used. Due to space limitation, only the main formulas are mentioned hereunder. More details are presented in the main paper [27]. According to this method the future position is computed as follows:

$$x(f) = (2 + \psi)x(f - 1) + (-1 - 2\psi)x(f - 2) + \psi x(f - 3) \tag{7}$$

$$\psi = \frac{r_1}{r_0} \tag{8}$$

$$r_k := \frac{c_k}{c_0} \tag{9}$$

$$c_k := E[x(i)x(i - k)] \tag{10}$$

where $k = 0, 1$ and $E[.]$ denotes mathematical expectation and i is defined in (1).

In order to predict the ball position in the next q steps, the following expression is used:

$$x(f + q) = (2 + \psi)x(f + q - 1) + (-1 - 2\psi)x(f + q - 2)$$
$$+ \psi x(f + q - 3) \tag{11}$$

where $q = 1, ..., n - f$. In an exactly same manner, (7) to (11) are used for predicting position in y direction. Now $C_{on}(f : n)$ is defined by the following expression

$$C_{on}(f : n) := \Big(x(f : n), y(f : n)\Big)^T \tag{12}$$

2.4   Combination of Offline and Online Portions

In this paper, we design a combination of offline and online methods in order to use both the prior knowledge and the current position data. Due to low efficiency of the offline method in the lack of sufficient dataset size, and also reducing the calculations performance in the presence of a huge dataset because of the high time constraints, using offline method alone seems inefficient. On the other hand, online method suffers from problems such as being unable to predict the stop position of the ball and lack of learning from the previous ball paths. As a consequence, each method can cover the disadvantages of the other by being combined together. Our proposed method is introduced by the following expression

$$C(f : n) = \alpha C_{off}(f : n) + (1 - \alpha)C_{on}(f : n) \tag{13}$$

where $0 \leq \alpha \leq 1$. Equation (13) is called the *fixed prediction scheme*, in which both online and offline portions of the prediction are determined merely once at the beginning of the motion. However, if an unexpected change in ball movement due to an external disturbance occurs in the middle of the motion, the above-mentioned scheme fails to accurately predict the ball path. To tackle this issue, we propose a novel approach which is called *adaptive prediction scheme* in which the online prediction method is updated in predefined steps. In this method $n - f$ steps ahead is divided into j equal parts and online method Eqs. (7) to (11) are repeated for each part. In other words, online portion coefficients are recalculated for the first $f + j'n'$ steps, where $n' = \frac{n-f}{j}$ is the length of each part and $j' = 1, ..., j$, and then prediction is made for the remaining points. Therefore we have:

$$
C_{on}(f : j'n') = \Big(x(f : f + n'), y(f : f + n'), ...,
$$
$$
x(f + (j' - 1)n' : f + j'n'), y(f + (j' - 1)n' : f + j'n') \Big)^T \tag{14}
$$

Now the new $C_{on}(f : n)$ is put into (13) and the path prediction is conducted while the online portion coefficients are updated in fixed steps during the actual path. It should be noted that here j or n' are chosen such that for both of them we have $j \in N$ and $n' \in N$.

3   Results

3.1   Description

Two scenarios are designed in order to carry out the simulation and experiment:

- Scenario 1: The ball moves normally in an x-y direction.
- Scenario 2: The ball initiates a normal movement, but an unknown disturbance is applied to the ball during its path in an unknown moment.

  Note that:

- The initial speed of the ball in both the simulations and the experiments is random and less than $2\,\text{m/s}$.
- An Obstacle is put on the way of the ball while shooting that causes a change in the direction of the shot ball; this is similar to the scenario of what happens to the ball in real passing/shooting situations. This is the allowed "external disturbance" in this research, which is not of any specific kind and has been chosen by chance. Based on the collision angle that the ball makes while hitting the obstacle, its path changes to a direction which we could not have known.
- Some disturbances like the friction in the artificial grass are considered in the offline method. These disturbances are intrinsically presented in the ball's trajectory. Hence, we are learning the system's dynamics without building our model.
- It is assumed that the ball's movement is always in x-y, ahead in the direction of the x-axis.

3.2 Simulation Results

Gazebo is used as our simulation environment. It is selected because of its integrity with ROS, the framework that is utilized in the robots. Gazebo's world is consisted of two models; RoboCup 3D soccer simulation field and RoboCup 3D soccer simulation ball with their corresponding friction force in order to achieve the real world conditions and ball movements. Our dataset is collected by simulating the ball movement 155 times with different linear and angular velocities for being used in offline prediction. Ball position in 2D axis is captured each 40 ms, 100 times to occupy the whole ball movement in 4 s. The 2D position of the ball is then sent to ROS for capturing data. We collected 139 sample ball paths for the dataset. Gazebo simulation environment is depicted in Fig. 1.

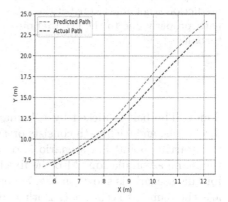

Fig. 1. Gazebo simulation environment.

Fig. 2. Simulation result for scenario 1 using fixed prediction scheme.

For scenario 1, $\alpha = 0.9$, $m = 10$, $\rho = 5$ and $s = 10$ and the fixed prediction scheme is utilized. The result for this scenario is shown in Fig. 2.

For scenario 2, $\alpha = 0.1$ and other parameters are as same as scenario 1. Both fixed and adaptive schemes are adopted for this scenario. In the adaptive scheme, the online method is updated every 15 steps ($n' = 15$). The results for this scenario are illustrated in Fig. 3 and Fig. 4. Note that the actual path is the same in these two figures.

3.3 Experimental Results

Experiments are carried out utilizing soccer artificial grass field and standard soccer ball as shown in Fig. 5. A fixed camera is placed above the soccer field, which is shown in Fig. 6. The Shared Vision System for the RoboCup Small Size League [29] is used in order to implement detection and localization of the ball. 166 sample ball paths were collected for the dataset (166 real experiments were

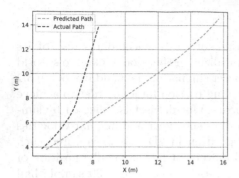

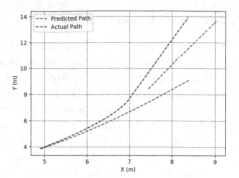

Fig. 3. Simulation result for scenario 2 using fixed prediction scheme. Fixed prediction is not able to predict the ball path properly due to the external disturbance.

Fig. 4. Simulation result for scenario 2 using adaptive prediction scheme. The actual path is the same as Fig. 3. Adaptive prediction is able to predict the ball path despite the external disturbance.

done). The ball is kicked by a human from a fixed starting point in different directions, and each path consists of samples from position of the ball relative to the starting point. For scenario 1, $\alpha = 0.9$, $\rho = 1$ and the other parameters are the same as simulation. Also the fixed prediction scheme is adopted. The result for this scenario is shown in Fig. 7. For scenario 2, $\alpha = 0.1$ and other parameters are the same as scenario 1. Both fixed and adaptive schemes are used in this scenario. In the adaptive scheme, the online method is updated every 15 steps ($n' = 15$). Figure 8 and Fig. 9 show the results for this scenario. Note that the actual path is the same in these two figures.

3.4   Analysis of Results

In scenario 1, the fixed scheme with only offline portion (i.e. $\alpha = 1$) can be efficient, but this approach strongly depends on the size and variation of the dataset and because of this dependency, it is possible that it does not lead to the best prediction. Hence, by combining it with the online method, the position data of the current path can also be involved in the prediction. However, the online method weakly predicts the position at which the ball stops. For this reason, it seems better to use a low coefficient for the online method. As can be seen in Fig. 2 and Fig. 7, both path and stop position are predicted well (The final position at which the ball stops is the end of the actual path). The root mean square errors (RMSE) are 1.00 m and 0.36 m, respectively, and the normalized root mean square errors (NRMSE) are 3.96% and 10.27%, respectively. It should be noted that NRMSE is calculated by dividing RMSE by the length of the actual path. However, for scenario 2, the fixed scheme can not predict the disturbance effect on the ball path as can be seen in Fig. 3 and Fig. 8. The RMSE for these two

Fig. 5. Ball and soccer grass field used for experimental setup.

Fig. 6. Camera configuration used for experimental setup.

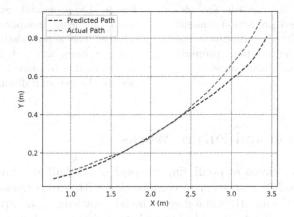

Fig. 7. Experimental result for scenario 1 using fixed prediction scheme.

figures are 5.38 m and 0.45 m and NRMSEs are 31.59% and 10.86%, which seem relatively high. As a result, the adaptive scheme is used in this scenario with the same actual path in order to account for the sudden change in the ball direction and decrease the prediction error. Figure 4 and Fig. 9 show that this approach can effectively update the primary prediction. The RMSE for these two figures are 0.61 m and 0.08 m and NRMSEs are 3.59% and 2.07%. Since the actual paths are the same, these errors show significant improvement in the prediction process, both in simulation and experiment. Note that the discontinuities and overlaps in the prediction curves in Fig. 4 and Fig. 9 are due to the updates made at the corresponding steps. In other words, they do not indicate lack of or duplicate predictions at the specified positions, they are simply due to the step-wise corrections during the update procedure in order to modify the predictions made at the previous steps. Finally, it should be pointed out that it is important to choose the coefficient of the online method (i.e. $1 - \alpha$) considerably larger than the coefficient of the offline method in the adaptive scheme, because the online method is responsible for updating the prediction.

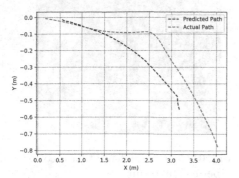 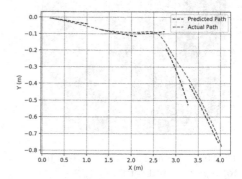

Fig. 8. Experimental result for scenario 2 using fixed prediction scheme. Same as Fig. 3, Fixed prediction is not able to predict the ball path properly due to the external disturbance.

Fig. 9. Experimental result for scenario 2 using adaptive prediction scheme. The actual path is the same as Fig. 8. Same as Fig. 4, Adaptive prediction is able to predict the ball path despite the external disturbance.

4   Conclusion and Future Works

In this paper, we aimed at predicting the path of the ball for humanoid robots. First, we used k-NN regression in combination with autoregression method in order to benefit from both previously gathered knowledge and current ball path. Furthermore, in order to be able to predict an unexpected change in the ball movement due to an external disturbance, we proposed an adaptive prediction scheme in which the online method coefficients are updated in fixed intervals. Simulation and experimental results showed that the fixed prediction scheme can predict the path in a proper way, but in the presence of an external disturbance this method can not carry out the prediction task accurately. However, it could be deduced from the results that the adaptive scheme can robustify the prediction against an external disturbance which alters the preliminary path and, thus, can make the prediction more accurate. For the future contributions, a suggestion is to consider more neighbours in offline method for the k-NN algorithm. Another suggestion to mention is to calculate the parameters adaptively instead of setting them as constant values. Moreover, a study on the effect of the initial speed of the ball could be considered as a future contribution.

References

1. Ayhan, S., Samet, H.: Aircraft trajectory prediction made easy with predictive analytics. In: Proceedings of the 22nd ACM SIGKDD International Conference on Knowledge Discovery and Data Mining, pp. 21–30 (2016)
2. Duca, A.L., Bacciu, C., Marchetti, A.: A K-nearest neighbor classifier for ship route prediction. In: OCEANS 2017-Aberdeen, pp. 1–6 (2017)
3. Ma, Y., Zhu, X., Zhang, S., Yang, R., Wang, W., Manocha, D.: Trafficpredict: trajectory prediction for heterogeneous traffic-agents. In: Proceedings of the AAAI Conference on Artificial Intelligence, pp. 6120–6127 (2019)
4. Baltes, J., Tu, K.-Y., Sadeghnejad, S., Anderson, J.: HuroCup: competition for multi-event humanoid robot athletes. Knowl. Eng. Rev. **32**, 1–14 (2017)
5. Lin, H.-I., Yu, Z., Huang, Y.-C.: Ball tracking and trajectory prediction for table-tennis robots. Sensors **20**(2), 333 (2020)
6. Cong, V.D., Hanh, L.D., Phuong, L.H.: Real-time measurement and prediction of ball trajectory for ping-pong robot. In: 2020 5th International Conference on Green Technology and Sustainable Development (GTSD), Ho Chi Minh City, Vietnam, pp. 9–14 (2020). https://doi.org/10.1109/GTSD50082.2020.9303148
7. Gerndt, R., Seifert, D., Baltes, J.H., Sadeghnejad, S., Behnke, S.: Humanoid robots in soccer: robots versus humans in RoboCup 2050. IEEE Robot. Autom. Mag. **22**, 147–154 (2015)
8. Shangari, T.A., Shamshirdar, F., Azari, B., Heydari, M., Sadeghnejad, S., Baltes, J.: Real-time ball detection and following based on a hybrid vision system with application to robot soccer field. In: Kim, J.-H., Karray, F., Jo, J., Sincak, P., Myung, H. (eds.) Robot Intelligence Technology and Applications 4. AISC, vol. 447, pp. 521–527. Springer, Cham (2017). https://doi.org/10.1007/978-3-319-31293-4_42
9. Lengagneua, S., Fraisse, P., Ramdani, N.: Planning and fast re-planning of safe motions for humanoid robots: application to a kicking motion. In: IEEE/RSJ International Conference on Intelligent Robots and Systems, pp. 441–446 (2009)
10. Gomez, M., Kim, Y., Matson, E.T.: Iterative learning system to intercept a ball for humanoid soccer player. In: 6th International Conference on Automation, Robotics and Applications (ICARA), pp. 507–512 (2015)
11. Zhao, Y., Xiong, R., Zhang, Y.: Model based motion state estimation and trajectory prediction of spinning ball for ping-pong robots using expectation-maximization algorithm. J. Intell. Robot. Syst. **87**, 407–423 (2017)
12. Zhang, Y., Xiong, R., Zhao, Y., Chu, J.: An adaptive trajectory prediction method for ping-pong robots. In: Su, C.-Y., Rakheja, S., Liu, H. (eds.) ICIRA 2012. LNCS (LNAI), vol. 7508, pp. 448–459. Springer, Heidelberg (2012). https://doi.org/10.1007/978-3-642-33503-7_44
13. Liu, Y., Liu, L.: Accurate real-time ball path estimation with onboard stereo camera system for humanoid ping-pong robot. Robot. Auton. Syst. **101**, 34–44 (2018)
14. Hattori, M., et al.: Fast tennis swing motion by ball trajectory prediction and joint trajectory modification in standalone humanoid robot real-time system (2020)
15. Carneiro, D., Silva, F., Georgieva, P.: The role of early anticipations for human-robot ball catching. In: IEEE International Conference on Autonomous Robot Systems and Competitions (ICARSC), pp. 10–16 (2018)
16. LaViola, J.J.: Double exponential smoothing: an alternative to Kalman filter-based predictive tracking. In: Proceedings of the Workshop on Virtual Environments, pp. 199–206 (2003)

17. Stolzenburg, F., Obst, O., Murray, J.: Qualitative velocity and ball interception. In: Jarke, M., Lakemeyer, G., Koehler, J. (eds.) KI 2002. LNCS (LNAI), vol. 2479, pp. 283–298. Springer, Heidelberg (2002). https://doi.org/10.1007/3-540-45751-8_19
18. Janati, F., Abdollahi, F., Ghidary, S.S., Jannatifar, M., Baltes, J., Sadeghnejad, S.: Multi-robot task allocation using clustering method. In: Kim, J.-H., Karray, F., Jo, J., Sincak, P., Myung, H. (eds.) Robot Intelligence Technology and Applications 4. AISC, vol. 447, pp. 233–247. Springer, Cham (2017). https://doi.org/10.1007/978-3-319-31293-4_19
19. Baltes, J., Bagot, J., Sadeghnejad, S., Anderson, J., Hsu, C.-H.: Full-body motion planning for humanoid robots using rapidly exploring random trees. KI - Künstliche Intelligenz 30(3), 245–255 (2016)
20. Remus, W., O'Connor, M.: Neural networks for time-series forecasting. In: Armstrong, J.S. (ed.) Principles of Forecasting. ISOR, vol. 30, pp. 245–256. Springer, Boston (2001). https://doi.org/10.1007/978-0-306-47630-3_12
21. Kolarik, T., Rudorfer, G.: Time series forecasting using neural networks. In: ACM SIGAPL APL Quote Quad, pp. 86–94 (1994)
22. Gheyas, I.A., Smith, L.S.: A neural network approach to time series forecasting. In: Proceedings of the World Congress on Engineering, pp. 1–3 (2009)
23. Zhao, Y., Yang, R., Chevalier, G., Shah, R.C., Romijnders, R.: Applying deep bidirectional LSTM and mixture density network for basketball trajectory prediction. Optik 158, 266–272 (2018)
24. Mironov, K., Pongratz, M.: Applying neural networks for prediction of flying objects trajectory. Newsl. UGATU 17(6), 28–32 (2013)
25. Mironov, K., Vladimirova, I., Pongratz, M.: Processing and forecasting the trajectory of a thrown object measured by the stereo vision system. IFAC-PapersOnLine 48, 28–35 (2015)
26. Mironov, K., Pongratz, M.: Fast kNN-based prediction for the trajectory of a thrown body. In: 24th Mediterranean Conference on Control and Automation (MED), pp. 512–517 (2016)
27. Yazdankhoo, B., Shahsavari, M.N., Sadeghnejad, S., Baltes, J.: Prediction of a ball trajectory for the humanoid robots: a friction-based study. In: Holz, D., Genter, K., Saad, M., von Stryk, O. (eds.) RoboCup 2018. LNCS (LNAI), vol. 11374, pp. 387–398. Springer, Cham (2019). https://doi.org/10.1007/978-3-030-27544-0_32
28. Klanke, S., Ritter, H.: Variants of unsupervised kernel regression: general cost functions. Neurocomputing 70(7–9), 1289–1303 (2007)
29. Zickler, S., Laue, T., Birbach, O., Wongphati, M., Veloso, M.: SSL-vision: the shared vision system for the RoboCup small size league. In: Baltes, J., Lagoudakis, M.G., Naruse, T., Ghidary, S.S. (eds.) RoboCup 2009. LNCS (LNAI), vol. 5949, pp. 425–436. Springer, Heidelberg (2010). https://doi.org/10.1007/978-3-642-11876-0_37

Enabling Modern Application Development with Swift on the Nao/Pepper Robots

Callum McColl[1]($\boxtimes$), Vladimir Estivill-Castro[2], Eugene Gilmore[1], Morgan McColl[1], and René Hexel[1]

[1] MiPal, Griffith University, Brisbane, QLD, Australia
`callum.mccoll@griffithuni.edu.au`
[2] MiPal, Universitat Pompeu Fabra, Barcelona, Spain

Abstract. We show the advantages of using `Swift` as the programming language for behaviours on the `Pepper` and `Nao` robots as used with the RoboCup Standard Platform League and the RoboCup@Home - Social Standard Platform. We show that `Swift` is not only incorporating modern features of object-oriented programming and functional programming, but is also now a stable systems programming language that enables both high-level development as well as fine hardware control. Deterministic memory management makes `Swift` suitable for real-time, embedded systems, and thus for robotic applications. Moreover, we show in this paper we can apply model-driven software-development by deploying behaviours coded as executable arrangements of logic-labelled finite-state machines (LLFSMs). We also show LLFSMs are not only suitable for reactive architectures, but also for deliberative architectures.

Keywords: Functional programming languages · Logical programming languages · Model-driven software development · Deliberative architectures

1 Introduction

While there have been long-ranging debates on the most relevant programming language for Software Engineering as well as robotics [29,31,38], there is agreement on important characteristics that a programming language for robotics and embedded systems needs to satisfy. Number one is to be Turing complete[1]. Importantly, it should be a systems programming language, able to provide fine grained, standardised control over devices, hardware drivers, and communication mechanisms, with predictable performance to enable integration across hardware, from sensors to actuators. The capability to have control over the temporal domain in execution, task control, and parallelism is crucially important.

---

[1] This formally means that it should be as expressive as a Turing machine, including sequencing, conditionals, and iteration found in most imperative languages [17].

© Springer Nature Switzerland AG 2022
R. Alami et al. (Eds.): RoboCup 2021, LNAI 13132, pp. 15–27, 2022.
https://doi.org/10.1007/978-3-030-98682-7_2

We argue here that such a language should also enable a seamless transition to higher behaviour-based descriptions and model-driven development.

We port `Swift` and its supporting environment to the virtual machine development environment associated with the SoftBank Pepper and Nao robots, as well as to the robots themselves. `Swift` has long produced fast and predictable executables for iOS and macOS, but is Open Source and features modern and safe language concepts. Complex data testbeds show `Swift` code to be about two times faster than Objective-C [39] and four to eight times faster than Python [1], while being similarly discoverable to programmers (e.g. through *Playgrounds* that facilitate interactivity during development and enable programmers to quickly test new algorithms). `Swift`'s modern features include closures, generics, and type inference, which have been shown to result in higher productivity and more adherence to common software patterns.

The clean syntax of `Swift` is a major factor for its higher readability [40] and thus maintainability, while its semantics make it harder to make mistakes common to systems programming languages and add a layer of quality control during development. Functional language features that provide referential transparency and avoid implicit state or mutable data allow writing performant code in more functional style [8]. This also facilitates pure functions and idempotence (i.e. lack of side-effects and the same output regardless how many times a function is called), enabling parallelisation as function calls become independent.

With `Swift` being Open Source, while being a relatively young language, and still somewhat of a moving target [33], it has become popular very quickly, including on the server side and cloud computing. The `Swift` language won first place for *Most Loved Programming Language* in the *Stack Overflow Developer Survey* 2015 and second place in 2016. Three years ago, `Swift` became the 12th most popular language, overtaking Objective-C, Go, Scala, and R. Now, in 2021, the reviews of the full-stack academy place `Swift` second just below JavaScript. For robotics, `Swift` provides the capability dynamic libraries and, vitally, a low memory footprint through value types and Automatic Reference Counting (ARC) that offers similar convenience as tracing garbage collectors, but vastly superior and deterministic performance. This is in contrast to languages such as Python, Java, C♯, or Go, whose lack of ability to bound memory usage and garbage collection performance implies unpredictability of CPU usage, suggesting that every single thread on board of the robot could be denied vital CPU time, potentially resulting in catastrophic consequences. For example, what would be the use of a Kalman filter if the time-stamp of the sensor reading was unpredictable or seriously jeopardised? The literature has plenty of discussion [3] why, e.g., the versions of Java for real-time and/or embedded systems are not completely satisfactory.

While IDE integration is not as mature as with other languages and despite some blogs criticising `Swift`, suggesting that Objective-C can use C and C++ libraries more smoothly, we demonstrate that we can use in-memory middleware for module/package/node communication quite effectively, integrating applicable C and C++ libraries for robotics applications.

2   Cross Compiling

The goal of cross-compilation is to be able to build a program for a specific platform on a different platform. When compiling for the Nao and Pepper robots, SoftBank Robotics provides GNU tools commonly found in linux systems for C and C++ which have been specifically built to allow cross-compilation. The tools include binutils [15] which contains tools such as the linker (ld), glibc [16] which contains the C standard library, and the gcc project [14] which contains the C compiler (gcc) as well as other compilers such as the C++ compiler g++. This, for example, allows us to build Nao-robot applications from a 64-bit Linux or macOS. We note that the Nao and the Pepper use some version of the linux kernel (for us, we use version 2.6). The kernel is simply a C program, thus a C compiler is needed to compile the kernel.

When cross-compiling, two things are required on the host (the system executing the cross-compiler): the tools (the cross-compiler and linker), and, the sysroot folder containing all necessary files needed for compilation for the target platform, such as the Nao. The sysroot folder is usually setup to mimic the folder structure of the target and generally contains headers and libraries which are needed at runtime by the programs being compiled. When using the GNU tools (as Aldebaran did originally), a compiler must be provided for each host and target combinations. So in order to build for the Pepper and Nao robots on two separate hosts—for example macOS and linux—then you need a total of four compilers. Two compilers for each host which build for the Nao and Pepper respectively. However, we can use alternatives to this approach.

Our Swift project is built using LLVM [20], built on top of the GNU stack and provides compilers (clang for the C language and clang++ for C++) that allow programs to be cross-compiled without having to build a separate cross-compiler. In other words, the same compiler that is built for the host is able to cross-compile for other targets (as already utilised, e.g., for iOS and tvOS applications). We potentiate this further here for Swift, which already leverages LLVM, by creating an environment that allows us to cross-compile for Nao robots using only one cross-compiler.

3   Swift for the Pepper

To enable Swift for a new host system and target system, such as the Pepper, we need to build the Swift compiler (and libraries), often passing platform-specific flags to the C/C++ compilers to fix compiler errors or warnings. To ensure consistency, alleviate setup-specific issues, and document the process, we provide a Docker container which builds the Swift project [27]. Docker allows OS-level virtualisation in what is called containers, similar to virtualisation; however, rather than a host OS emulating the hardware in favour of a guest OS [37], containers share the host kernel. Containers are now a de-facto standard to share the environment for a package of applications.

Another challenge when building for the Pepper is the fact the Swift project does not support compiling for 32-bit linux targets. That is, none of the build scripts that are provided by the Swift project will allow such cross-compilation. Instead, we release our own scripts that our Docker container [27] automatically downloads and uses.

To cross-compile Swift for the Pepper, we need to replace existing binutils with gold enabled binutils (--enable-gold), build the LLVM tools for the host and the target, and then build the Swift standard library for the target. This allows us to create a swiftenv toolchain that enables building vital infrastructure libraries for the target such as libdispatch and Foundation.

3.1 Replacing Binutils and Building the LLVM Toolchain

SoftBank's toolchain provides an older ld linker that does not have the capabilities required by more modern languages such as Swift. The Swift project requires the gold linker [41], ld.gold, a more modern alternative to ld. Our scripts download binutils and recompile them, enabling the gold linker and allowing it to be executed on the 64-bit host, but cross-compile for the 32-bit Pepper.

The Swift project uses a series of git repositories, utilising a consistent version tag, to distribute a specific version of the language and the tools that are used within the Swift toolchain. The version of Swift that we have built is version 5.1.4 (tagged as swift-5.1.4-RELEASE).

We then build the LLVM project, creating C/C++ compilers that are capable of running on the host, but also cross-compile for the Pepper. We recommend building the C/C++ compilers using our Swift project since subsequent cross-compilation of robotic applications with Swift is simpler and more convenient. In particular, fewer flags are necessary for cross-compilation than with the GNU cross-compilers provided by the original SoftBank toolchain.

Using the host tools built in the previous step, a second build cross-compiles the LLVM toolchain for the Pepper delivering pre-requisites for the Swift cross-compiler and standard library. This requires several flags that inform the host C/C++ compiler where the shared objects, headers and C standard library exist within the Pepper toolchain. This is necessary to redirect the compiler away from the usual locations in the 64-bit host environment.

3.2 Building the Swift Environment for the Pepper

As we cross compile, we can skip building a Swift compiler to run on the Pepper, but, the Swift standard library must still be built, which is now possible with our cross-compilers. However, The Swift standard library consists of several modules written in different languages, some are C/C++ while others (such as the main standard library) are written in Swift itself and needs to be compiled and installed into the sysroot. Importantly here, since the standard library is written in Swift, a Swift compiler with a specific version is needed within the Docker container. We use swiftenv [13] in order to download the appropriate compiler for the version of Swift that we are compiling, to ensure that the host

Swift compiler and all the other tools that exist within the toolchain match the versions of the tools that we are building for the Pepper.

The Swift project follows a folder structure where the actual Swift standard library folders are placed within a Swift folder under the installation directories lib folder (typically /usr/lib for a normal installation). The installation folder that our scripts use is $SYSROOT/home/nao/swift-tc where $SYSROOT represents the absolute path of the sysroot directory on the build system. The reason why we use this installation prefix is to follow Pepper's security policy where the only folder with write access is the /home/nao folder. This swift directory follows the following format:

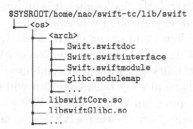

In this folder structure <os> and <arch> represent the target operating system and architecture (e.g. linux and i686 for the Pepper). These folders contain the Swift standard library files, consisting of the shared objects or dynamic libraries required by the compiler. The glibc.modulemap file includes the C standard library which allows developers to import into their programs by a simple import statement, for example (import Glibc).

This folder structure is important because when building the Pepper Swift toolchain, some of these files need to change. Recall that we leverage swiftenv to install a version of Swift that matches the version of Swift that we are building for the host. This makes it so that we can use the host Swift compiler to cross-compile Swift programs. However, the host Swift toolchain contains the standard library for the host 64-bit linux. We copy this toolchain into a new Pepper toolchain folder, and replace the Swift folder contents with the cross-compiled toolchain that was installed into the sysroot, replacing the 64-bit standard library with the 32-bit standard library built for the Pepper. Then we patch the glibc.modulemap file to correct the hardcoded paths to point to the Pepper C standard library within sysroot.

3.3   Building Libdispatch and Foundation for the Pepper

Once the Pepper swiftenv toolchain has been created, we can use it to build the remaining projects that make up the required Swift infrastructure. The libdispatch project is a C project, but the Swift variant contains wrappers that enable simple access to libdispatch from Swift programs. The Foundation framework was once written in Objective-C, but has since been rewritten in pure Swift. This allows it to be deployed to linux platforms, adding extra functionality on top of the Swift standard library. By using the swiftenv, we are able to compile these components and install them within the sysroot.

4   Swift on Legacy Robots

Older versions of the Nao (version 5 or earlier) use older versions of the C compiler and standard library that fail to meet the minimum system requirements for cross-compiling the swift toolchain. To overcome this issue, we need to take the extra step of installing an entirely separate *root* directory within the home directory of the Nao that will contain all files required for a newer linux system containing a suitable version of glibc. However, we avoid installing an entire linux system. Instead, we install the minimum amount of software that Swift needs in order to minimise disk space.

Installing a newer version of glibc is particularly challenging, it is an integral part of the system, i.e., there is a mutual inter-dependence between the kernel and the GNU C compiler (gcc) on the one hand and glibc on the other hand. This circular dependency creates close coupling, and if the newer version of glibc breaks ABI (application binary interface) stability (meaning that symbols within the library have changed), programs that have already been compiled will stop working. Since the linux kernel is itself a C program which links against glibc, this means that nothing will work. Upgrading an existing glibc to a newer version is therefore only possible if the new glibc version does not break ABI stability. In our illustration (Nao V5), the minimum version of glibc supported by the swift toolchain does break ABI stability.

An additional challenge is that the glibc version that is needed for the swift toolchain does not compile under the Nao kernel. For our approach of a parallel system root, the new toolchain must not depend on anything outside of this parallel system root. If we were to simply compile glibc using the existing gcc compiler, then the new glibc would link against libgcc.so which is outside of the system root directory. Hence, we needed to compile an entirely new linux systems from source, following [2]. This book provides a comprehensive guide for creating new Linux distributions without any prior knowledge, particularly, the details for compiling a self-contained system root [2]. Akin to this approach, we created a parallel system root containing the new glibc, kernel and gcc, taking the opportunity to upgrade the gcc compiler to a more modern version. From this point, the same steps as in Sect. 3 apply.

5   Efficient Robot Software Architectures Through Swift

5.1   Behaviour-Based Architectures

Finite-State Machines are ubiquitous models of behaviour. In robotics, they have been used in several forms, perhaps most notably with the introduction of the subsumption architecture [4] and therefore, in behaviour-based control by the seminal description of Toto [22–24]. Finite-state machines are typically associated with reactive software architectures for robotics, because of the prevalence of the state-chart format introduced by Harel [18]. However, Harel's semantics of finite-state machines is event-driven, implying that the driver of any activity is the environment who generates events to state-charts waiting and expecting events [7]. Harel's vision was the creation of mechanisms to compose more sophisticated behaviours by hierarchies of state-charts as nesting one sub-machine in a parent sub-machine created an appealing mechanism nesting behaviours from other behaviours. This idea gained acceptance in OMT [35] and latter became the dominant semantics of UML's model for describing behaviour [32]: that is the semantics of *run until completion* [7,36].

However, the original time-augmented finite-state machines of the subsumption architecture were essentially logic-labelled; that is, what labels a transition between two states is a Boolean expression. In such models, the machine runs at its own pace, evaluating the expressions of the transitions and performing a transition only when the expression evaluates to **true**. Expressions labelling transitions can be as sophisticate as decision trees [21,34]. Logic-Labelled Finite State Machines (LLFSMs) use this alternative paradigm of execution enabling much safer elaboration of behaviours [30]. Rather than using nesting, LLFSMs can use stacking like the subsumption architecture [4] or create versatile dynamic executions by **suspend**, **resume** and **restart** calls. Concurrency of arrangements of LLFSMs is achieved by a sequential pre-defined schedule of execution, enabling smaller state-spaces for formal verification and model checking [12].

5.2 Formal Verification

Implementations of LLFSMs were based on interpreters until **clfsm** [12] offered their compilation into loadable libraries in **C++**. However, doing so left them unverifiable as the C++ language does not posses any means of being able to query the state of the variables making up the LLFSM at run time. Our porting of **Swift** to the SoftBank robots enables efficient execution on board of the robot of compiled **swift** LLFSMs while still enabling formal verification. Here we argue for the use of **swiftfsm** [25,26]: a scheduler for LLFSMs enabling formal verification.

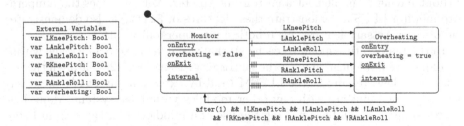

Fig. 1. The temperature monitor LLFSM

We now present a small illustration of the efficacy and usefulness of our **Swift** toolchain. We use **swiftfsm** to perform verification of a small piece of infrastructure: a module which monitors the temperature levels of the motors on the robot. The corresponding LLFSM is presented in Fig. 1. For the sake of this example, we represent the temperature sensors as Boolean values. This is to minimise the resulting Kripke Structure from the verification for this simple example. Each Boolean variable in the external variables represents whether or not that particular sensors is overheating. If the sensor is overheating, then the value is `true`, otherwise the value is `false`. The `overheating` external variable represents a control message which notifies any other modules that a joint is overheating. Thus, this LLFSM simplifies the process of checking whether the robot is overheating by distilling the sensors into one overheating message.

The machine starts in the Monitor state indicated by the initial pseudo-state icon. The Monitor sets `overheating` to `false` and contains a number of transitions to the Overheating state. We have labelled each of these transitions with a check for each external variable. Therefore, if any of these external variables evaluate to `true`, then the machine will transition to the Overheating state. Our machine takes advantage of the LLFSM semantics [10] implemented by `swiftfsm` to continuously poll the external variables throughout its execution. This simple fact also demonstrates the advantages of `swiftfsm` in handling issues of concurrency without any overhead created by the user. Lastly, if the machine transitions to the Overheating state, then the overheating external variable is set to `true`. After a second and when all sensors are not overheating, the machine transitions back to the Monitor state thus setting `overheating` back to `false`.

One of the advantages of using `Swift` and `swiftfsm` is that `swiftfsm` utilises an extensive set of protocols to enforce its semantics. A protocol in `Swift` is a construct similar to an interface in Java, but more powerful. This *protocol oriented design* (a paradigm widely used in the `Swift` community) establishes the desired semantics of the scheduler which enables formal verification. Only by enforcing LLFSMs to follow these semantics—through the use of protocols—is a verification possible [28]. Performing the actual verification is only possible because of the reflection capabilities of the language. As stated earlier, the C++ variants of LLFSMs were only able to verify LLFSMs through the implementation of an interpreter. With `Swift`, we are able to verify LLFSMs natively without having to implement a custom interpreter. Not only does the temperature monitor LLFSM demonstrate these features of `Swift`, it also demonstrates one of the necessary features for robotics: interoperability with C.

In the temperature monitor, each external variable maps to a message within a middleware implemented in C: the `gusimplewhiteboard` [12]. Through the use of this middleware, any `Swift` LLFSM (and by extension any `Swift` program) is able to communicate with any other modules within the system. Many languages support C bindings making the use of a middleware a key step in being able to communicate between modules written in different languages including C++. The temperature monitor demonstrates that the use of `Swift` does not demand that existing modules must be rewritten. `Swift` modules can add extra functionality and coexist with existing modules written in different languages. Other LLFSMs written in C++ or `Swift` can now use the output of the `Swift` machine in Fig. 1 through the use of the same middleware. Moreover, using LLFSMs enables Model-Driven Software Development. That is, the LLFSMs can be defined using a language agnostic meta-model and editor. Then, model-to-text transformation produces the equivalent behaviour for C++, Swift, and LISP [5]. More importantly for formal verification, a model-to-text transformation produces the equivalent NuSMV model (see coming up example in Fig. 3b) which can be co-simulated by the model-checker (that is, by NuSMV) as well as verifying properties against it.

5.3   Deliberative Architectures

Importantly, LLFSMs enable the ability to create declarative and deliberative architectures, as the expression labelling the transitions can be a query to a reasoning agent [11] or a task planning system [9].

We now illustrate LLFSMs capability to describe behaviours beyond a reactive architecture. Our example is part of an application of a social robot that plays the game of Spanish dominoes with a human partner against another pair of players [19]. Figure 2 shows a small Prolog program that defines whether a player can play one of the tiles in their hand or must pass. Figure 3a shows an executable (compiled, not interpreted) of deliberative LLFSMs of a player that plays with the most naive strategy, play the first tile playable in the hand or pass. A more sophisticated player can be produced by sophistication of the Prolog program of Fig. 2. Nevertheless, the current version is sufficient to implement the server of the game that monitors players following the rules to play valid tiles and not revoke (claim to pass when it is possible to play).

```
% Return what tile a player can play
% Can play on end with value X the tile [X,Y]
tile_playable_on_end(X,[X,Y]).
tile_playable_on_end(Y,[X,Y]).
% Can play on end with value X with a tile on
%the list that starts with a tile the given tile
can_play_on_end(X,[T|R],T) :- tile_playable_on_end(X,T).
can_play_on_end(X,[T|R],T) :- can_play_on_end(X,R,O).
%Can the player with hold H play on a chain with ends X and Y the tile T
can_play_low_end(X,Y,H,T) :- can_play_on_end(X,H,T).
can_play_high_end(Y,X,H,T) :- can_play_on_end(X,H,T).
can_play(X,Y,H T) :- can_play_low_end(X,Y,H,T).
can_play(X,Y,H,T) :- can_play_high_end(X,Y,H,T).
```

Fig. 2. Determine a tile to play in the players hand.

The experience of enabling Swift is crucial to port GNU-Prolog [6] to the robots. Porting the interpreter gprolog and the compiler gplc for interfacing with C amounts to downloading and patching the sources of a suitable version and using out C/C++ cross-compilers. However, calling prolog from Swift LLF-SMs requires cross-compiling a C/C++ wrapper. In our illustration we wrap the querying whether a player holding a specific hand can lay a tile on the board and must pass. This wrapper is now a C-function that is in itself wrapped and linked by Swift and thus, we can invoked in the label of a transition of the LLFSM defining the player's behaviour. However, this is easier said than done. While

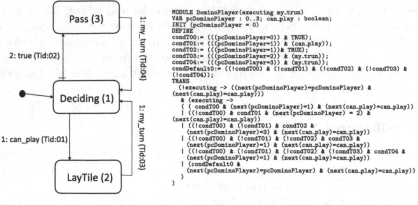

(a) Executable behaviour.   (b) Corresponding NuSMV code.

Fig. 3. Small example of an LLFSMs that enables deliberation. LLFSMs use a cross-action language semantics that enables automatic translation to NuSMV.

our earlier infrastructure enables to install gprolog on the host (the docker container) and to cross-compile gprolog for the Pepper, the gplc compiler offers no options to specify target architectures. Thus, although we can invoke our C cross-compiler for the .c files in the prolog project, we need to compile the .pl (the pure Prolog files) on the Pepper .s assembly files:

1. pl2wam -o step.wam step.pl
2. wam2ma -o step.ma step.wam
3. ma2asm -o step.s step.ma

We then copy the .s files back to the Docker host and continue with the cross compilation of the .s files to .o (object) files using the Pepper cross-assembly compiler. Now all files are linked in the host using our cross-linker and we have an executable (binary) that once copied to the Pepper executes as expected.

6 Conclusions

Model-driven software development promises high levels of abstraction. In this paper we have shown how to incorporate a modern systems programming language, Swift, with the most advanced features of object orientation that enables complete execution time control. We incorporated features of functional and logic programming. All this enables a high-level of abstraction that define executable behaviour models. Moreover, we can automatically produce input code for a model-checker for formal verification. We believe that these paradigms significantly improve the quality of the robotic behaviours and the facility to produce correct code both in the value domain as well as the time domain. With the combination of paradigms, we are not advocating just a choice of programming language, we are enabling safety through adherence to widely accepted design principles and philosophies. This is more important than the specific language; however, we believe the experience reported in this paper for enabling Swift as well as our Docker container constitute immediate, valuable contributions and pieces of knowledge for broadening the available tools in the RoboCup community.

References

1. The computer language benchmarks game, April 2018. https://benchmarksgame-team.pages.debian.net/benchmarksgame/compare/swift-gcc.html
2. Beekmans, G., Burgess, M., Dubbs, B.: Linux from scratch, April 2021. http://www.linuxfromscratch.org/lfs/
3. Bouyssounouse, B., Sifakis, J.: Programming languages for real-time systems. In: Bouyssounouse, B., Sifakis, J. (eds.) Embedded Systems Design. LNCS, vol. 3436, pp. 338–351. Springer, Heidelberg (2005). https://doi.org/10.1007/978-3-540-31973-3_25
4. Brooks, R.: A robust layered control system for a mobile robot. IEEE J. Robot. Autom. **2**(1), 14–23 (1986)
5. Carrillo, M., Estivill-Castro, V., Rosenblueth, D.A.: Verification and simulation of time-domain properties for models of behaviour. In: Hammoudi, S., Pires, L.F., Selić, B. (eds.) MODELSWARD 2020. CCIS, vol. 1361, pp. 225–249. Springer, Cham (2021). https://doi.org/10.1007/978-3-030-67445-8_10
6. Diaz, D., Codognet, P.: The GNU prolog system and its implementation. In: ACM Symposium on Applied Computing, SAC 2000, NY, USA, vol. 2, pp. 728–732 (2000). https://doi.org/10.1145/338407.338553
7. Drusinsky, D.: Modeling and Verification Using UML Statecharts: A Working Guide to Reactive System Design, Runtime Monitoring and Execution-Based Model Checking. Newnes (2006)
8. Eidhof, C., Kugler, F., Swierstra, W.: Functional Programming in Swift. Florian Kugler (2014)
9. Estivill-Castro, V., Ferrer-Mestres, J.: Path-finding in dynamic environments with PDDL-planners. In: 16th International Conference on Advanced Robotics, ICAR, pp. 1–7. IEEE (2013)
10. Estivill-Castro, V., Hexel, R.: Arrangements of finite-state machines-semantics, simulation, and model checking. In: International Conference on Model-Driven Engineering and Software Development, pp. 182–189. SCITEPRESS (2013)
11. Estivill-Castro, V., Hexel, R., Ramirez Regalado, A.: Architecture for logic programing with arrangements of finite-state machines. In: 1st CPS Week Workshop on Declarative Cyber-Physical Systems, DCPS, pp. 1–8. IEEE (2016)
12. Estivill-Castro, V., Hexel, R., Lusty, C.: High performance relaying of C++11 objects across processes and logic-labeled finite-state machines. In: Brugali, D., Broenink, J.F., Kroeger, T., MacDonald, B.A. (eds.) SIMPAR 2014. LNCS (LNAI), vol. 8810, pp. 182–194. Springer, Cham (2014). https://doi.org/10.1007/978-3-319-11900-7_16
13. Fuller, K.: swiftenv documentation – release 1.4.0, 10 September 2018. http://buildmedia.readthedocs.org/media/pdf/swiftenv/latest/swiftenv.pdf
14. GNU Project: GCC, the GNU Compiler Collection. https://gcc.gnu.org/
15. GNU Project: GNU Binutils. https://www.gnu.org/software/binutils/
16. GNU Project: GNU C Library (glibc). https://www.gnu.org/software/libc/

17. Harel, D.: On folk theorems. Commun. ACM **23**(7), 379–389 (1980)
18. Harel, D., Politi, M.: Modeling Reactive Systems with Statecharts: The Statemate Approach. McGraw-Hill, New York (1998)
19. Javaid, M., Estivill-Castro, V.: Explanations from a robotic partner build trust on the robot's decisions for collaborative human-humanoid interaction. Robotics **10**(1), 51 (2021)
20. The LLVM Project: The LLVM Compiler Infrastructure. https://llvm.org/
21. Lötzsch, M., Bach, J., Burkhard, H.-D., Jüngel, M.: Designing agent behavior with the extensible agent behavior specification language XABSL. In: Polani, D., Browning, B., Bonarini, A., Yoshida, K. (eds.) RoboCup 2003. LNCS (LNAI), vol. 3020, pp. 114–124. Springer, Heidelberg (2004). https://doi.org/10.1007/978-3-540-25940-4_10
22. Mataric, M.J.: Behavior-based control: examples from navigation, learning, and group behavior. J. Exp. Theor. Artif. Intell. **9**, 323–336 (1997)
23. Mataric, M.J.: The Robotics Primer. MIT Press, Cambridge (2007)
24. Mataric, M.: Integration of representation into goal-driven behavior-based robots. IEEE Trans. Robot. Autom. **8**(3), 304–312 (1992)
25. McColl, C., Estivill-Castro, V. Hexel, R.: An OO and functional framework for versatile semantics of logic-labelled finite state machines. In: The 12th International Conference on Software Engineering Advances, ICSEA, pp. 238–243 (2017)
26. McColl, C.: SwiftFSM - a finite state machines scheduler. Honours thesis (2016)
27. McColl, C., Gilmore, E.: Swift on Pepper. https://github.com/mipalgu/SwiftOnPepper
28. McColl, C., Estivill-Castro, V., Hexel, R.: Versatile but precise semantics for logic-labelled finite state machines. Int. J. Adv. Softw. **11**(3 & 4), 227–238 (2018)
29. Nicolescu, M.: Lecture 6: Lecture notes autonomous mobile robots CPE 470/670 (2016). http://slideplayer.com/slide/5382727/
30. Nicolescu, M.N., Mataric, M.J.: Deriving and using abstract representation in behavior-based systems. In: The 17th National Conference on Artificial Intelligence and 12th Conference on on Innovative Applications of Artificial Intelligence, p. 1087. AAAI Press (2000)
31. Owen-Hill, A.: What is the best programming language for robotics? (2016). https://blog.robotiq.com/what-is-the-best-programming-language-for-robotics-0
32. Pilone, D., Pitman, N.: UML 2.0 in a Nutshell. O'Reilly Media, Inc. (2005)
33. Rebouças, M., Pinto, G., Ebert, F., Torres, W., Serebrenik, A., Castor, F.: An empirical study on the usage of the swift programming language. In: 2016 IEEE 23rd International Conference on Software Analysis, Evolution, and Reengineering (SANER), vol. 1, pp. 634–638 (2016)
34. Risler, M., von Stryk, O.: Formal behavior specification of multi-robot systems using hierarchical state machines in XABSL. In: AAMAS08-Workshop on Formal Models and Methods for Multi-Robot Systems, Estoril, Portugal (2008)
35. Rumbaugh, J., Blaha, M.R., Lorensen, W., Eddy, F., Premerlani, W.: Object-Oriented Modelling and Design. Prentice-Hall, Englewood Cliffs (1991)
36. Samek, M.: Practical UML Statecharts in C/C++: Event-Driven Programming for Embedded Systems, 2nd edn. Newnes, Newton (2008)
37. Scheepers, T.: Virtualization and containerization of application infrastructure: a comparison. In: 21st Twente Student Conference on IT (2014)
38. Sheu, P.C.Y., Xue, Q.: Intelligent Robotic Planning Systems. World Scientific Publishing, River Edge (1993)
39. Singh, H.: Speed performance between swift and objective-C. Int. J. Eng. Appl. Sci. Technol. **1**(10), 185–189 (2016). http://www.ijeast.com

40. Solt, P.: Swift vs. Objective-C: 10 reasons the future favors Swift. InfoWorld (2015). https://www.infoworld.com/article/2920333/mobile-development/swift-vs-objective-c-10-reasons-the-future-favors-swift.html
41. Taylor, I.L.: A new elf linker. In: Proceedings of the GCC Developers' Summit, pp. 29–36 (2008). http://ols.fedoraproject.org/GCC/Reprints-2008/taylor-reprint.pdf

Step Adjustment for a Robust Humanoid Walk

Philip Reichenberg[1] and Thomas Röfer[1,2(✉)]

[1] Fachbereich 3 – Mathematik und Informatik, Universität Bremen,
Postfach 330 440, 28334 Bremen, Germany
{s_ksfo6n,roefer}@uni-bremen.de
[2] Deutsches Forschungszentrum für Künstliche Intelligenz, Cyber-Physical Systems,
Enrique-Schmidt-Str. 5, 28359 Bremen, Germany

Abstract. A stable and fast walk for humanoid robots is a challenging problem. In particular for multiple robots with different degrees of wear, it is necessary to tune several control parameters, which consumes a lot of time and wears down the hardware even more. In this paper, we present the latest improvements of our current walk, which enable a significant boost in the walking speed and stability, basically independent of the robot's hardware state. Based on a linear inverted pendulum model and thresholds determined statistically, the feet positions are adapted to follow the center of mass' direction of movement and let the robot walk in the direction of a potential fall if necessary. In addition, we ensure that the movement of the swing foot is parallel to the ground with a closed-loop feedback controller over the measured rotation errors of the support foot, without the direct use of the inertial measurement unit. The approaches presented allow for a up to 40% faster walk on different robots of the same type, without the need for a manual calibration.

1 Introduction

In the RoboCup Standard Platform League (SPL), all teams use the same humanoid robot, the NAO manufactured by SoftBank Robotics (currently, most teams use the NAO[6]). Although a number of different walks were developed in the past [2,4,8,9,12,14], in actual competitions, the current walks [1,3,6,10,11,13] all reach similar speeds. In addition, even after 12 years of development, the robots still fall down quite frequently in actual games. Falls often result from colliding with other robots while fighting for the ball, but often enough they also happen when a robot is simply walking from one point to another.

The NAO is equipped with 26 joints that are driven by 25 motors. Each leg contains six joints of which the only one that allows a rotation around the vertical axis is mechanically linked to the same joint in the other leg. All joints are position-controlled by motor controllers that are not accessible by the user. The NAO is also equipped with four pressure sensors under each of its feet and an inertial measurement unit (IMU) in its chest. The robot operates at a cycle time of 12 ms (i.e., 83.33 Hz). However, there is a delay of 3–4 cycles between sending

© Springer Nature Switzerland AG 2022
R. Alami et al. (Eds.): RoboCup 2021, LNAI 13132, pp. 28–39, 2022.
https://doi.org/10.1007/978-3-030-98682-7_3

joint commands and measuring the effects of these commands. This control delay makes the development of a fast and stable walk difficult. In addition, the joints typically also have 1°–3° of play, depending on the wear of the robot hardware.

Since 2017 in the SPL, robots play on artificial grass of 8 mm height, which many walks developed before could not handle. Many teams switched to the walk developed by Hengst [3], because of its high stability under such conditions. The walk, which is often called the *rUNSWift* walk, has four core properties: Firstly, it creates fixed trajectories for both the swing foot (lifted up in the walking direction) and the support foot (on the ground against the walking direction) based on the step size required to walk at the requested speed at the begin of each step. The trajectories are generated in Cartesian space, relative to the robot's torso (i.e., the robot's coordinate system), and converted to the joint space during the execution using inverse kinematics [10]. Although the trajectories of the support foot and the swing foot are not perfect mirrors of each other (because the first one is linear, the second one parabolic), the torso-relative center of mass (COM) of the robot basically stays above the middle between both feet all the time. Secondly, the walk uses a natural swinging motion to shift the weight between the two legs, i.e., it does not actively move the hip sideways, but simply lets gravity do its work. Thirdly, it uses the pressure sensors under the feet to determine when the weight shifts from one leg to the other and starts the next step in that moment. Fourthly, it uses the measurements of the sagittal gyroscope to press the support foot against the fall direction by increasing the ankle pitch angle proportional to the rotational speed of the torso.

The works in this paper are based on the version of that walk that was adapted by the team B-Human [10]. The paper is organized as follows. In Sect. 2, we discuss some of the related work. In Sect. 3, we present the first approach for a more robust walk, the step adjustment. It uses a tolerance range that is relative to an actual foot support area, the calibration of which is shown in Sect. 4. The second approach for a more stable walk is described in Sect. 5, which is keeping the swing foot parallel to the ground. Both approaches are evaluated in Sect. 6. Finally, we conclude the paper in Sect. 7.

2 Related Work

Tilgner *et al.* [13] use a similar approach as Hengst [3]. However, in their work, the support foot switch is predicted to compensate for the delay of 48 ms. In addition, the steps are adjusted by a stability controller based on the error in the body tilt. For example, if the robot is tilting backwards the step duration is increased and the forward velocity reduced.

In the approach by Schwarz *et al.* [11], a step size is calculated based on the requested walking speed. With the resulting foot positions, a trajectory for the zero moment point (ZMP) is determined. With a flexible linear inverted pendulum (FLIP) [15], a COM trajectory is calculated, which shall follow the ZMP one. The FLIP is extended with a second COM, which in theory models the flexibility of the limbs and pulls on the first COM. In addition, several PID controllers are used to compensate various errors. The COM is shifted based on body angle errors. The hip and ankle joints are adjusted based on gyroscope and body angle errors. The legs are rotated based on body angle errors to keep the feet parallel to the ground.

Mellmann et al. [6] calculate a sequence of ZMPs based on a requested walking direction, one for each execution cycle of the following step. Afterwards with a linear inverted pendulum model [5] (LIPM), the COM trajectory is determined and with that the 3D trajectory of the feet and the corresponding joint angles for each motion cycle. For a higher stability, a PD controller is used in the step target generation based on the COM. In addition, if the average COM error exceeds a threshold, the robot must come to a full stop as long as the error does not drop below a certain threshold. During the step execution, three stabilization mechanisms are applied. The height and the roll angle of the legs are adjusting in the moment a foot is lifted. Another controller balances the body to keep it upright. Thirdly, the ankles are adjusted based on the body orientation.

Similar to the walk used in the paper, the one developed by Missura et al. [7] first determines the foot target positions for each step and then interpolates between the current positions and the target ones. With a LIPM, those foot target positions are modified instantly when responding to a disturbance. As a result, the robot starts to walk backwards when pushed from the front and is walking forward when pushed from the back. The difference to the approach presented in this paper is that we do not calculate new target positions for the feet but just let the swing foot follow the COM without the use of the ZMP and move the support foot against the swing foot's direction.

A general approach to reduce the risk of falling when fighting for the ball is to move the arms to the back of the robot and shifting or tilting the upper body forward. This reduces the overall footprint of the robot and reduces the likelihood of colliding with another robot. Such an approach is used by most teams. Basler et al. [1] are tilting the upper body even more to the front in a tackling situation, which makes the robot more stable, as disturbances, such as collisions with other robots, from the front are less harmful.

3   Step Adjustment

Although the two stability mechanism of the *rUNSWift* walk, i.e., detecting the change of the support foot and gyro-based balancing, can counter a certain amount of disturbances while walking, there are situations which require to change the steps itself to prevent falls. For instance, the gyro-based balancing has its limits, in particular for preventing falls to the back, because the soles of the feet extend less to the back than to the front and therefore, they cannot exert that much force against the ground to keep the body upright. In addition, the available torque of the motors is limited, so even some swings to the front cannot be compensated although the foot might be long enough to do so. Therefore, the goal of the step adjustment is to modify the step trajectories themselves instead of just pitching the ankle joints. However, these adjustments are only applied when the robot reaches a state the original walk cannot cope with.

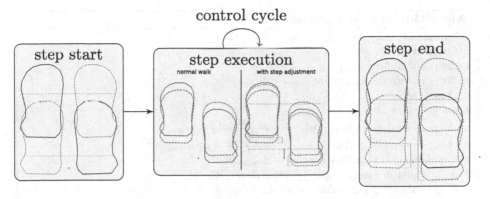

Fig. 1. The step adjustment. The planned step (cyan) is to swing the right foot forward, while the left (support) foot is moved backward. The projected COM (green) is outside the tolerance range (yellow) by an, in this case negative, offset δ (red). In each control cycle, the feet (dark blue) are moved closer to their planned end positions (brown). Meanwhile, the step adjustment adds δ to the position of the swing foot and thereby moves the foot slowly backwards in the direction of the COM, and half of the offset is subtracted from the position of the support foot (violet). At the end of the step, the robot effectively walked backwards for a small step (dark green). At the start of the step, the tolerance range is shown relative to the initial foot positions (black). At the end of the step, it is shown relative to the new foot positions (dark green). (Color figure online)

For example in a situation in which the robot is walking forward and its body starts tilting backwards, the torso does not seem to keep up with the legs. Therefore, the step size is reduced (up to a full backward step), which allows the upper body to "catch up". This is achieved with the approach that is shown in Fig. 1. The COM of the robot is projected onto the plane of the feet (m). The robot is considered to be stable if the projected COM is located inside a tolerance range ($T_{\min}, T_{\max}$) that is spanned by fixed regions on both feet. If the COM leaves this area, the swing foot is moved in that direction by the amount that the COM left the area (δ) and the support foot is moved in the opposite direction by half that amount, until the COM is once again inside the tolerance range. This adjustment is only applied in the sagittal direction and the adjustment size is clipped (by $p_{\max}$), to ensure that the feet do not move with too much speed. Also half of δ is applied on the support foot, because in test trials applying nothing or the full value on the support foot resulted in a significantly less stable walk, while the half showed a significant boost in the stabilization. This is due the fact that the full value results in an overcompensation. Not adjusting the position of the support foot results in both feet being placed too far backward or forward. Therefore, it would not adapt the walking direction based on the fall direction. The projected COM is lowpass-filtered to avoid any jerky movements due to measurement noise. As shown in Fig. 1, this can lead to a step in the opposite direction of the current walking direction. In this case, the next step will be very

---

Algorithm 1: Step Adjustment

Input: $w_t, w_{t-1}, \bar{w}_{t-1}, u_t, m, p_{\max}, T_{\min}, T_{\max}$
Output: $\bar{w}_t, \bar{u}_t$

1 $\Delta w_{t-1} = \bar{w}_{t-1} - w_{t-1}$
2 $\Delta \hat{w}_{t-1} = \max(-p_{\max}, \min(p_{\max}, -\Delta w_{t-1}))$
3 $\Delta w_t = w_t - w_{t-1}$
4 $\hat{w}_t = \bar{w}_{t-1} + \Delta w_t$
5 $\Delta_{min} = \min(\hat{w}_t + \Delta \hat{w}_{t-1}, u_t - \frac{\Delta w_{t-1} + \Delta \hat{w}_{t-1}}{2}) + T_{\min}$
6 $\Delta_{max} = \max(\hat{w}_t + \Delta \hat{w}_{t-1}, u_t - \frac{\Delta w_{t-1} + \Delta \hat{w}_{t-1}}{2}) + T_{\max}$
7 $\delta = \min(m - \Delta_{\min}, 0) + \max(m - \Delta_{max}, 0)$
8 $\hat{p}_{\min} = \min(0, -p_{\max} - \Delta w_t) - \max(\Delta \hat{w}_{t-1}, 0)$
9 $\hat{p}_{\max} = \max(0, p_{\max} - \Delta w_t) - \min(\Delta \hat{w}_{t-1}, 0)$
10 $\bar{w}_t = \hat{w}_t + \max(\hat{p}_{\min}, \min(\hat{p}_{\max}, \delta))$
11 $\bar{u}_t = u_t - \frac{(\bar{w}_t - w_t)}{2}$
12 return $\bar{w}_t, \bar{u}_t$

---

small, because the swing foot is already in front and the support foot is in the back. In combination, this results in two steps on the spot (or even more) that stabilize the robot, after which it can continue to walk normally.

The step adjustment algorithm is shown in Algorithm 1. All variables are in the robot's system of coordinates. w and u describe the forward components of the swing foot's and support foot's position, respectively, as computed by the original walk. Variables with a hat represent temporary variables. Variables with a bar describe the adjusted forward components of both feet. t addresses the current control frame, $t-1$ the previous one. The tolerance range was determined beforehand by statistically analyzing the projected COM of one of our robots from the log files of a competition game, with the calibration that will be discussed in Sect. 4 applied. Both values are distances relative to the feet sole origins in the sagittal direction. Since the relative positions of the feet towards each other always change while walking, we distinguish between three different regions in the joint area of both soles of the feet that are separated by the origins (i.e., the points below the ankles) of both feet (cf. Fig. 2). The COM positions in the middle region are considered to be stable. Therefore, this region is ignored in the analysis. The two remaining regions together always extent the length of a single foot, independent of the relative positions of the two feet. The heatmap of the COM positions is shown in Fig. 4. For the tolerance range, using the range $[-2\sigma \ldots 2\sigma]$ seems to give good results.

To compensate for the sensor delay of up to 48 ms (i.e., four control cycles), the behavior of the COM is predicted using a LIPM. Thus, the relation between the COM and tolerance range is estimated based on the commanded joint angles and the estimated current position of the COM, reducing the reaction time significantly. In addition, we apply an automatic per-robot calibration procedure for the support area of the feet to compensate for variances between different robots. This is described in the next section.

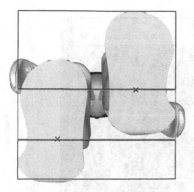

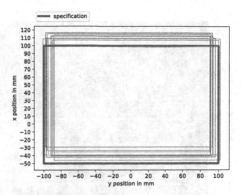

Fig. 2. The three supporting areas. The blue area is defined from the heel of the furthest backward foot to its origin point. The green one is defined between the origin points of both feet. If they are parallel to each other then the green area does not exist. The red area is defined from the origin of the furthest forward foot to its tip. (Color figure online)

Fig. 3. The calibrated support rectangles, relative to the origin of both feet, of several NAO[6] robots. The support polygon based on the specification of the robot is shown in red. (Color figure online)

4   Foot Support Rectangle Calibration

The NAO is equipped with joint position sensors and an IMU. Both are used to determine the COM position projected to the foot area. The joints can have play and IMUs in different robots might return slightly different results. This can result in deviations in the computation of the projected COM in relation to the tolerance range between different robots. Instead of calibrating each joint and calibrating the IMU, we use an abstraction that is sufficient for walking: the support rectangle. This is the rectangle in the foot plane that spans all the projected COM values of a standing robot that do not result in a fall. To determine the support rectangle, the robot executes a semi-automatic calibration procedure, in which it determines, how far it can shift its torso in all four directions while standing normally on both feet, before it topples over. The beginning of the fall is detected using the gyroscopes. At this moment, the COM projected onto the foot plane defines a border of the support rectangle of both feet. The robot is caught manually to prevent it from actually falling down. The calibrated support rectangle is used to interpret the boundaries of the tolerance range (which are given as percentages of the foot length) as described in Sect. 3. In addition, they are used as tipping edges for the LIPM used to predict the current COM.

Figure 3 shows the calibrated foot areas of several NAO[6] robots, in comparison to the foot area resulting from the hardware specification of the robot. There seems to be a shift of between one and two cm in the forward and backward direction and a small shift to the sides.

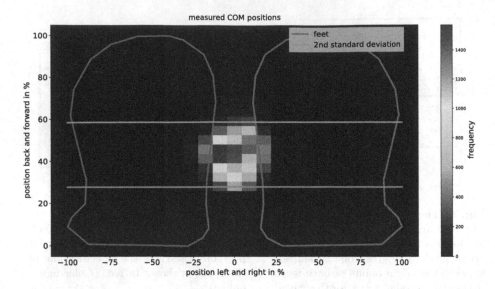

Fig. 4. The COM positions relative to the foot area during a of a robot during a half of a competition game. The actual dimensions of the feet are abstracted to percentages. The positions of two times the standard deviation σ are marked at 27.8% and 58.6%. The average is located at 43.2%.

To get a fully automatic calibration procedure without the need of a person to catch the robot, the robot can approximate the forward and backward edges while it walks. From a calibrated robot we can measure the average COM position in the foot plane (see Fig. 4). As long as the robots do not walk too fast, they can walk stable without much deviation in the torso tilt. Therefore, a non-calibrated robot can measure its average COM position for a short period of time while walking slowly. Afterwards, the difference of the desired and measured average is used to shift the calibrated forward and backward foot support edges. This procedure is currently used during the preparation for remote soccer games. A robot automatically walks to certain positions on the field to perform an automatic extrinsic camera calibration. While walking, also its foot support rectangle is calibrated.

5   Swing Foot Leveling

A problem of the NAO robots is the limited strength of the joint motors. A typical observation when a robot falls to the front without colliding with another robot is shown in Fig. 5. Here the robot is walking forward, with the right foot being the supporting one and the left foot being the swing foot. The swing foot is moving parallel to the theoretical ground (red line), as if the robot would have a perfectly straight upper body. The supporting foot is assumed to be parallel to the real ground (green line) and has full ground contact. Therefore the rotation

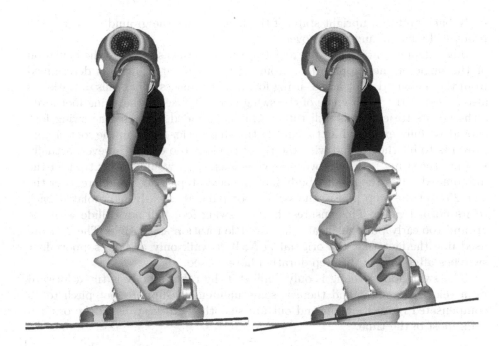

Fig. 5. The feet rotations of a robot while walking. Left: the feet under normal circumstances. Right: The robot's body swings quickly forward and is already tilted a lot. The right foot is the support foot, the left foot the swing foot. The ground is shown in green. The movement direction of the swing foot is shown in red. (Color figure online)

of the supporting foot equals the rotation of the ground. To keep the robot upright, the supporting foot must also move parallel to the theoretical ground, i.e., both feet should be parallel to each other. But in situations in which the robot already starts to tilt forward, even with a small angular velocity, the joint motors are too weak to press against the robot's weight. As a result the hip joint of the supporting foot gets stuck, while the other joints continue their movement, because those are not pressing against the robot's weight. This tilts the robot even further forward and the swing foot will inevitably touch the ground earlier than expected. The tip of the swing foot moves really fast into the ground, which is then measured as a support foot switch. Afterwards, the new support foot, in this case the left foot, is really far backward while the robot is still tilted forward a lot. In most cases the robot will fall shortly afterwards in the same step phase.

Since hardware changes are not allowed in the SPL and we also do not have access to the parameters of the motor controllers, the problem can only be changed by adapting the trajectory of the swing foot. The goal is that the swing foot should reach its intended target position as close as possible, because its support is required in that position to counter a possible fall and to bring the body back up to an upright state. If the foot touches the ground too early, the robot will stumble and topple over.

The adaptation of the swing foot trajectory works as follows: The deviation of the angle of the support foot from its intended pitch angle is determined from the measured joint angles using forward kinematics. Then this deviation is also added to the pitch angle of the swing foot. This keeps the swing foot level, although its trajectory is still tilted. This is intended, because the swing foot should be fully extended at the end of the step cycle. Leveling the foot simply prevents to hit the ground with the tip of the foot too early. However, actually keeping the swing foot level over the whole step cycle would simply transfer the unintended tilt of the robot's body into the next step cycle. Therefore, over the last 25% of the step phase, the swing foot pitch is linearly interpolated back to its normal value. This ensures that the swing foot will not collide with the ground too early but that it also has as little rotation as possible. The 25% are used due the fact that the original *rUNSWift* walk only accepts support foot switches after 75% of the step duration have passed.

The swing foot leveling is only applied if the robot's body is tilted forward by a relevant amount and there is some unintended support foot pitch to be compensated (transitions in and out are smoothed) to keep using the original walk most of the time.

6   Evaluation

We evaluated our adjustments with a test setup (see Fig. 6)[1]. We let several robots walk over the field with different configurations: The old walk (Old), the old walk with only the walk step adjustment (wsa), the old walk with only the swing foot leveling (sfl), and the new walk with both adjustments (New). Each configuration was tested eight times, distributed over four different NAO[6] robots. We counted how often the robots fell at each obstacle with the default forward walking speed of $250\frac{mm}{s}$ used by our team B-Human. The results are shown in Table 1.

All configurations except for the new walk showed similar result. With the first three configurations, the robots fell on average 2.5 times in each try, while the robots with the new walk fell less than once per try, which is only one third compared to the old walk.

We also compared the old and new walk with higher forward walking speeds of $300\frac{mm}{s}$ and $350\frac{mm}{s}$. Here we tested both configurations only four times each, distributed over two different Nao[6] robots. The results are shown in Table 2. Once again the new walk performed significantly better than the old one, with about 45.5% less falls. Also even with a 40% higher walking speed, the new walk fell about 33% less than the old walk with the default walking speed. However, there were two main problems with the new walk: On one hand the step adjustment sometimes started too late, while the robots were already falling backwards too

---

[1] A comparison between the old and the new walk is shown here: https://www.youtube.com/watch?v=N_Q7qLDYqyY.

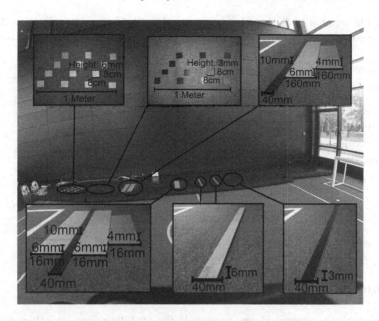

Fig. 6. The construction of the test setup. The robots walked from the right to the left, with the obstacles hidden under the field carpet.

Table 1. The number of fallen robots for the different walk configurations, with the default forward walking speed of $250\frac{mm}{s}$. Each configuration was tested eight times.

Obstacle configuration	Old	WSA	SFL	New	Sum
First three meters	0	0	0	0	0
3 mm edge	0	0	0	0	0
First 6 mm edge	6	4	4	2	16
Second 6 mm edge	5	4	4	1	14
First 1 cm ramp	3	4	5	0	12
Second 1 cm ramp	3	5	3	0	11
3 mm wooden blocks	0	0	0	0	0
6 mm wooden blocks	4	1	4	4	13
Sum	21	18	20	7	66

fast. On the other hand, especially at the last obstacle, the step duration was a lot longer for a few walking steps. The walk has no balancing for the sideways swinging, therefore the robot can only keep walking until the sideways swinging reduced itself and the step duration becomes normal again. This resulted in a few falls, in which the robots fell diagonally or even sideways.

Table 2. The number of fallen robots, compared between the old and new walk with walking speeds of $300\frac{mm}{s}$ and $350\frac{mm}{s}$. Both configurations were tested four times.

Obstacle configuration	Old $300\frac{mm}{s}$	New $300\frac{mm}{s}$	Old $350\frac{mm}{s}$	New $350\frac{mm}{s}$	Sum
First three meters	0	0	0	0	0
3 mm edge	0	0	0	0	0
First 6 mm edge	0	1	2	2	5
Second 6 mm edge	0	1	3	0	4
First 1 cm ramp	3	0	4	0	7
Second 1 cm ramp	1	0	2	1	4
3 mm wooden blocks	2	0	0	1	3
6 mm wooden blocks	3	3	2	3	11
Sum	9	5	13	7	34

7   Conclusion and Future Work

In this paper, we presented an approach for stabilizing an existing walk for the NAO robot. It is based on two ideas: On the one hand, the positions of the feet are adapted to ensure that the COM stays above a safe area in the foot plane. On the other hand, the swing foot is kept parallel to the ground to avoid ramming the tip of the foot into the ground when the robot is tilted too far forward. Together, both approaches result in a faster and more stable walk. However, the evaluation also showed that the step adjustment sometimes adapts the foot positions too late and the support foot switch sometimes takes longer than expected, which brings the robot into a diagonal or sideways fall. Unfortunately, the approaches presented in this paper do not reduce the number of falls resulting from collisions with other robots. We are currently investigating how such falls could be prevented as well.

Acknowledgements. We thank the team rUNSWift and in particular Bernhard Hengst for releasing the source code of their walking engine. We also thank the past and current members of the team B-Human for developing the software that is the basis for the work presented in this paper. Without them, this work would not have been possible.

References

1. Basler, J., et al.: HULKs team research report 2019 (2019). https://hulks.de/_files/ TRR_2019.pdf
2. Graf, C., Röfer, T.: A center of mass observing 3D-LIPM gait for the RoboCup standard platform league humanoid. In: Röfer, T., Mayer, N.M., Savage, J., Saranlı, U. (eds.) RoboCup 2011. LNCS (LNAI), vol. 7416, pp. 102–113. Springer, Heidelberg (2012). https://doi.org/10.1007/978-3-642-32060-6_9

3. Hengst, B.: rUNSWift Walk 2014 report. Technical report, School of Computer Science & Engineering University of New South Wales, Sydney 2052, Australia (2014). http://cgi.cse.unsw.edu.au/~robocup/2014ChampionTeamPaperReports/20140930-Bernhard.Hengst-Walk2014Report.pdf
4. Jahn, K.U., Borkmann, D., Reinhardt, T., Tilgner, R., Rexin, N., Seering, S.: Team research report 2009 (2009). https://robots.htwk-leipzig.de/fileadmin/portal/m_nao/Publikationen/TRR_2009.pdf?lang=de
5. Kajita, S., et al.: Biped walking pattern generation by using preview control of zero-moment point. In: Proceedings of the IEEE International Conference on Robotics and Automation, ICRA 2003, vol. 2, pp. 1620–1626, September 2003
6. Mellmann, H., et al.: Berlin United - Nao Team Humboldt team report 2018 (2018). https://github.com/NaoDevils/CodeRelease/blob/master/TeamReport2019.pdf
7. Missura, M., Bennewitz, M., Behnke, S.: Capture steps: robust walking for humanoid robots. Int. J. Humanoid Rob. 16(06), 1950032 (2019)
8. Qian, Y., et al.: The UPennalizers RoboCup 2015 Standard Platform League team description paper (2015). https://fling.seas.upenn.edu/~robocup/files/2015Report.pdf
9. Riebesel, N., Hasselbring, A., Peters, L., Poppinga, F.: Team research report 2016 (2016). https://hulks.de/_files/TRR_2016.pdf
10. Röfer, T., et al.: B-Human team report and code release 2019 (2019). https://github.com/bhuman/BHumanCodeRelease/raw/coderelease2019/CodeRelease2019.pdf
11. Schwarz, I., Urbann, O., Larisch, A., Brämer, D.: Nao Devils team report 2019 (2019). https://github.com/NaoDevils/CodeRelease/blob/master/TeamReport2019.pdf
12. Tilgner, R., et al.: Team research report Nao-Team HTWK (2018). https://robots.htwk-leipzig.de/fileadmin/portal/m_nao/Publikationen/TRR_2017.pdf?lang=de
13. Tilgner, R., et al.: Team research report Nao-Team HTWK (2020). https://drive.google.com/file/d/13s28gGVsKkxd8ogoNfEf4Ic5Gyysi137/view
14. Tsogias, A.: Laufen für den NAO-Roboter mittels Zero-Moment Point Preview Control. Master thesis, Faculty 3 - Mathematics and Computer Science, University of Bremen (2016)
15. Urbann, O., Schwarz, I., Hofmann, M.: Flexible linear inverted pendulum model for cost-effective biped robots. In: 2015 IEEE-RAS 15th International Conference on Humanoid Robots (Humanoids), pp. 128–131. IEEE (2015)

Inter-task Similarity Measure
for Heterogeneous Tasks

Sergio A. Serrano[1]([⊠]) [iD], Jose Martinez-Carranza[1,2] [iD], and L. Enrique Sucar[1] [iD]

[1] Óptica y Electrónica, Computer Science Department,
Instituto Nacional de Astrofísica, Sta. María Tonantzintla, Puebla, Mexico
{sserrano,carranza,esucar}@inaoep.mx
[2] Computer Science Department, University of Bristol, Bristol, UK

Abstract. A long term goal in robotics is *lifelong learning*, in which a robot learns to perform new tasks without human intervention. For this a promising alternative is reinforcement learning (RL), in which an agent learns how to solve sequential decision-making problems by interacting with its environment. Despite the effectiveness of RL, learning in a trial-and-error way can be infeasible in robotics applications, in which long training periods can significantly deteriorate hardware. For robots that face long sequences of tasks, transfer learning represents an alternative to reduce training time, by transferring knowledge from previously learned tasks. However, in domains such as service robotics, identifying reusable pieces of knowledge and transferring them across tasks can be challenging, due to the mismatch between the state-action spaces (heterogeneous tasks). Thus, in this article we present an inter-task similarity measure and a transfer learning method for heterogeneous tasks. Through experimental evaluations, we show that the proposed measure is able to rank tasks in a way that prioritizes those that cause a larger increment of the learning performance in a target task. Additionally, results show that for some tasks the similarity measure can be computed with few data, enabling significant speedups in the learning process by transferring knowledge at an early stage.

Keywords: Inter-task similarity · Reinforcement learning · Transfer learning · Heterogeneous tasks

1 Introduction

In Reinforcement Learning (RL) the goal is to have a sequential decision-making system (agent) learn certain behavior by interacting with its environment. In the context of robotics, the robot is expected to interact with a real physical environment, that contains intricacies that are sometimes difficult to model with precision in a simulator. Thus, the robot is sometimes forced to learn by interacting with the real environment. By doing so, the robot hardware is prone to suffer from wear and tear, also known as *curse of real-world samples* [8]. Hence,

© Springer Nature Switzerland AG 2022
R. Alami et al. (Eds.): RoboCup 2021, LNAI 13132, pp. 40–52, 2022.
https://doi.org/10.1007/978-3-030-98682-7_4

it is particularly important for robotic agents to learn with the least amount of data as possible.

Lifelong learning constitutes a scenario in which a service robot will face a long sequence of tasks during its lifetime, that presents an opportunity for transferring knowledge across tasks and, hopefully, reduce the training time in some of them. In lifelong learning, the agent strives to exploit common traits between previously learned tasks and the one currently being learned to transfer knowledge. For instance, if a robot has so far learned to pour a glass of water and go from the dining room to the kitchen, then it would be useful to transfer knowledge when it learns to go to the dining room and pour a glass of wine. However, due to the mismatch between the state-action space of the former tasks and the latter, most lifelong learning methods would not be able to identify the common features across tasks for knowledge transfer purposes.

Thus, in order to employ a transfer/lifelong learning approach in a scenario with tasks that differ in their state-action space (*i.e.*, heterogeneous tasks [9]), in this article we present an inter-task similarity measure and a transfer learning method for heterogeneous tasks. In order to assess the similarity of two tasks that differ in their state-action space, we compare their Q matrices by applying a clustering process across states and actions, from which two "intersection" matrices are derived and summarized in a similarity score. This score is used to rank the potential source tasks to transfer to a target task. To transfer knowledge from the more "promising" task, the intersection matrices computed for a pair of Q matrices are employed to transfer *Q-values* between them.

The proposed inter-task similarity measure and transfer learning method are evaluated in a set of six different RL tasks. We show how the similarity measure is able to correctly select a source task that will improve the learning in a target task, using the proposed TL algorithm. Additionally, we present an analysis on the data required by the similarity measure to produce a good estimate, showing that employing our proposal in a model-free learning setting is a feasible option.

2   Background and Related Work

In RL, sequential decision-making learning problems are modeled as a Markov Decision Process (MDP). An MDP is defined by a tuple $M = \langle S, A, T, R \rangle$, where S is the of states a system can adopt, A is the set of actions that can be performed to modify the state of the system, $T : S \times A \times S \rightarrow [0, 1]$ is the transition function that describes the probability of the system transiting between a pair of states given that an action was taken, and $R : S \times A \times S \rightarrow \mathbb{R}$ is the reward function, which assigns a scalar value to every state-action-state tuple, representing which state transitions are preferred [10]. An MDP policy $\pi : S \rightarrow A$ is a function that indicates which action should be taken at any state of the system. To solve an MDP, one must find an optimal policy π^*, as described in Eq. 1 (which is derived from Bellman's equation [2], see Eq. 2), where γ is a discount factor.

$$\pi^*(s) = argmax_a \left\{ R(s,a) + \gamma \sum_{s' \in S} T(s,a,s')V^{\pi^*}(s') \right\} \tag{1}$$

$$V^{\pi}(s) = max_a \left\{ R(s,a) + \gamma \sum_{s' \in S} T(s,a,s')V^{\pi}(s') \right\} \tag{2}$$

Depending on the information that is available about the system one will select an algorithm to find the optimal policy. In the model-free learning setting, only sets S and A are known *a priori*. The agent must interact with the environment (system) to learn an action-value function $Q : S \times A \to \mathbb{R}$ by backing up the rewards that have been observed through time. $Q(s,a)$ represents the expected return after action a is taken from state s, and the best current policy can be obtained by selecting the highest valued action form the current state, *i.e.*, $a^* = \text{argmax}_a Q(s,a)$. Q-learning [17] is an example of a model-free learning algorithm in which, for MDPs with discrete state-action spaces, the Q function can be represented as a matrix, also called Q table or Q matrix.

Considering that to obtain a good estimate of the Q function can take long periods of interactions with the environment, there are methods concerned with reducing the time required to learn. Transfer learning (TL) refers to a collection of techniques whose goal is to reduce the training time and/or improve the final performance of a learning system in a target task by transferring knowledge from a source task [14]. One way to evaluate the proficiency of TL methods in RL is by comparing the performance of the agent when knowledge was transferred to when it learns from scratch.

However, one of the main challenges in TL is to select the source of the knowledge. Hence, it is crucial to have a way to identify when the learning agent has at its disposal useful knowledge. A task similarity measure (TSM) is a function that assigns a scalar value to a pair of tasks to express how similar they are. Under the assumption that similar tasks share common features, relevant for TL, a TSM could be used as a heuristic for a TL system through time. For instance, in [4] three TSM are proposed, based on the immediate reward, the policy overlap in states, and the mean square error between the Q functions. Their TSMs are used to approximate the speedup that a source task will bring, however, they require tasks to be completely learned in order to work.

In [12] the concept of homomorphism is extended to MDPs, where the structure that should be maintained are the transition and reward function. A soft-homomorphism is introduced, so that the closer a pair of MDPs is to maintain a hard-homomorphism, the more similar these MDPs. Similarly, in [5,6] the concept of bisimulation is employed to define a class of equivalence for states within the same MDP. In [11] the bisimulation-based metric for states is extended with the Kantorovich and Hausdorff metrics [7] to propose two metrics that asses the distance between a pair of different MDPs. Alternatively, in [1] the inter-task similarity is assessed based on the transition functions. A Restricted Boltzmann Machine (RBM) is trained on a data set sampled form one task, and then a data set sampled from the other task is reconstructed with the trained RBM. The reconstruction error is regarded as the similarity value for the pair of tasks.

One aspect that the works reviewed so far have in common is that they asses the similarity between MDPs that share the same state-action space. Despite the potential benefit of transferring knowledge across heterogeneous tasks [16], very little efforts have been taken towards this direction. In [13] is proposed a TL algorithm and a TSM for heterogeneous tasks, based on state variable and action mappings. Their algorithm creates an approximate model of the transition function in the target task, and then evaluates how well the model predicts the transition model in the source task with different mappings. The mapping with the lowest mean square error is selected. However, the main drawbacks of this approach is the exhaustive search in the space of all mappings, and that it does not take into account differences between the reward function of a pair of tasks.

In contrast to the works covered in this section, the TSM we propose is applicable for tasks that do not share the state-action space, and considers both the reward and the transition function to compare tasks. Additionally, by adopting a data-driven approach, our method can be applied to model-free learning settings.

3   Similarity Measure for Heterogeneous Tasks

This section introduces a novel method to compute the similarity between heterogeneous tasks with discrete state-action spaces (Sects. 3.1 and 3.2), and a technique to transfer knowledge based on the similarity measure (Sect. 3.3).

3.1   Intersection Matrices

In order to assess the similarity of two tasks that differ in their state-action space, we compare their Q matrices. For a pair of matrices Q_1 and Q_2, an actions-intersection matrix I^A and a states-intersection matrix I^S are computed following the procedure that is summarized in Fig. 1 and described below.

Let Q_1 and Q_2 be matrices with dimensions $N_1 \times M_1$ and $N_2 \times M_2$, respectively. Then, for each matrix $Q \in \{Q_1, Q_2\}$ (where $N \times M$ are the dimensions of Q) the following steps are performed:

1. Computation of $C^{row} \in \mathbb{R}^{N \times M}$: Let $Q(i, *) = [Q_{i,0}, ..., Q_{i,M-1}]$ be the i-th row of matrix Q. K-means is applied to the elements of $Q(i, *)$ to produce K clusters. The i-th row of matrix C^{row}, $C^{row}(i, *) = [C_{i,0}^{row}, ..., C_{i,M-1}^{row}]$, contains the cluster labels assigned to each element of $Q(i, *)$. That is, $C_{i,j}^{row}$ holds the label assigned to $Q_{i,j}$ after producing K clusters with the elements of $Q(i, *)$.

2. Computation of $C^{col} \in \mathbb{R}^{N \times M}$: Let $Q(*, j) = [Q_{0,j}, ..., Q_{N-1,j}]^T$ be the j-th column of matrix Q. K-means is applied to the elements of $Q(*, j)$ to produce K clusters. The j-th column of matrix C^{col}, $C^{col}(*, j) = [C_{0,j}^{col}, ..., C_{N-1,j}^{col}]^T$, contains the cluster labels assigned to each element of $Q(*, j)$. That is, $C_{i,j}^{col}$ holds the label assigned to $Q_{i,j}$ after producing K clusters with the elements of $Q(*, j)$.

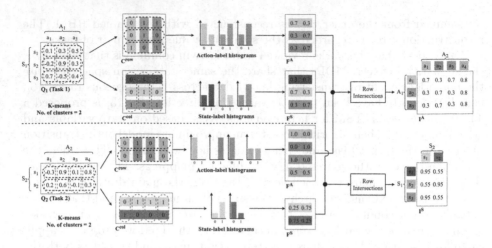

Fig. 1. Computation of the intersection matrices I^A and I^S for a pair of Q matrices Q_1 and Q_2. Matrices C^{row} and C^{col} contain the labels assigned to the elements of the Q matrix if they were clustered row-wise (red dotted ovals) and column-wise (blue dotted ovals), respectively. Each row in matrix F^A is a histogram for the label frequency of each column in C^{row}, whereas in matrix F^S rows count the label frequency of each row in C^{col}. The elements of matrices I^A and I^S represent the intersection value between the rows of two F^A and F^S, respectively. (Best seen in color)

3. Computation of $F^A \in \mathbb{R}^{M \times K}$: The j-th row of F^A, $F^A(j, *) = [F^A_{j,0}, ..., F^A_{j,K-1}]$, represents a normalized histogram for the frequencies of labels in the j-th column of C^{row}. That is, $F^A_{j,k}$ holds the proportion of times label k appeared in the j-th column of C^{row}.

4. Computation of $F^S \in \mathbb{R}^{N \times K}$: The i-th row of F^S, $F^S(i, *) = [F^S_{i,0}, ..., F^S_{i,K-1}]$, represents a normalized histogram for the frequencies of labels in the i-th row of C^{col}. That is, $F^S_{i,k}$ holds the proportion of times label k appeared in the i-th row of C^{col}.

After F^A_1, F^S_1 and F^A_2, F^S_2 have been computed for Q_1 and Q_2, respectively, the intersection matrices I^A and I^S are computed as follows:

1. Computation of $I^A \in \mathbb{R}^{M_1 \times M_2}$: The element $I^A_{i,j}$ holds the intersection value between the i-th row of F^A_1 and the j-th row of F^A_2, i.e., $Intersection(F^A_1(i, *), F^A_2(j, *))$ (see Eq. 3).

2. Computation of $I^S \in \mathbb{R}^{N_1 \times N_2}$: The element $I^S_{i,j}$ holds the intersection value between the i-th row of F^S_1 and the j-th row of F^S_2, i.e., $Intersection(F^S_1(i, *), F^S_2(j, *))$ (see Eq. 3).

$$Intersection(u, v) = \sum_i min(u(i), v(i)) \tag{3}$$

3.2   Similarity Scores

Once the intersection matrices have been computed for a pair of Q matrices, the mean value is computed on each intersection matrix. As a result, two values are obtained: $mean(I^A)$ and $mean(I^S)$, which are used to assess the similarity between the Q matrices of two tasks with different state-action spaces. Additionally, the larger $mean(I^A)$ and $mean(I^S)$, the greater the similarity between a pair of tasks.

3.3   Knowledge Transfer

To transfer knowledge between a pair of heterogeneous tasks, the intersection matrices computed for a pair of Q matrices are employed to transfer Q-values between them. Let Q_1, Q_2 be the Q matrices of MDPs M_1 and M_2, I^A, I^S their intersection matrices, and (s_i, a_j) an element from the state-action space of M_2 ($i.e.$, $(s_i, a_j) \in S_2 \times A_2$). To determine which value should be transferred from Q_1 to $Q_2(s_i, a_j)$ the following procedure is performed:

1. Identification of the most similar state: Find the index k that maximizes $I^S_{k,i}$. That is, the most similar state from S_1 (the state space of M_1) to s_i should be the one with the largest intersection value.
2. Identification of the most similar action: Find the index l that maximizes $I^A_{l,j}$. That is, the most similar action from A_1 (the action space of M_1) to a_j should be the one with the largest intersection value.
3. Q-value transfer: Assign the value of $Q_1(s_k, a_l)$ to $Q_2(s_i, a_j)$.

In order to transfer knowledge from Q_1 to Q_2, steps 1–3 are repeated for every state-action pair in $S_2 \times A_2$. Figure 2 illustrates an example of how to transfer a Q-value.

4   Experiments

4.1   Environments

To evaluate the proposed similarity measure, a collection of six environments with different state-action spaces were selected as test scenarios from OpenAI Gym [3], a collection of RL environments. Since the proposed similarity measures works in discrete state-action spaces, some environments were discretized (Acrobot, Mt. Car and Pendulum). Table 1 summarizes the state and action space dimensions of each environment, as well as what type of goal the agent must accomplish: to reach a particular state as soon as possible, or maintain the system within a subset of states as long as possible.

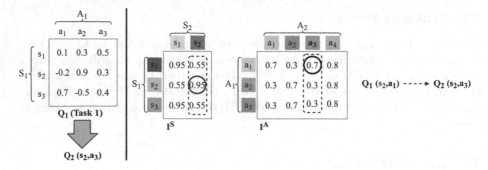

Fig. 2. Example of a Q-value transfer using the Q and intersection matrices form Fig. 1. To transfer from Q_1 to $Q_2(s_2, a_3)$ the state $s \in S_1$ and action $a \in A_1$ with the largest intersection value to $s_2 \in S_2$ and $a_3 \in A_2$ are selected. In this example, $a_1 \in A_1$ is the most similar action to $a_3 \in A_2$, whereas state $s_2 \in S_1$ is the most similar to $s_2 \in S_2$. Therefore, the Q-value $Q_1(s_2, a_1)$ is transferred to $Q_2(s_1, a_3)$.

Table 1. Collection of test environments. Columns present (left to right): the name of the environment, the size of the state space, the size of the action space, and the type of goal. *Reach* indicates that the end-goal is to take the system to a goal state, while *Maintain* represents the fact that the agent should keep the system within a subset of states as long as possible.

Environment	$|S|$	$|A|$	Goal
Frozen Lake (FL)	16	4	*Reach*
Frozen Lake 8x8 (F8)	64	4	*Reach*
Taxi (TA)	500	6	*Reach*
Acrobot (AC)	6400	3	*Reach*
Mt. Car (MC)	400	3	*Reach*
Pendulum (PE)	640	20	*Maintain*

4.2   Experimental Configurations

Considering that the purpose of the proposed similarity measure is to assess the potential benefit of transferring knowledge between a pair of tasks, our experiments evaluate: i) how the a set of source tasks is ranked for a target task, ii) the benefit the target task experiences from transferring knowledge from each source task, and iii) how much data is required to produce a good estimation of the similarity between a source and target task.

In our experiments, Q-learning [17] was employed as learning algorithm. In every environment, the agent was trained for 300,000 episodes, and was evaluated for 10 episodes every 100 training episodes. Regarding the learning rate and exploration probability values, these were varied depending on whether knowledge was being transferred or not. Each stage of the experiments is detailed below.

1. Learning from scratch: In each environment, an agent was trained from scratch, with an initial and final value of 0.95 and 0.01 for both the learning rate and exploration probability.
2. Measuring similarity: The inter-task similarity was measured between each pair of tasks, using a constant of $K = 3$ (*i.e.*, amount of clusters) and K-means was applied to compute the C^{row} and C^{col} matrices.
3. Learning with transferred knowledge: For each ordered pair of tasks (excluding same-task pairs), the method presented in Sect. 3.3 was used to initialize the Q matrix of the target task. Then, the agent was trained with an initial and final value of 0.5 and 0.01 for the learning rate, while the initial and final exploration probability were set to 0.25 and 0.01, respectively. The difference in performance between the learner with transferred knowledge and the scratch learner was determined by the transfer ratio [15].
4. Estimating similarity during training: To evaluate how the similarity score between a source task and target task evolves (throughout the training process of the target task), the similarity between the final Q matrix and the Q matrix at twenty different points of the training process was computed. The objective of this evaluation is to determine how fast a lifelong learning agent could have a good estimate of the similarity measure between previous tasks and a new task; and even realize by itself that it has previously learned the current task that its trying to learn.

4.3   Results

Table 2 shows the similarity scores $mean(I^S)$ and $mean(I^A)$ between each pair of the evaluation tasks. For most tasks, both $mean(I^S)$ and $mean(I^A)$ scores were able to correctly assign the highest similarity score with the same task. This feature is critical for a similarity measure, as it would prevent the learning agent from unnecessarily spending time to learn a Q matrix it already learned. Furthermore, in the case of $mean(I^A)$, the similarity score was above 0.84 when a task was correctly identified as the most similar one to itself. This is worth emphasizing, since a high similarity score provides a greater confidence to the learning system on the selection of a promising source task.

In Table 3 are shown the rankings based on the similarity scores from Table 2. By selecting the most similar source task, according to the rankings based on $mean(I^S)$, one would get the same task as the target task, or a source task that would produce an improvement of the performance in the target task. That is, the $mean(I^S)$ score deemed AC to be the most similar task to PE. However, as Table 4 shows the transfer ratios, by transferring from AC to PE the performance in PE is better than to the one obtained by learning from scratch.

Table 2. Inter-task similarity scores based on the mean value of matrices I^S and I^A. The larger the value, the more similar the tasks. Values in the main diagonal that are the largest value in its row and column are in bold.

	$mean(I^S)$						$mean(I^A)$					
	FL	F8	TA	AC	MC	PE	FL	F8	TA	AC	MC	PE
FL	**0.49**	0.46	0.48	0.13	0.35	0.24	0.78	0.76	0.62	0.58	0.79	0.76
F8	–	**0.51**	0.48	0.13	0.42	0.25	–	**0.85**	0.64	0.50	0.80	0.71
TA	–	–	**0.51**	0.16	0.40	0.27	–	–	0.62	0.50	0.62	0.57
AC	–	–	–	**0.81**	0.37	0.56	–	–	–	**0.98**	0.61	0.77
MC	–	–	–	–	**0.46**	0.38	–	–	–	–	**0.89**	0.80
PE	–	–	–	–	–	0.45	–	–	–	–	–	**0.88**

Additionally, as shown in Table 4, despite that there are some tasks that do not seem to be affected by which task is used as source of knowledge (*e.g.*, AC, MC, PE), other tasks can be completely hindered from learning if the wrong source task is selected (*e.g.*, FL, F8, TA). It is worth mentioning that the tasks that were not harmed by any source of knowledge were all control tasks. It seems that the Q matrix learned in control tasks was more similar to the Q matrices of all the other tasks than to a random initialization. In contrast, the non-control tasks seem to be more similar to the random initialization than to other tasks. In the context of a transfer learning agent, it is important to keep in mind that there might scenarios in which none of the sources of knowledge available will be useful. For this reason, it is critical to have a reliable similarity measure for knowledge transfer purposes.

Table 3. Ranking of source tasks for a target task based on the inter-task similarity measures $mean(I^S)$ and $mean(I^A)$.

Target task	Source task ranking											
	$mean(I^S)$						$mean(I^A)$					
	1st	2nd	3rd	4th	5th	6th	1st	2nd	3rd	4th	5th	6th
FL	FL	TA	F8	MC	PE	AC	MC	FL	F8	PE	TA	AC
F8	F8	TA	FL	MC	PE	AC	F8	MC	FL	PE	TA	AC
TA	TA	F8	FL	MC	PE	AC	F8	MC	TA	FL	PE	AC
AC	AC	PE	MC	TA	FL	F8	AC	PE	MC	FL	F8	TA
MC	MC	F8	TA	PE	AC	FL	MC	F8	PE	FL	TA	AC
PE	AC	PE	MC	TA	F8	FL	PE	MC	AC	FL	F8	TA

Table 4. Transfer ratio values obtained as a result of transferring knowledge with the method described in Sect. 3.3. Columns present the task from which knowledge was transferred, while rows present the task in which the agent trained with the additional knowledge. Values above 1 represent a performance improvement in comparison to learning from scratch. Alternatively, values below 1 represent a performance deterioration as a consequence of transferring knowledge. In the case of the target and source tasks TA and PE, the negative transfer ratio is a result of having a negative accumulated reward when knowledge was transferred and a positive accumulated reward when the agent learned from scratch.

Target task	Source task					
	FL	F8	TA	AC	MC	PE
FL	–	1.67	0.35	0.001	0	0
F8	1.27	–	0.05	0.0002	0.0006	0
TA	0.99	0.99	–	1.01	1.01	−23.96
AC	1.15	1.16	1.17	–	1.17	1.18
MC	1.08	1.08	1.08	1.08	–	1.08
PE	1.32	1.31	1.32	1.31	1.31	–

Regarding the amount of data required to compute the similarity scores, Fig. 3 shows the progression of both $mean(I^S)$ and $mean(I^A)$ scores during the training of an agent that learned from scratch in each task. In the cases of TA, AC, MC and PE, the $mean(I^S)$ score gets quite close to the final similarity value before the first quarter of the training process. However, in FL the $mean(I^S)$ score does not seem to converge to the final similarity value, which makes it unreliable. On the other hand, the $mean(I^A)$ score behaves in a more stable manner. In the case of FL, AC, MC and PE, the $mean(I^A)$ score gets considerably close to the final similarity value before the 50,000th episode. Hence, given the stability of the estimation for $mean(I^A)$, a lifelong learning system could rely on it to select a source task at a an early training stage.

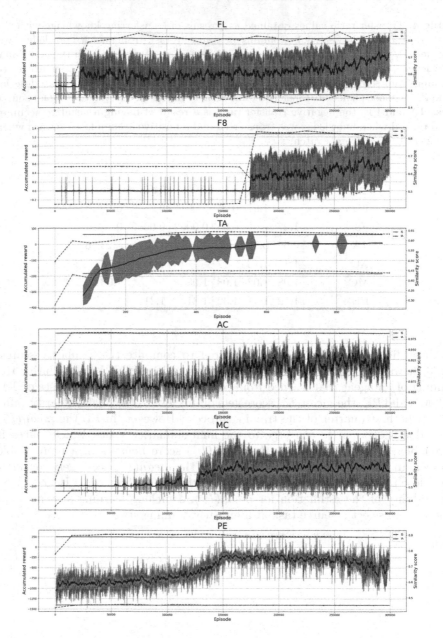

Fig. 3. Progression of the similarity score between the Q matrix being learned and its final version ($mean(I^S)$ and $mean(I^A)$ colored in red and blue, respectively). Horizontal axes represent training episodes, while the left and right vertical axes show the accumulated evaluation reward and the similarity score, respectively. The solid horizontal lines represent the similarity score of the final Q matrix with itself, while the dotted lines show the similarity score between the Q matrix partially trained at episode t and the final Q matrix. Green graphs show the average and standard deviation of the accumulated evaluation rewards. (Color figure online)

5 Conclusions

In this work we have presented an inter-task similarity measure and a transfer learning method for heterogeneous tasks. By measuring similarity across heterogeneous tasks, a lifelong learning system is able to operate in scenarios with high degree of task diversity, such as service robotics. Instead of assuming that the tasks within a domain hold a minimum degree of similarity (*e.g.*, share the same state and action spaces), evaluating their similarity endows a learning agent with the capability of making informed decisions about under which circumstances it is safe to transfer knowledge. Experimental results showed how the similarity measure is able to rank a set of source tasks, in a way that prioritizes those that would improve the performance in the target task. Additionally, it was also shown that for some tasks the similarity score can be computed with a low error before the first quarter of the learning process. Hence, with the proposed similarity measure and transfer learning method we hope to contribute towards the robustness and autonomy of lifelong learning systems.

References

1. Ammar, H.B., et al.: An automated measure of MDP similarity for transfer in reinforcement learning. In: Workshops at the Twenty-Eighth AAAI Conference on Artificial Intelligence (2014)
2. Bellman, R.E.: Dynamic programming (1957)
3. Brockman, G., et al.: Openai gym (2016)
4. Carroll, J.L., Seppi, K.: Task similarity measures for transfer in reinforcement learning task libraries. In: Proceedings of the 2005 IEEE International Joint Conference on Neural Networks, vol. 2, pp. 803–808. IEEE (2005)
5. Ferns, N., Panangaden, P., Precup, D.: Metrics for finite Markov decision processes. In: UAI, vol. 4, pp. 162–169 (2004)
6. Ferns, N., Panangaden, P., Precup, D.: Metrics for Markov decision processes with infinite state spaces. arXiv preprint arXiv:1207.1386 (2012)
7. Henrikson, J.: Completeness and total boundedness of the Hausdorff metric. MIT Undergraduate J. Math. **1**, 69–80 (1999)
8. Kober, J., Bagnell, J.A., Peters, J.: Reinforcement learning in robotics: a survey. Int. J. Robot. Res. **32**(11), 1238–1274 (2013)
9. Lin, K., Wang, S., Zhou, J.: Collaborative deep reinforcement learning. arXiv preprint arXiv:1702.05796 (2017)
10. Puterman, M.L.: Markov Decision Processes: Discrete Stochastic Dynamic Programming. Wiley, Hoboken (2014)
11. Song, J., Gao, Y., Wang, H., An, B.: Measuring the distance between finite Markov decision processes. In: Proceedings of the 2016 International Conference on Autonomous Agents & Multiagent Systems, pp. 468–476 (2016)
12. Sorg, J., Singh, S.: Transfer via soft homomorphisms. In: Proceedings of the 8th International Conference on Autonomous Agents and Multiagent Systems, vol. 2, pp. 741–748 (2009)
13. Taylor, M.E., Kuhlmann, G., Stone, P.: Autonomous transfer for reinforcement learning. In: AAMAS (1), pp. 283–290. Citeseer (2008)

14. Taylor, M.E., Stone, P.: Representation transfer for reinforcement learning. In: AAAI Fall Symposium: Computational Approaches to Representation Change during Learning and Development, pp. 78–85 (2007)
15. Taylor, M.E., Stone, P.: Transfer learning for reinforcement learning domains: a survey. J. Mach. Learn. Res. **10**(Jul), 1633–1685 (2009)
16. Wan, M., Gangwani, T., Peng, J.: Mutual information based knowledge transfer under state-action dimension mismatch. arXiv preprint arXiv:2006.07041 (2020)
17. Watkins, C.J., Dayan, P.: Q-learning. Mach. Learn. **8**(3–4), 279–292 (1992)

Dataset and Benchmarking of Real-Time Embedded Object Detection for RoboCup SSL

Roberto Fernandes$^{(\boxtimes)}$, Walber M. Rodrigues, and Edna Barros

Centro de Informática, Universidade Federal de Pernambuco, Recife, Brazil
{rcf6,wmr,ensb}@cin.ufpe.br
http://robocin.com.br

Abstract. When producing a model to object detection in a specific context, the first obstacle is to have a dataset labeling the desired classes. In RoboCup, some leagues already have more than one dataset to train and evaluate a model. However, in the Small Size League (SSL), there is not such dataset available yet. This paper presents an open-source dataset to be used as a benchmark for real-time object detection in SSL. This work also presented a pipeline to train, deploy, and evaluate Convolutional Neural Networks (CNNs) models in a low-power embedded system. This pipeline is used to evaluate the proposed dataset with state-of-art optimized models. In this dataset, the MobileNet SSD v1 achieves 44.88% AP (68.81% AP_{50}) at 94 Frames Per Second (FPS), while running on an SSL robot.

Keywords: Dataset · Benchmark · Deep learning · Object detection

1 Introduction

The Small Size League (SSL) is one of the most traditional leagues in the RoboCup. In this league, it is possible to precisely perform a wide range of dynamic plays every moment during a game. The decision-making process at each play needs to be fast to keep up with the fast-paced game, in which robots usually move at 3 m/s, and the ball reaches 6.5 m/s. These actions are possible due to the use of omnidirectional wheeled robots, and the use of SSL-Vision [25] as a global vision system.

Due to the use of the SSL-Vision, all robots have all the field information, making it easy to design and develop a tactic. With this external vision system, a team in the SSL is considered a semi-autonomous system. As a comparison, in Middle Size League (MSL) and Standard Platform League (SPL) instead of using external information, each robot has its camera and vision system, limiting the information to which they have access. Thus, they are considered a fully autonomous system because each robot can perform a tactic without receiving external information.

© Springer Nature Switzerland AG 2022
R. Alami et al. (Eds.): RoboCup 2021, LNAI 13132, pp. 53–64, 2022.
https://doi.org/10.1007/978-3-030-98682-7_5

A technical challenge [18] was introduced in 2019 to evolve the league, encouraging the teams to develop and propose a local vision system. This challenge aims to bring autonomy to an SSL robot, in a similar way to MSL and SPL. A MSL robot fits in $52 \times 52 \times 80$ cm, which can equip a full-size computer, and a SPL robot can not be modified, since it uses the NAO as standard platform. However, an SSL robot needs to fit in a cylinder with a height of 15cm and a diameter of 18cm [19], which constrains the robot's vision system complexity.

In the first three steps of this challenge, a robot has to grab a stationary ball, find a goal, and score against a static defender robot without receiving any information from the SSL-Vision. Therefore, a robot has to detect a Robot, a Ball, and a Goal autonomously. It also has to respect the league requirements, except for the height restriction, creating a small room for hardware improvements.

The straightforward option to detect these objects uses scan lines and color segmentation to detect the ball [16], as the league uses an orange golf ball. However, this approach can not detect robots and goals because they do not have a unique pattern. For instance, a team can use robots of any color, making it harder to use this technique. Besides, the color segmentation approach needs to be re-calibrated on each slight environment variation, as uneven illumination or field changes [10].

The state-of-the-art of object detection relies on Convolutional Neural Networks (CNNs) [2], which given a labeled dataset, trains a model once, and does not need any other calibration or modification. Besides, this approach is robust to deal with occlusion, scale transformation, and background switch [24], which makes CNNs strong candidates to use in the SSL.

For other RoboCup's leagues, like SPL [1] and MSL [9], there are public object detection datasets. Although, in the SSL does not exist an open-source labeled dataset and creating a new one takes time, making the research and development of object detection models in this league even harder.

Therefore, given the SSL technical challenge, the league constraints, and the lack of an open-sourced dataset, this paper has two main contributions:

- Propose a novel open-source dataset for SSL, containing labels for Robot, Ball, and Goal, intended to benchmark object detection in this league.
- Evaluate and compare CNNs models, respecting the league's hardware constraints while achieving an inference frequency of at least 24 Frames Per Second (FPS), real-time rate, necessary during actual games.

This paper's remainder is organized as follows: Sect. 2 will present some related works. Section 3 will detail the dataset. Section 4 will explain the evaluation methodology. Section 5 will show and discuss the achieved results. Section 6 will present what can be concluded and propose some future works.

2   Related Work

Object detection has been one of the most studied fields in computer vision since the first use of CNNs [7]. Since that, datasets have been released to improve object detection models. Among these released datasets, some label many classes, as COCO with 91 classes, and others are task-specific, with less than three classes. This section will present some of these datasets, as the COCO and some datasets used in other RoboCup leagues.

The most famous and used dataset for object detection is COCO [8], released in 2014. This dataset contains 328.000 images, collected from Flickr, to avoid iconic-object images containing a single object centered in the image. Thus, the COCO dataset focus on non-iconic images, which means images with multiples categories in a diverse context. This strategy helps trained models to generalize objects instance, given the multiple contexts.

The classes used in the COCO dataset were chosen among 255 candidates given by children from 4 to 8 years old. The authors then voted on these categories based on how often each category occurred, and the most voted ones were selected, resulting in 80 classes. This dataset consists of 2.5 million instances, and as a result, each image averages 7.7 instances per image. It took 77.000 working hours to label all of these instances.

Moreover, in other RoboCup leagues, some datasets appear as good options. For instance, on MSL, there is an open object detection dataset [9], which consists of 1456 images, divided into train and test using 70/30 proportion. This dataset uses images taken from the robot camera and images taken from outside of the field from different competitions to increase the variety of the dataset. This dataset provides the annotations in Pascal VOC and YOLO format, although it has only one class, labeling robot instances.

The SPL has an open-source tool to create and share dataset for object detection [3] that has several images labeling Robot, Ball, and Goalpost. Besides, teams have been regularly releasing their datasets, as, per instance, the SPQR dataset [1], that labels the same three classes. The SPQR dataset contains 2411 images collected from various game conditions, as natural and artificial light.

Other SPL dataset focus only on detecting Ball, as [11]. This dataset has 6564 images collected from RoboCup logs and the authors' laboratory, varying lighting conditions. The images have a fixed size of 640 × 480 pixels from static and moving balls, resulting in 5209 ball examples.

3 Dataset

3.1 Dataset Creation

The first step to create a labeled dataset is to select images to be part of it. The proposed dataset's images come from three different sources to use images under different conditions and angles.

The first set of images consists of 259 pictures taken outside of the SSL field, obtained from public image repositories of league teams. This set contains a variety of robot models and images taken under various light conditions. The second set has 516 brand-new images taken for this dataset from a smartphone camera inside a university laboratory field. Furthermore, the remaining 156 images were collected similarly to the second set but came from the final configuration, a camera placed on the SSL robot. The images from this last set came from videos, where it was used a frame rate of 10 FPS to avoid using similar images. The combination of those sets results in a dataset of 931 images.

After collecting the images, they were resized to a standard resolution of 224×224 pixels as used by [4,15]. Figure 1 shows some labeled examples from this dataset, each column of this image has two examples of each set of images.

Fig. 1. Sample images from the dataset, showing ground-truth detection. The leftmost column has images from public SSL images, the middle column has images collected from a smartphone inside the field, and the rightmost column has images taken in a camera placed in the robot.

The next step of creating the proposed dataset was to add labels to the objects in images. In the proposed dataset were defined three objects class to label: Robot, Ball, and Goal. These classes are the distinctive and relevant ones to detect in an SSL game. Each image on this dataset can contain multiple labels, including none of it in the image. LabelImg [20] was used to label the images. This tool outputs squared detection in Pascal VOC and YOLO format.

After labeling the images, they were randomly divided into train and test set using the 70/30 proportion as in other robotics' object detection works [9], Table 1 shows the final result of this division. This creation process took 160 working hours, most of them manually adding labels to each image. The proposed dataset is fully available on the author's GitHub[1].

Table 1. Number of images divided into train and test set.

	Number of images
Train	651 (69,92%)
Test	280 (30,08%)
Dataset size	931

---

[1] https://github.com/bebetocf/ssl-dataset.

3.2   Dataset Statistics

The proposed dataset's main objective is to detect objects in distinct game situations, so it is important to have multiple instances in each image. Figure 2 shows the number of instances per image. It is possible to see that most images have more than one instance, so there are more class instances than images. The dataset has 4182 instances, averaging 4.5 instances per image, which helps mitigate the low number of images.

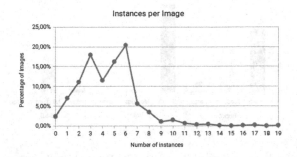

Fig. 2. Number of instances per image.

Table 2 shows the instance division on the proposed dataset. The Goal class has fewer examples than Robot and Ball classes because not all images have a Goal instance, and when it appears, there is only one instance per image. Besides, the Goal instances are characteristics since they are very similar to each other. As COCO [8], some datasets also have some imbalanced class, and some techniques could be used to balance a dataset [12].

Table 2. Number of instances of each class in the dataset.

Object class	Instances per class
Robot	1886
Ball	1711
Goal	585
Number of instances	4182

The proposed dataset classifies the objects by their area, Small, Medium, and Large, similarly to COCO [8]. Small objects have less than 32×32 (1024) pixels and represent 2919 instances. Medium objects are 1225 instances and have an area between 32×32 (1024) pixels and 96×96 (9216). Moreover, Large objects are bigger than 96×96 (9216) pixels, representing 38 instances. Most objects concentrate in the Small area class, approximately 70% of all objects, due to the low-resolution images.

Figure 3 shows each instance's division by the class and their area size. It is possible to see that almost all Ball instances are Small due to their actual size. More than half of the Robots' examples are Small due to images from the first set taken from outside the field, where robots are far from the camera. Furthermore, most of the Goals' samples are in Medium class.

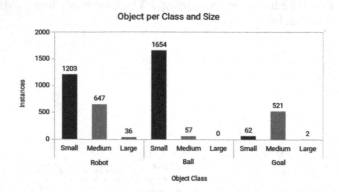

Fig. 3. Instance division per class and size. Small objects have less than 32×32 (1024) pixels, medium objects have a size between 32×32 (1024) pixels and 96×96 (9216) pixels, and large objects are bigger than 96×96 (9216) pixels.

4   Evaluation Methodology

4.1   Environment

One of the main drawbacks of using a CNNs is the requirement of a Graphical Processing Units (GPUs) to infer in a frequency to use in a real-time detection [22]. Besides, GPUs are too big to use in an SSL robot, and they have a power consumption too high for the battery that fits in one of these robots. However, improvements in CNNs inference time in an embedded system make this method an excellent option to solve this technical challenge.

The primary constraint to this work is the environment delimitation due to the league's restrictions [19]. The robot used to test was a modified version on the RobôCIn v2020 [17]. As the technical challenge does not have a height restriction, another floor was added to the robot to fit additional hardware. All the modifications should have low power consumption, as the robot uses a LiPo 2200 mah 4S 35C battery. This battery is enough to supply four brushless motors of 50W each and all the other robot's necessities.

A Raspberry Pi 4 Model B, a Google Coral Edge TPU accelerator, and a camera module were added to the robot, composing the vision system. The camera can capture images up to 90 FPS in a resolution of 640×480 pixels. These new components aim to tackle the lack of computational power in the main microcontroller, an STM32F767ZI. The power consumption of a Raspberry Pi

4 with the camera module is up to 7.5 W, and the Google Coral is 4.5 W, which fits the power supply of the robot's battery.

The vision system's inclusion is desirable to avoid modifying the architecture and data flow on the current robot. In the current robot, the microcontroller controls the motors to operate at the desired speeds. In the new system, the Raspberry Pi receives the camera's captured frames and uses them to input the inference model running on the Google Coral Edge TPU. After the inference, the model outputs the detected objects to the Raspberry Pi, which computes where the robot should go, and sends this position to the microcontroller. Figure 4 shows the new system architecture of the robot.

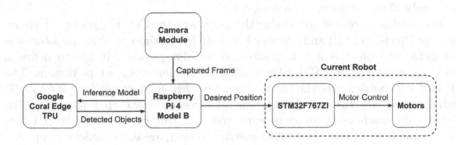

Fig. 4. Modifications on the architecture and data flow of the new robot.

4.2   Models and Experiments

The pipeline to train, run and evaluate any model follows the same standards to each approach. Transfer Learning was used due to the proposed dataset size and the system restrictions, which speeds up training and takes advantage of low-level learned features [14]. This technique uses a model pre-trained with another dataset to them train it with the proposed dataset. The proposed dataset was evaluated using MobileNet SSD v1 [4], MobileNet SSD v2 [15], MobileDet [23] and YOLO v4 Tiny [21], which are state-of-the-art object detection models.

TensorFlow Object Detection API [5] was used to train MobileNets' and MobileDet's models. These models' train was improved using data augmentation techniques as Horizontal Flip, Image Crop, Image Scale, Brightness Adjustment, Contrast Adjustment, Saturation Adjustment, and Black Patches.

YOLO v4 tiny is a shallow version of the YOLO v4 [2], designed to run in an embedded system. It already uses CutMix, Mosaic, Class Label Smoothing, and Self-Adversarial Training, so this architecture does not need any extra data augmentation technique. Furthermore, due to limitations of the portability process for Google Coral Edge TPU, the YOLO v4 tiny uses ReLU rather than Leaky ReLU as activation functions.

These models were optimized using Integer Quantization, which increases the inference speed while maintaining network precision [6]. This method consists of converting the network weight from floating-point numbers to integer values. After training, the models were quantized and converted to a TensorFlow Lite compatible model, which is required to compile the model to run on a Google Coral Edge TPU accelerator.

4.3 Running and Evaluating

The primary constraint to use a trained model on an SSL robot is inferring in real-time. A model has to run in at least 24 FPS to be considered a real-time inference. This frame rate is acceptable with the league's objects' speed since a ball, the fastest object in the field, with a maximum speed of 6.5 m/s [19], would move only 27 cm between inferences.

The models were evaluated using the metrics as the COCO dataset, which are Average Precision (AP) and Average Recall (AR). In those metrics, to determine if a detected object is a true positive or a false positive, it has to define a Intersection over Union (IoU) threshold to consider a correct prediction. The AP and AR metrics uses the mean of ten IoU threshold values from 0.5 to 0.95 with a step of 0.05. Besides, these metrics are presented by each object's size. The evaluation is made using an open-source tool [13], that given ground-truth labels and predictions, output the COCO metrics to compare each model's result.

5   Results

Table 3 shows the AP for the four models separated by IOU threshold and object area. AP for Medium and Large objects shows how powerful these models can be in less challenging scenarios, where the object is much closer to the robot. However, the results for Small objects are worse than for Medium and Large objects, which indicates a high false-positive rate. This error occurs due to the low information on objects of Small size.

Table 3. Average Precision (AP) for each model by Intersection over Union (IoU) threshold, in AP_{50} the threshold used is 0.5 and AP_{75} is 0.75, and detected object area, where AP_S, AP_M, and AP_L stands for the result by each detection size, Small, Medium or Large.

Method	AP	AP	AP_{75}	AP_S	AP_M	AP_L
MobileNet SSD v1	**44.88%**	68.81%	47.51%	26.83%	68.54%	**89.62%**
MobileNet SSD v2	43.42%	**74.41%**	44.83%	23.06%	62.55%	82.93%
MobileDet	35.96%	64.95%	36.62%	16.63%	60.48%	82.97%
YOLOv4 Tiny	42.17%	62.24%	**54.09%**	**27.34%**	**69.05%**	58.84%

From the AP perspective, the MobileNet SSD v1 had the best result overall and for Large objects. The AP for Large objects on the YOLO v4 tiny model was worse than for Medium objects, which is a peculiar behavior since the other models achieve better AP when detecting Large objects. This result can indicate that YOLO v4 tiny needs more labeled data with Large size, as there are only 38 objects with this size on the proposed dataset.

Table 4 shows the AR results separated by maximum detection per image and detected object size. A high AR is important for Robot and Goal classes, as the robot uses it to avoid colliding with another robot when navigating and helps the robot identify the Goal faster. The Robot and Goal classes' represents all of the Large objects and 95% of Medium objects, as shown in Fig. 3.

Table 4. Average Recall (AR) for each model by maximum detection per image, AR_1 for at most 1 object per image and AR_{10} for 10 objects per image, and detected object area, where AR_S, AR_M, and AR_L stands for the result by each detection size, Small, Medium or Large.

Method	AR_1	AR_{10}	AR_S	AR_M	AR_L
MobileNet SSD v1	**37.75%**	**62.87%**	**40.62%**	**82.18%**	**91.00%**
MobileNet SSD v2	34.76%	50.60%	29.28%	66.21%	87.00%
MobileDet	30.62%	43.66%	22.96%	65.41%	85.00%
YOLOv4 Tiny	36.72%	45.36%	30.41%	74.16%	64.00%

The obtained result of AR for Medium and Large objects sizes shows a high detection rate, with the MobileNet SSD v1 as the best AR results overall. It was also observed that YOLO v4 tiny had worse results for Large objects, which supports the necessity of more samples of Large objects for this model.

Table 5 shows each model's inference frequency, where the MobileNet SSD v1 had the best FPS overall, but MobileNet SSD v2 and MobileDet had a rate that fits the requirement of at least 24 FPS. However, the YOLO v4 Tiny had a bad result with only 10 FPS, which is caused by the lack of architectural optimizations on the network compared with the other evaluated models. This shortage of optimization results in a bad mapping to the Google Coral.

Table 5. Mean inference frequency in Frames Per Second (FPS) for each tested model.

Method	FPS
MobileNet SSD v1	94
MobileNet SSD v2	78
MobileDet	87
YOLOv4 Tiny	10

Figure 5 shows the Precision-Recall curve for each model, separated by class, and using a IoU threshold of 0.5. The Ball class is the most difficult class to detect due to the object size. The MobileNet SSD v2 in this IoU had a good result in all the three classes but has a smaller recall in the Goal class. The YOLO v4 tiny had a good precision when detecting all classes but could detect only 20% of the Ball in the test set. This result explains why the AP_{50} for this model is lower than MobileNet SSD v2 since it is calculated averaging precision across recalls values from 0 to 1. This figure also shows that the fewer examples in the Goal class were not a problem since the Precision x Recall curve for this class is very similar to the other classes.

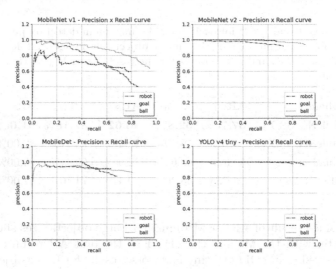

Fig. 5. Precision x Recall graphs for trained models, using IoU = 0.5. When the line disappears, it means that the value of precision is zero.

6   Conclusion

This paper presented an open-source labeled dataset and a benchmark for object detection for SSL. The proposed dataset guarantees variety with images extracted from different sources under distinct lighting conditions and camera configurations. The labeled objects are Robot, Ball, and Goal, which are the essential objects found during an SSL game. The dataset's images can contain multiple instances of these objects, including no objects per image.

It was also presented a pipeline to train a CNNs and deploy it on an embedded device with limited computational power. The results show that CNNs are robust to variable light conditions and can also detect robots with different structures. This result contrasts with using color segmentation with scan lines. Color segmentation can be easily disturbed by these circumstances since it needs fine-tuning parameters that rely on image saturation and brightness.

The presented dataset has a similar size as other datasets used on other RoboCup leagues. However, it is smaller than general propose object detection datasets. So, data augmentation techniques were applied to increase diversity and model generalization. A future improvement to the dataset is to add images from game situations and different field configurations. Besides, increasing the number of distinctive robots' instances and the number of Large images will boost the dataset robustness.

This paper uses the proposed dataset to evaluate AP, AR, and FPS of four different CNNs models on constrained hardware. Furthermore, this paper highlights the importance of model architectural optimizations. Future works will analyze other models and modifications to hyperparameters, as input size, to enhance Small object detection. Further work will also analyze other techniques, such as tracking, to continuously detect objects in multiple frames in a real game environment.

Acknowledgements. The authors would like to acknowledge the RoboCIn's team and Centro de Informática - UFPE for all the research support. The first and second authors were also funded by the Conselho Nacional de Desenvolvimento Científico e Tecnológico (CNPq). The authors appreciate all the SSL's teams for the open-source images from past competitions.

References

1. Albani, D., Youssef, A., Suriani, V., Nardi, D., Bloisi, D.D.: A deep learning approach for object recognition with NAO soccer robots. In: Behnke, S., Sheh, R., Sariel, S., Lee, D.D. (eds.) RoboCup 2016. LNCS (LNAI), vol. 9776, pp. 392–403. Springer, Cham (2017). https://doi.org/10.1007/978-3-319-68792-6_33
2. Bochkovskiy, A., Wang, C.Y., Liao, H.Y.M.: YOLOv4: optimal speed and accuracy of object detection (2020)
3. Fiedler, N., Bestmann, M., Hendrich, N.: ImageTagger: an open source online platform for collaborative image labeling. In: Holz, D., Genter, K., Saad, M., von Stryk, O. (eds.) RoboCup 2018. LNCS (LNAI), vol. 11374, pp. 162–169. Springer, Cham (2019). https://doi.org/10.1007/978-3-030-27544-0_13
4. Howard, A.G., et al.: MobileNets: efficient convolutional neural networks for mobile vision applications (2017)
5. Huang, J., et al.: Speed/accuracy trade-offs for modern convolutional object detectors (2017)
6. Jacob, B., et al.: Quantization and training of neural networks for efficient integer-arithmetic-only inference (2017)
7. LeCun, Y., et al.: Backpropagation applied to Handwritten zip code recognition. Neural Comput. **1**(4), 541–551 (1989). https://doi.org/10.1162/neco.1989.1.4.541
8. Lin, T.-Y., et al.: Microsoft COCO: common objects in context. In: Fleet, D., Pajdla, T., Schiele, B., Tuytelaars, T. (eds.) ECCV 2014. LNCS, vol. 8693, pp. 740–755. Springer, Cham (2014). https://doi.org/10.1007/978-3-319-10602-1_48
9. Luo, S., Lu, H., Xiao, J., Yu, Q., Zheng, Z.: Robot detection and localization based on deep learning. In: 2017 Chinese Automation Congress (CAC), pp. 7091–7095 (2017). https://doi.org/10.1109/CAC.2017.8244056

10. Neves, A.J., Pinho, A.J., Martins, D.A., Cunha, B.: An efficient omnidirectional vision system for soccer robots: from calibration to object detection. Mechatronics **21**(2), 399–410 (2011)
11. O'Keeffe, S., Villing, R.: A benchmark data set and evaluation of deep learning architectures for ball detection in the RoboCup SPL. In: Akiyama, H., Obst, O., Sammut, C., Tonidandel, F. (eds.) RoboCup 2017. LNCS (LNAI), vol. 11175, pp. 398–409. Springer, Cham (2018). https://doi.org/10.1007/978-3-030-00308-1_33
12. Oksuz, K., Cam, B.C., Kalkan, S., Akbas, E.: Imbalance problems in object detection: a review (2020)
13. Padilla, R., Passos, W.L., Dias, T.L.B., Netto, S.L., da Silva, E.A.B.: A comparative analysis of object detection metrics with a companion open-source toolkit. Electronics **10**(3) (2021). https://doi.org/10.3390/electronics10030279. https://www.mdpi.com/2079-9292/10/3/279
14. Pan, S.J., Yang, Q.: A survey on transfer learning. IEEE Trans. Knowl. Data Eng. **22**(10), 1345–1359 (2010). https://doi.org/10.1109/TKDE.2009.191
15. Sandler, M., Howard, A., Zhu, M., Zhmoginov, A., Chen, L.C.: MobileNetV2: inverted residuals and linear bottlenecks (2019)
16. Seel, F., Jut, S.: On-board computer vision for autonomous ball interception (2019). https://tigers-mannheim.de/download/papers/2019-BallIntercept-TC-Seel_Jut.pdf. Accessed 12 Apr 2021
17. Silva, C., et al.: Robôcin 2020 team description paper (2020)
18. RoboCup 2020 SSL vision blackout technical challenge rules (2020). https://ssl.robocup.org/wp-content/uploads/2020/07/2020-ssl-vision-blackout-rules.pdf. Accessed 12 Apr 2021
19. Laws of the RoboCup small size league 2021 (2021). https://robocup-ssl.github.io/ssl-rules/sslrules.pdf. Accessed 12 Apr 2021
20. Tzutalin: Labelimg (2015). https://github.com/tzutalin/labelImg. Accessed 12 Apr 2021
21. Wang, C.Y., Bochkovskiy, A., Liao, H.Y.M.: Scaled-YOLOv4: scaling cross stage partial network (2021)
22. Wang, Y., Wei, G., Brooks, D.: Benchmarking TPU, GPU, and CPU platforms for deep learning. CoRR abs/1907.10701 (2019). http://arxiv.org/abs/1907.10701
23. Xiong, Y., et al.: MobileDets: searching for object detection architectures for mobile accelerators (2020)
24. Zhao, Z.Q., Zheng, P., Xu, S., Wu, X.: Object detection with deep learning: a review (2019)
25. Zickler, S., Laue, T., Birbach, O., Wongphati, M., Veloso, M.: SSL-vision: the shared vision system for the RoboCup small size league. In: Baltes, J., Lagoudakis, M.G., Naruse, T., Ghidary, S.S. (eds.) RoboCup 2009. LNCS (LNAI), vol. 5949, pp. 425–436. Springer, Heidelberg (2010). https://doi.org/10.1007/978-3-642-11876-0_37

TORSO-21 Dataset: Typical Objects in RoboCup Soccer 2021

Marc Bestmann, Timon Engelke, Niklas Fiedler, Jasper Güldenstein,
Jan Gutsche, Jonas Hagge, and Florian Vahl$^{(\boxtimes)}$

Hamburg Bit-Bots, Department of Informatics, Universität Hamburg,
Vogt-Kölln-Straße 30, 22527 Hamburg, Germany
{bestmann,7engelke,5fiedler,5guelden,7gutsche,
5hagge,7vahl}@informatik.uni-hamburg.de
https://robocup.informatik.uni-hamburg.de

Abstract. We present a dataset specifically designed to be used as a benchmark to compare vision systems in the RoboCup Humanoid Soccer domain. The dataset is composed of a collection of images taken in various real-world locations as well as a collection of simulated images. It enables comparing vision approaches with a meaningful and expressive metric. The contributions of this paper consist of providing a comprehensive and annotated dataset, an overview of the recent approaches to vision in RoboCup, methods to generate vision training data in a simulated environment, and an approach to increase the variety of a dataset by automatically selecting a diverse set of images from a larger pool. Additionally, we provide a baseline of YOLOv4 and YOLOv4-tiny on this dataset.

Keywords: Computer vision · Vision dataset · Deep learning

1 Introduction

In recent years, similar to other domains, the approaches for computer vision in the RoboCup soccer domain moved nearly completely to deep learning based methods [2]. Still, a quantitative comparison between the different approaches is difficult, as most approaches are evaluated using their custom-made dataset. The presented performance of the approaches is therefore not only related to its detection quality but also the specific challenge posed by the used dataset. Especially, if images are only from a single location or without natural light, they can hardly be an indicator for actual performance in a competition.

Outside of the RoboCup domain, this problem is addressed by creating standardized datasets for various challenges in computer vision [7,9,20,32]. These datasets are used as a benchmark when comparing existing approaches with each other, allowing a quantitative evaluation (e.g. [4]). Tsipras et al. investigated how well results of evaluations with the ImageNet dataset [7] reflect the performance

---

All authors contributed equally.

© Springer Nature Switzerland AG 2022
R. Alami et al. (Eds.): RoboCup 2021, LNAI 13132, pp. 65–77, 2022.
https://doi.org/10.1007/978-3-030-98682-7_6

of approaches in their actual tasks [31]. They observed that in some cases, the scores achieved in the ImageNet challenge poorly reflect real-world capabilities. In the RoboCup domain, participants are challenged with restricted hardware capabilities resulting in computer vision approaches specifically designed for the given environment (e.g. [28]). Thus, existing datasets are even less applicable to evaluate the vision pipelines designed for RoboCup soccer.

We propose a standardized dataset for the RoboCup Humanoid Soccer domain consisting of images of the Humanoid League (HSL) as well as the Standard Platform League (SPL). We provide two image collections. The first one consists of images from various real-world locations, recorded by different robots. It includes annotations for the ball, goalposts, robots, lines, field edge, and three types of line intersections. The second collection is generated in the Webots simulator [22] which is used for the official RoboCup Virtual Humanoid Soccer Competition[1]. Additionally to the labels of the first collection, labels for the complete goal, crossbar, segmentation images for all classes, depth images, 6D poses for all labels, as well as the camera location in the field of play, are provided. For both collections, we give a baseline using YOLOv4 [4].

Most of the existing popular image datasets are only designed to compare image classification approaches. In RoboCup Soccer, object localization, as well as segmentation, are also commonly used (see Table 1).

While the creation and sharing of datasets were already facilitated by the ImageTagger platform [13], it did not help increase the comparability of vision pipelines since teams use different parts of the available images. Furthermore, many teams published the datasets that they used in their publications (see Table 1). Still, none of these papers have compared their work directly to others.

While this lack of using existing datasets could simply result from missing knowledge about their existence, since they are often only mentioned briefly as a side note in the publications, this is not probable. In our experience, we chose to create a new dataset for our latest vision pipeline publication [14] since the other datasets did not include the object classes required. Another issue is a lack of variety in some sets, e.g. only including the NAO robot or being recorded in just one location. Furthermore, the label type of the dataset may also limit its uses, e.g. a classification set is not usable for bounding box based approaches.

The remainder of this paper is structured as follows: Our methods of image collection and annotation are presented in Sect. 2 and Sect. 3 respectively. We evaluate and discuss the proposed dataset in Sect. 4 followed by a conclusion of our work in Sect. 5.

2   Image Collection

The dataset presented in this work is composed out of images recorded in the real world as well as in simulation using the Webots simulator. In the following, we describe the methods of image collection and also our method to reduce the number of similar images for greater variety in the dataset.

---

[1] https://humanoid.robocup.org/hl-2021/v-hsc/ (last accessed: 2021/06/14)

Table 1. Comparison of approaches to vision in RoboCup Humanoid Soccer leagues. Detection types are abbreviated as follows: classification (C), bounding box (B), segmentation (S), keypoints (K). Detection classes are abbreviated as follows: ball (B), goal (G), goalpost (P), field (F), robot (R), obstacles (O), lines (L), line intersections (I). The ○ sign means the data is publicly available, but the specific dataset is not specified. (✓) means it is partially publicly available. The sources are as follows: ImageTagger (IT), SPQR NAO image dataset (N), self created (S), not specified (?). The locations are competition (C), lab (L), and not specified (?).

Year	Paper	League	Approach Detection Type	Approach Classes	Dataset # Images	Dataset Synthetic	Dataset Source	Dataset Public	Dataset Location
2016	[1]	SPL	C	B,G,R	6,843	×	N	✓	?
2016	[10]	HSL	B,C,K	R	1,500	×	?	?	?
2016	[25]	HSL-K	S	B	1,160	×	S	×	?
2017	[24]	HSL-A	K	B,I,P,O,R	2,400	×	S,YouTube	×	C,L
2017	[6]	SPL	C	R	6,843	×	N	✓	?
2017	[17]	SPL	C	B,F,P,R	100,000	✓	S	?	–
2017	[21]	SPL	C	B	16,000	×	S	×	?
2017	[18]	HSL	S	R	4,000	×	S,N	✓	?
2018	[27]	SPL	S	B,R,P,L	syn: 5,000 real: 570	(✓)	S	×	C,L
2018	[12]	SPL	C	B	40,756	×	S	×	C,L
2018	[15]	HSL-T	B,S	B,F	?	×	S	?	?
2018	[8]	HSL-K	S	B	1,000	×	IT	✓	C
2018	[11]	HSL-A	K	B,P,R	3,000	×	(IT)	(○)	?
2018	[26]	HSL-K	S	B	35,327	×	IT	✓	C,L
2019	[19]	HSL-A	K	B	4,562	×	S	✓	C,L
2019	[30]	HSL-K	B	B	1,000	×	S	×	C,L
2019	[16]	HSL-K	C	B,P	?	×	Rhoban Tagger	○	C
2019	[23]	SPL	B	R	syn: 28,000 real: 7,000	(✓)	IT, SimRobot	✓	C,L
2019	[3]	HSL-K	B	B,P	1,423	×	S, IT	✓	C
2019	[14]	HSL-K	B,S	B,F,L,O,P,R	?	×	IT	✓	C
2021	[28]	SPL	B	B,I,P,R	syn: 6,250 real: 710	(✓)	Unreal Engine, S	✓	C,L
2021	[5]	SPL	B	B,R,I	?	(✓)	N, S	✓	?
2021	[29]	SPL	B,S	B,P,R,L,I	syn: 6,250 real: 3,000	(✓)	Unreal Engine, S	✓	C,L
	Ours	HSL-K SPL	B,S,K	B,P,F,R,L,I,(G)	syn: 10,000 real: 10,464	(✓)	IT, Webots	✓	C,L

2.1 Reality

To create a diverse dataset, we collected images from multiple sources. First, from our recordings during different RoboCup competitions and our lab. Second, we investigated the data other teams uploaded publicly to the ImageTagger. Finally, we asked other teams to provide images especially from further locations, and for situations that were not already represented in the existing images. While this provided a large set of images, most of them had to be excluded to prevent biasing the final dataset. First, the number of images from the SPL was limited, as these only include the NAO robot and this could have easily lead to an over-representation of the robot model. Many imagesets were excluded to limit one of the following biases: the ball is always in the image center, the camera is stationary, there are no robots on the field, other robots are not moving, or the camera always points onto the field. Generally, the selection focus was on including images that were recorded by a robot on a field, rather than images that were recorded by humans from the side of the field. Using images recorded by different teams is also crucial to include different camera and lens types, locations, and perspectives.

2.2   Simulation

As the RoboCup world championship in the HSL is held virtually in 2021, we deemed a data collection recorded in a simulated environment necessary. Diverse data can be generated as required. We chose the Webots simulator because it is used for the official competition. The official KidSize environment of the competition including the background, ball, goals, and turf as well as lighting conditions was used. During data generation, we used six robot models (including our own) which were published for this year's competition in the league.

Four setups are used per matchup of these robots. These vary by the robot team marker color and the team from whose perspective the image is captured. Scenes were generated in four scenarios per setup. In the first one, images are taken at camera positions uniformly distributed over the field. To prevent a bias of always having the ball included, we created a second scenario without a ball, but the same distribution of camera positions. Similar to the previous two, we also include two scenarios with the camera position normally distributed around a target on the field with and without a ball present. These last two scenarios imitate a robot that is contesting the ball.

We generated 100 images for each of the presented scenarios resulting in a total of: $\binom{6}{2} \cdot 2 \cdot 2 \cdot 4 \cdot 100$ images = 24000 images. The data is split into a 85% training and 15% test set.

For each image, a new scene is generated. The scenes are set up randomly by first sampling a target position. The ball is placed at the target position or out of sight depending on the scenario. Then the field players are placed by sampling from a normal distribution around the target position since it occurs often that multiple robots are grouped. To prevent robots from standing inside of each other, we resample the robot's position in the case of a collision. The heading of each robot is sampled from a normal distribution around facing the ball for the images where the ball is at the target position and from a uniform distribution otherwise. We assume each team to have a goalie, which stands on a random position on the goal line with its heading sampled from a normal distribution with the mean being the robot looking towards the field. The postures of the robots with our own robot model are each sampled from a set of 260 postures. These were recorded while the robot was performing one of six typical actions. The sampling is weighted by the estimated probability of an action occurring in a game (walking: 50%, standing: 20%, kicking: 10%, standup: 10%, falling: 5%, fallen: 5%). We chose these samplings to cover the majority of situations a robot could realistically face in a match.

The camera position is sampled in the field either from a uniform distribution or from a normal distribution around the target position depending on the scenario. The camera floats freely in space instead of being mounted on a robot. We chose to do this to be able to simulate various robot sizes. Thus, edge cases such as the robot looking at its shoulder, are not included in this collection. The camera is generally oriented towards the target position. To avoid a bias towards the ball being in the center of the image, the camera orientation is offset so the position of the target position is evenly distributed in the image space.

Since the robot sizes (and thereby camera height) and fields of view (FOVs) are very different in the league, we decided to also model this in the dataset. We collected these parameters from the robot specifications from the last RoboCup competition. On this basis, we calculated the mean FOV and height as well as its standard deviations (FOV: $\mu = 89.3°, \sigma^2 = 28.1$, height: $\mu = 0.64\,\mathrm{m}$, $\sigma^2 = 0.12$) for the HSL-KidSize. Based on this, for each image, we sample an FOV and a camera height from a normal distribution around the mean and with the standard deviation of the league. If the sampled FOV or height is smaller or larger than the extreme values used by a team (FOV: $60° - 180°$, height: $0.45\,\mathrm{m}-0.95\,\mathrm{m}$), we resample for a new value.

2.3   Avoiding Similarity

How well a dataset represents a domain is not only related to its size but also the diversity between the images. In the Pascal VOC dataset [9] special attention was put on removing exact and near-duplicate images from the set of images to reduce redundancy and unnecessary labeling work. This approach worked well on their raw data taken from a photo-sharing website. However, the RoboCup domain poses additional challenges, as the images are typically recorded in a sequence. Therefore, most images are similar to the one before, since the robots only move slowly or are even standing (especially prevalent with goalkeepers). While a naive approach of taking every nth image can address this problem, it can also remove short events which rarely occur in the dataset. Additionally, the robots typically have some version of capture bias such as continuously tracking the ball or looking back to positions where they expect objects to be. Finally, the position of the robot on the field is not evenly distributed. Positions like the goal area, the center circle, and the sides of the field where the robots walk in are more commonly represented than for example the corners.

To avoid these issues, we used unsupervised machine learning to train a variational autoencoder. It was trained on a dataset consisting of low-resolution images (128×112 pixels) from the various imagesets we decided to include. The autoencoder has $3,416,987$ trainable parameters and is based upon the *conv-vae*[2] GitHub repository using the original model architecture. We trained it to represent the images of this domain in a 300 dimensional latent space. To prune

---

[2] https://github.com/noctrog/conv-vae (last accessed: 2021/06/14)

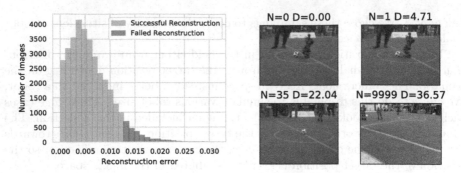

Fig. 1. Distribution of the reconstruction error from the variational autoencoder on the unfiltered dataset (**left**) and exemplary images with distance to a reference point in latent space (**right**). **D** describes the Euclidean distance in the latent space of the **N**'th distant neighbor of the reference image.

similar images, we used this latent space representation to remove images with close proximity to a given image. Neighbors within a given Euclidean distance were determined using a k-d tree. During the greedy sampling process, we start with the set E containing all the unfiltered images and a k-d tree representing the latent space relations. An image is randomly selected from E and all its close neighbors including the image itself are removed from E while the sampled image itself is added to our filtered set O. We repeat this process until E is empty and O contains our filtered imageset. This algorithm is based on the assumption that the variational autoencoder can represent a given image in its latent space. This may not be the case for edge cases. Therefore we check the reconstruction performance of the autoencoder on a given image by comparing the original image against the decoder output and calculating the mean squared error between both of them. Outliers with an error of more than 1.64σ (which equals 10% of the dataset) are added to O regardless of their latent space distance to other images. The error distribution is shown in Fig. 1. Since a high error implies that a situation is not represented significantly in our existing dataset to be encoded into the latent space, it is assumed to be sufficiently distinct from the other images in the set. To filter our real-world dataset, we used 44,366 images as an input to this selection algorithm and reduced it to 10,464 images.

3   Image Annotation

In the following, we define the label types we used in the dataset. Additionally, we explain the process of image annotation for both the images gathered in the real world and in simulation. We provide labels for the classes ball, robot, goalpost, field area, lines, T-, L-, and X-line intersections. Only features that are relevant for a robot in a RoboCup Soccer game were labeled. Thus, no balls or robots outside of the current field and no other fields are labeled. Parts of the recording robot, e.g. its feet, are not labeled. Additionally, each label might be marked as concealed or blurred. Concealed means that the object is partially covered by another object that is in front of it. Labels of objects, that are truncated as they are located on the border of the image, are not marked as concealed. The exception to this are the line crossings, they are concealed if they are not entirely visible. A blurred annotation is affected by either motion or camera blur, resulting in a significantly changed appearance of the object, e.g. a ball might appear oval rather than circular. A concealed or blurred object is significantly harder to detect. For example, this information could be used in the calculation of the loss function to specifically focus on also detecting blurred and concealed objects. It could also be used to focus on them less since a team might have no issues with motion blur because they use a different camera setup.

To avoid ambiguities, we define each object class in detail:

Ball: The ball is represented as a bounding box. It is possible to compute a near pixel-precise ellipse from the bounding box [26]. In some images, multiple balls are present on the field of play. We label all of them even though this would not occur in a regular game.

Robot: We define robot labels as a bounding box. Unlike the ball, it is not as easy to generate an accurate shape of the robot with just a bounding box, because the form of a robot is not as easy to define. However, to make labeling feasible, we compromise by using bounding boxes.

Goalpost: The label for goalposts is a four-point polygon. This allows to accurately describe tilted goalposts. Because the polygon encompasses the goalpost tightly, this method allows the computation of a segmentation image, the middle point, and the lowest point, which is required for the projection of the goalpost position from image space into Cartesian space. Only the goalposts on the goal line are labeled, excluding other parts of the goal.

Field Area: The field area is relevant as everything outside of the field provides no useful information for the robot. We define it with a series of connected lines, the ends are connected to the right and left borders of the image, assuming the end of the field area is visible there. A segmentation is computed from the area between the lines and the bottom of the image.

Lines: We offer a segmentation image for lines as the ground truth because there is no other option to annotate lines with sufficient precision, as their width in image space is highly variable.

Field Features: We define the T-Intersections, L-Intersections, and X-Intersections (including penalty mark and center point) of lines as field features. For this feature, we only define a single point in the center of the intersection.

To create labels for the real-world images, we used the ImageTagger. It provides all the necessary labeling types we used, other than for the annotation of lines. For these, we created a specialized tool. First, it allows the user to specify smoothing and adaptive threshold parameters for a given image. Based on this, a proposed segmentation mask is generated which can then be corrected manually. In the last step, all balls, robots, goalposts, and the area above the field are excluded from the line segmentation using the existing labels for these classes. In general, features are only labeled when they are detectable by a human considering only the respective image (i.e. no context information from a previous image should be necessary). Some imagesets were already labeled for some of the classes. The rest of the labels were created by us. Additionally, we manually verified all labels in the set.

One of the main advantages of training data generation in simulated environments is the availability of ground truth data. Webots offers the functionality to generate bounding boxes and segmentation images for the objects present in a scene. Each individual object has a distinct color in the segmentation image. Furthermore, we provide bounding box annotations for the classes ball and robot, four-point polygons for goalposts and the goal top bar, and a single image coordinate for T-, L-, and X-intersections. Since the bounding boxes provided by Webots were inaccurate in some cases, we computed the minimum enclosing rectangle from the segmentation images. The bounding boxes for robots and the ball are calculated from this. For goalposts, we used rotated bounding boxes to account for the fact they may be tilted yielding similar annotations as the 4-point polygons used for manual annotation of real-world images. Line intersections were annotated by projecting their known positions into the image space of the camera. To detect whether they are visible, we verify in the segmentation image that lines are visible close to the intersection point. If the intersection is occluded, we still include it in the annotations, but mark it as "not in image". The remaining classes (i.e. goal, field area, and lines) are only provided in the segmentation images.

4   Evaluation

To evaluate the dataset, we performed a statistical analysis of the data and assess the performance of a YOLOv4 on it. We focus our evaluation on the real-world images since the images from simulation were generated as described in Sect. 2.2. The real-world dataset contains 10,464 images and 101,432 annotations

Table 2. Detailed distribution of annotations (**left**) and general statistics (**right**) of the real-world collection.

Annotation Type	Total	Annotations per Image					
		0	1	2	3	4	5+
Ball	10,959	46.6%	49.6%	2.9%	0.9%	0.0%	0.0%
Goalpost	12,780	46.8%	31.4%	21.6%	0.3%	0.0%	0.0%
Robot	14,383	64.2%	18.6%	7.6%	4.3%	2.1%	3.1%
L-Intersection	15,458	48.6%	19.3%	22.4%	5.6%	3.1%	1.1%
T-Intersection	13,479	46.1%	35.1%	12.7%	3.5%	1.8%	0.9%
X-Intersection	13,445	59.0%	24.0%	9.6%	4.2%	2.3%	0.9%
Field Area	10,464	Segmentation Mask					
Lines	10,464						
Sum	101,432						

Ball Types	6
Locations	12
Camera Types	5
On Robot	76%
During Game	59%
Natural Light	38%
League	
SPL	25%
HSL	75%
Perspective	
Field	93%
Goalie	4%
From Outside	3%

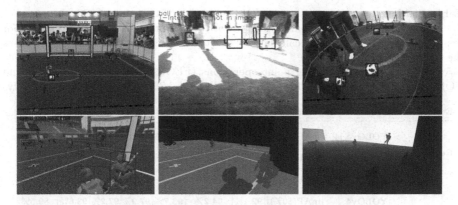

Fig. 2. Examples from the dataset. First row from the real-world collection, second row shows one image of the simulation collection with the corresponding segmentation and depth images.

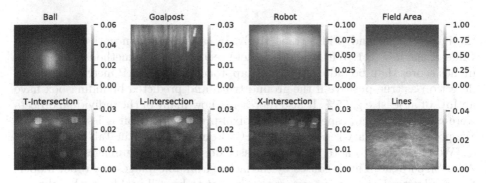

Fig. 3. Visualization of the position density of the respective annotations in the image space over all images of the real-world collection.

in eight different classes. In Table 2 we showcase metadata about the images and annotations present in the collection. Figure 2 shows exemplary annotations on images from the dataset. Also, we investigated the positions of annotations in image space. This was done by plotting the heatmaps shown in Fig. 3. Many of the patterns evident in the heatmaps are caused by the typical positions of the robots in the field and especially prominent by their head behavior as they are often programmed to look directly at a ball.

Based on metrics used in related work, we decided to present detection results using the mean average precision (mAP) and intersection over union (IoU) metrics. The IoU metric compares how well pixels of the ground truth and the detection overlap. Since the ball is round, but the labels are rectangular, we computed an ellipse in the bounding box as the ground truth for the IoU. Similarly, the line intersections are labeled as a single coordinate, but since the intersection itself is larger, we assumed a bounding box with height and width as 5% of

Table 3. Mean average precision of YOLOv4 and YOLOv4-tiny on this dataset. For the intersections, we used a bounding box of 5% of the image size. The mAP values for the goalpost and crossbar are calculated from a bounding box that fully encompasses the polygon. The values are IOU, mAP with IOU threshold of 50%, mAP with IOU threshold of 75%. The floating point operations (FLOPs) required by YOLOv4 and YOLOv4-tiny per sample are 127 billion FLOPs and 6.79 billion FLOPs respectively.

Environment	Approach	Metric	Ball	Goalpost	Robot	T-Int.	L-Int.	X-Int.	Crossbar
Real World	YOLOv4 [4]	IoU	91.1%	70.0%	91.7%	77.3%	79.2%	83.6%	-
		mAP(50%)	98.8%	91.9%	96.0%	95.1%	94.4%	93.5%	
		mAP(75%)	89.7%	54.9%	72.7%	23.6%	23.8%	23.1%	
	YOLOv4-tiny	IoU	89.2%	69.9%	89.3%	75.5%	75.8%	82.2%	-
		mAP(50%)	97.5%	89.6%	91.4%	89.8%	88.8%	92.6%	
		mAP(75%)	80.0%	42.9%	47.7%	43.3%	39.7%	38.9%	
Simulation	YOLOv4	IoU	88.5%	51.2%	87.2%	70.5%	69.3%	78.9%	58.1%
		mAP(50%)	92.1%	94.2%	93.7%	97.9%	97.2%	98.6%	89.5%
		mAP(75%)	84.6%	76.4%	82.7%	86.7%	87.1%	91.1%	66.2%
	YOLOv4-tiny	IoU	85.1%	51.4%	82.5%	63.1%	60.9%	73.2%	58.9%
		mAP(50%)	80.4%	91.0%	83.5%	89.8%	85.8%	91.7%	91.2%
		mAP(75%)	59.5%	64.8%	57.8%	55.4%	50.6%	63.4%	59.2%

the image height and -width respectively. In case of a true negative, we set the value of the IoU to 1. With the IoU, pixel-precise detection methods can achieve higher scores than bounding box based approaches. The mAP metric classifies a detection as true positive if the ground truth and predicted bounding box have an IoU of at least e.g. 75%. It also represents how many of the individual objects were correctly found, especially when pixel-precise detection is less important. We present exemplary results of a YOLOv4 on the dataset in Table 3.

We would like to note that the dataset does not include images of the HSL AdultSize league. This is caused by the lack of available images and robot models for simulation. However, we expect the dataset to be still usable as a benchmark as the HSL KidSize and AdultSize leagues are visually very similar from a robot's perspective.

5   Conclusion

Efforts to share training data between teams have eased the transition to machine learning based approaches and were a good starting point for new teams. However, as we have shown in Table 1, many of the existing and new approaches were hard to compare quantitatively to each other as there was no common benchmark available. This work closes this gap by providing a benchmark dataset that is specific to the RoboCup Humanoid Soccer domain. Additional contributions of this paper are a system for vision training data generation in a simulated environment and an approach to increase the variety of a dataset by automatically selecting a diverse set of images from a larger pool.

The quality of the dataset is limited by the availability of images. Therefore, we hope that more teams start recording images on their robots during games and publish them so that future datasets can profit from this. Future datasets could include image sequences to allow detection of robots' actions, e.g. a kick, and include images of outdoor fields with real grass. This dataset could also be used as a qualification metric for future competitions.

The dataset and tools used to create it are available at https://github.com/bit-bots/TORSO_21_dataset.

Acknowledgments. Thanks to all individuals and teams that provided data and labels or helped to develop and host the ImageTagger.

This research was partially funded by the Ministry of Science, Research and Equalities of Hamburg as well as the German Research Foundation (DFG) and the National Science Foundation of China (NSFC) in project Crossmodal Learning, TRR-169.

References

1. Albani, D., Youssef, A., Suriani, V., Nardi, D., Bloisi, D.D.: A deep learning approach for object recognition with NAO soccer robots. In: Behnke, S., Sheh, R., Sariel, S., Lee, D.D. (eds.) RoboCup 2016. LNCS (LNAI), vol. 9776, pp. 392–403. Springer, Cham (2017). https://doi.org/10.1007/978-3-319-68792-6_33
2. Asada, M., von Stryk, O.: Scientific and technological challenges in robocup. Ann. Rev. Control Robot. Auton. Syst. **3**, 441–471 (2020)
3. Barry, D., Shah, M., Keijsers, M., Khan, H., Hopman, B.: xYOLO: a model for real-time object detection in humanoid soccer on low-end hardware. In: International Conference on Image and Vision Computing New Zealand (IVCNZ), pp. 1–6. IEEE (2019)
4. Bochkovskiy, A., Wang, C.Y., Liao, H.Y.M.: Yolov4: optimal speed and accuracy of object detection. arXiv preprint arXiv:2004.10934 (2020)
5. Cruz, N., Leiva, F., Ruiz-del-Solar, J.: Deep learning applied to humanoid soccer robotics: playing without using any color information. Auton. Robot. **45**(3), 335–350 (2021). https://doi.org/10.1007/s10514-021-09966-9
6. Cruz, N., Lobos-Tsunekawa, K., Ruiz-del-Solar, J.: Using convolutional neural networks in robots with limited computational resources: detecting NAO robots while playing soccer. In: Akiyama, H., Obst, O., Sammut, C., Tonidandel, F. (eds.) RoboCup 2017. LNCS (LNAI), vol. 11175, pp. 19–30. Springer, Cham (2018). https://doi.org/10.1007/978-3-030-00308-1_2
7. Deng, J., Dong, W., Socher, R., Li, L.J., Li, K., Fei-Fei, L.: ImageNet: a large-scale hierarchical image database. In: IEEE Conference on Computer Vision and Pattern Recognition, pp. 248–255. IEEE (2009)
8. van Dijk, S.G., Scheunemann, M.M.: Deep learning for semantic segmentation on minimal hardware. In: Holz, D., Genter, K., Saad, M., von Stryk, O. (eds.) RoboCup 2018. LNCS (LNAI), vol. 11374, pp. 349–361. Springer, Cham (2019). https://doi.org/10.1007/978-3-030-27544-0_29
9. Everingham, M., Van Gool, L., Williams, C.K., Winn, J., Zisserman, A.: The pascal visual object classes (VOC) challenge. Int. J. Comput. Vision **88**(2), 303–338 (2010). https://doi.org/10.1007/s11263-009-0275-4
10. Farazi, H., Behnke, S.: Real-time visual tracking and identification for a team of homogeneous humanoid robots. In: Behnke, S., Sheh, R., Sariel, S., Lee, D.D. (eds.) RoboCup 2016. LNCS (LNAI), vol. 9776, pp. 230–242. Springer, Cham (2017). https://doi.org/10.1007/978-3-319-68792-6_19

11. Farazi, H., et al.: NimbRo robots winning RoboCup 2018 humanoid AdultSize soccer competitions. In: Holz, D., Genter, K., Saad, M., von Stryk, O. (eds.) RoboCup 2018. LNCS (LNAI), vol. 11374, pp. 436–449. Springer, Cham (2019). https://doi.org/10.1007/978-3-030-27544-0_36

12. Felbinger, G.C., Göttsch, P., Loth, P., Peters, L., Wege, F.: Designing convolutional neural networks using a genetic approach for ball detection. In: Holz, D., Genter, K., Saad, M., von Stryk, O. (eds.) RoboCup 2018. LNCS (LNAI), vol. 11374, pp. 150–161. Springer, Cham (2019). https://doi.org/10.1007/978-3-030-27544-0_12

13. Fiedler, N., Bestmann, M., Hendrich, N.: ImageTagger: an open source online platform for collaborative image labeling. In: Holz, D., Genter, K., Saad, M., von Stryk, O. (eds.) RoboCup 2018. LNCS (LNAI), vol. 11374, pp. 162–169. Springer, Cham (2019). https://doi.org/10.1007/978-3-030-27544-0_13

14. Fiedler, N., Brandt, H., Gutsche, J., Vahl, F., Hagge, J., Bestmann, M.: An open source vision pipeline approach for RoboCup humanoid soccer. In: Chalup, S., Niemueller, T., Suthakorn, J., Williams, M.-A. (eds.) RoboCup 2019. LNCS (LNAI), vol. 11531, pp. 376–386. Springer, Cham (2019). https://doi.org/10.1007/978-3-030-35699-6_29

15. Gabel, A., Heuer, T., Schiering, I., Gerndt, R.: Jetson, where is the ball? Using neural networks for ball detection at RoboCup 2017. In: Holz, D., Genter, K., Saad, M., von Stryk, O. (eds.) RoboCup 2018. LNCS (LNAI), vol. 11374, pp. 181–192. Springer, Cham (2019). https://doi.org/10.1007/978-3-030-27544-0_15

16. Gondry, L., et al.: Rhoban football club: RoboCup humanoid KidSize 2019 champion team paper. In: Chalup, S., Niemueller, T., Suthakorn, J., Williams, M.-A. (eds.) RoboCup 2019. LNCS (LNAI), vol. 11531, pp. 491–503. Springer, Cham (2019). https://doi.org/10.1007/978-3-030-35699-6_40

17. Hess, T., Mundt, M., Weis, T., Ramesh, V.: Large-scale stochastic scene generation and semantic annotation for deep convolutional neural network training in the RoboCup SPL. In: Akiyama, H., Obst, O., Sammut, C., Tonidandel, F. (eds.) RoboCup 2017. LNCS (LNAI), vol. 11175, pp. 33–44. Springer, Cham (2018). https://doi.org/10.1007/978-3-030-00308-1_3

18. Javadi, M., Azar, S.M., Azami, S., Ghidary, S.S., Sadeghnejad, S., Baltes, J.: Humanoid robot detection using deep learning: a speed-accuracy tradeoff. In: Akiyama, H., Obst, O., Sammut, C., Tonidandel, F. (eds.) RoboCup 2017. LNCS (LNAI), vol. 11175, pp. 338–349. Springer, Cham (2018). https://doi.org/10.1007/978-3-030-00308-1_28

19. Kukleva, A., Khan, M.A., Farazi, H., Behnke, S.: Utilizing temporal information in deep convolutional network for efficient soccer ball detection and tracking. In: Chalup, S., Niemueller, T., Suthakorn, J., Williams, M.-A. (eds.) RoboCup 2019. LNCS (LNAI), vol. 11531, pp. 112–125. Springer, Cham (2019). https://doi.org/10.1007/978-3-030-35699-6_9

20. Lin, T.-Y., et al.: Microsoft COCO: common objects in context. In: Fleet, D., Pajdla, T., Schiele, B., Tuytelaars, T. (eds.) ECCV 2014. LNCS, vol. 8693, pp. 740–755. Springer, Cham (2014). https://doi.org/10.1007/978-3-319-10602-1_48

21. Menashe, J., et al.: Fast and precise black and white ball detection for RoboCup soccer. In: Akiyama, H., Obst, O., Sammut, C., Tonidandel, F. (eds.) RoboCup 2017. LNCS (LNAI), vol. 11175, pp. 45–58. Springer, Cham (2018). https://doi.org/10.1007/978-3-030-00308-1_4

22. Michel, O.: Cyberbotics ltd. webots^{TM}: professional mobile robot simulation. Int. J. Adv. Robot. Syst. **1**(1), 5 (2004)

23. Poppinga, B., Laue, T.: JET-Net: real-time object detection for mobile robots. In: Chalup, S., Niemueller, T., Suthakorn, J., Williams, M.-A. (eds.) RoboCup 2019. LNCS (LNAI), vol. 11531, pp. 227–240. Springer, Cham (2019). https://doi.org/10.1007/978-3-030-35699-6_18

24. Schnekenburger, F., Scharffenberg, M., Wülker, M., Hochberg, U., Dorer, K.: Detection and localization of features on a soccer field with feedforward fully convolutional neural networks (FCNN) for the adult-size humanoid robot sweaty. In: Proceedings of the 12th Workshop on Humanoid Soccer Robots, IEEE-RAS International Conference on Humanoid Robots, Birmingham. Sn (2017)

25. Speck, D., Barros, P., Weber, C., Wermter, S.: Ball localization for Robocup soccer using convolutional neural networks. In: Behnke, S., Sheh, R., Sarıel, S., Lee, D.D. (eds.) RoboCup 2016. LNCS (LNAI), vol. 9776, pp. 19–30. Springer, Cham (2017). https://doi.org/10.1007/978-3-319-68792-6_2

26. Speck, D., Bestmann, M., Barros, P.: Towards real-time ball localization using CNNs. In: Holz, D., Genter, K., Saad, M., von Stryk, O. (eds.) RoboCup 2018. LNCS (LNAI), vol. 11374, pp. 337–348. Springer, Cham (2019). https://doi.org/10.1007/978-3-030-27544-0_28

27. Szemenyei, M., Estivill-Castro, V.: Real-time scene understanding using deep neural networks for RoboCup SPL. In: Holz, D., Genter, K., Saad, M., von Stryk, O. (eds.) RoboCup 2018. LNCS (LNAI), vol. 11374, pp. 96–108. Springer, Cham (2019). https://doi.org/10.1007/978-3-030-27544-0_8

28. Szemenyei, M., Estivill-Castro, V.: ROBO: robust, fully neural object detection for robot soccer. In: Chalup, S., Niemueller, T., Suthakorn, J., Williams, M.-A. (eds.) RoboCup 2019. LNCS (LNAI), vol. 11531, pp. 309–322. Springer, Cham (2019). https://doi.org/10.1007/978-3-030-35699-6_24

29. Szemenyei, M., Estivill-Castro, V.: Fully neural object detection solutions for robot soccer. Neural Comput. Appl. 1–14 (2021). https://doi.org/10.1007/s00521-021-05972-1

30. Teimouri, M., Delavaran, M.H., Rezaei, M.: A real-time ball detection approach using convolutional neural networks. In: Chalup, S., Niemueller, T., Suthakorn, J., Williams, M.-A. (eds.) RoboCup 2019. LNCS (LNAI), vol. 11531, pp. 323–336. Springer, Cham (2019). https://doi.org/10.1007/978-3-030-35699-6_25

31. Tsipras, D., Santurkar, S., Engstrom, L., Ilyas, A., Madry, A.: From ImageNet to image classification: contextualizing progress on benchmarks. In: International Conference on Machine Learning, pp. 9625–9635. PMLR (2020)

32. Xiao, H., Rasul, K., Vollgraf, R.: Fashion-MNIST: a novel image dataset for benchmarking machine learning algorithms. arXiv preprint arXiv:1708.07747 (2017)

6D Object Pose Estimation Using Keypoints and Part Affinity Fields

Moritz Zappel, Simon Bultmann$^{(\boxtimes)}$, and Sven Behnke

Autonomous Intelligent Systems, Computer Science Institute VI,
University of Bonn, Bonn, Germany
s6mozapp@uni-bonn.de, {bultmann,behnke}@ais.uni-bonn.de
https://www.ais.uni-bonn.de

Abstract. The task of 6D object pose estimation from RGB images is an important requirement for autonomous service robots to be able to interact with the real world. In this work, we present a two-step pipeline for estimating the 6 DoF translation and orientation of known objects. Keypoints and Part Affinity Fields (PAFs) are predicted from the input image adopting the OpenPose CNN architecture from human pose estimation. Object poses are then calculated from 2D-3D correspondences between detected and model keypoints via the PnP-RANSAC algorithm. The proposed approach is evaluated on the YCB-Video dataset and achieves accuracy on par with recent methods from the literature. Using PAFs to assemble detected keypoints into object instances proves advantageous over only using heatmaps. Models trained to predict keypoints of a single object class perform significantly better than models trained for several classes.

Keywords: Object pose estimation · Robot perception · Deep learning

1 Introduction

Object pose estimation is essential for autonomous robots to be able to interact with their environment. It has numerous real-world applications, such as robotic manipulation and human-robot interaction for autonomous service robots which are the focus of RoboCup@Home [17].

The task addressed in this work consists of detecting known objects and estimating their 6 DoF orientation and translation in 3D space from a single RGB image. In recent years, two-stage approaches, which first detect keypoints and then solve a Perspective-n-Point (PnP) problem to infer the object pose [14–16], have been shown to provide robust and accurate results. However, keypoint detection remains difficult for occluded or truncated objects.

In this paper, we propose a two-stage pipeline for 6D object pose estimation in real-world scenes. We adopt the OpenPose architecture [2], well known from person pose estimation, to detect keypoints and Part Affinity Fields (PAFs) of everyday objects. Keypoints are predicted as local maxima of a heatmap indicating the confidence of a part being present at the image location. PAFs are

R. Alami et al. (Eds.): RoboCup 2021, LNAI 13132, pp. 78–90, 2022.
https://doi.org/10.1007/978-3-030-98682-7_7

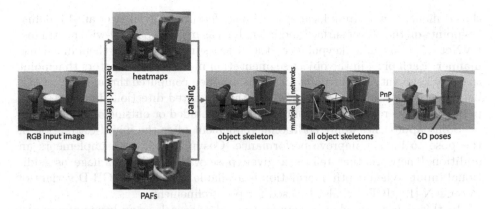

Fig. 1. Pose estimation approach: Heatmaps and PAFs are inferred for each object and 6D poses are calculated from detected keypoints via PnP.

vector fields connecting the keypoints of an object. They are used to assemble keypoints to object instances. As the OpenPose architecture is a bottom-up approach, keypoints are directly estimated from the input image. No prior object detection or segmentation is required, which is advantageous in terms of complexity and runtime [2]. Correspondences between the predicted 2D keypoints from the image and the keypoints defined on the 3D object models are then used to calculate the 6 DoF object poses via the PnP-RANSAC algorithm. An overview of the proposed method is given in Fig. 1. Two different ways to define keypoints and PAFs on the object models are proposed in this work and the method is extensively evaluated on the challenging YCB-V dataset [19].

2   Related Work

6D object pose estimation methods from the literature can roughly be divided into two classes. Direct methods infer pose parameters directly from the image [9,19]. PoseCNN [19] defines a CNN architecture that segments objects in 2D images, predicts their depth, and regresses the 6D pose parameters. Capellen et al. [3] extend this approach to a fully convolutional network for dense prediction of pose parameters not depending on prior object segmentation. The direct pose regression is, however, difficult—especially for the rotation parameters as the 3D rotation space is highly nonlinear.

In contrast, Keypoint-based approaches adopt a two-step pipeline: First, 2D keypoints are predicted for each object instance in the image and the 6 DoF pose is computed in a second step from 2D-3D correspondences with a variant of the PnP-Algorithm [11]. Approaches mainly differ in how the keypoints are defined on the object model and how they are inferred from the image. In BB8 [16], a segmentation mask is computed for each object and the keypoints are then inferred as the eight corners of the 3D object bounding box. The coordinates of the keypoints are directly regressed by the network. The corners of the 3D bounding box, however, often are not located on the object surface and are thus difficult to infer from local object image features. Pavlakov et al. [14] define keypoints on the object surface and infer them as maxima of pixel-wise heatmaps. PVNet [15] also defines keypoints on the object surface but infers them in a dense manner: Each pixel in the object segmentation mask predicts vectors that point to every keypoint. The keypoint locations are then computed through RANSAC-based voting, choosing locations where the predicted directions intersect. This permits to also represent keypoints that are occluded or outside of the image.

Some approaches apply additional refinement after the initial estimation of the pose to further improve performance. Cosypose [10], e.g., implements an additional network that refines a given pose with the input image as additional input. When depth information is available, e.g., in the RGB-D variant of PoseCNN [19], ICP can also be used for pose refinement.

In this paper, we adopt a keypoint-based approach using keypoints on the object surface. The 6D object pose is computed via a combination of the PnP [11] and RANSAC [4] algorithms to increase the robustness of the estimation. Only RGB images are used as input and no further refinement steps are employed, keeping our pipeline simple and efficient. The OpenPose architecture [2] is adopted for 2D keypoint estimation. OpenPose is a keypoint-based bottom-up approach for human pose estimation in images. Together with heatmaps of the keypoints, the CNN computes vector fields, called Part Affinity Fields (PAFs), connecting the keypoints of an object instance. This permits to directly predict keypoints on the input image without prior segmentation or detection required. Local maxima in the heatmaps are then assembled into instances via the PAFs.

3   Method

In this section, we detail design choices and workflow of the proposed approach for 6 DoF object pose estimation.

For evaluation, we employ the YCB-V dataset [19]. It comprises over 130k images at VGA resolution of 21 different object classes and is widely used for robot manipulation and object pose estimation tasks. For each object, a textured mesh is included as 3D model with the origin of the object coordinate frame defined at its center. All objects are household objects relevant for real-world robot experiments in domestic service scenarios (cf. Fig. 2). The images contain multiple objects in realistic settings with changing lighting conditions, significant image noise and cluttered backgrounds.

3.1   Selection of Keypoints and PAFs

The choice of keypoints and PAFs is an important design parameter of our method. They need to be well localized on the object geometry and texture, to facilitate their CNN-based detection, and should be spread out on the object surface such that a stable and well-defined solution of the PnP-problem can be found. Keypoints and PAFs are defined based on the 3D object models in two different ways: They are chosen manually or automatically. Eight keypoints and twelve PAFs are defined per object class. The manually defined keypoints are

01   02   03   04   05   06   07   08   09   10

11   12   13   14   15   16   17   18   19   20   21

Fig. 2. Objects of the YCB-V dataset with heatmaps of the manually defined keypoints and their interconnections.

located on easy-to-find spots of the object geometry and texture and represent the object contour. If applicable, the keypoints are placed to form a cuboid. This set of keypoints is shown in Fig. 2. The automatically defined set of keypoints is chosen with the farthest-point-algorithm, inspired by PVNet [15]: Starting with the object center, points on the object surface which are farthest from the already chosen points are added to the keypoint set. Eight points on the object surface are retained—the center point is not part of the final keypoint set. The set of automatically chosen keypoints is shown in Fig. 3. The PAFs for both sets of keypoints are defined by hand. The objective is to choose connections, which run along distinctive features and to form one upper and one lower polygon, which are connected with vertical PAFs. The PAFs run along the keypoint connections displayed in Figs. 2 and 3 and have a fixed width. The automatically picked keypoints are less intuitively placed and harder to find than the manually picked ones. The reason for this is, that the automatically picked keypoints are often located on edges instead of corners and on surfaces instead of edges. Furthermore, the texture is ignored in the automatic selection although it is important to localize keypoints. The inferior performance of the automatically chosen keypoints is confirmed by the evaluation results (cf. Sect. 4). Therefore, the manually chosen keypoints are used for the main results of this paper.

The YCB-V dataset contains several symmetric objects: 13, 16, 19, 20, and 21. The bowl (Obj. 13) is rotationally symmetric while the other objects possess discrete symmetry transformations. For each symmetric object, some poses are not distinguishable from each other. Hence, keypoints of the symmetric objects cannot be learned by the network if the symmetries are ignored. A simple elimination of symmetric poses during training is implemented in this work. All symmetry-equivalent poses are mapped to the same pose which ensures same relative position of keypoints on the image plane.

3.2 Network

We extend a public implementation of the OpenPose framework [18]. The network architecture is adjusted to the YCB-V dataset as well as the used keypoints

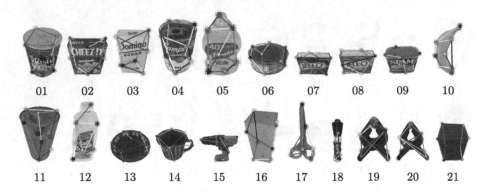

Fig. 3. Objects of the YCB-V dataset with heatmaps of the automatically defined keypoints and their interconnections.

and PAFs. For an input image of size $H \times W$ and C object classes, the output shape is $\frac{H}{8} \times \frac{W}{8} \times (C \cdot 8 + 1)$ for the heatmaps and $\frac{H}{8} \times \frac{W}{8} \times (C \cdot 12 \cdot 2)$ for the PAFs. Heatmaps consist of 8 keypoint channels per object class and background, while PAFs consists of x and y channels for the 12 keypoint connections per class. Training labels are generated from the object model keypoints projected into the images of the video sequences using the annotated poses. A Gaussian blob is rendered at the keypoint position in the respective heatmap channel and the respective PAF channels represent the unit vector in the direction of the connection, within a fixed width along the connecting line, as in [2].

To enable the network to estimate the poses for multiple object classes, the layer width of the intermediate stages needs to be scaled accordingly to the output layers. A network for all 21 object classes would require more GPU memory than most graphic cards possess. Because of this, we train a separate model for each object class. We verify in the evaluation (Sect. 4), that the performance of these 1-object models is superior to models trained for multiple object classes.

3.3 Workflow

Figure 1 illustrates the general workflow of our pipeline for 6D object pose estimation. The input image is processed by the network and heatmaps and PAFs are estimated. The local maxima of each heatmap are candidates for the respective keypoint. These keypoint candidates are grouped into object instances using the PAFs, as in the OpenPose framework [2]. This step is repeated for every object class. The PnP and RANSAC algorithms are used to calculate the 6D poses of the found object instances with four or more valid keypoints[1] using correspondences between detected 2D image keypoints and 3D model keypoints. In datasets with only one instance of an object per image, the best guess will be kept. In multi-instance datasets, each estimated object pose will be assigned to the closest ground truth object pose of this class for evaluation.

---

[1] The PnP algorithm requires at least four correspondences for a unique solution.

4   Evaluation

We evaluate our approach on the YCB-Video dataset [19], compare the results to other approaches from the literature, and perform ablation studies to understand the influences of different components of our method. All experiments run on a workstation PC with RTX 2080 GPU, i7-8700K CPU, and 32 GB of RAM. Pose estimation takes 50 ms in average per object and image, thereof 8 ms for pre-processing, 8 ms for inference, and 34 ms for post-processing and PnP. The network requires 1.24 GB of GPU memory.

4.1   Metrics

We employ two standard metrics for evaluation: average 3D distance of model points (ADD) [5] and 2D projection error [1]. Both metrics employ the meshes of the object models to calculate the pose error. The ADD metric is defined as:

$$\epsilon_{\text{ADD}} = \frac{1}{|P|} \sum_{\vec{p} \in P} \| (\vec{R}\vec{p} + \vec{t}) - (\tilde{\vec{R}}\vec{p} + \tilde{\vec{t}}) \|, \tag{1}$$

with $\tilde{R}$ and $\tilde{\vec{t}}$ being the estimated rotation and translation, $\vec{R}$ and $\vec{t}$ defining the ground-truth pose and P the set of vertices of the object model mesh. For symmetric objects, the point-to-point correspondences can be ambiguous and the metric is adapted to compute the average distance using the closest point from the mesh [19]:

$$\epsilon_{\text{ADD-S}} = \frac{1}{|P|} \sum_{\vec{p}_1 \in P} \min_{\vec{p}_2 \in P} \| (\vec{R}\vec{p}_1 + \vec{t}) - (\tilde{\vec{R}}\vec{p}_2 + \tilde{\vec{t}}) \|. \tag{2}$$

The 2D projection metric computes the average 2D pixel distances between corresponding points projected onto the image plane of the evaluated view:

$$\epsilon_{\text{2DProj}} = \frac{1}{|P|} \sum_{\vec{p} \in P} \| \text{proj}(\vec{R}\vec{p} + \vec{t}) - \text{proj}(\tilde{\vec{R}}\vec{p} + \tilde{\vec{t}}) \|. \tag{3}$$

The evaluation scores are given in terms of the area under the accuracy-threshold curve (AuC). For this, the threshold for the respective distance metric is varied and the pose accuracy is computed for each threshold value. The maximum thresholds are set to 10 cm for ADD(-S) and 40 px for the 2D projection metric.

4.2   Results on the YCB-Video Dataset

In Table 1, we give detailed evaluation results of the AuC scores for all 21 objects of the YCB-V dataset and compare them to the results of PoseCNN [19]. The proposed approach outperforms PoseCNN in terms of ADD for most of the non-symmetric objects and on average over all objects. The improvement is most significant for the box-shaped Objects 2, 3, 7, and 8 as well as for Objects 11,

Table 1. Area under accuracy Curve (AuC) for pose estimation of YCB-V objects. * denotes symmetric objects. Best results are marked bold.

Object	Ours			PoseCNN [19]	
	ADD	ADD-S	2D Proj.	ADD	ADD-S
1	49.9	80.7	54.8	**50.9**	**84.0**
2	**80.5**	**88.4**	84.3	51.7	76.9
3	**85.5**	**92.4**	88.8	68.6	84.3
4	**68.5**	**81.4**	84.8	66.0	80.9
5	**87.0**	**93.3**	89.8	79.9	90.2
6	**79.3**	**89.7**	81.7	70.4	87.9
7	**81.8**	**89.5**	88.7	62.9	79.0
8	**89.4**	**94.0**	92.9	75.2	87.1
9	**59.6**	70.0	69.0	**59.6**	**78.5**
10	36.5	58.3	55.0	**72.3**	**85.9**
11	**78.1**	**86.9**	78.0	52.5	76.8
12	**56.7**	67.1	66.2	50.5	**71.9**
*13	**12.2**	23.5	4.1	6.5	**69.7**
14	54.0	76.9	75.2	**57.7**	**78.0**
15	**82.8**	**91.0**	88.2	55.1	72.8
*16	16.7	29.6	29.5	**31.8**	**65.8**
17	**46.0**	**64.1**	76.7	35.8	56.2
18	9.8	11.9	20.8	**58.0**	**71.4**
*19	20.0	47.4	8.9	**25.0**	**49.9**
*20	14.1	45.5	3.5	**15.8**	**47.0**
*21	12.1	29.7	2.3	**40.4**	**87.8**
Average	**59.0**	72.7	65.0	53.7	**75.9**

15, and 17 which have a more complex shape (cf. Fig. 2). PoseCNN, on the other hand, achieves better results for the symmetric objects in terms of ADD-S. The proposed approach provides less accurate results for these objects, where several keypoint configurations can result in visually equivalent poses. This makes the keypoint estimation harder to learn and cannot be fully compensated by the symmetry handling during training (cf. Sect. 3). Also, keypoints are difficult to infer for objects with little prominent geometric features (e.g., edges or corners) such as Objects 10 and 18. The 2D projection metric scores per object are not reported by the authors of PoseCNN.

In Table 2, we further compare the overall results of our method with the recent Benchmark for 6D Object Pose Estimation (BOP) challenge 2020 [6,7]. The BOP challenge defines slightly different evaluation metrics: The MSSD and MSPD metrics are similar to the ADD and 2D projection metrics, but give the

Table 2. Results on YCB-V of the five best candidates using only RGB images of the BOP challenge 2020 [7] in comparison with our work.

Name	AR	AR_{VSD}	AR_{MSSD}	AR_{MSPD}	Training data
CosyPose [10]	0.821	0.772	0.842	0.850	pbr+real
EPOS [8]	0.696	0.626	0.677	0.783	pbr
Ours	0.575	0.506	0.567	0.654	pbr+real
CosyPose [10]	0.574	0.516	0.554	0.653	pbr
Leaping from 2D to 6D [13]	0.543	0.443	0.499	0.687	pbr+real
CDPNv2 [12]	0.532	0.396	0.570	0.631	pbr+real

(a) Object skeletons   (b) 6D Poses

Fig. 4. Qualitative results on the YCB-V dataset: (a) keypoints and connections, (b) transformed object models overlay on input image.

maximum value instead of the average error and deal with symmetries. The VSD metric is the percentage of pixels, which are visible in the estimated and ground truth pose and are close in the image space. The formal definitions are given in [7]. We achieve the third-best result. In comparison to CosyPose [10], which achieves the best result by a significant margin, we do not refine the initially estimated pose, which could further improve our result.

In Fig. 4, qualitative results on the YCB-V dataset are shown. 6D poses are estimated accurately despite occlusions and outlier keypoint detections.

4.3   Ablation Studies

Several systematic ablation studies have been conducted in this work to evaluate the influences of different components and parameters of the proposed method.

PAFs: We investigate the benefit of PAFs for the YCB-V dataset, where a maximum of one instance per object class is present in an image. For this, we infer the keypoints of an object instance as the global maximum of the respective heatmaps and do not use the PAFs computed by the CNN to assemble keypoints into object instances. This heatmaps-only approach is compared to the full approach using the PAF output. The results are presented in Table 3. Using the PAFs improves the pose estimation result for almost all objects as well as the average accuracy. Without PAFs, recovering from wrong or ambiguous heatmap

Table 3. AuC when using PAFs to connect keypoints into instances vs. only using global heatmap maxima. * denotes symmetric objects. Best results marked bold.

Object	Using PAFs			Heatmaps only		
	ADD	ADD-S	2D Proj.	ADD	ADD-S	2D Proj.
1	**49.9**	**80.7**	**54.8**	48.0	80.1	50.2
2	**80.5**	**88.4**	**84.3**	73.1	83.3	72.7
3	**85.5**	**92.4**	**88.8**	79.2	89.4	76.6
4	**68.5**	**81.4**	**84.8**	59.5	75.6	75.0
5	**87.0**	**93.3**	**89.8**	80.4	90.8	79.3
6	**79.3**	**89.7**	**81.7**	68.3	84.5	72.4
7	**81.8**	**89.5**	**88.7**	74.0	84.3	81.2
8	**89.4**	**94.0**	**92.9**	81.8	90.3	81.0
9	**59.6**	**70.0**	**69.0**	54.3	66.3	60.4
10	**36.5**	**58.3**	**55.0**	35.2	55.3	53.0
11	**78.1**	**86.9**	**78.0**	72.9	84.3	67.4
12	**56.7**	**67.1**	**66.2**	51.7	64.3	57.8
*13	**12.2**	**23.5**	**4.1**	11.5	23.2	**4.1**
14	**54.0**	**76.9**	**75.2**	49.1	72.0	63.3
15	**82.8**	**91.0**	**88.2**	76.8	88.3	77.1
*16	**16.7**	**29.6**	**29.5**	15.7	27.4	23.2
17	**46.0**	**64.1**	**76.7**	37.3	56.2	65.1
18	9.8	11.9	20.8	**36.1**	**43.1**	**65.1**
*19	**20.0**	**47.4**	8.9	17.8	45.1	**10.1**
*20	**14.1**	**45.5**	3.5	11.8	43.0	**4.7**
*21	**12.1**	**29.7**	**2.3**	6.2	18.3	0.2
Average	**59.0**	**72.7**	**65.0**	54.5	70.4	58.9

maxima is not possible, leading to inaccurate results especially in the case of occlusions and truncation. An exception is Object 18, where the pose estimation is more accurate without using PAFs. This is probably due to the small size of the object leading to very short PAF vectors at the ends of the marker (cf. Fig. 2). These cannot be well detected by the model, leading to problems parsing the object skeleton. Figure 5 shows the accuracy-threshold curves for each metric with and without using PAFs. The improvement using PAFs is most significant for small accuracy thresholds, demanding a precise estimation of the object pose. The two curves approach each other for higher thresholds.

Selection of Keypoints on Object Models: In Table 4, we compare evaluation results using manually and automatically chosen object keypoints for an exemplary subset of the object classes. The estimated pose generally is more

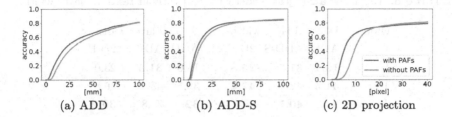

(a) ADD   (b) ADD-S   (c) 2D projection

Fig. 5. Accuracy curves for all YCB-V objects using PAFs vs. heatmaps only.

Table 4. AuC for manually and automatically picked keypoints.

Object	Manually picked keypoints			Automatically picked keypoints		
	ADD	ADD-S	2D Proj.	ADD	ADD-S	2D Proj.
1	**49.9**	**80.7**	54.8	47.7	78.5	**56.7**
2	80.5	88.4	84.3	**81.0**	**89.8**	**87.1**
3	**85.5**	**92.4**	88.8	82.4	90.8	**89.6**
4	**68.5**	**81.4**	**84.8**	68.4	80.8	84.3
5	**87.0**	**93.3**	89.8	83.7	92.0	**92.0**
6	**79.3**	**89.7**	81.7	77.3	88.9	**85.2**
7	**81.8**	**89.5**	**88.7**	75.9	85.0	85.2
8	**89.4**	**94.0**	**92.9**	81.0	89.6	92.4

Table 5. AuC for ADD(-S) and 2D-projection metrics comparing models trained to detect one object class versus models detecting two object classes.

Object	1-Object models			2-Object models		
	ADD	ADD-S	2D Proj.	ADD	ADD-S	2D Proj.
1	**49.9**	**80.7**	**54.8**	18.0	31.5	23.0
4	**68.5**	**81.4**	**84.8**	38.5	43.6	46.8
5	**87.0**	**93.3**	**89.8**	20.3	23.8	23.9
6	**79.3**	**89.7**	**81.7**	53.6	63.1	60.3
7	**81.8**	**89.5**	**88.7**	38.5	42.3	42.5
8	**89.4**	**94.0**	**92.9**	39.8	44.4	45.3
9	**59.6**	**70.0**	**69.0**	25.2	33.3	35.5
10	**36.5**	**58.3**	**55.0**	8.3	12.4	16.9
Average	**66.2**	**81.3**	**75.2**	32.2	39.8	39.2

accurate using the manually defined keypoints. As discussed in Sect. 3, these keypoints are easier to find and can be more precisely localized by the CNN architecture, as they are placed on distinct spots of the object geometry and

Table 6. AuC using a 2-object model with and without rescaling layer width.

Object	Doubled layer width			Normal layer width		
	ADD	ADD-S	2D Proj.	ADD	ADD-S	2D Proj.
1	**19.1**	**31.5**	**25.8**	18.0	**31.5**	23.0
4	**41.5**	**47.1**	**47.4**	38.5	43.6	46.8
Average	**32.2**	**40.7**	38.5	**32.2**	39.8	**39.2**

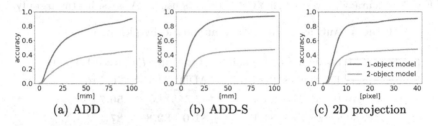

(a) ADD   (b) ADD-S   (c) 2D projection

Fig. 6. Accuracy curves for all YCB-V objects using models that detect one object class vs. models detecting two object classes.

texture (cf. Figs. 2 and 3). The locations of the automatically chosen keypoints, on the other hand, are often weakly constrained along edges or on the object surface, thus being predicted less precisely.

Number of Object Classes per Model: We also investigate the influence of training the CNN model to detect keypoints and PAFs for objects of one or of several classes. The results of this comparison are shown in Table 5 exemplary for a subset of the object classes. The performance of models trained for one object class only is significantly better. The plot of the accuracy-threshold curves shown in Fig. 6 confirms these results. Also, rescaling the width of the CNN model, i.e., doubling the number of channels at each stage of the network, does not significantly improve the results of the 2-object model, as is shown in Table 6. Therefore, a separate model per object class has been used in this work.

5   Conclusion

In this work, we introduce a pipeline for 6D object pose estimation adopting the OpenPose CNN architecture [2] to predict keypoints and Part Affinity Fields (PAFs) on objects. Keypoints are defined on prominent geometric features of the object contour (i.e., corners) and interconnected by PAFs to form a cuboid-like structure. They are predicted as local maxima of a pixel-wise heatmap and assembled into instances using the PAFs. This bottom-up approach permits to infer keypoints directly from the input image, without prior object detection or segmentation. Object poses are then calculated via the PnP-RANSAC algorithm using 2D-3D correspondences between detected and model keypoints. The proposed approach is evaluated on the YCB-Video dataset, containing 21 typical household objects important for domestic service robot applications. Our method achieves accuracy comparable to recent state-of-the-art methods using RGB images only, without employing further pose refinement. The usage of PAFs is shown to be advantageous compared to directly using global maxima of the heatmaps as keypoint detections. Models trained for a single object class perform significantly better than models trained for multiple object classes.

Directions for future work include improved handling of symmetric objects and evaluating the method in scenarios where multiple instances of the same object class occur. Furthermore, a method for automatic keypoint and PAF selection without sacrificing accuracy compared to manual selection should be investigated, enabling to efficiently extend the method with novel object models.

Acknowledgments. This work was funded by grant BE 2556/18-2 of the German Research Foundation (DFG).

References

1. Brachmann, E., Michel, F., Krull, A., Yang, M.Y., Gumhold, S., Rother, C.: Uncertainty-driven 6D pose estimation of objects and scenes from a single RGB image. In: IEEE/CVF Conference on Computer Vision and Pattern Recognition (CVPR), pp. 3364–3372 (2016)
2. Cao, Z., Hidalgo Martinez, G., Simon, T., Wei, S., Sheikh, Y.A.: OpenPose: real-time multi-person 2D pose estimation using part affinity fields. IEEE Trans. Pattern Anal. Mach. Intell. (TPAMI) **43**(1), 172–186 (2019)
3. Capellen, C., Schwarz, M., Behnke, S.: ConvPoseCNN: dense convolutional 6D object pose estimation. In: International Conference on Computer Vision Theory and Applications (VISAPP), pp. 162–172 (2020)
4. Fischler, M.A., Bolles, R.C.: Random sample consensus: a paradigm for model fitting with applications to image analysis and automated cartography. Commun. ACM **24**(6), 381–395 (1981)
5. Hinterstoisser, S., et al.: Model based training, detection and pose estimation of texture-less 3D objects in heavily cluttered scenes. In: Asian Conference on Computer Vision (ACCV), pp. 548–562 (2012)
6. Hodaň, T., et al.: BOP: benchmark for 6D object pose estimation. In: Ferrari, V., Hebert, M., Sminchisescu, C., Weiss, Y. (eds.) ECCV 2018. LNCS, vol. 11214, pp. 19–35. Springer, Cham (2018). https://doi.org/10.1007/978-3-030-01249-6_2
7. Hodan, T., et al.: BOP challenge 2020 on 6D object localization. arXiv:2009.07378 [cs] (2020)
8. Hodaň, T., Baráth, D., Matas, J.: EPOS: estimating 6D pose of objects with symmetries. In: IEEE/CVF Conference on Computer Vision and Pattern Recognition (CVPR), pp. 11700–11709 (2020)
9. Kendall, A., Grimes, M., Cipolla, R.: PoseNet: a convolutional network for real-time 6-DOF camera relocalization. In: IEEE International Conference on Computer Vision (ICCV), pp. 2938–2946 (2015)
10. Labbé, Y., Carpentier, J., Aubry, M., Sivic, J.: CosyPose: consistent multi-view multi-object 6D pose estimation. In: Vedaldi, A., Bischof, H., Brox, T., Frahm, J.-M. (eds.) ECCV 2020. LNCS, vol. 12362, pp. 574–591. Springer, Cham (2020). https://doi.org/10.1007/978-3-030-58520-4_34

11. Lepetit, V., Moreno-Noguer, F., Fua, P.: EPnP: an accurate O(n) solution to the PnP problem. Int. J. Comput. Vision **81**(2), 155 (2008). https://doi.org/10.1007/s11263-008-0152-6

12. Li, Z., Wang, G., Ji, X.: CDPN: coordinates-based disentangled pose network for real-time RGB-based 6-DoF object pose estimation. In: IEEE/CVF International Conference on Computer Vision (ICCV), pp. 7677–7686 (2019)

13. Liu, J., et al.: Leaping from 2D detection to efficient 6DoF object pose estimation. In: Bartoli, A., Fusiello, A. (eds.) ECCV 2020. LNCS, vol. 12536, pp. 707–714. Springer, Cham (2020). https://doi.org/10.1007/978-3-030-66096-3_47

14. Pavlakos, G., Zhou, X., Chan, A., Derpanis, K.G., Daniilidis, K.: 6-DoF object pose from semantic keypoints. In: IEEE International Conference on Robotics and Automation (ICRA), pp. 2011–2018 (2017)

15. Peng, S., Liu, Y., Huang, Q., Zhou, X., Bao, H.: PVNet: pixel-wise voting network for 6DoF pose estimation. In: IEEE/CVF Conference on Computer Vision and Pattern Recognition (CVPR), pp. 4561–4570 (2019)

16. Rad, M., Lepetit, V.: BB8: a scalable, accurate, robust to partial occlusion method for predicting the 3D poses of challenging objects without using depth. In: IEEE International Conference on Computer Vision (ICCV) (2017)

17. Stückler, J., Schwarz, M., Behnke, S.: Mobile manipulation, tool use, and intuitive interaction for cognitive service robot Cosero. Front. Robot. AI **3**, 58 (2016)

18. Wangpeng, A.: Multi person pose estimation by pytorch (2020). https://github.com/tensorboy/pytorch_Realtime_Multi-Person_Pose_Estimation

19. Xiang, Y., Schmidt, T., Narayanan, V., Fox, D.: PoseCNN: a convolutional neural network for 6D object pose estimation in cluttered scenes. In: Robotics: Science and Systems (RSS) (2018)

Real-Time Pose Estimation from Images for Multiple Humanoid Robots

Arash Amini[✉], Hafez Farazi, and Sven Behnke

Computer Science Institute VI, Autonomous Intelligent Systems, University of Bonn,
Friedrich-Hirzebruch-Allee 8, 53115 Bonn, Germany
amini@uni-bonn.de, {farazi,behnke}@ais.uni-bonn.de

Abstract. Pose estimation commonly refers to computer vision methods that recognize people's body postures in images or videos. With recent advancements in deep learning, we now have compelling models to tackle the problem in real-time. Since these models are usually designed for human images, one needs to adapt existing models to work on other creatures, including robots. This paper examines different state-of-the-art pose estimation models and proposes a lightweight model that can work in real-time on humanoid robots in the RoboCup Humanoid League environment. Additionally, we present a novel dataset called the HumanoidRobotPose dataset. The results of this work have the potential to enable many advanced behaviors for soccer-playing robots.

1 Introduction

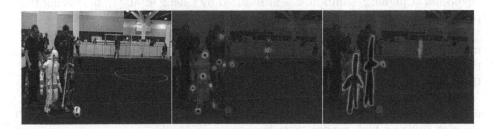

Fig. 1. One sample image of the introduced dataset with the estimated poses is shown on the left. Our model's predicted heatmaps of all keypoints and limbs are displayed in the middle and right, respectively.

The 2D humanoid pose estimation problem aims to detect and localize keypoints and parts and infer the limb connections to reconstruct the existing human poses from images. The human pose estimation problem's importance arises from the fact that this task has many applications in various areas such as human-computer interaction and action recognition. In this work, we address the real-time pose estimation problem for humanoid robots (see Fig. 1). The shape

R. Alami et al. (Eds.): RoboCup 2021, LNAI 13132, pp. 91–102, 2022.
https://doi.org/10.1007/978-3-030-98682-7_8

similarity between humanoid robots and persons is a double-edged sword. On the one hand, it enables us to start with existing methods designed for persons, but on the other hand, it adds additional difficulty to our problem not to confuse humans with humanoid-robots, especially in adult-size league. In general, the attempts to address the pose estimation problem for multiple persons can be categorized as either top-down or bottom-up approaches.

In the top-down models, the procedure includes two distinct steps. The first step is to detect individual people, while the particular pose is estimated in the next step. One of these models' disadvantages is that the performance of the model is tightly correlated to the person detector performance. Although the state-of-the-art (SOTA) results are derived from this type of models, including Cascaded Pyramid Network [3] and High-Resolution Net (HRNet) [24], the runtime of such approaches is negatively affected by the number of persons present, as a single-person pose estimator is run for each detection. Hence, the computational cost linearly increases with more persons, so the performance is often not real-time.

In contrast, bottom-up approaches detect body joints and group them into individuals simultaneously; therefore, they are less dependant on the number of persons in the image. One of the bottom-up method's main challenges is to group the detected keypoints in a real-time manner accurately. Recent approaches [2,11,19] utilize a greedy algorithm to group the detected keypoints into individual instances. Moreover, the bottom-up method's performance is more vulnerable to the different scales of the persons in a given image compared to the top-down approaches. To alleviate this issue, previous works exploit the scale search method [2] or rely on high-resolution input size [19]. These solutions are increasing the inference time though. A time-efficient method predicting keypoints at higher resolution was introduced by Cheng et al. [4], narrowing the performance gap between bottom-up and top-down models.

This paper opts for a bottom-up approach designed for 2D pose estimation of multiple humanoid robots. We made this choice because, in top-down methods, the inference time is generally much higher than in bottom-up approaches, so they will not be suitable for RoboCup real-time applications. Furthermore, we wanted to avoid the cost of annotating bounding boxes. We remedy our bottom-up model scale variations problem by using feature pyramid structure [13] through utilizing high-resolution feature maps.

Despite the availability of several large-scale benchmark datasets such as MPII Human Pose [1] and MS COCO [14] for the task of human pose estimation, we cannot fully utilize them because of differences between robots and humans, such as types and sizes. Thus, we present a new pose dataset of robots from the RoboCup Humanoid League. The code and dataset of this paper are publicly available.[1] In summary, we make the following contributions:

- We propose a deep learning model specifically designed to address the 2D pose estimation problem for multiple humanoid robots.

---

[1] https://github.com/AIS-Bonn/HumanoidRobotPoseEstimation.

– We introduce a new dataset, namely the HumanoidRobotPose dataset, consisting of robots from the RoboCup Humanoid League.
– We demonstrate that the proposed real-time light-weight model outperforms the SOTA bottom-up methods in our application.

2 Related Work

Although there are some works on the detection and tracking of humanoid robots [6,7], to the best of our knowledge, there is no previous work that addresses humanoid robot's pose estimation, which works on a variety of robots. Giambattista et al. [5] propose a gesture-based communication between Nao robot that utilizes OpenPose [2] for Nao robot pose estimation. Note that pose estimation on a single standardized Nao robot type is significantly easier than what we need in the Humanoid League. We have to address various unseen robots with different colors, kinematic shapes, and sizes.

Top-down: Most of the existing top-down methods exploit human detector models such as Feature Pyramid Networks [13], and Faster R-CNN [21]. Papandreou et al. [20] propose one of the first top-down models which employ the Faster R-CNN for the person detector step and present a new representation for keypoints, which is a mixture of binary activation heatmap and the corresponding offset. The most recent top-down approaches which obtain SOTA accuracy are the Cascaded Pyramid Network (CPN) introduced by Chen et al. [3], where multi-scale feature maps from different layers of the GlobalNet are integrated with an online hard keypoint mining loss for difficult-to-detect joints, and the model presented by Sun et al. [24] that improves the heatmap estimation using high-resolution representations and multiple branches of different resolutions.

Bottom-up: The recent architectures [2,12,16,18,19] take advantage of the confidence maps to detect the keypoints. Kreiss et al. [11] introduce a combination of confidence maps and vectorial parts for keypoints detection. Moreover, there are different approaches for encoding the part association used in the SOTA bottom-up models. OpenPose [2] introduces the Part Affinity Fields (PAFs) method to learn the body parts associations by encoding the location and direction, offset regression that uses the displacements of the keypoints [18,19], and tag heatmap, which produces a heatmap as a tag for each keypoint heatmap [12,16]. Pose Partition Networks [18] present a dense regression approach over all the keypoints to generate individuals' partitions using the embedding spaces.

3 Pose Estimation Model

In this section, we present our real-time bottom-up approach to pose estimation of multiple humanoid robots. The aim is to predict the part coordinates and

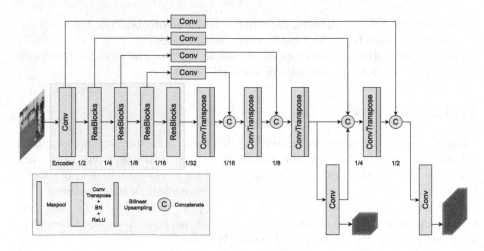

Fig. 2. The architecture of the proposed single-stage encoder-decoder model. The model predicts heatmaps of both keypoints and limbs for scale 1/4 and only heatmaps of keypoints for scale 1/2, where each scale is supervised with an intermediate loss.

the part associations to build robot poses. In the following, we first describe the model, then explain the keypoint detection and the part association methods in detail.

3.1   Network Architecture

Following the successful results of NimbRo-Net [8] and NimbRo-Net2 [22], we decided to utilize a similar architecture. This decision ensures that later we can combine this model with NimbRo-Net2 to have a unified network for multiple tasks related to the humanoid league. The proposed network is depicted in Fig. 2.

Our model is an encoder-decoder network which takes an RGB image of size $w \times h$. We observe that it is required to use a deeper encoder than the decoder to create a powerful feature extractor. The encoder is a pre-trained ResNet model [10], in which the last fully connected and global average pooling layers are eliminated. The first layer is a 7×7 convolutional with stride 2, followed by a max-pooling layer. The rest of the encoder network consists of four modules of residual blocks with higher depths and lower resolutions as the number of modules increases. Each residual block consists of two or three convolutional layers, depending on the selected ResNet architecture, followed by batch normalization and ReLU activation and a shortcut connection. More fine-grained spatial information is present in the early layers, while in the final layers, the network extracts more semantic information.

In the decoder part, we utilize lateral connections from different parts of the encoder, which allows us to maintain the high-resolution information. For every lateral connection, we apply 1×1 convolution to generate a fixed number of channels. The decoder network has a feature pyramid structure involving four modules. At each level of the pyramid, the previous level's output is fed to the 3×3 transposed convolution followed by a bilinear upsampling to obtain a fixed number of higher-resolution features. These upsampled features are concatenated with the features from the corresponding lateral connection. Similar to the encoder, ReLU and batch normalization is used to get the final output of the module.

As high-resolution feature maps are essential for precise keypoint localization [25], we leverage two scales of the feature pyramid hierarchy, i.e., $1/4$ and $1/2$ resolutions. As a result, the keypoints heatmaps $\hat{\mathbf{K}}^s$ at each scale s is generated by performing a final convolution on extracted features. As depicted in Fig. 2, we have two scales of keypoint heatmaps with intermediate supervision, inspired by HigherHRNet [4]. The final keypoints heatmaps $\hat{\mathbf{K}}$ are the average over the predictions generated by these two scales after upsampling to the same resolution as the input image in order to achieve accurate high-resolution predictions. Note that only one scale of limbs heatmaps $\hat{\mathbf{L}}$ is utilized, as we observe that following the same approach as keypoints yields performance drop.

3.2 Keypoint Detection and Part Association

The ground truth heatmaps of the keypoints in a given image can be represented as the set $\mathbf{K} = \{\mathbf{K}_1, \mathbf{K}_2, ..., \mathbf{K}_P\}$, where $\mathbf{K}_p \in \mathbb{R}^{w' \times h'}$, $p \in \{1, 2, ..., P\}$, and P is the total keypoints of a robot instance, which is equal to six for our dataset (see Fig. 3 (left)). The heatmap $\mathbf{K}_p$ with the resolution of $w' \times h'$ includes the Gaussian heatmaps of the pth part of all the robot instances. Let $x_{p,n}$ and $y_{p,n}$ be the location of the pth part of the nth instance, where $n \in \{1, 2, ..., N\}$ and N is the total number of existing robots with the visible pth part in an image. To embed the position of the annotated pth part, we use the 2D unnormalized Gaussian distribution with the center of $(x_{p,n}, y_{p,n})$ and the standard deviation σ, which is fixed for all the parts:

$$\mathbf{K}_p(x, y) = \exp(-\frac{(x - x_{p,n})^2 + (y - y_{p,n})^2}{2\sigma^2}). \tag{1}$$

Due to occlusion or proximity of the robot instances in a given image, we utilize the pixel-wise max operation on Eq. 1 to preserve the Gaussian peak of the pth part for each instance.

For limbs, the ground truth heatmaps in a given image can be expressed as the set $\mathbf{L} = \{\mathbf{L}_1, \mathbf{L}_2, ..., \mathbf{L}_C\}$, where $\mathbf{L}_c \in \mathbb{R}^{w' \times h'}$, $c \in \{1, 2, ..., C\}$, and C is the total limbs of a robot instance that is five in this work (see Fig. 3 (left)). Note that the intended utility of limbs is only to encode the relations between keypoints, so they do not necessarily lie on actual robot limbs. Therefore, to encode a limb's position, first, we compute a line segment between two keypoints and mark all of the points that lie on such limb, following the approach proposed by Li et al. [12]. Then having these offsets, the final Gaussian heatmap of each limb is generated by an unnormalized Gaussian distribution with the standard deviation 4σ that controls the spread of the Gaussian peak in the same way as for the keypoint heatmap. The final limb heatmap is the average of all the robots' limb appearing in the image. In contrast to the PAFs method that encodes each limb in two channels as vector directions, we encode each limb type in a single channel. This simpler approach for encoding the limbs is enough for our application since our experiments show better performance than the PAF method.

3.3 Loss

We use the mean square error to compute the loss between the predicted heatmaps and the ground truth heatmaps for both keypoints and the limbs.

$$\mathcal{L}_{keypoints} = \frac{1}{2P} \sum_{s \in \{\frac{1}{4}, \frac{1}{2}\}} \sum_{p=1}^{P} \mathbf{W} \cdot \left\| \mathbf{K}_p^s - \hat{\mathbf{K}}_p^s \right\|_2^2, \tag{2}$$

$$\mathcal{L}_{limbs} = \frac{1}{C} \sum_{c=1}^{C} \mathbf{W} \cdot \left\| \mathbf{L}_c - \hat{\mathbf{L}}_c \right\|_2^2, \tag{3}$$

where $\mathbf{W}$ is a binary mask with $\mathbf{W} = 0$ when the annotation is missing in the image, and s is the scale of the predicted heatmaps. Finally, the total loss used to train the network is the sum of the keypoint loss (2) and the limb loss (3).

3.4 Post Processing

By performing Non-Maximum Suppression (3×3 kernel) on the predicted keypoint heatmaps, we obtain the peak of each Gaussian heatmap and the location of its corresponding keypoint for the robot instances. We use the detected limb's heatmaps to acquire the candidate connections between the keypoints as [2]. As there are multiple robot instances in an image, it is required to group the keypoints to determine the poses corresponding to the correct individuals. Having the set of keypoints and the connection candidates, we employed the proposed greedy algorithm by Cao et al. [2] to solve the assignment problem and obtain the final pose of all robot instances. In this algorithm, instead of considering the fully connected graph, the goal is to obtain the minimum spanning tree of the pose instance and assign the adjacent tree nodes independently, resulting in a well-approximate solution with efficient computational cost.

4   Dataset

This section explains the paper's additional contribution, the HumanoidRobot-Pose dataset, including data collection and annotation procedures and the evaluation metrics used for this dataset.

Our goal was to collect a dataset containing both single and multiple robots to simulate the RoboCup's real conditions. We gathered many YouTube videos from the RoboCup Humanoid League, as well as some in-house videos and ROS bags. Some videos originate from the qualification videos, which only demonstrate a

  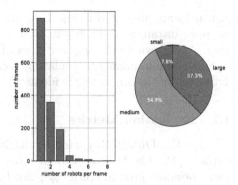

Fig. 3. An example of the annotations depicted in left. Visualization for the distribution of pose variability by considering the head as the origin is shown in right. Note that we did not choose trunk joint as the origin to show the dataset's variability better.

Fig. 4. Statistics for our dataset. The diversity of the number of robot instances is illustrated in left, and the scale proportions of robot instances is shown in right. The definition of small, medium and large scale is identical to the COCO dataset.

specific robot; therefore, they only consist of a single pose. To include videos with multiple robots and increase the diversity of robots in the dataset, we also employ videos from drop-in games and round-robin competitions. These videos are from recent years and contain various view angles, lens distortions, brightness, and robots. Note that in most of the videos, there are humans present in the pictures, e.g., the robot handler, the referee, and audiences around the field. Overall, we annotated over 1.5K manually selected frames from 23 videos with around 2.3K robot instances. These frames include teen and adult sized robots and contain more than ten different robot types. About 30 percent of the dataset was exclusively used for testing. Note that testing frames were collected from different videos than the training videos.

4.1 Data Annotation

For data annotation, we used Supervise.ly[2], a web-based data annotations and management tool. We decided to ignore the truncated or severely occluded points in the image, which are usually considered invisible keypoints. For each robot, six keypoints are annotated, including head, trunk, hands, and feet. The head keypoint is important, for instance, to estimate the height of the goalie robot. We use these few keypoints to avoid annotation costs; however, they can be easily extended to more keypoints. We define a minimal pose representation by five limbs from these keypoints, which would be sufficient for the current soccer behavior level. The annotation for a robot instance is illustrated in Fig. 3 (left).

To show the diversity of our dataset, we visualize the variability of annotated poses in Fig. 3 (right) and statistics of the number and scales of the robot

---

[2] https://supervise.ly.

instances are presented in Fig. 4. About 60% of the collected frames contain single pose instances and robot instances with medium scale, i.e., $[32^2 < \text{segment area} < 96^2]$, where the segment area of a robot instance is measured using the size of the minimum encapsulating rectangle of the annotated keypoints. Our definition of the size scales is identical to the COCO dataset[3].

4.2 Evaluation Metrics

We use the Object Keypoint Similarity (OKS) metric from COCO keypoint dataset [23]. The OKS of a robot r between the detected keypoint $(\hat{y}_{r_i})$ and its corresponding ground truth (y_{r_i}) can be written as follows:

$$OKS(\hat{y}_r, y_r) = \frac{\sum_i e^{-\frac{\|\hat{y}_{r_i} - y_{r_i}\|_2^2}{2a^2 k_i^2}} \delta(v_i > 0)}{\sum_i \delta(v_i > 0)}, \tag{4}$$

where k_i is a constant specific to each keypoint, which is equal for all keypoints in our dataset, a is the segment area of the robot instance measured in pixels, and v_i is the keypoint visibility flag in the ground truth ($v_i = 0$ for the invisible keypoint). The OKS metric is robust to the number of visible keypoints as it gives equal importance to the robot instances with different numbers of visible keypoints. The evaluation metrics used for the proposed dataset are as following: AP (the mean average precision over 10 OKS thresholds = [0.50:0.05:0.95]), AP^{50} (AP at OKS threshold = 0.50), AP^{75}, AP^M for medium scale robot instances, AP^L for large scale instances, and AR (the mean of average recall over 10 OKS thresholds).

5 Experiments

We compare the proposed method with SOTA bottom-up approaches on the HumanoidRobotPose dataset. These approaches are OpenPose [2], Associative Embedding (AE) [16], PifPaf [11], and HigherHRNet [4]. OpenPose [2] utilizes confidence maps to localize the keypoints and PAFs to encode the body parts' location and orientation. For grouping the detected keypoints, the greedy algorithm is proposed in which each part is scored, computing the line integral on the corresponding PAF. Associative Embedding (AE) [16], merges the stacked hourglass architecture [17] with associative embedding.

PifPaf [11] proposes Part Intensity Field to detect and localize the keypoints and Part Association Fields to associate body parts with each other.

HigherHRNet [4] is using an adopted top-down model as the backbone with a transposed convolution module to predict higher resolution heatmaps for the keypoints detection. Similar to the AE approach, in HigherHRNet, the associative embedding is employed to parse the poses. Following the configurations provided by the original papers, we reported the details of models and the inference time evaluated on NimbRo-OP2X robot hardware [9] in Table 1.

---

[3] https://cocodataset.org/#keypoints-eval.

Fig. 5. Four sample results from the test set. Methods used from top to bottom: Open-Pose [2], AE [16], PifPaf [11], HigherHRNet [4], and our model.

For all methods, the hyperparameters are tuned to achieve the best possible results. Our model is trained using the AdamW [15] optimizer with learning rate of 10^{-4}, batch size 16 and weight decay of 10^{-4} for the total 200 epochs. Note that the encoder is initialized by pre-trained ResNet weights on ImageNet. We conduct data augmentation that includes random horizontal flip, random rotation, random scaling, and random translation during training.

The results on the test set are reported in Table 2. The reported results are achieved without performing the flip test or the multi-scales test for preserving the methods to be real-time. Our proposed method with ResNet18 backbone outperforms the best existing methods in all metrics except for large scale when we train the models from scratch on our dataset (see Table 2). Note that compared to other baselines, our model can utilize our limited dataset better. Based on AP results of medium and large scales, our model can better handle the different scales than the other approaches. Moreover, the strict metric results

Table 1. Details for the used methods.

Method	Input Size	Backbone	Params	GFLOPs	FPS
OpenPose [2]	368	VGG19	25.8M	159.8	14
AE [16]	512	Hourglass	138.8M	441.6	5
PifPaf [11]	385	ShuffleNetV2	**9.4M**	46.3	13
HigherHRNet [4]	512	HRNet-W32	28.6M	94.7	13
Ours	384	ResNet18	12.8M	**28.0**	**48**

Table 2. Results on the test set.

Method	AP	AP^{50}	AP^{75}	AP^M	AP^L	AR	AR^{50}	AR^{75}	AR^M	AR^L
OpenPose [2]	67.9	80.0	70.0	73.8	73.1	68.7	80.1	70.4	74.8	74.4
AE [16]	62.9	71.9	64.1	64.0	72.9	64.6	73.9	65.6	64.7	76.0
PifPaf [11]	76.1	81.6	75.6	76.0	**91.0**	77.9	83.6	77.2	77.7	**93.0**
HigherHRNet [4]	73.4	84.1	75.6	80.3	78.7	76.2	85.3	77.2	81.4	83.0
Ours	**78.1**	**84.6**	**79.6**	**87.5**	80.2	**79.4**	**85.4**	**80.6**	**88.4**	81.6

demonstrate that the predicted pose instances are more accurate compared to the other methods due to the high-resolution predictions. Fig. 5 illustrates some samples of estimated poses for all the approaches.

6   Ablation Study

This section investigates different backbones for the encoder part of our model and the importance of employing multi-scale predictions in our approach. As shown in Table 3, although applying a deeper encoder helps achieve better performance, it negatively affects the inference time of the model. Moreover, AP results demonstrate that without multi-scale heatmaps, the accuracy of predicted keypoints drops.

Table 3. Ablation study: the effectiveness of backbones and multi-scale predictions on the test set.

Backbone	Multi-scale	AP	AP^M	AP^L	Params	GFLOPs	FPS
ResNet18		76.6	83.6	82.0	**12.4M**	**17.8**	**83**
ResNet18	✓	78.1	**87.5**	80.2	12.8M	28.0	48
ResNet50	✓	**78.6**	86.0	**82.1**	27.0M	47.7	25

7   Conclusion

In this paper, we presented a lightweight bottom-up model for estimating multiple humanoid robot poses in real-time. We showed that our proposed model is capable of multi-robot pose estimation on NimbRo-OP2X robot hardware and is more suitable for the RoboCup humanoid league in comparison with other SOTA models. For the future, we will use this model for advanced soccer behavior decisions like recognizing rival robots' actions or anticipating the ball's movement direction before the kicking motion. Since the developed model is very similar to NimbRo-Net2, we will combine them to produce a unified network for diverse perception tasks in RoboCup.

Acknowledgment. This work was partially funded by grant BE 2556/16-2 (Research Unit FOR 2535 Anticipating Human Behavior) of the German Research Foundation (DFG).

References

1. Andriluka, M., Pishchulin, L., Gehler, P., Schiele, B.: 2D human pose estimation: new benchmark and state of the art analysis. In: IEEE Conference on Computer Vision and Pattern Recognition (CVPR) (2014)
2. Cao, Z., Hidalgo, G., Simon, T., Wei, S.E., Sheikh, Y.: OpenPose: realtime multi-person 2D pose estimation using part affinity fields. IEEE Trans. Pattern Anal. Mach. Intell. (2021)
3. Chen, Y., Wang, Z., Peng, Y., Zhang, Z., Yu, G., Sun, J.: Cascaded pyramid network for multi-person pose estimation. In: IEEE Conference on Computer Vision and Pattern Recognition (CVPR) (2018)
4. Cheng, B., Xiao, B., Wang, J., Shi, H., Huang, T.S., Zhang, L.: HigherHRNet: scale-aware representation learning for bottom-up human pose estimation. In: IEEE Conference on Computer Vision and Pattern Recognition (CVPR) (2020)
5. Di Giambattista, V., Fawakherji, M., Suriani, V., Bloisi, D.D., Nardi, D.: On field gesture-based robot-to-robot communication with NAO soccer players. In: Chalup, S., Niemueller, T., Suthakorn, J., Williams, M.-A. (eds.) RoboCup 2019. LNCS (LNAI), vol. 11531, pp. 367–375. Springer, Cham (2019). https://doi.org/10.1007/978-3-030-35699-6_28
6. Farazi, H., Behnke, S.: Real-time visual tracking and identification for a team of homogeneous humanoid robots. In: Behnke, S., Sheh, R., Sariel, S., Lee, D.D. (eds.) RoboCup 2016. LNCS (LNAI), vol. 9776, pp. 230–242. Springer, Cham (2017). https://doi.org/10.1007/978-3-319-68792-6_19
7. Farazi, H., Behnke, S.: Online visual robot tracking and identification using deep LSTM networks. In: IEEE/RSJ International Conference on Intelligent Robots and Systems (IROS) (2017)
8. Farazi, H., et al.: NimbRo robots winning RoboCup 2018 humanoid AdultSize soccer competitions. In: Holz, D., Genter, K., Saad, M., von Stryk, O. (eds.) RoboCup 2018. LNCS (LNAI), vol. 11374, pp. 436–449. Springer, Cham (2019). https://doi.org/10.1007/978-3-030-27544-0_36
9. Ficht, G., et al.: NimbRo-OP2X: adult-sized open-source 3D printed humanoid robot. In: IEEE-RAS 18th International Conference on Humanoid Robots (Humanoids) (2018)

10. He, K., Zhang, X., Ren, S., Sun, J.: Deep residual learning for image recognition. In: IEEE Conference on Computer Vision and Pattern Recognition (CVPR) (2016)
11. Kreiss, S., Bertoni, L., Alahi, A.: PifPaf: composite fields for human pose estimation. In: IEEE/CVF Conference on Computer Vision and Pattern Recognition (CVPR) (2019)
12. Li, J., Su, W., Wang, Z.: Simple pose: rethinking and improving a bottom-up approach for multi-person pose estimation. In: AAAI (2020)
13. Lin, T.Y., Dollar, P., Girshick, R., He, K., Hariharan, B., Belongie, S.: Feature pyramid networks for object detection. In: IEEE Conference on Computer Vision and Pattern Recognition (CVPR) (2017)
14. Lin, T.-Y., et al.: Microsoft COCO: common objects in context. In: Fleet, D., Pajdla, T., Schiele, B., Tuytelaars, T. (eds.) ECCV 2014. LNCS, vol. 8693, pp. 740–755. Springer, Cham (2014). https://doi.org/10.1007/978-3-319-10602-1_48
15. Loshchilov, I., Hutter, F.: Decoupled weight decay regularization. In: International Conference on Learning Representations (ICLR) (2019)
16. Newell, A., Huang, Z., Deng, J.: Associative embedding: end-to-end learning for joint detection and grouping. In: Advances in Neural Information Processing Systems (2017)
17. Newell, A., Yang, K., Deng, J.: Stacked hourglass networks for human pose estimation. In: Leibe, B., Matas, J., Sebe, N., Welling, M. (eds.) ECCV 2016. LNCS, vol. 9912, pp. 483–499. Springer, Cham (2016). https://doi.org/10.1007/978-3-319-46484-8_29
18. Nie, X., Feng, J., Xing, J., Yan, S.: Pose partition networks for multi-person pose estimation. In: Ferrari, V., Hebert, M., Sminchisescu, C., Weiss, Y. (eds.) ECCV 2018. LNCS, vol. 11209, pp. 705–720. Springer, Cham (2018). https://doi.org/10.1007/978-3-030-01228-1_42
19. Papandreou, G., Zhu, T., Chen, L.-C., Gidaris, S., Tompson, J., Murphy, K.: PersonLab: person pose estimation and instance segmentation with a bottom-up, part-based, geometric embedding model. In: Ferrari, V., Hebert, M., Sminchisescu, C., Weiss, Y. (eds.) Computer Vision – ECCV 2018. LNCS, vol. 11218, pp. 282–299. Springer, Cham (2018). https://doi.org/10.1007/978-3-030-01264-9_17
20. Papandreou, G., et al.: Towards accurate multi-person pose estimation in the wild. In: IEEE Conference on Computer Vision and Pattern Recognition (CVPR) (2017)
21. Ren, S., He, K., Girshick, R., Sun, J.: Faster R-CNN: towards real-time object detection with region proposal networks. In: Advances in Neural Information Processing Systems (2015)
22. Rodriguez, D., Farazi, H., Ficht, G., Pavlichenko, D., Brandenburger, A., Hosseini, M., Kosenko, O., Schreiber, M., Missura, M., Behnke, S.: RoboCup 2019 AdultSize winner NimbRo: deep learning perception, in-walk kick, push recovery, and team play capabilities. In: Chalup, S., Niemueller, T., Suthakorn, J., Williams, M.-A. (eds.) RoboCup 2019. LNCS (LNAI), vol. 11531, pp. 631–645. Springer, Cham (2019). https://doi.org/10.1007/978-3-030-35699-6_51
23. Ruggero Ronchi, M., Perona, P.: Benchmarking and error diagnosis in multi-instance pose estimation. In: IEEE International Conference on Computer Vision (ICCV) (2017)
24. Wang, J., et al.: Deep high-resolution representation learning for visual recognition. IEEE Trans. Pattern Anal. Mach. Intell. (2020)
25. Xiao, B., Wu, H., Wei, Y.: Simple baselines for human pose estimation and tracking. In: Ferrari, V., Hebert, M., Sminchisescu, C., Weiss, Y. (eds.) ECCV 2018. LNCS, vol. 11210, pp. 472–487. Springer, Cham (2018). https://doi.org/10.1007/978-3-030-01231-1_29

Improving Sample Efficiency in Behavior Learning by Using Sub-optimal Planners for Robots

Emanuele Antonioni(✉), Francesco Riccio, and Daniele Nardi

Department of Computer, Control, and Management Engineering,
Sapienza University of Rome, Rome, Italy
{antonioni,riccio,nardi}@diag.uniroma1.it

Abstract. The design and implementation of behaviors for robots operating in dynamic and complex environments are becoming mandatory in nowadays applications. Reinforcement learning is consistently showing remarkable results in learning effective action policies and in achieving super-human performance in various tasks – without exploiting prior knowledge. However, in robotics, the use of purely learning-based techniques is still subject to strong limitations. Foremost, sample efficiency. Such techniques, in fact, are known to require large training datasets, and long training sessions, in order to develop effective action policies. Hence in this paper, to alleviate such constraint, and to allow learning in such robotic scenarios, we introduce SErP (Sample Efficient robot Policies), an iterative algorithm to improve the sample-efficiency of learning algorithms. SErP exploits a sub-optimal planner (here implemented with a monitor-replanning algorithm) to lead the exploration of the learning agent through its initial iterations. Intuitively, SErP exploits the planner as an expert in order to enable focused exploration and to avoid portions of the search space that are not effective to solve the task of the robot. Finally, to confirm our insights and to show the improvements that SErP carries with, we report the results obtained in two different robotic scenarios: (1) a cartpole scenario and (2) a soccer-robots scenario within the RoboCup@Soccer SPL environment.

Keywords: Automated planning · Reinforcement learning · Decision-making

1 Introduction

Nowadays, robots can operate in very challenging scenarios such as healthcare, security, industry, and domestic aid [3]. These contexts are highly dynamic, not structured, and characterized by unpredictable events [22]. Consequently, the deployment of robots with predefined decision-making processes or static behavioral rules is not recommended and often not effective. Instead, they must be provided with the capability of (1) learning through continuous interaction

© Springer Nature Switzerland AG 2022
R. Alami et al. (Eds.): RoboCup 2021, LNAI 13132, pp. 103–114, 2022.
https://doi.org/10.1007/978-3-030-98682-7_9

with their environment; (2) adapting to an unexpected situation; (3) recovering from faults; and (4) generalize their behavior to a new situation.

In the literature, proposed solutions can be coarsely categorized into two main classes: planning-based [12] and learning-based [16] approaches. In the former case, the robot behavior can be explicitly formalized over a model of the environment, which results in immediate solutions and robust action policies. Nevertheless, planning-based techniques usually lack generalization to similar states and could require expert domain knowledge to be correctly designed. Instead, the latter category aims to learn an optimal action policy through continuous interaction with the environment. In particular, reinforcement learning (RL) techniques have been widely adopted to determine robust action policies that can generalize to unknown situations. However, learning approaches are sample inefficient, and to converge to competitive policies, they require a tremendous amount of iterations and training samples [2], which make their use less appealing in robotics.

In this paper, we attack the problem of sample efficiency by combining the main advantages both of planning and learning paradigms for obtaining a robust decision-making process. We introduce SERP (Sample Efficient Robot Policies), which is specifically designed to enable and support the focused exploration of learning algorithms by exploiting a sub-optimal planner. In particular, SERP is an iterative algorithm that uses a sub-optimal planner based on an incomplete transition model as an expert for (1) initializing the robot policy; and for (2) preventing the exploration of state-action space portions that do not contribute to task completion. SERP is configured to follow the planner policy throughout its first iterations, accumulate training samples, and then gradually switch to the action policy learned at training time. Importantly, the planner remains active during the entire learning routine, and it is exploited to maintain a focused and safe exploration. Such a configuration allows the robot to achieve competitive performance with a reduced number of training samples and to avoid the choice of actions that are not focused on the current task.

The goal of this work is to introduce a novel methodology in robot learning that improves sample efficiency, making learning approaches more practical and safe in robotics. In Fig. 1 is shown the selection mechanism of the planner, which marks with utilities the possible future actions, assigning low utilities to potentially useless ones (highlighted in red) and with good ones the promising useful actions (highlighted in blue). Another key feature of this algorithm is assigning the lowest possible utilities to actions that could negatively impact robot safety. To confirm this feature we assign extremely negative reward signals to actions that can impact the robot's safety, in order to have an high impact of such actions in the overall collected reward. It is important to remember that we consider robot safety during learning as the learner's ability to ensure research space configurations that do not damage the robot embodiment, the environment and nearby people. In fact the planner contains information that regulates the behavior of the robot to prevent these situations. We validate SERP in two different robotic scenarios: a cart-pole task and robot soccer task. In the first

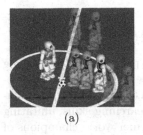
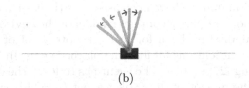

(a)   (b)

Fig. 1. The figure shows SERP sample efficiency that avoids the exploration of red actions and promotes portions of the state space that are meaningful to the task (blue). (Color figure online)

scenario, the algorithm is used to balance the cart-pole within a reduced number of iterations. In the second scenario, the proposed approach is exploited to learn a defender robot's action policy when opposing an attacker. The proposed tasks have been learned using simulated environments; however, the action policy has also been deployed in real settings in the RoboCup scenario.

2   Related Work

SERP relies on both planning and learning approaches. Accordingly, we survey existing literature, and we focus on approaches that use RL or Automated Planning to face decision-making problems for robots.

Automated planning techniques have been widely used in the recent years to implement articulated decision-making processes; for example, in [8], authors formalize all the robot behaviors are by defining the tuple of static axioms, effect axioms, action preconditions, and initial state. Due to such a formalization, the authors can promptly trace the entire robot behavior and recover from the planners' failures. In a different context, [13] propose a formal language $\mathcal{KL}$ to express planning domains with incomplete knowledge and to generate plans in partially observable environments. Also, in the context of soccer robots, there are some planning-based solutions for robot behaviors; in [20] authors propose a work based on the exploration of future states. They introduce a method for fast decision-making. The outcome of each possible action is simulated based on the estimated state of the situation. The simulation of a single action is split into several simple deterministic simulations, considering the uncertainties of the action model's estimated state. However, planning-based approaches cannot generalize to unknown situations, and the contributions mentioned above all rely on solid domain expertise to define the planning procedure. On the other hand, learning-based approaches are receiving increasing interest in the last years. Several steps have been taken in this direction in robotics, although, due to demanding computational requirements, many RL solutions cannot be easily adopted in robotics [25]. To alleviate computational constraints, learning algorithm are used for system identification of high-dimensional problems [29] and learning control policies in dynamic environments [5]; advanced manipulation [26]; and optimizing robot behaviors [23]. Moreover, several model-based RL techniques for decision making have been used over time, such as [9] and [6]. However, these applications require a complete model of the environment to be provided to the learning algorithm. Even for soccer robots, a lot of work has been done using reinforcement learning for learning players' skills. In [1] authors discuss an imitation learning [27] system. The agent has to learn the dribble and searching skills, imitating the motion of the Striker agent (model-based) of the former world champions of the RoboCup@Soccer SPL competition. However, this approach still suffers the requirement of a previously modeled and efficient player to imitate. The dribble with the ball problem is also addressed in [19]. The paper describes and compares several hierarchical learning strategies for designing robot skills. However, the results show that there is a trade-off between sample efficiency and the final performance of the model. More closely related to our approach, exploiting both planning and learning approaches, [18] propose DARLING, a method that uses planning to bound the agent's behavior to reasonable choices during reinforcement learning to adapt it to the environment. However, DARLING does not evaluate the actions of the planner during training. Thus, the learner agent can explore undesired portions of the state-action space and does not preserve a focused exploration. Differently, [14] introduces TMP-RL to integrate Task Motion Planning TMP and RL, while [10] exploits a planning algorithm to model the rewards function of a learning algorithm in a multi-agent system. However, these contributions' focus is to improve policy generalization and not to guarantee sample efficiency. [4] present R-Max, a model-based RL algorithm that learns a complete transition model of the environment that can be used to define planning algorithms. However, differently from our solution, R-Max is randomly initialized, and thus, does not guarantee a focused and safe exploration since the first iterations. The problem of learning from sub-optimal teachers has been addressed in several recent works. In [17], authors present a learning algorithm that uses an ensemble of sub-optimal teachers. The robot successfully manages to outperform the teacher performances and to complete the task. Nevertheless, in this work, the teachers are meant to solve part of the problem. In our work, the teacher cannot solve any part of the problem itself, but it is only used for deciding which action to avoid or to explore in the initial part of the training phase. This allows the teacher to be way simpler to model both with a handcrafted or a learning-based technique. Similarly, in [15], the authors introduce a residual method to correct the robot control performed by a sub-optimal controller using an RL-based approach. In this case, the method differs strongly from the one that we propose. The cited work, in fact, acts on the correction of a continuous control signal, which is not applicable to a decision-making process like the ones addressed in this paper. In [7] a method that alternates Imitation Learning phases to Reinforcement Learning ones starting the imitation from a sub-optimal teacher is introduced. This work manages to outperform the teacher performances and speed up the RL algorithm's learning process. Differently, our work also introduces a method for avoiding actions that are risky for robot safety keeping the planner always active in the background.

Summarizing, several procedures for efficient decision-making processes have been created using automated planning and reinforcement learning, and competitive results can be achieved with both. This work investigates the use of both planning and learning to improve sample efficiency by exploiting a planner for guaranteeing focused exploration of the state-action space. Hence, the contribution of SErP is to generate competitive action policies already since the first iterations of the algorithm using just a partial model of the environment, then use this to prevent the learner from exploring invalid portions of the search space.

3   SErP

In order to iteratively refine an action policy, SErP relies upon two main building blocks: a planner and a learner. These two components are used to achieve focused search-space exploration and to learn effective action policies with a reduced number of training samples. To formalize SErP we adopt the MDP notation, where decision-making is expressed as a tuple

$$MDP = (S, A, \mathcal{T}, R, \gamma), \tag{1}$$

where S and A represent the set of states and actions respectively, $\mathcal{T} : S \times A \times S \to [0, 1]$ is a stochastic transition model from state $s \in S$ to $s' \in S$, when taking action $a \in A$, $R : S \times A \to \mathbb{R}$ is the reward function, and γ is a discount factor in $[0, 1)$. At each iteration, the output of the algorithm is a policy π_i that is used to determine the next action to perform.

3.1   Algorithm

During the first phase of the algorithm, SErP achieves sample efficiency by exploiting a planner, as an expert, to collect training samples. In fact, the planner is used to explore the search-space with a sub-optimal action policy and provide prior knowledge to the learner, which is refined at each time a state-action transition is observed. During in the initial phase, the agent only considers the planner's actions and disregards the learner's output. Afterward, once enough samples are collected, the agent's focus gradually shifts toward the learner policy. To guarantee safety during the learning process the planner is always active and available to validate the learner's choices. It is worth noting that the concept of safety expressed in this paper refers to the robot embodiment, the environment, and the people involved in the task.

In particular, SErP follows the policy generated by the planner in its first iterations. In fact, the planner guarantees that the learner collects only training samples from useful portions of the search space. This is especially important during policy initialization since the majority of learning algorithms require demanding exploration phases. Then, with a ρ probability, increasing over time, SErP selects actions in accordance with the policy π of the learner. Algorithm 1

Algorithm 1: SErP.

Input: D_0 dataset of random state-action pairs, π_P planner policy
Output: π_I learner policy
Data: I number of iterations, ρ learner probability, $\Delta\rho$ learner probability increment, R_{min} reward minimum value
begin

1[Train π_0 on D_0
    for $i = 1$ **to** I **do**
       $p \leftarrow UniformRandom(0, 1)$
2[**if** $p > \rho$ **then**
          | Get action a from $\pi_P(s_{t-1})$.
       end
       else
          Get action a from $\pi_{i-1}(s_{t-1})$.
          $s' \leftarrow \mathcal{T}(a, s_{t-1})$
3[**if** $\mathcal{R}(s') < R_{min}$ **then**
4[| Get action a from $\pi_P(s_{t-1})$.
          end
       end
       $s' \leftarrow \tau(a, s_{t-1})$
       $r \leftarrow \mathcal{R}(s')$
5[$D^{0:i} \leftarrow \{s, a, r, s'\} \cup D^{0:i-1}$
6[Train π_i on $D^{0:i}$
       $\rho \leftarrow \rho + \Delta\rho$
    end
    return π_I
end

---

reports the SErP procedure: (1) policy π_0 with a random dataset d_0; (2) sample an action from the learner or the planner according to a probability ρ; (3) if the action is sampled from the learner, it is evaluated with the minimum reward threshold R_{min}; (4) if it is lower than R_{min}, then the action is selected from the planner policy; (5) upon action completion, a new sample is generated and aggregated to the dataset; (6) finally the learner policy is updated with a gradient descent algorithm and the ρ probability is increased. It is important to highlight that SErP is agnostic to the planner and the learner implementation. This is an important feature that allows an effective instantiation to various domains that require specific planners and/or learners. Here, we provide a description of SErP when the planner and the learner are instantiated with a monitor replanning algorithm [24] and with DQN [21] respectively.

3.2   Planner

On-line planning techniques have demonstrated satisfactory results when physical agents are deployed in dynamic and unpredictable environments. In the literature, monitor-replanning (MrP) [24] has shown promising results being responsive and easy to configure. MrP algorithms replan the agent actions at each iteration and after each action is executed. This guarantees that each action of the agent is informed, and the plan is generated by observing the current state of the environment. The MrP algorithm implemented in SERP executes four steps at each iteration: (1) monitors the environment to get the current state; (2) expands the planning graph in accordance to predefined actions effects, and preconditions; (3) visits the graph to select the path that maximizes the reward of the agent R – usually defined by an expert of the domain; (4) executes the first action of the path. It is important to highlight that we define a planning graph as a structure in which nodes represent states of the environment, and edges represent actions that transition from a state to another.

3.3   Learner

Deep RL has shown super-human performance in various applications demonstrating remarkable generalization capability and competitive action policies. In this work, we take advantage of the success of such approaches, and we implement the learner of SERP with a basic Deep RL algorithm – DQN [21]. In this work, we formalize the state of the agent as a feature vector characterizing meaningful landmarks of the search space. While the output of the learner is a policy π that is refined iteratively. The DQN algorithm implemented executes the following three steps: (1) aggregates training samples to the original dataset (a reply-buffer) each time a transition is observed; (2) randomly samples state-action pairs from the dataset to compose mini-batches of i.i.d samples; (3) updates the learner policy by minimizing the loss function. Such a loss function is defined as the mean squared error (MSE) between the Q-value obtained by the Bellman equation and the network output (Eq. 2).

$$L\left(\theta_i\right) = \mathbb{E}_{s,(\cdot)}\left[\left(y_i - Q\left(s, a; \theta_i\right)\right)^2\right] \tag{2}$$

where θ is the set of parameters of the approximator and y_i us defined as in Eq. 3.

$$y_i = \begin{cases} R_T & \text{for terminal state } s_T \\ R_{t+1} + \gamma \max_{a'} Q\left(s_{t+1}, a'\right) & \text{for non-terminal state } s_t \end{cases} \tag{3}$$

4   Experimental Evaluation

In this section, we aim to demonstrate the performances of the SERP algorithm in terms of sample efficiency. Hence, we configured two applications: a cart-pole robot environment and a RoboCup@Soccer environment. In both experiments, the learner is implemented as DQN. The training is configured with an Adam optimizer with learning rate = 0.001 and decay factor = 0.9. The ϵ for the DQN $\epsilon - greedy$ policy is set to 0.3. The learner probability ρ takes values in $(0, 1]$, and increase at each iteration by a $\Delta\rho$ selected depending on the application. In this evaluation, the CartPole scenario is configured with $\Delta\rho = 0.01$, the robot soccer environment $\Delta\rho = 0.1$ this is given by the different amount of samples that the two environments have. To validate SERP, we compare its performance with vanilla-MrP and vanilla-DQN algorithms, as well as PPO, which represent a state-of-the-art baseline [11,28].

4.1   CartPole

The CartPole scenario is composed of an under-actuated platform made by a pole with an un-actuated joint attached to a cart that moves over a track (see Fig. 1, bottom). The robot can execute two actions: Left and Right. The former applies a force to the cart pushing it to the left while the latter to the right. The pendulum starts upright, and the goal is to prevent it from falling. An episode ends when (1) the distance between the pole and its upright position is greater than 15 degrees or (2) when the cart is pushed beyond a certain limit on the track. To formalize the cartpole scenario as a planning problem, we define the planner's state as a tuple of four elements: pole position, pole velocity, cart position, and cart velocity.

In this scenario, SERP is compared with OpenAI baselines[1] of the vanilla-DQN and PPO and with a vanilla-MrP implementation. All algorithms are let run for 1000 episodes, and the cumulative average reward of each episode is reported in Fig. 2(a). On the y-axis, the average cumulative reward value while on the x-axis the training iterations. The solid line represents the average value, while the light area represents their standard deviation. The figure shows that the prior knowledge allows SERP to rapidly increase during the time, due to the exploration of meaningful portions of the search space. In fact, PPO and DQN (that are initialized randomly) require a larger amount of training samples and result to be sample inefficient. Moreover, DQN standard deviation is considerably larger, which suggests that random factors in the initial exploration can significantly affect the action policy's overall performance and accuracy. The plot confirms our insights and shows that SERP converges to competitive results with a reduced number of training samples being extremely sample efficient. Moreover, it is worth noticing that the reward signal never decays also in the first iterations that confirms that the planner prevents the learner from exploring not useful portions of the search space.

4.2   Soccer Defender

RoboCup@Soccer is a challenging test-bed for decision-making algorithms due to unpredictability, partial observability, unstructured environments, and highly dynamic events. In this experimental evaluation, we validate sample efficiency and confirm that SERP is practical in complex robotic environments such as multi-robot adversarial setting. Specifically, we task SERP to learn a defensive robot's behavior in fighting for the ball with an opponent attacker. Hence, the experiment configures two robots, a defender that runs SERP, and an attacker

---

[1] https://github.com/openai/baselines.

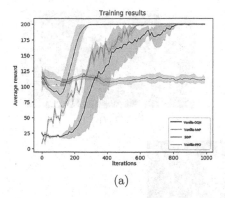
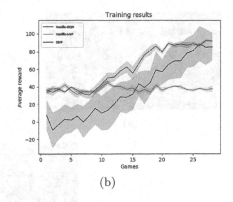

(a)   (b)

Fig. 2. a) Training results on CartPole. (b) Training results on Robocup@Soccer. Full line: average, Dull area: Standard deviation

that plays-out a predefined action policy. The goal of the defender is to contrast the attacker and to prevent it from scoring. We configured three possible actions that the defender can perform, and we let SERP decide which is the appropriate depending on the current state of the environment. Namely, in order to block the attacker, the defender can: cover the goal not allowing the opponent to move towards or kick (Fig. 3)(a); advance and push the ball on the side of the attacker (Fig. 3)(b); make a frontal contrast (Fig. 3)(c). In order to configure the planner in this scenario, the state is represented as a tuple of 3 elements: robot pose, ball position, and opponent pose. It is important to notice that in this environment, some robot actions could damage the platforms. For example, while learning, the robot could learn to kick other robots to prevent them from scoring. Conversely, the SERP planner not only guarantees focused exploration but also prevents the learner from exploring such actions.

In this scenario, SERP and baseline algorithms are compared in different games lasting ten minutes. A training episode is started each time the agent robot and the nearest opponent enter within a radius of 70 centimeters of the ball. It is considered finished when at least one of the robots exits such an area, or the ball is secured by the defender, or the attacker scores. Each episode is then given a cumulative reward depending on: (1) the robots' positions with respect to the ball, (2) the coverage of the goal, and (3) the final outcome of the contrast. To best simulate learning on a real robot, the simulations have been run in real-time. Each training cycle is set to last 28 games. Thus, the time required to complete a training session of about 280 min. Algorithms are tested by repeating the training session five times and reporting their cumulative average rewards and standard deviation. Due to PPO long training time, the algorithm proved itself to be not a practical solution in such scenarios, and therefore it has been not included in this evaluation.

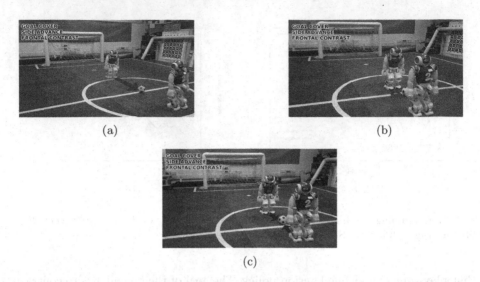

Fig. 3. a) Goal cover action, (b) Side advance action (c) Frontal contrast action

As for the cartpole scenario, Fig. 2(b) reports the cumulative average reward of the soccer scenario. A similar analysis can also be conducted in this experiment. SErP outperforms both vanilla-MrP and vanilla-DQN algorithms since first iterations and demonstrates to be a more practical solution that easily generates competitive action policies. In the end, both models converge on similar cumulative reward values even though SErP is more sample-efficient. The avoidance of execution of critical actions for the robot's safety in this scenario is also confirmed by the obtained results in terms of cumulative reward, in fact, very negative rewards have been assigned to this type of situations.

5 Conclusion

In this work, we introduce SErP, a new methodology for performing robot behavior learning using a partial model. The SErP algorithm is based on the use of a model-free RL algorithm and a model-based planning one. To realize the required online planner, only a basic model of the environment is needed; in fact, the planner itself does not need to completely solve the problem. This implies that it is not required the figure of an expert to define the transition model of this kind of planning system. With this simple shaping in the initial action selection, we can significantly improve the sample efficiency of the model-free DQN algorithm. Also, using elementary modeling of harmful actions for robot safety, it is possible to avoid selecting them and preventing potential damages on robots.

There are several directions to extend the work presented in this paper. One overall is to scale this algorithm over different behaviors and demonstrate its applicability to several environments and situations. For example, in the soccer domain, different situations can benefit from the use of our approach. Corner kick situations, in fact, can be easily addressed with SERP. Differently, another way to extend the proposed approach is to generalize it to a hierarchical problem formulation. In this way, the problem can be divided, and the learner can be challenged to learn smaller tasks in a more efficient way.

References

1. Aşık, O., Görer, B., Akın, H.L.: End-to-end deep imitation learning: robot soccer case study. In: Holz, D., Genter, K., Saad, M., von Stryk, O. (eds.) RoboCup 2018. LNCS (LNAI), vol. 11374, pp. 137–149. Springer, Cham (2019). https://doi.org/10.1007/978-3-030-27544-0_11
2. Baker, B., et al.: Emergent tool use from multi-agent autocurricula (2019)
3. Ben-Ari, M., Mondada, F.: Robots and their applications. In: Elements of Robotics, pp. 1–20. Springer, Cham (2018). https://doi.org/10.1007/978-3-319-62533-1_1
4. Brafman, R.I., Tennenholtz, M.: R-max - a general polynomial time algorithm for near-optimal reinforcement learning. J. Mach. Learn. Res. **3**, 213–231 (2003). https://doi.org/10.1162/153244303765208377
5. Böhmer, W., Springenberg, J.T., Boedecker, J., Riedmiller, M., Obermayer, K.: Autonomous learning of state representations for control: an emerging field aims to autonomously learn state representations for reinforcement learning agents from their real-world sensor observations. KI - Künstliche Intelligenz **29**(4), 353–362 (2015). https://doi.org/10.1007/s13218-015-0356-1
6. Chatzilygeroudis, K., Rama, R., Kaushik, R., Goepp, D., Vassiliades, V., Mouret, J.: Black-box data-efficient policy search for robotics. In: 2017 IEEE/RSJ International Conference on Intelligent Robots and Systems (IROS), pp. 51–58 (2017)
7. Cheng, C.A., Yan, X., Wagener, N., Boots, B.: Fast policy learning through imitation and reinforcement. arXiv preprint arXiv:1805.10413 (2018)
8. De Giacomo, G., Iocchi, L., Nardi, D., Rosati, R.: Planning with sensing for a mobile robot. In: Steel, S., Alami, R. (eds.) ECP 1997. LNCS, vol. 1348, pp. 156–168. Springer, Heidelberg (1997). https://doi.org/10.1007/3-540-63912-8_83
9. Deisenroth, M., Rasmussen, C.E.: PILCO: a model-based and data-efficient approach to policy search. In: Proceedings of the 28th International Conference on machine learning (ICML-11), pp. 465–472 (2011)
10. Devlin, S., Kudenko, D.: Plan-based reward shaping for multi-agent reinforcement learning. Knowl. Eng. Rev. **31**(1), 44–58 (2016). https://doi.org/10.1017/S0269888915000181
11. Henderson, P., Islam, R., Bachman, P., Pineau, J., Precup, D., Meger, D.: Deep reinforcement learning that matters. In: Thirty-Second AAAI Conference on Artificial Intelligence (2018)
12. Ingrand, F., Ghallab, M.: Deliberation for autonomous robots: a survey. Artif. Intell. **247**, 10–44 (2017). https://doi.org/10.1016/j.artint.2014.11.003. http://www.sciencedirect.com/science/article/pii/S0004370214001350. Special Issue on AI and Robotics
13. Iocchi, L., Nardi, D., Rosati, R.: Generation of strong cyclic plans with incomplete information and sensing **2**(4), 58–65 (2005)
14. Jiang, Y., Yang, F., Zhang, S., Stone, P.: Integrating task-motion planning with reinforcement learning for robust decision making in mobile robots. ArXiv abs/1811.08955 (2018)

15. Johannink, T., et al.: Residual reinforcement learning for robot control. In: 2019 International Conference on Robotics and Automation (ICRA), pp. 6023–6029. IEEE (2019)

16. Kober, J., Peters, J.: Reinforcement learning in robotics: a survey. In: Learning Motor Skills. STAR, vol. 97, pp. 9–67. Springer, Cham (2014). https://doi.org/10.1007/978-3-319-03194-1_2

17. Kurenkov, A., Mandlekar, A., Martin-Martin, R., Savarese, S., Garg, A.: AC-Teach: a Bayesian actor-critic method for policy learning with an ensemble of suboptimal teachers. arXiv preprint arXiv:1909.04121 (2019)

18. Leonetti, M., Iocchi, L., Stone, P.: A synthesis of automated planning and reinforcement learning for efficient, robust decision-making. Artif. Intell. **241**, 103–130 (2016). https://doi.org/10.1016/j.artint.2016.07.004

19. Leottau, D.L., Ruiz-del-Solar, J., MacAlpine, P., Stone, P.: A study of layered learning strategies applied to individual behaviors in robot soccer. In: Almeida, L., Ji, J., Steinbauer, G., Luke, S. (eds.) RoboCup 2015. LNCS (LNAI), vol. 9513, pp. 290–302. Springer, Cham (2015). https://doi.org/10.1007/978-3-319-29339-4_24

20. Mellmann, H., Schlotter, B., Blum, C.: Simulation based selection of actions for a humanoid soccer-robot. In: Behnke, S., Sheh, R., Sarıel, S., Lee, D.D. (eds.) RoboCup 2016. LNCS (LNAI), vol. 9776, pp. 193–205. Springer, Cham (2017). https://doi.org/10.1007/978-3-319-68792-6_16

21. Mnih, V., et al.: Playing Atari with deep reinforcement learning. arXiv preprint arXiv:1312.5602 (2013)

22. Mohanan, M., Salgoankar, A.: A survey of robotic motion planning in dynamic environments. Robot. Auton. Syst. **100**, 171–185 (2018). https://doi.org/10.1016/j.robot.2017.10.011. http://www.sciencedirect.com/science/article/pii/S09218890 17300313

23. Noda, K., Arie, H., Suga, Y., Ogata, T.: Multimodal integration learning of robot behavior using deep neural networks. Robot. Auton. Syst. **62**(6), 721–736 (2014). https://doi.org/10.1016/j.robot.2014.03.003. http://www.sciencedirect.com/science/article/pii/S0921889014000396

24. Onaindia, E., Sapena, O., Sebastia, L., Marzal, E.: SimPlanner: an execution-monitoring system for replanning in dynamic worlds. In: Brazdil, P., Jorge, A. (eds.) EPIA 2001. LNCS (LNAI), vol. 2258, pp. 393–400. Springer, Heidelberg (2001). https://doi.org/10.1007/3-540-45329-6_38

25. Pierson, H.A., Gashler, M.S.: Deep learning in robotics: a review of recent research. CoRR abs/1707.07217 (2017). http://arxiv.org/abs/1707.07217

26. Polydoros, A., Nalpantidis, L., Krüger, V.: Real-time deep learning of robotic manipulator inverse dynamics (2015). https://doi.org/10.1109/IROS.2015.7353857

27. Schaal, S.: Is imitation learning the route to humanoid robots? Trends Cogn. Sci. **3**(6), 233–242 (1999)

28. Schulman, J., Wolski, F., Dhariwal, P., Radford, A., Klimov, O.: Proximal policy optimization algorithms. arXiv preprint arXiv:1707.06347 (2017)

29. Watter, M., Springenberg, J.T., Boedecker, J., Riedmiller, M.A.: Embed to control: a locally linear latent dynamics model for control from raw images. CoRR abs/1506.07365 (2015). http://arxiv.org/abs/1506.07365

Soccer Robots Modeling Project Based on RoboCupJunior: Simulation Environment for Physical Robot Improvement

Breno Cunha Queiroz[1,2](✉) and Fábio Ferreira[1,3](✉)

[1] CIC Robotics, Salvador, BA, Brazil
cic.robotics@gmail.com
[2] University of São Paulo, São Carlos, SP, Brazil
brenocqueiroz@usp.br
[3] Federal University of Bahia, Salvador, BA, Brazil
joao.fabio@ufba.br

Abstract. This article aims to present the contributions of the soccer robot project based on RoboCupJunior Soccer Open. The project proposes the 3D modeling of the robot in order to create a virtual version before the physical robot. In the virtual robot, it is implemented the algorithm, are validated the game strategies, and tested the design functionality in the robot structure through the 3D simulation environment. This virtual environment was developed within the parameters of the competition to provide greater consistency and integrity during the simulations, which allows time optimization, project improvement, problem correction and solution implementation before robot construction. The potential of the simulation environment is visible, which can encourage a 3D Simulation modality of Soccer at RoboCupJunior.

Keywords: 3D simulation · RoboCupJunior · Soccer

1 Introduction

The Soccer category of RoboCupJunior (RCJ) requires the construction of 02 mobile robots capable of cooperating in search of a common goal: the goal. The soccer game is a sport that requires countless skills for humans, ranging from speed to space localization. The challenge of building robots able to play a soccer game is precisely in the ability to develop a cooperative robotics, in which the robot needs to interact with the elements of the context of the game and establish strategies as a team. For this, a level of sensing is necessary to self location, locate the ball, the opponents and establish a communication with the team partner to exchange messages [1]. The process of developing a robot can come at a high cost, when you add the sensors, actuators, controller, chassis, devices, everything is doubled.

© Springer Nature Switzerland AG 2022
R. Alami et al. (Eds.): RoboCup 2021, LNAI 13132, pp. 115–126, 2022.
https://doi.org/10.1007/978-3-030-98682-7_10

The prototyping stage of the robot is the first stage of testing of what was idealized. At this moment, one can see the need for changes, corrections or propose new solutions, which means starting from the beginning.

The high cost of digital chassis manufacturing, devices, wheels and printed circuit boards can greatly burden the design. Other concerns are the time for quotation, contracting, and execution of services, import deadline, foreign currency exchange and taxes. At this time, the project can be stopped, depending on these variables.

In this way, how to optimize time and reduce costs in a RCJ Soccer based robot soccer project? The use of Virtual Simulation Environment (VSE), according to the rules of RCJ Soccer Open, as a development environment for soccer robots. For this, the project was digitized: the 3D modeling of the robots was developed using the SolidWorks tool [2]; prototyping of printed circuits was designed in Altium [3]; the VSE configuration, based on the RCJ Soccer Open, used V-Rep [4]; and the coding was written in C++, in the Visual Studio. In this way, compatible for the virtual environment, but obeying the criteria for physical robots according to the rules of the competition.

The relevance of the project is in the possibility of optimizing the time and reducing the cost of development of the robot. However, VSE for RCJ Soccer can become an important tool for teams in the category, with great potential for evolution to a simulation server. As with RoboCup's major soccer and rescue categories, the RCJ could expand the participation of students from all over the world, who face many difficulties due to the cost of developing the soccer project. A simulated category would also serve as a trampoline for beginning teams, reducing the challenges to popularize educational robotics in schools. These suggestions become even more necessary during the Covid-19 pandemic, which since November 2019 imposed social isolation as a barrier against the spread of the virus. This article can be the first step towards the creation of RCJ Soccer 3D (simulated soccer league) in the RoboCup Federation.

The sections of this article are divided into the following sections: Sect. 1, Problem Introduction; Sect. 2, the Robot 3D Digital Model; Sect. 3, the 3D Simulation Environment; Sect. 4, Results and Discussion of Results are presented; and Sect. 5, Conclusion and Future Proposals.

2   3D Digital Modeling

2.1   Layered Chassis

The structure of the physical robot is composed of 3 layers of polycarbonate printed in 3D (Fig. 1), which guarantee greater resistance to the robot and simultaneously structural complexity. Heavier components like motors and battery are designed for the lower portion of the robot, distributed over the surface to ensure stability. While, in the upper layer, is located the compass due to the sensitivity to the electromagnetic distortions caused by the motors. In Fig. 2 it is possible to see the robot from different perspectives.

Fig. 1. Robot layers.

Fig. 2. Perspectives of the robot.

2.2   Dribbler Device

The dribbler device, located in the front portion of the robot, is composed of a 1500 RPM motor and a rubber roller to make contact with the ball, to keep this joint to the robot during the movement and to guarantee a better ball possession.

2.3   Camera Support

The omnidirectional support of the camera has the function of locating the ball in the field. We use a Pixy camera for its precision and its pre-processing of data. The bracket has increased the degree of freedom of the camera vertically, and it is possible to frame the ball in the image. The horizontal remains fixed, so as to depend on the degree of rotation of the robot.

2.4   Omni Wheels

The omni-directional wheels are made of aluminum, because it is lighter and ensures better stiffness than plastic. The use of them allows the robot to move in all directions, ensuring a high maneuverability both in rotation and translation, as used by [5] during the robot's spatial orientation process.

2.5   Devices

The robot has 4 DC motors of 320 RPM arranged at 90° to ensure consistent omnidirectional movement in conjunction with the wheels. Ultrasonic sensors URM37 were used to locate the robot in the field and detect obstacles. LDRs (Light Dependent Resistor) were distributed in the lower layer along with LEDs to read the field lines.

3   3D Simulation Environment

The V-Rep program was used to simulate the game environment due to its compatibility with the C++ language, which allows the same programming logic to be used in both the simulation and the physical robot, which will work through the arduino IDE. In [6], was used the Webots program for simulation, given their specific needs to simulate the game with robots NAO (robot made by the company Aldebaran Robotics for RoboCup Simulation 3D League). In this project, we previously modeled the robot, field and ball (Fig. 3) and then imported into the simulation environment. The physical engine ODE was used during all tests to simulate the behavior of real physics. However, it was necessary to make adaptations of form to the sensors and controllers available in the simulated environment to represent more precisely the same ones of the physical robot. In addition, it was necessary to decrease the resolution of the robot structure to avoid slowness due to the number of polygons during the collision check phase of the physics engine.

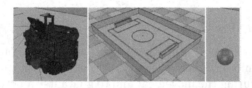

Fig. 3. 3D objects inserted in the simulation environment.

Virtual Robots. When imported into the VSE, the mass properties are configured; sensors and virtual controllers are created and added to the robot. These that later, exchange of information with the programming environment used; here, Visual Studio.

The code compatibility, both for the simulation and for the physical robot, is due to use of the Object Oriented Programming (OOP) paradigm. When creating each object it is detected if the Arduino IDE is being used for programming (Fig. 4). If it is being used, the called functions will be those of the physical robot. However, if it is not detected, only the code related to the simulation is activated. In this way, it is possible to program using the same classes in both the simulated environment and the Arduino environment.

The Vision Sensor used in the simulated environment returns the captured objects on the scene in a similar way to the Pixy camera, as shown in Table 1, which presents the comparison between the actual camera settings and the Vision Sensor of the simulation.

Although, use of higher fps and better image resolution was allowed during the simulation, their use resulted in slow processing of information during the

Fig. 4. Code OOP excerpt.

Table 1. Comparison between Pixy CAM and simulated vision sensor.

Comparative items	Pixy CAM	Vision sensor
FPS (fps)	50	20
Vertical FoV (degrees)	47	75
Horizontal FoV (degrees)	75	75
Resolution (pixels)	1280 × 800	256 × 256

tests. In addition, because in the simulated environment only quadrangular fields of view are allowed, the values of the vertical reading were treated in the Camera class to return values corresponding to a field of view of 47°.

The dribbler, which in the physical robot is composed of a rotating silicone roller has been replaced by a suction pad in the simulated environment, because the ball does not remain fixed in the dribbler by the friction while it rotates. In the real robot there is a CMPS11 compass sensor, which has an internal magnetometer, accelerometer and gyroscope to detect the robot's inclination. In the simulation was used the value of rotation relative to the robot object created in the VSE.

The ultrasonic sensors (US) used in the simulation environment partially represent the actual sensor, since the reading of this in the physical robot does not have a constant amplitude of 15° at any distance. In addition, contrasting to the simulation, in real sensors the reflection of the sound signal occurs when reaching surfaces with 45 degrees of inclination, indicating the wrong distance of the sensor to the first object hit by the sound wave.

The first proposals for field recognition consisted of 8 sonars arranged at 45° around the robot (Fig. 5 top), however, when carrying out the tests in the simulation the simulated robot presented large blind spots for the detection of other robots in the field. In this way, the current version of the robot has 12 sonars arranged at 30° (Fig. 5 bottom). Thus, ensuring a more accurate reading of the field and reducing the area not detected by the sensors.

Strategies Tested with the Virtual Robot in the Simulation Environment. The absolute position of the robot in the game is calculated in relation to the origin of the game field (Fig. 6). To estimate the location, the 12 ultra-

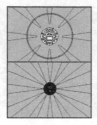

Fig. 5. Ultrasonic sensors reading areas. Top: Robot with 8 ultrasonics. Bottom: Robot with 12 ultrasonics.

sonic sensors were initially used to calculate the location from straight triangles formed with the walls of the field. However, the use of this strategy was not demonstrated to be effective alone, since the results with the ultrasonic with beam angle of 2° are close to the actual walls (Fig. 7a), but with 15° - closer to the actual sensor - obtained relatively inaccurate data (Fig. 7b); red dots represent the ultrasonic readings.

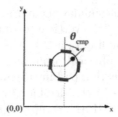

Fig. 6. Absolute robot position.

To determine the positioning in the field we compare the encoder readings of the four motors, ultrasonic sensors, accelerometer, gyroscope and magnetometer, and used Kalman Filter for error handling as shown in [7] and [8].

The location of the ball in the field, in turn, occurs in two steps. The first one (Fig. 8), from the angle of inclination of the camera θ_c, calculates the distance of the ball to the center of the robot, where D_{bc} is the distance from the camera to the ball, D_{bcY} is the projection of D_{bc} on the Y axis (1), D_c is the distance from the camera lens to the support base of the omnidirectional camera (2) and D_{cr} is the distance from the omnidirectional support base to the center of the robot, which is constant. From this moment angles referred to as θ have their intervals between [0.360[, while angles symbolized by β have their intervals in] −180,180] for the purpose of simplifying the calculations.

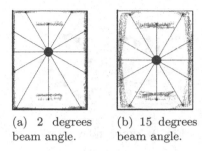

(a) 2 degrees beam angle.   (b) 15 degrees beam angle.

Fig. 7. Ultrasonic reading points. (Color figure online)

$$D_{bcY} = D_{cb}sin\theta_c \tag{1}$$

$$D_c = Y_{max}cos\theta_c \tag{2}$$

Thus, the total distance D_t from the ball to the center of the robot is given by the sum of D_{bcY}, D_c and D_{cr}.

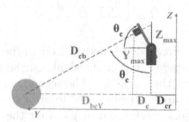

Fig. 8. Variables to calculate ball position.

The second part consists in transforming the distance of the ball relative to the robot in an absolute distance to the origin of the field through (3).

$$\begin{bmatrix} X_b \\ Y_b \end{bmatrix} = D_t \begin{bmatrix} sin(-\theta_{cmp}) \\ cos(-\theta_{cmp}) \end{bmatrix} \tag{3}$$

One of the approaches used to facilitate the power control of the motors and the reading of the ultrasonic sensors was the relativization of these devices during the programming. That is, when they have components distributed evenly along a circumference, store them in an array 0..(n − 1), where n is the number of devices, and perform a treatment on the index i of according to the angle of rotation of the robot, so that each index corresponds to a specific arc of this circumference. Thus, in the distribution of the 4 motors around the robot (Fig. 9), for the length of the arc of each index being i, which varies to perform the control of the engine with index 0, will always control the device that is the bow 0–90.

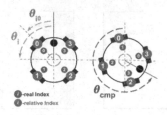

Fig. 9. Motor index rotation.

Therefore, for an array with $0..(n-1)$ components, where the index i_r corresponds to the real index and i correspond to the relative index - the one used by the user. Being: θ_{cmp} the angle of rotation of the robot and θ_{i0} being the angle between the first index and the front of the robot. The arc of θ_i can be calculated by (4) and the relative index i by (5):

$$\theta_i = \frac{360}{n} \tag{4}$$

$$i = \left\lfloor \frac{\theta_f + \frac{\theta_i}{2} - \theta_{io}}{\theta_i} \right\rfloor \tag{5}$$

In addition, the robot drive, developed entirely in the VSE, is based on angles and is divided into two stages. The first calculates the power in each motor to realize the movement with the angle β_m. The second, uses PID control to adjust the front to the angle θ_f (angle to where the front of the robot will be directed).

The power calculation is performed in pairs for the motors, since the robot motion vector can be decomposed into two diagonals parallel to the motors. In this way, the power calculation of each diagonal can be realized through β_m (desired angle of movement) and the reading value β_{cmp} (compass value converted from θ_{cmp} to βcmp) for compensation (Fig. 10).

Fig. 10. Angle to calculate motors power.

Thus, the resulting angle θ_r for the calculation of the left and right diagonals is:

$$\theta_r = 45 - \beta_{cm} + \beta_m \tag{6}$$

Being D_l and D_r the resulting vector projections on the axes of the robot (Fig. 11) with values in the range $[-255, 255]$, $D_l = sinr$ power is applied to motors with a relative index 0 and 2, and $D_r = cosr$ the power applied to motors 3 and 1 (Fig. 9) via PWM control:

Fig. 11. Diagonal bundles of the resulting vector.

The second stage for movement consists of the alignment of the front of the robot with θ_f using proportional-integral-derivative (PID) to reduce or increase the power of the motors to the right or left of the robot, ensuring that the angle θ_{cmp} will be very near to θ_f. The error used for the PID control is the difference between θ_f and θ_{cmp}, where the resulting value of the PID calculation, C_m, varies from $[0,1]$. Thus, where P is the power of the motor, the compensation is applied as follows: if the robot needs to rotate to the left, the motors with relative index 0 and 1 suffer a reduction of power with $P = P \cdot C_m$.

While the motors with relative index 2 and 3 suffer an increase in the power equivalent to $P = \frac{P}{C_m}$.

The inverse happens when the robot needs to rotate right to align θ_f with θ_{cmp}. The Fig. 12 represents a test with the use of this method in the simulation.

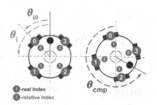

Fig. 12. Test for robot $\theta_f = 150$ and $\theta_m = -160$ movement.

The locomotion of the robot is performed from the displacement between points of stored coordinates of an array, which is generated taking as parameters a goal, the current location and obstacles along the way. We are working to implement an obstacle avoidance approach based on the AG approach proposed by [9].

Point-based locomotion allows a more precise displacement during play, for example, the path to the ball is generated as follows: a sequence of dots (represented in red from Fig. 13) along a straight line from the robot to the point tangent to the radius circumference r - the minimum distance between the robot and the ball - is created. From this point the coordinate sequence is generated along the radius r until it reaches the position in front of the ball. Figure 14 shows the generation of locomotion path generated during the simulation.

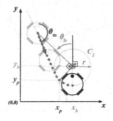

Fig. 13. Alignment with the ball. (Color figure online)

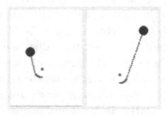

Fig. 14. Path generated to get the ball in the simulation.

The coordinates X_p and Y_p of the point can be determined by (7) and (8), respectively.

$$X_p = \begin{cases} X_b - cos(90 - (\theta_b + 90)) \cdot r, & \text{if } X_r \leq X_b \\ X_b - cos(90 - (\theta_b - 90)) \cdot r, & \text{otherwise} \end{cases} \quad (7)$$

$$Y_p = \begin{cases} Y_b - sin(90 + (\theta_b + 90)) \cdot r, & \text{if } X_r \leq X_b \\ Y_b - sin(90 + (\theta_b - 90)) \cdot r, & \text{otherwise} \end{cases} \quad (8)$$

After adding the points of the line to the point tangent to the circle C_1 in the displacement array are added the points belonging to the circumference C_1.

3.1   Game Dynamics

From the object-oriented programming it is possible to generalize the program in terms of creating Robot objects. In this way, we started to perform real game simulations, with the formation of two teams, each one initially with two robots to simultaneously test the defense and attack strategies, allowing to evaluate which strategy is the most effective and to detect in which points defense and attack strategies can improve. In [10] it is discussed as the auxiliary simulation to increase the performance of real robots. Figure 15 shows sequential images of a game in which the attack algorithm managed to score a goal over the defense algorithm.

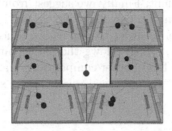

Fig. 15. Simulated game 1 × 1 that resulted in a goal.

We are working to improve the monitoring and control of matches in order to simulate the supervised game according to the rules of RCJ Soccer, with the creation of a class responsible for detecting the output of the ball and players to reposition and penalty, respectively, and of detecting goals and timing the starting time.

4   Impact of Project Cost and Time Savings

Every project requires the necessary planning to achieve the proposed goals. This planning includes the physical definitions of the robots, which impact on the sensing, actuators, physical layers for organizing their structure, weight and dimensions), which generate impacts on the strategy and, also, on the investment of the project development. Defining how many motors to move the robot or how many sensors to determine its position, for example, can have a direct impact on increasing costs. In the simulation, these strategies can be tested and validated, either to confirm an investment or to change it. Many devices are imported making purchases by unit, which increases the cost of the project and development time.

5   Conclusion and Future Work

The use of simulation and previous tests with a virtual robot made it possible to propose new ideas and validate strategies without having the physical robot, which allowed a greater use of time. A significant part of this work was done, requiring only adjustments. This saves time and has resulted in more efficient and effective strategies, as we can test strategy and defense simultaneously during simulated matches.

In the future, we intend to implement the rules of RCJ Soccer in the VSE, such as Kick-off, Pushing, Lack of progress, Off the field, Multiple Defense and Goalkeeper and Striker, in order to guarantee games closer to real competitions. In addition, the creation of libraries to mediate between simulation and programming that accelerate and facilitate the creation and programming of robots in the simulated environment. Finally, we suggest from the experience obtained in this project the creation of a new league in the RCJ, the RoboCupJunior 3D Soccer Simulation League, in order to popularize educational robotics through the RCJ Soccer modality, which allows the participation of students of basic education who are new to RCJ Soccer competitions and/or who do not have the investment capacity to develop physical robots in the soccer challenge.

References

1. RoboCupJunior Soccer - Rules (2020). https://junior.robocup.org/wp-content/uploads/2020Rules/final_2020rules/RCJ2020-Soccer-final.pdf. Accessed 24 Apr 2021
2. Solidworks. https://www.solidworks.com/. Accessed 24 Apr 2021
3. Altium. https://www.altium.com/. Accessed 24 Apr 2021
4. V-Rep. http://www.coppeliarobotics.com/. Accessed 24 Apr 2021. HuangYu-WeiShiao
5. Huang, S., Shiao, Y.: 2D path control of four omni wheels mobile platform with compass and gyroscope sensors. Sensors Actuators A: Phys. **234**, 302–310 (2005)
6. Magalhães, G., Colombini, L.: Detecção de objetos no futebol de robôs, Campinas-SP, Brazil (2017)
7. Anjum, L., Park, J., Hwang, W.: Sensor data fusion using unscented Kalman filter for accurate localization of mobile robots. In: IEEE International Conference on Control, Automation and Systems, pp. 947–952 (2010)
8. Li, Q., et al.: Accurate, fast fall detection using gyroscopes and accelerometer-derived posture information. In: IEEE Sixth International Workshop on Wearable and Implantable Body Sensor Networks, pp. 138–143 (2009)
9. Mujahed, M., Mertsching, B.: The admissible gap (AG) method for reactive collision avoidance. In: IEEE International Conference on Robotics and Automation, ICRA, pp. 1916–1921 (2017)
10. Marco, A., et al.: Virtual vs. real: trading off simulations and physical experiments in reinforcement learning with Bayesian optimization. In: IEEE International Conference on Robotics and Automation, ICRA, pp. 1557–1563 (2017)

Closing the Reality Gap with Unsupervised Sim-to-Real Image Translation

Jan Blumenkamp[1(✉)], Andreas Baude[2], and Tim Laue[2]

[1] Department of Computer Science and Technology, University of Cambridge, Cambridge, UK
jb2270@cam.ac.uk
[2] Fachbereich 3 – Mathematik und Informatik, Universität Bremen, Postfach 330 440, 28334 Bremen, Germany
{an_ba,tlaue}@uni-bremen.de

Abstract. Deep learning approaches have become the standard solution to many problems in computer vision and robotics, but obtaining sufficient training data in high enough quality is challenging, as human labor is error prone, time consuming, and expensive. Solutions based on simulation have become more popular in recent years, but the gap between simulation and reality is still a major issue. In this paper, we introduce a novel method for augmenting synthetic image data through unsupervised image-to-image translation by applying the style of real world images to simulated images with open source frameworks. The generated dataset is combined with conventional augmentation methods and is then applied to a neural network model running in real-time on autonomous soccer robots. Our evaluation shows a significant improvement compared to models trained on images generated entirely in simulation.

1 Introduction

In recent years, deep learning approaches became the standard solution to many problems in computer vision, such as classification [5], object detection [16], or semantic segmentation [18]. Efforts were made to reduce the computational complexity in order to deploy them to mobile devices [9]. These approaches usually require a vast amount of training data which can either be generated through human labor or be generated synthetically. Generating training data through human labor can result in datasets of high quality, but it is a cumbersome and expensive task. The CamVid dataset [4] contains detailed semantic labels and uses preprocessing to assist human labelers, but annotating a single frame takes 20 to 25 min. Multiple volunteers were tasked to perform the labeling, but only about 15% of the volunteers delivered acceptable results. Similar problems exist in other datasets such as the PASCAL VOC challenge [6] or in the COCO dataset [14].

Recently, a trend can be seen to approaches that rely on simulated and synthetic data. The SYNTHIA dataset, for instance, consists of 213400 images and

R. Alami et al. (Eds.): RoboCup 2021, LNAI 13132, pp. 127–139, 2022.
https://doi.org/10.1007/978-3-030-98682-7_11

pixel-accurate semantic annotations as well as depth maps generated with the Unity framework [19]. Computer games can also be used to generate images that can then be labeled manually [17]. Unfortunately, data generated in a simulated environment often does not directly transfer to reality. This issue is referred to as the *reality gap* [12].

Hess *et al.* [8] introduced an environment to create annotated training data in a RoboCup Standard Platform League (SPL) setting and demonstrated the feasibility of performing a semantic segmentation on that data. A major challenge in the RoboCup SPL is the perception of the field in a diverse set of lighting conditions. Low quality cameras result in images with low contrasts and limited processing power usually requires using fast conventional computer vision approaches. Frameworks such as TensorFlow Lite [1] or CompiledNN [25] made utilizing neural networks in mobile and low-end devices more feasible.

In our work, we synthetically generate images with the tools provided by [8] and transform them with unsupervised image-to-image translation [10] and domain randomization [26] so that they can be used as training data for any kind of deep learning task. We use this dataset to train a semantic segmentation that is able to run in real-time on a NAO v6 robot. Our approach can generally be applied to any other domain where computing power is sparse and flexibility and reliability plays an important role. All required software dependencies are open source. Our evaluation shows that models trained with our method perform noticeably better than models trained with data directly generated from simulation as well as with generated data that is expanded with conventional augmentation techniques. In summary, our main contributions are:

- We developed a method using publicly available state of the art image-to-image transformation frameworks and demonstrate that it can be used to generate high quality datasets that allow training highly performing models.
- We introduce a multi-class semantic segmentation model architecture that is capable of running in real-time on a NAO v6 robot.

The remainder of this paper is organized as follows: After summarizing the related work in Sect. 2, we describe our data generation approach in Sect. 3. In Sect. 4, we present our semantic segmentation model architecture. Lastly, multiple models generated with different data augmentations are evaluated and discussed in Sect. 5 and Sect. 6 respectively. An overview of the proposed method is depicted in Fig. 1.

2   Related Work

There are two remarkable works in the area of *closing the reality gap with image-to-image translation*: Bousmalis *et al.* [3] use domain adaptation and domain-adversarial neural networks to utilize synthetic training data in an end-to-end learning approach in order to learn robotic grasping. Bewley *et al.* [2] use image-to-image translation to transfer a vision-based driving policy from simulation to reality. Instead of explicit representations such as a semantic segmentation,

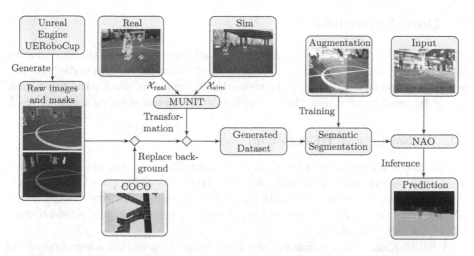

Fig. 1. The general workflow of our proposed method: images and corresponding masks are generated in simulation. The background of the generated images is replaced with a random image from the COCO dataset. MUNIT image-to-image translation is applied to these enhanced images, which are now the intermediate dataset.

their end-to-end approach uses more implicit representations. In contrast to our proposed method, both approaches have in common that they utilize the image-to-image translation in an end-to-end approach. Flexibility in the postprocessing plays an important role in RoboCup settings, which is not given with the current state of the art of end-to-end approaches. Using intermediate representations such as pixel-accurate labels allows a higher flexibility and versatility. A dataset using such low level representations can be used both for semantic segmentation and for high level classification and object detection.

Deep learning approaches for robot vision in RoboCup were first applied in the humanoid league, where Schnekenburger *et al.* [20] use a segmentation to detect different field features such as line intersections and objects. All classes except for the detection of other robots performed satisfactory. Van Dijk *et al.* [27] propose a novel model architecture without any residual connections for a semantic segmentation, which was able to be executed in close to real-time on a typical smartphone CPU, but lacks the ability to properly detect complex features or multiple classes at once. In contrast to the humanoid league, the SPL, which uses the SoftBank NAO robots, is more constrained in terms of hardware. Nevertheless, Hess *et al.* [8] trained a simple classifier model to demonstrate the feasibility of using synthetic images in such a scenario. Szemenyei *et al.* [24] propose a novel, small semantic segmentation model that uses images generated with *UERoboCup* for pre-training the model and eventually tune it with real images. However, this approach does not focus on the more extreme conditions that games in environments with natural lighting require. Furthermore, Poppinga *et al.* [15] proposed a robot detection framework for which data obtained in a simulation was used to learn additional features that are hard to label manually, such as robot distances.

3   Data Generation

In this section, after briefly describing the background and the tools generating the simulated data, we give insights into the Multimodal Unsupervised Image-to-Image Translation (MUNIT) framework [10], which we use for the sim-to-real image translation, and describe the online data augmentation methods we used.

3.1   RoboCup and UERoboCup

While RoboCup provides a benchmark to quantitatively compare the progress over time, the community is small and lacks labeled training data for deep learning approaches. Efforts were made to create a community-driven database for labeled real images [7], but the data required for specific tasks and pixel-accurate labels are rarely available.

UERoboCup is an application based on *Unreal Engine* that allows generating game situations with multiple robots from the view of a specific robot [8] and is capable of generating pixel-accurate semantic annotation. To provide a more accurate representation of the environment, we added additional labels relevant to the SPL context, such as the penalty mark and the goal bar as well as an adapted appearance of the robots to that of the latest NAO robot generation. In addition, we increased the variation in the generated images to reflect reality more properly. This is achieved by a variable camera pitch instead of a fixed one and the definition of a skeleton for the previously static robot mesh, which allows dynamic robot poses. This procedure is referred to as domain randomization [26]. Furthermore, the robot skeleton can be used for a more detailed segmentation of individual robot limbs, allowing, for instance, a pose detection. We also export meta data such as the extrinsic camera parameters and the poses of robots in the standardized JSON format. Such information is difficult to annotate manually, therefore learning further characteristics, such as the distance to another robot, as shown in [15], mainly relies on synthetic data.

We generated a set of 10000 images and labels with UERoboCup. A generated image with the corresponding converted segmentation mask can be seen in the overview in Fig. 1.

3.2   Image Post Processing

UERoboCup only creates images of a plain RoboCup scene taking place in a white room. However, during an actual game, the background is cluttered with a wide range of different objects, such as people walking around. In order to make potential deep learning applications understand the concept of unwanted background clutter, we replace the background with structured images, similar to [26]. This can be considered another variation of domain randomization. We use images from the COCO test set [14]. Even though these images do not exactly represent how a scene would look like at a RoboCup event, we found that they are well-suited to help deep learning applications differentiate between relevant foreground and irrelevant background clutter.

3.3 MUNIT

MUNIT assumes images from two different domains $x_1 \in \mathcal{X}_1$ and $x_2 \in \mathcal{X}_2$ and, given samples drawn from the two marginal distributions $p(x_1)$ and $p(x_2)$, without access to the joint distribution $p(x_1, x_2)$, estimate the conditionals $p(x_1|x_2)$ and $p(x_2|x_1)$ with the image-to-image translation models $p(x_{1 \to 2}|x_2)$, where $x_{1 \to 2}$ is a sample resulting from translating x_1 to $\mathcal{X}_2$ [10]. Due to the unsupervised nature of MUNIT, no explicit labeling has to be performed on any of the sample images. The learned mapping is multimodal, thus multiple different images with different styles from domain $x_1 \in \mathcal{X}_1$ can be applied to the same image $x_2 \in \mathcal{X}_2$ and each time a different image with the style from domain $x_1 \in \mathcal{X}_1$ is computed.

3.4 Style Transfer

MUNIT requires a test set and a training set of images for the two classes $\mathcal{X}_1$ and $\mathcal{X}_2$. For this application, the two classes are real images recorded by a robot's camera $\mathcal{X}_{real}$ and simulated images created with UERoboCup $\mathcal{X}_{sim}$. For the real domain, we select images from previous RoboCup events and from ImageTagger [7], accumulating to an overall of 885 images in the training set and 155 images in the test set. We found that a large variance in the training images is essential for MUNIT to generate useful results. Since the images generated by UERoboCup are random, any subset with about the same size can be used. Note that in this subset, we already replaced the background with a random image from the COCO dataset. In the simulated domain, we used 1000 images for training and 200 for testing. We train on an NVidia Titan V with MUNIT default settings for 70000 epochs. Due to memory limitations, we slightly decreased the amount of the generator and discriminator filters. We noticed a convergence after 50000 epochs, with no further significant improvements from that point. To generate the processed images, we took three random style images from the set of real images and applied them to each image generated by UERoboCup, resulting in 30000 different images. An example can be seen in Fig. 2.

3.5 Data Augmentation

Data augmentation is a type of data regularization and helps to avoid overfitting. Additionally, data augmentation can be used to enhance the size and quality of datasets with warping or oversampling methods [21].

We used the following online data augmentations during training: Vertical image flipping, Gaussian noise, multiply, add (RGB and HSV), simplex noise, motion blur, contrast normalization, and simulated sun patches.

It is essential that the model learns to handle extreme environmental situations with patches of light and shadow. Since this is not captured with sufficient variance in our dataset, we introduce an additional domain randomization method during online data augmentation by simulating patches on the field that

Fig. 2. After changing the background in the simulated image to a random image from the COCO dataset (left), we apply the image-to-image translation learned by MUNIT to it (middle). In addition to the offline augmentation obtained with the sim-to-real translation, we perform an online augmentation during training (right). Beside standard augmentations such as blur, we also introduce a simple simulation of sun light patches on the field.

are illuminated by the sun. We implement this augmentation by generating multiple random polygons consisting of three to six points in the frame and multiply these areas with a random factor. A sample augmentation is shown in Fig. 2.

4   Semantic Segmentation

Designing models that are capable of being executed in real-time on platforms with limited resources is difficult due to computing constraints. In our application, the performance baseline for the design of the model is the NAO's camera frame rate of 30 fps. We allocate one CPU core for the processing of the frames of one camera, which means that the model must process each frame at the same rate. As inference framework, we use *CompiledNN* [25].

The model architecture is based on the U-Net architecture [18] and incorporates features from MobileNet [9]. The U-Net architecture consists of an encoder and a decoder with multiple residual connections between the encoder and the decoder. The reduced model from this work uses only two residual connections and downscales the image twice. MobileNet was designed to be deployed to mobile devices and is therefore optimized to run with limited computing power. This is mainly realized by replacing convolutions with separable convolutions [9]. For an additional acceleration, pooling layers are replaced with convolutions with a corresponding stride, as proposed in [23]. We use batch normalization for regularization [11] and LeakyReLU [28] as activation functions. The resulting model has 12909 learnable parameters and is shown in Table 1.

Our proposed model is capable of performing multi-class predictions (in our case ball, goal posts, lines, and robots). Due to limitations in CompiledNN, no softmax activation is applied to the last layer. This means that the model detects all mentioned classes independently from each other. Note that a binary cross entropy or something similar must be used as the loss function. Furthermore, it can be desirable to have multiple independent classifications outputs. For instance, if the model is not certain if the arm of a robot is a similarly looking goal

Table 1. Our proposed segmentation model architecture. The scale refers to the tensor size relative to the input size. N is the amount of how often the layer in the row is repeated and F represents the amount of filters.

Layer	Scale	N	F
Input	1	1	3
3 × 3-SConv2D, BN, LeakyReLU	1	1	8
3 × 3-SConv2D, BN, LeakyReLU	1	1	8
3 × 3-SConv2D, BN, LeakyReLU	1/2	1	8
3 × 3-SConv2D, BN, LeakyReLU	1/2	2	16
3 × 3-SConv2D, BN, LeakyReLU	1/4	1	16
3 × 3-SConv2D, BN, LeakyReLU	1/4	6	24
Up2D	1/2	1	24
Concat	1/2	1	40
3 × 3-SConv2D, BN, LeakyReLU	1/2	3	16
Up2D	1	1	16
Concat	1	1	24
3 × 3-SConv2D, BN, LeakyReLU	1	3	8
3 × 3-SConv2D, BN, LeakyReLU	1	1	5

post, the likelihood of both outputs would be small with a softmax activation. By keeping the output layers independent from each other, the model can classify the arm of a robot both as part of a robot but also as a goal post. This can be validated in the postprocessing by applying additional domain knowledge and thus discarding false positives. Note that ideally, the model is able to capture this from context, but we found that increasing the model size more leads to an unacceptably low inference time. The maximum amount of features is limited by the complexity of the model. We achieved good results with predicting five and less classes, but it is to be expected that a larger amount of independent output predictions yields worse predictions, if the base model is not adapted.

We perform different experiments to find a working model architecture and look for a compromise between detection accuracy and inference time. The runtime was measured on a single CPU core of the NAO v6 (Intel Atom E3845@1.91 GHz [22]) using CompiledNN [25]. The results for different image resolutions are shown in Table 2. As the maximum feasible input resolution for real-time operation is 14 ms, the original input image is subsampled accordingly. The resulting aliasing should not affect the neural model as it should learn to ignore it.

Table 2. Inference time on the NAO v6 with CompiledNN

Size [px × px]	40 × 32	80 × 64	108 × 80	120 × 88	160 × 120	320 × 240
Duration [ms]	1.6	6.7	11.2	14.0	27.3	116.0

5   Results

In order to evaluate the performance of the model and the synthetic dataset, we manually labeled 348 images, which we also used in the MUNIT augmentation resembling varying environment conditions with the five classes field, lines, robots, goal post, and ball. We evaluate the mean Average Precision (mAP) metric. In order to evaluate the effect of the different augmentation techniques, we use five different configurations of our dataset to train the previously described model:

1. no augmentation at all (only the raw images generated by UERoboCup are used, this is the baseline)
2. conventional augmentation without sun (all the augmentations described in Sect. 3.5 except for the sun patch augmentation)
3. conventional augmentation (including the sun patch augmentation)
4. only the image-to-image translation augmentation performed with MUNIT
5. the image-to-image translation combined with all previously described conventional augmentations.

We train all five models with a subset of 8000 images and 2000 images as test set with the same augmentations in a batch size of 128 using the Adam optimizer [13] with an initial learning rate of 0.1. We decay the learning rate by 0.5, if the loss on the validation set does not decrease for 10 epochs and we terminate training after 20 epochs without improvement, which was usually reached in less than 100 epochs.

The different precision-recall curves are visualized in Fig. 3. The mAPs for all models and all classes can be seen in Table 3. We report the precision-recall curves for the individual classes as well as micro-averaged for all classes. Note that the computed mAP represents the classification performance of each individual pixel over all test images and not the classification performance of the object instances.

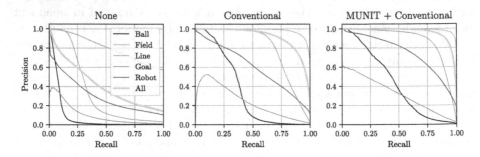

Fig. 3. Precision-recall curves for a model trained without any augmentation (left), a model trained with conventional online augmentation as described before (middle), and a model trained with sim-to-real image translation and conventional augmentation (right). A significant improvement can be seen due to the augmentation with MUNIT.

Table 3. All mAP values for all tested models and all classes

	None	Conventional without sun	Conventional	MUNIT	MUNIT and conventional
Ball	0.0843	0.3927	0.3440	**0.4577**	0.4277
Field	0.8037	0.9846	0.9835	0.9877	**0.9917**
Line	0.3404	0.7866	0.7952	0.8745	**0.8779**
Goal	0.1024	0.1418	0.2367	**0.3554**	0.3207
Robot	0.3059	0.5361	0.5983	0.6529	**0.7478**
All	0.4203	0.9140	0.9165	0.9536	**0.9647**

6   Discussion

As expected, the model without any augmentation performs worst with an overall mAP of 0.4203, which shows that reality gap is an issue for plain images generated in UERoboCup. The ball and the goals are rarely detected with a slightly higher mAP for robots and lines. Since a quantitative comparison with related works [20,24,27] is not possible due to different metrics that do not capture the problem well, this model is used as baseline of what is possible with purely synthetic data generated in UERoboCup.

Just by performing basic augmentation (all augmentations mentioned above except for the sun patch augmentation), the performance of the model increases drastically to an overall mAP of 0.914. Most classes receive a significant increase in mAP, particularly the robot, line, and ball classes. The goal classes' mAP only increase slightly. Adding the sun patch augmentation increases the overall mAP again slightly to 0.9165. The sun patches augmentation helps improving the line, goal, and robot classification, but results in a drop in the ball class, while the field prediction stays about the same. This demonstrates that the sun patch augmentation in fact helps.

When considering the model trained solely with data augmented with MUNIT, a clear rise in overall mAP to 0.9536 can be seen, with an improvement for all classes. Adding conventional augmentation to the MUNIT augmentation results in a slight overall mAP increase to 0.9647. While the ball and goal classes' mAPs drop again slightly, all other classes' performances increase. This shows that our proposed method yields the desired result. Particularly highly unbalanced classes benefit from the image-to-image translation augmentation.

The ball class is consistently the one with the lowest mAP, which is likely due to highly unbalanced training samples (with the ball being significantly smaller than any other objects). The same applies to the goal post class. The ball is one of the most challenging objects to detect in different lighting conditions since it is small, very close to the ground and throws shadows due to its spherical shape. Lastly, the model operates on a small resolution which makes it impossible to detect the ball at large distances.

Fig. 4. Examples demonstrating the final performance of the neural network on an easy sample with constant lighting (left) and two hard samples with extreme lighting conditions (middle and right). The best performing model was trained on the full dataset (30000 images) with a termination patiency of 40 epochs. The classes are encoded as follows: field (green), line (white), robot (pink), ball (red), goal post (blue), and background (black). None of these images were used for the MUNIT training. Despite the extreme lighting conditions, the segmentation performs reasonably well and even underrepresented classes such as the ball are mostly detected successfully. (Color figure online)

Despite its little size with only 12909 trainable parameters (opposed to 300000 parameters in [20]), our proposed model trained with our synthetically generated training data seems to perform better than the approaches proposed by van Dijk *et al.* [27] and by Szemenyei *et al.* [24]. A quantitative comparison is difficult due to the differing capabilities of the models. While our model operates at a low resolution of only 120 × 88 pixels, van Dijk *et al.* operates at QVGA resolution and Szemenyei *et al.* use QQVGA resolution while Schnekenburger *et al.* [20] use an image of 640 × 512 as input. In contrast to van Dijk *et al.*, our model is successful in predicting multiple classes at once. In contrast to Szemenyei *et al.*, our model seems to predict a subjectively more precise multi-class classification for each independent prediction, which Szemenyei *et al.* solve with an expensive label propagation. Due to the same reasons, a runtime comparison is difficult, as van Dijk *et al.* and Schnekenburger *et al.* utilize GPUs for the inference. With 14 ms, our model is faster than the fastest model proposed by Szemenyei *et al.* (22 ms + 170 ms label propagation).

The segmentation model was applied to images recorded in extreme lighting conditions. Multiple samples can be seen in Fig. 4.

7   Conclusion

We proposed a method for segmenting an image in real-time at a reduced resolution into five different classes by utilizing a deep learning approach. We generated all training data synthetically and evaluated the results on a test set made of manually labeled real data.

We demonstrated our proposed method of generating a dataset with image-to-image translation with publicly available simulation tools. With this dataset, we showed that a small semantic segmentation model is capable of running in real-time on low-end hardware with while producing results that outperform related work. In contrast to end-to-end solutions such as [2, 3], which integrate the image augmentation into the model, our approach allows to generate a versatile and high quality dataset, which we share with the community[1], without the need to have access to high performance GPUs required to generate such datasets or the knowledge to design image-to-image translation models.

References

1. Abadi, M., et al.: TensorFlow: large-scale machine learning on heterogeneous systems (2015). http://tensorflow.org/
2. Bewley, A., et al.: Learning to drive from simulation without real world labels. In: 2019 International Conference on Robotics and Automation (ICRA). IEEE (2019)
3. Bousmalis, K., et al.: Using simulation and domain adaptation to improve efficiency of deep robotic grasping. In: 2018 IEEE International Conference on Robotics and Automation (ICRA) (2018)
4. Brostow, G.J., Fauqueur, J., Cipolla, R.: Semantic object classes in video: a high-definition ground truth database. Pattern Recogn. Lett. **30**(2), 88–97 (2009)
5. Cireşan, D.C., Meier, U., Gambardella, L.M., Schmidhuber, J.: Deep, big, simple neural nets for handwritten digit recognition. Neural Comput. **22**(12), 3207–3220 (2010)
6. Everingham, M., Van Gool, L., Williams, C.K., Winn, J., Zisserman, A.: The PASCAL visual object classes (VOC) challenge. Int. J. Comput. Vis. **88**(2), 303–338 (2010)
7. Fiedler, N., Bestmann, M., Hendrich, N.: ImageTagger: an open source online platform for collaborative image labeling. In: Holz, D., Genter, K., Saad, M., von Stryk, O. (eds.) RoboCup 2018. LNCS (LNAI), vol. 11374, pp. 162–169. Springer, Cham (2019). https://doi.org/10.1007/978-3-030-27544-0_13
8. Hess, T., Mundt, M., Weis, T., Ramesh, V.: Large-scale stochastic scene generation and semantic annotation for deep convolutional neural network training in the RoboCup SPL. In: Akiyama, H., Obst, O., Sammut, C., Tonidandel, F. (eds.) RoboCup 2017. LNCS (LNAI), vol. 11175, pp. 33–44. Springer, Cham (2018). https://doi.org/10.1007/978-3-030-00308-1_3
9. Howard, A.G., et al.: MobileNets: efficient convolutional neural networks for mobile vision applications. CoRR abs/1704.04861 (2017)

---

[1] https://sibylle.informatik.uni-bremen.de/public/datasets/semantic_segmentation.

10. Huang, X., Liu, M.-Y., Belongie, S., Kautz, J.: Multimodal unsupervised image-to-image translation. In: Ferrari, V., Hebert, M., Sminchisescu, C., Weiss, Y. (eds.) ECCV 2018. LNCS, vol. 11207, pp. 179–196. Springer, Cham (2018). https://doi.org/10.1007/978-3-030-01219-9_11

11. Ioffe, S., Szegedy, C.: Batch normalization: accelerating deep network training by reducing internal covariate shift. In: Proceedings of the 32nd International Conference on International Conference on Machine Learning, ICML 2015, vol. 37. JMLR.org (2015)

12. Jakobi, N., Husbands, P., Harvey, I.: Noise and the reality gap: the use of simulation in evolutionary robotics. In: Morán, F., Moreno, A., Merelo, J.J., Chacón, P. (eds.) ECAL 1995. LNCS, vol. 929, pp. 704–720. Springer, Heidelberg (1995). https://doi.org/10.1007/3-540-59496-5_337

13. Kingma, D., Ba, J.: Adam: a method for stochastic optimization. In: International Conference on Learning Representations (2014)

14. Lin, T.-Y., et al.: Microsoft COCO: common objects in context. In: Fleet, D., Pajdla, T., Schiele, B., Tuytelaars, T. (eds.) ECCV 2014. LNCS, vol. 8693, pp. 740–755. Springer, Cham (2014). https://doi.org/10.1007/978-3-319-10602-1_48

15. Poppinga, B., Laue, T.: JET-net: real-time object detection for mobile robots. In: Chalup, S., Niemueller, T., Suthakorn, J., Williams, M.-A. (eds.) RoboCup 2019. LNCS (LNAI), vol. 11531, pp. 227–240. Springer, Cham (2019). https://doi.org/10.1007/978-3-030-35699-6_18

16. Ren, S., He, K., Girshick, R., Sun, J.: Faster R-CNN: towards real-time object detection with region proposal networks. In: Proceedings of the 28th International Conference on Neural Information Processing Systems, NIPS 2015, vol. 1. MIT Press (2015)

17. Richter, S.R., Vineet, V., Roth, S., Koltun, V.: Playing for data: ground truth from computer games. In: Leibe, B., Matas, J., Sebe, N., Welling, M. (eds.) ECCV 2016. LNCS, vol. 9906, pp. 102–118. Springer, Cham (2016). https://doi.org/10.1007/978-3-319-46475-6_7

18. Ronneberger, O., Fischer, P., Brox, T.: U-net: convolutional networks for biomedical image segmentation. In: Navab, N., Hornegger, J., Wells, W.M., Frangi, A.F. (eds.) MICCAI 2015. LNCS, vol. 9351, pp. 234–241. Springer, Cham (2015). https://doi.org/10.1007/978-3-319-24574-4_28

19. Ros, G., Sellart, L., Materzynska, J., Vazquez, D., Lopez, A.M.: The SYNTHIA dataset: a large collection of synthetic images for semantic segmentation of urban scenes. In: The IEEE Conference on Computer Vision and Pattern Recognition (CVPR) (2016)

20. Schnekenburger, F., Scharffenberg, M., Wülker, M., Hochberg, U., Dorer, K.: Detection and localization of features on a soccer field with feedforward fully convolutional neural networks (FCNN) for the adult-size humanoid robot Sweaty. In: Proceedings of the 12th Workshop on Humanoid Soccer Robots, 17th IEEE-RAS International Conference on Humanoid Robots. Birmingham (2017)

21. Shorten, C., Khoshgoftaar, T.M.: A survey on image data augmentation for deep learning. J. Big Data 6(1), 60 (2019)

22. SoftBank Robotics Documentation: What's new in NAOqi 2.8? (2019). http://doc.aldebaran.com/2-8/index.html. Accessed 15 Sept 2019

23. Springenberg, J., Dosovitskiy, A., Brox, T., Riedmiller, M.: Striving for simplicity: the all convolutional net. In: ICLR (Workshop Track) (2015). http://lmb.informatik.uni-freiburg.de/Publications/2015/DB15a

24. Szemenyei, M., Estivill-Castro, V.: Real-time scene understanding using deep neural networks for RoboCup SPL. In: Holz, D., Genter, K., Saad, M., von Stryk, O. (eds.) RoboCup 2018. LNCS (LNAI), vol. 11374, pp. 96–108. Springer, Cham (2019). https://doi.org/10.1007/978-3-030-27544-0_8
25. Thielke, F., Hasselbring, A.: A JIT compiler for neural network inference. In: Chalup, S., Niemueller, T., Suthakorn, J., Williams, M.-A. (eds.) RoboCup 2019. LNCS (LNAI), vol. 11531, pp. 448–456. Springer, Cham (2019). https://doi.org/10.1007/978-3-030-35699-6_36
26. Tremblay, J., et al.: Training deep networks with synthetic data: bridging the reality gap by domain randomization. In: The IEEE Conference on Computer Vision and Pattern Recognition (CVPR) Workshops (2018)
27. van Dijk, S.G., Scheunemann, M.M.: Deep learning for semantic segmentation on minimal hardware. In: Holz, D., Genter, K., Saad, M., von Stryk, O. (eds.) RoboCup 2018. LNCS (LNAI), vol. 11374, pp. 349–361. Springer, Cham (2019). https://doi.org/10.1007/978-3-030-27544-0_29
28. Xu, B., Wang, N., Chen, T., Li, M.: Empirical evaluation of rectified activations in convolutional network. CoRR abs/1505.00853 (2015). http://arxiv.org/abs/1505.00853

Engineering Features to Improve Pass Prediction in Soccer Simulation 2D Games

Nader Zare[1]($\boxtimes$), Mahtab Sarvmaili[1], Aref Sayareh[3], Omid Amini[4],
Stan Matwin[1,2], and Amilcar Soares[5]

[1] Institute for Big Data Analytics, Dalhousie University, Halifax, Canada
{nader.zare,mahtab.sarvmaili}@dal.ca, stan@cs.dal.ca
[2] Institute for Computer Science, Polish Academy of Sciences, Warsaw, Poland
[3] Shiraz University, Shiraz, Iran
[4] Qom University of Technology, Qom, Iran
[5] Memorial University of Newfoundland, St. John's, Canada
amilcarsj@mun.ca

Abstract. Soccer Simulation 2D (SS2D) is a simulation of a real soccer game in two dimensions. In soccer, passing behavior is an essential action for keeping the ball in possession of our team and creating goal opportunities. Similarly, for SS2D, predicting the passing behaviors of both opponents and our teammates helps manage resources and score more goals. Therefore, in this research, we have tried to address the modeling of passing behavior of soccer 2D players using Deep Neural Networks (DNN) and Random Forest (RF). We propose an embedded data extraction module that can record the decision-making of agents in an online format. Afterward, we apply four data sorting techniques for training data preparation. After, we evaluate the trained models' performance playing against 6 top teams of RoboCup 2019 that have distinctive playing strategies. Finally, we examine the importance of different feature groups on the prediction of a passing strategy. All results in each step of this work prove our suggested methodology's effectiveness and improve the performance of the pass prediction in Soccer Simulation 2D games ranging from 5% (e.g., playing against the same team) to 10% (e.g., playing against Robocup top teams).

Keywords: Feature engineering · Agent systems · Machine learning · Soccer simulation 2D

1 Introduction

Soccer is the world's most popular sport where two teams of eleven players play against each other, and the team with the highest number of goals wins the game. Shooting, dribbling, and passing are examples of possible actions that can lead the ball to the goal. Possessing the ball for a more extended period

© Springer Nature Switzerland AG 2022
R. Alami et al. (Eds.): RoboCup 2021, LNAI 13132, pp. 140–152, 2022.
https://doi.org/10.1007/978-3-030-98682-7_12

not only reduces the chance of losing the game to the opposing team but may also create more opportunities to shoot at the opponent's goal. The team with a smart passing strategy dictates the play, saves energy, and makes the best use of their resources (e.g., player's stamina).

Due to technological development, the idea of robotic soccer players was introduced as a new research area in 1992 [1]. Since then, the RoboCup[1] has been known as an international competition for promoting ideas in A.I. and robotics. Within this competition, the 2D soccer simulation league works as an abstraction of real soccer games into a two-dimensional environment.

The RoboCup Soccer Simulation Server (RCSSServer) is responsible for simulating the environment and the connection between the game elements. For this simulation each player (agent) is an individual program that communicates with the server to send actions and to receive its observations.

As in real soccer, passing behavior in a Soccer Simulation 2D (SS2D) game plays a critical role in increasing the chance of winning. The prediction of agents' passing behavior has the advantages of improving a team's passing strategy, increasing the accuracy of passing actions, enhancing agents' decision-making, managing agents' stamina, and enhancing an agent's unmark behavior. In this work, we propose an embedded Data Extractor module that collects events of an SS2D game and creates features that can be used to train models to enhance the passing actions in a game.

This module generates data containing features of the ball, our players, and opponent players. We also propose three sorting methods along with two modes of placing kicker's features as the first element of each data instance to create. We trained a Deep Neural Network (DNN) and Random Forest (RF) models on a generated dataset with 3,000 games to predict our teammates' passing behavior to validate our module. Our experimental results show that these sorting algorithms, along with suggested feature groups, improve the team's passing prediction accuracy. To assess the quality of the suggested feature groups, we investigated the robustness of these feature groups in the face of changes in the opponent team.

The rest of this paper is organized as follows. Section 2 presents some related works in the area of soccer simulation 2D. In Sect. 3, we provide definitions of the environment and some detail about soccer simulation. Section 4 explains the data gathering step. Section 5 shows the experimental results of our model. Finally, Sect. 6 concludes the work and also discusses future works.

2 Related Works

The prediction of players' behavior is an active research topic in robotic soccer. The work of [2] tries to predict the tactical strategy of opponent by analyzing the kicking distribution of agents from the records of the game. Similarly, [3] has evaluated the kicking distribution and action trajectories of players from records of games to analyze teams' offensive strategy. The positional features

---

[1] www.robocup.org.

of the players and the ball extracted from the records of the game have been a source of data for the behavioral analysis of players, such as the proposed methods in these papers [4–6] extracted 46 positional features of players and ball in the field for trajectory analysis, formation detection and assessment of games' state respectively, without any further investigation of the effect of other features groups. All these works had applied machine learning algorithms to the records of the game that were extracted when the game was finished; therefore the observation of agents and the process of decision making remains unclear.

Unlike all previous approaches, we propose an online data extractor inserted in the players of a team, which continuously records the agent's action from the environment. In this case, not only do we have access to the decision of agents but also, we can record the live observations of the agent from the environment. Additionally, we have introduced different feature groups and sorting methods. Our idea is to evaluate the impact of these feature groups on the prediction of passing behavior.

To the best of our knowledge, implementing the data generator module inside the players and performing the online recording of the game's information is done for the first time in Soccer Simulation 2D research. None of the previous researches have explored the significance of other positional feature groups rather than Cartesian positions of elements in the field. Alternatively, investigate the robustness of a trained model against changes in the opponent team has never been explored in the literature.

3   The Environment

Soccer Simulation 2D (SS2D) League is part of the RoboCup [7] research project and presents a dynamic, continuous, real-time, incomplete, and distributed environment. Like real soccer, the teams of eleven players compete against each other in a two-dimensional field set up on a computer server. All the players are mapped to this two-dimensional space, and they are represented by circles (Fig. 1).

Each team consists of 12 agents (11 players and one coach), and each agent is executed as an independent program. A game in this league consists of 6,000 cycles, and one cycle is represented in 0.1 s.

In a SS2D game, the players of a team are created before a match starts. The server will randomly generate 18 players with the attributes: *maximum speed*, *decay*, *size*, *effort max*, *effort min*, *kickable area size*, *kick power*, *margin*, *dash rate*. Afterwards, the server sends all 18 different players to the teams' coach, who has the task of selecting 11 players to start a game.

At the beginning of each cycle, the server sends distinct information to each agent based on its angle view in the previous cycle. At the end of each cycle, players send their actions along with their parameters to the server. After, the server adds a noise to the received actions from all players and it updates the state of game, moving to the next cycle at the end of this step. The result of repeated matches between two teams can be different every time a game is played since the noise values are randomly generated in each game, even if they use the same algorithms and parameters in those matches.

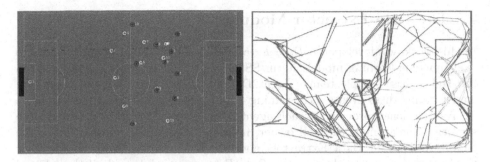

Fig. 1. Left: an overview of soccer simulation 2D environment. Right: visualization of all passes, dribbles and shoots between two agents from the left team.

3.1 The Helios Base

Most teams that play in the SS2D league use one of the popular released base codes [8–10,13]. The HELIOS base [8] is the most popular base code among the teams. It consists of a debugging monitor, a formation editor, and a sample team (known as *Agent2D*) that can connect to the server and plays a full game against other teams. Some of the fundamental behaviors such as passing, dribbling, and shooting have been developed in this sample team. In this work, we are giving an overview of the *Agent2D* Base but full details and documentation are available in [8].

The *Chain Action* is a decision-making module that has been developed for the player who holds the ball (i.e., ball owner or ball holder) in *Agent2D* base. The module uses the Breadth-First Search algorithm (BFS) [11] to find the best action for the ball holder. First, it creates a decision tree where the root node is the current state, and the actions are branches from this state. In the tree, each edge is a possible action selected (e.g., pass, shoot, dribble, etc.), and each node is a state (e.g., the position of the ball and players). Second, the *Field Evaluator* evaluates all nodes by using the position of the ball in that node. Finally, it selects the action that leads to the node with highest value of this metric. Figure 1 presents all selected action by players' of left team in a game.

The agent who has the ball can use the predictive model before receiving the ball to update his neck angle and to see the target player to enhance its pass accuracy.

This agent can also use the predicting model to deeply search the action tree, aiming to find the best chain of actions in the field. Finally, agents in the SS2D environment, like in real soccer games, should move to a position to receive the ball. In the SS2D league, each agent has limited stamina (i.e., players have a limited energy capacity in the game), and they can use this energy for kicking and moving. Efficient management of stamina is required, so all players can't go to a position to be the pass target. Therefore, deciding which player is the most likely to receive an accurate pass helps manage their available stamina.

4   The Data Extractor Module

In this work, we developed a *Data Extractor* Module to create training data to feed machine learning models in an SS2D game. Our module was designed in the Helios base sample team (Agent2D) and collects the events of the game, transforming these events into training data for machine learning models.

As mentioned previously, each agent receives its observation data from the server. If the agent is the ball owner, it feeds the observed information to the Chain Action and Data Extractor modules. The *Chain Action* module finds the best action and sends it to the *Data Extractor* module, only if the selected action is a pass. The *Data Extractor* Module has two sub-modules named *Feature Extractor* and *Label Generator*. The *Data Extractor* module gets the observation and the best action, and delivers the observation and action to the *Features Extractor* and *Label Generator*. The *Features Extractor* extracts the list of features shown in Sect. 4.1 from the observation. The *Label Generator* assigns one label "*Unum(Uniform Number)*" on the generated features. Finally, the *Data Extractor* saves the data to be used for training purposes. After completion of game, the generated dataset is sent to the *Sorting* module. This module reads the data features and sorts them based on six methods that are explained in Sect. 4.2. Eventually, the external *Trainer* Module receives sorted data and employs it for training the model. The structure of the agent and its processing modules are presented in the Fig. 2. Next, we discus the full procedure in details.

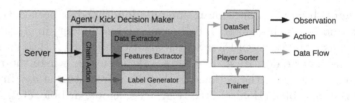

Fig. 2. Overview of the data extractor module.

4.1   Features and Values

For each cycle that one of our agents is the ball holder and the selected action is a pass, the agent creates a new data instance. This instance contains 12 features for the ball, 42 for each one of our players (42×11), and 24 for each of the opponent's players (24×11), in total 738 features. We used two labels for each data instance: Index Number and Uniform Number (Unum). The Uniform Number is the unique number of a target agent (who may receive the ball) in the game. Differently from Unum, the Index Number refers to the index of a target agent in the sorted data. The Index Number is assigned to the player in the *Player Sorter* module.

The list of extracted feature are broken down into nine feature subgroups that are measured for the ball, our agents, or the opponents' agents. Since at each time step, the ball holder is responsible for generating a data instance, the module creates all of these features for all agents on the field. In the following, we will discuss them in more detail.

Position. This feature group measures the position of an object in the field by using 4 parameters X, Y, R, and T. X and Y are the vector's coordinates in Cartesian system, R and T are the vector's coordinate in Polar system.

Kicker. This group measures the position of an object in the field with respect to the position of the ball holder. It contains four positional features similar to the Position feature group.

Velocity. This group measures the velocity of an object in the field by using positional parameters. It contains four positional features similar to the Position feature group.

Body. It measures the players' body angle with respect to the direct line between the center of two goals.

Team. This group contains two sets of parameters, Uniform number and "Is Kicker". Uniform number presents the unique number of players and "Is kicker" shows that the player is ball holder or not.

Player Type. This feature group contains nine values for player type.

Top k-th Riskiest Opponents. This feature group is measured for all of our players and helps to identify the top k riskiest opponents on the way of a pass to another teammate. The risk of an opponent is calculated by the difference between two angles: 1) angle of the ball to the opponent, 2) angle of the ball to the teammate.

The ball holder draws a direct line to all of the opponents and calculates it as the angle to the line between the ball and the target teammate. After identifying the two riskiest opponents, the agent will measure 1) the distance between the opponent and the ball, 2) the distance between the opponent and the direct pass line, 3) the angle of the line between the ball and the opponent, and the direct pass line, 4) the angle between the opponent body and the perpendicular line to the direct pass line, and 5) the distance between the projection point and the ball holder. Figure 3 illustrates the discussed features in the top k riskiest opponents' agents.

Top k-th Nearest Opponents. This feature group shows relative information of the k-th nearest opponents to the teammate. It is identified by three elements, *distance*, *angle*, and *body angle* of the opponent player to ours.

Goal. This feature group indicates the distance and the angle between teammates and the center of the opponent's goal.

The Position, Kicker and the Velocity groups are measured for all objects in the field. the Body, Team and the Player Type are measured for all players. The rest of feature groups are only measured for our players.

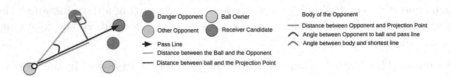

Fig. 3. Illustration of calculating "Top Kth riskiest" feature group

4.2   Sorting

The *Sorting* module is an essential component in the data preparation step since it organizes the input features and creates the training dataset. We proposed 4 distinct methods for the *sorting* sub-module.

Uniform Number Sorting. In this approach the sorting module arranges the data by uniform number. The data instance will be structured by: features of the Ball, features of Teammates sorted by Uniform number, and features of Opponents sorted by Uniform number.

X Sorting. For this method, the sorting module arranges the data based on the x coordinate, and the data will be structured by: features of the Ball, features of Teammates sorted, and features of Opponents sorted by X respectively.

Field Evaluator Sorting. This method sorts players based on an evaluation of their positions from the Field Evaluator sub module in the *Chain Action* [8]. The structure of the data will be as features of the Ball, features of Teammates, features of Opponents sorted by the evaluation criteria, respectively.

Kicker be First. This is a binary attribute that pushes the features of the ball holder as the first element of data.

After sorting the data, this module assigns a label to them which is based on the index of ball receiver. When the sorter module puts the information of players in one data instance, it finds the index of ball receiver in the sorted features. For example, the features of the ball receiver is the fifth elements of data. In this case the label of this data record will be five. Therefore applying three sorting methods and changing the **Kicker be First** attribute (i.e., true or false), we can generate six different datasets with a different order of the input data.

5   Experimental Results

5.1   Training Data Set

To obtain the training data[2], we enabled a "full state option" in the server that requires the server to dispense the exact observations of the environment to players. This feature improves the reproducibility of our model. For this work, we set the parameter of K (employed for the "Top Kth riskiest opponents" and "Top Kth nearest opponents") equal to two.

To create the dataset, we inserted the *Data Extractor* Module in Agent2D base, and we played against the same source code for 3,000 games (i.e. both teams are using the same source code, but only one of them has *Data Extractor* Module) and 1,361,126 data instances were generated.

We split the data into two subsets of training with $1,088,237$ instances and tested with $272,889$ instances. The distribution of acting as kicker players and being the ball's receiver is shown in Fig. 4. To sort the train and test data, we applied the three sorting methods (discussed in Sect. 4.2) in two modes where the *Kicker be First* attribute is *True* or *False*.

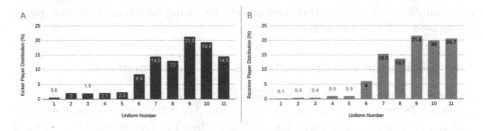

Fig. 4. The probability distribution of being the Kicker or the Receiver for all players

5.2   Early Results

For the prediction model, we employed a Deep Neural Network (DNN) and a Random Forest (RF).

The DNN model includes 6 layers of 1024, 512, 256, 64, 32, and 11 neurons. The activation function of internal layers is a RELU; the last layer uses the softmax function. Also, after the first layer, we added a dropout layer with 0.1 rate. The number of training epochs was 100. To identify the effect of presence or absence of features on the performance of the model, we followed two paradigms: 1) the training data includes all features listed in the Sect. 4.1, 2) the training data only has the *position group features*. Also, we trained two unique models for the prediction of Unum and Index as the data labels. Most of the previous works have employed the position features group with the "Uniform Number" sorting

---

[2] The dataset and source of this project for reproducing the results are available in "https://github.com/Cyrus2D/Agent2D-DataExtractor".

as their model's input to predict the UNUM of the target agent. Therefore, we can consider this feature group along with the UNUM as a baseline (Line 1 of Table 1) for comparing the proposed features and feature groups. Table 1 column *Test Data*, illustrates DNN and RF's performance on the prediction of passing behavior. The obtained results show that the prediction accuracy increased when all features were present in a range of 2.03 to 4.65. Predicting the Index of pass receiver is 3.41 more accurate than predicting its UNUM. Based on the obtained results, placing the ball holder's position as the first feature of data can increase the accuracy of prediction up to 0.83 on average and up to 1.94 when the *X Sorting* or *Field Evaluator Sorting* is employed for sorting the data. Finally, the *UNUM Sorting* has 1.27 higher accuracy in predicting the passing behavior.

Soccer Simulation 2D teams sometimes change their player's uniform number. To identify robustness of pass prediction models against changing uniform number, We randomly changed (0.1, 0.25, 0.50, 0.75, 1.0) proportions of player's uniform number in the test data, and then evaluate models' accuracy for the 16 trained DNN models. Figure 5 presents results of this experiment. This result shows that *Unum sorting* is not robust to changes of uniform number, but *X sorting is robust to this change, since changing uniform number does not impact the data when the sorter algorithm is X sorting*. Results of *Field Evaluator sorting* is similar to *X sorting*. It demonstrates that using all feature groups improve robustness of *Uniform sorting*.

5.3   Testing the Features in Games with Real Opponents

Similarly to real-world soccer, in SS2D league, the rules for a player can vary between different teams; for example, in the Agent2D, uniform numbers of 2 and 3 are assigned to Center Back players, but for Cyrus, player number 2 and 3 are the Center and Right back, respectively. Also, the formation strategies

Table 1. The prediction accuracy of DNN and RF on the test data using different features group and sorting algorithms

Data set			Test data				Real opponents			
Sorter algorithm	Kicker first	Features groups	DNN		RF		DNN		RF	
			Unum	Index	Unum	Index	Unum	Index	Unum	Index
Uniform	No	Position	79.40	79.40	80.90	80.89	55.91	54.97	57.73	57.40
Uniform	Yes	Position	79.99	79.94	81.42	81.43	55.99	56.43	58.69	59.19
X	No	Position	79.15	79.14	79.52	79.17	56.44	55.93	56.49	54.78
X	Yes	Position	79.45	79.32	80.32	80.38	57.13	55.68	58.55	58.93
Field evaluator	No	Position	79.09	79.15	79.40	79.17	57.37	55.68	55.86	54.39
Field evaluator	Yes	Position	79.27	79.35	80.23	80.26	57.43	55.80	57.88	58.70
Uniform	No	All	84.05	84.15	**84.41**	84.10	63.63	63.29	62.65	62.69
Uniform	Yes	All	83.74	84.00	84.09	84.07	63.03	63.50	62.66	62.47
X	No	All	81.64	81.98	82.01	83.24	60.76	63.61	59.99	64.28
X	Yes	All	81.90	82.59	82.35	83.43	61.64	65.10	60.65	64.62
Field evaluator	No	All	81.55	82.26	81.92	83.25	60.24	64.07	59.48	63.86
Field evaluator	Yes	All	81.97	82.93	82.33	83.32	62.17	**65.22**	60.22	64.12

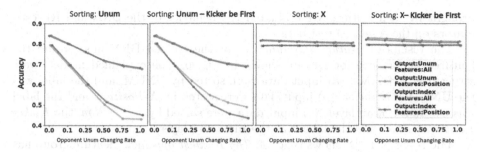

Fig. 5. The accuracy of predicting the passing behavior when different portions of opponents' UNUM were randomly changed. The percentage of players is shown in the X-Axis, and the accuracy of model on Y-Axis.

(e.g., defensive, offensive) of the teams are generally different, and the team's pass effectiveness depends strongly on how the opponent behaves. In this experiment, we examine our newly created features' performance by playing games with more sophisticated opponents aiming at verifying the impacts on the passing behavior.

To evaluate the pass improvements against different opponents, we ran 60 games between the Helios Base Sample Team with Feature Extractor module against the 6 top teams of RoboCup 2019, Helios [12], CYRUS [13], YuShan [14], MT2019 [15], Receptivity [16] and Razi [17]. After the games' execution, we generated 16,672 data samples; then, we exploited the sorter algorithms (Sect. 4.2) to sort the new data set. At the end, we evaluated the accuracy of trained models with the new dataset and reported the result in Table 1, column *Real Opponents*. Again, the baseline here is the first line of Table 1, where we do not use the kicker first strategy and use the position features. The results show that the presence of all features in the data improves by almost 10% (65.22% against 55.91% of the baseline) the prediction probability of the model; also *Field Evaluator Sorting* or *X Sorting* has higher accuracy in the prediction of passing behavior.

The obtained results show that when all features were present the prediction accuracy increased 5.86 in average. Predicting the Index of pass receiver is 3.71 more accurate than predicting its UNUM when all features were present and the *X Sorting* or *Field Evaluator Sorting* is employed for sorting the data. Based on the obtained results, placing the ball holder's position as the first feature of data can increase the accuracy of prediction up to 1.01 in average.

5.4   Feature Importance

Finally, to better understand the decisions of the DNN, the impact of input features on the prediction of passing strategy, we applied *feature permutation* strategy. This strategy measures the reduction of a model's score when a single feature value has been randomly shuffled [18]. For the RF model, the feature importance is the normalized total reduction of the Gini criterion in the RF brought by each feature. We evaluated the behavior of the DNN and RF estimators on the Agent2D test data.

The results of *Feature Permutation* for the trained DNN models and the features importance for RF are shown in Fig. 6. The explained models were structured as follows: (a) input data were sorted by UNUM, and the label was the UNUM of a player; (b) input data were sorted by *X Position*, and the label was the Index of a player; (c) input data were sorted by *X Position*, the *Kicker First* was *True*, and the label was the Index of player.

The result of DNN shows that the *Top Riskiest opponents* feature group has the greatest influence on the prediction probability of passing behavior among all of the models, as can be seen in Fig. 6. After the top-riskiest opponents, the *Kicker's position* has the next highest impact on the prediction of the DNN, mainly when the sorting algorithm uses the ball holder position player as the first element of the data. RF shows relatively similar behavior, in which the *kicker's position* and *top Riskiest* features groups have the most impact on the prediction of the model. Surprisingly for both of these models, the *Position* features have relatively low importance. From this chart, we can observe that although the process of learning is different for these models, similar results can be achieved when our newly engineered features are added.

Most previous works on this topic have exploited the *Position* features group of elements in the field. In this part, we want to observe the impact of *Kicker* features group on the prediction of DNN and RF even in the presence of *Position* features. Hence, we have compared the importance of the *Kicker* feature group regarding the *Position* features for 5 models. The obtained results are illustrated in Fig. 7.

In models A - C, all groups of features were used for the predictor model. In all of them, the *Kicker* features group has a higher impact on the prediction of the DNN and RF than *Position* features. The impact of *Kicker* features is more evident for model D when only two feature groups were used for this model. For model D, we employed both of *position* and *Kicker* features groups to examine the impact of positional features group on the prediction of the model.

Figure 7 shows the result of our experiment. The results show that the *Kicker* group is more important than the *Position* group; specially for DNN, *X* and *Y* of the *Kicker* group are the most important features in these two groups.

Since the *Kicker* feature group measures each element's position with respect to the ball holder, the location of objects is measured based on the ball's location. Using this feature group, our model can consider the similar situation in different locations of the field, and in this way becoming translation invariant. Additionally, similar to a real soccer game, if the players (teammates and opponents) are closer to the ball holder, the chance of receiving the ball or losing the ball is higher; hence the position of the objects near the kicker is crucial.

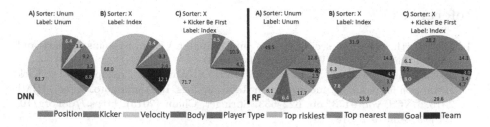

Fig. 6. The importance of different feature group in the presence of different sorting algorithms

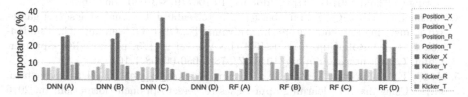

Fig. 7. The impact of "Kicker" feature group on the prediction of DNN and RF in the presence of other position related features

6   Conclusion

In this paper, we proposed an embedded data generator module in the Agent 2D base to record the information of a game SS2D game when the player is the ball holder aiming to create features to be used by machine learning algorithms to predict the best option for passing. To model our teammates' passing behavior in the game, we exploited the generated features and trained a Deep Neural Network and a Random Forest. We obtained an 84% accuracy on the prediction of passing behavior on the test data. Furthermore, we tested the trained models in terms of robustness against changes in the opponent's team, prediction of the accuracy facing the top five teams of RoboCup 2019, and the effectiveness of different feature groups on the prediction of passing behavior.

Our experiment shows that "X" sorting methods enhanced the models to predict agents' passing targets against varieties of opponents and situations. Also, the comparison of different features groups showed that features related to the position of the ball holder have higher importance for the prediction of pass target than other positional features.

We intend to explore several other directions in this work. First, we will disable the full state mode in the soccer simulation server to receive noisy information from the server and verify how the new features would impact in the result of games (i.e., win, tie, loss). We also intent to use other models with the newly engineered features such as recurrent neural networks.

References

1. Mackworth, A.K.: On seeing robots. In: Computer Vision: Systems, Theory and Applications, pp. 1–13. World Scientific (1993)
2. Nakashima, T., Mifune, S., Henrio, J., Obst, O., Wang, P., Prokopenko, M.: Kick extraction for reducing uncertainty in RoboCup logs. In: Yamamoto, S. (ed.) HIMI 2015. LNCS, vol. 9173, pp. 622–633. Springer, Cham (2015). https://doi.org/10.1007/978-3-319-20618-9_61
3. Fukushima, T., Nakashima, T., Akiyama, H.: Similarity analysis of action trajectories based on kick distributions. In: Chalup, S., Niemueller, T., Suthakorn, J., Williams, M.-A. (eds.) RoboCup 2019. LNCS (LNAI), vol. 11531, pp. 58–70. Springer, Cham (2019). https://doi.org/10.1007/978-3-030-35699-6_5
4. Michael, O., Obst, O., Schmidsberger, F., Stolzenburg, F.: Analysing soccer games with clustering and conceptors. In: Akiyama, H., Obst, O., Sammut, C., Tonidandel, F. (eds.) RoboCup 2017. LNCS (LNAI), vol. 11175, pp. 120–131. Springer, Cham (2018). https://doi.org/10.1007/978-3-030-00308-1_10
5. Asali, E., Valipour, M., Zare, N., Afshar, A., Katebzadeh, M., Dastghaibyfard, G.H.: Using machine learning approaches to detect opponent formation. In: 2016 Artificial Intelligence and Robotics (IRANOPEN), pp. 140–144. IEEE (2016)
6. Suzuki, Y., Nakashima, T.: On the use of simulated future information for evaluating game situations. In: Chalup, S., Niemueller, T., Suthakorn, J., Williams, M.-A. (eds.) RoboCup 2019. LNCS (LNAI), vol. 11531, pp. 294–308. Springer, Cham (2019). https://doi.org/10.1007/978-3-030-35699-6_23
7. Kitano, H., Asada, M., Kuniyoshi, Y., Noda, I., Osawa, E., Matsubara, H.: RoboCup: a challenge problem for AI. AI Mag. **18**(1), 73–73 (1997)
8. Akiyama, H., Nakashima, T.: HELIOS base: an open source package for the RoboCup soccer 2D simulation. In: Behnke, S., Veloso, M., Visser, A., Xiong, R. (eds.) RoboCup 2013. LNCS (LNAI), vol. 8371, pp. 528–535. Springer, Heidelberg (2014). https://doi.org/10.1007/978-3-662-44468-9_46
9. Prokopenko, M., Wang, P.: Gliders2d: source code base for RoboCup 2D soccer simulation league. In: Chalup, S., Niemueller, T., Suthakorn, J., Williams, M.-A. (eds.) RoboCup 2019. LNCS (LNAI), vol. 11531, pp. 418–428. Springer, Cham (2019). https://doi.org/10.1007/978-3-030-35699-6_33
10. Kok, J., Vlassis, N., Groen, F.: UvA Trilearn 2003 team description. In: Proceedings CD RoboCup 2003 (2003)
11. Mugnier, M.-L., Chein, M.: Conceptual graphs: fundamental notions. Rev. d'intell. Artif. **6**(4), 365–406 (1992)
12. Akiyama, H., Nakashima, T., Fukushima, T., Suzuki, Y., Ohori, A.: HELIOS2019: team description paper. In: RoboCup (2019)
13. Zare, N., et al.: Cyrus 2D simulation 2019. In: RoboCup (2019)
14. Cheng, Z., et al.: YuShan team description paper for RoboCup2019. In: RoboCup (2019)
15. Wang, X., et al.: MT2019 Robocup simulation 2D team description. In: RoboCup (2019)
16. Li, M.: Receptivity: team description paper 2018 fine tuning of agent decision evaluation. In: RoboCup(2019)
17. Noohpisheh, M., et al.: Razi soccer 2D simulation team description paper 2019. In: RoboCup (2019)
18. Breiman, L.: Random forests. Mach. Learn. **45**(1), 5–32 (2001)

Learning from the Crowd: Improving the Decision Making Process in Robot Soccer Using the Audience Noise

Emanuele Antonioni[1]([⊠])[iD], Vincenzo Suriani[1][iD], Filippo Solimando[2],
Daniele Nardi[1][iD], and Domenico D. Bloisi[2][iD]

[1] Department of Computer, Control, and Management Engineering,
Sapienza University of Rome, Rome, Italy
{antonioni,suriani,nardi}@diag.uniroma1.it
[2] Department of Mathematics, Computer Science, and Economics,
University of Basilicata, Potenza, Italy
domenico.bloisi@unibas.it

Abstract. Fan input and support is an important component in many individual and team sports, ranging from athletics to basketball. Audience interaction provides a consistent impact on the athletes' performance. The analysis of the crowd noise can provide a global indication on the ongoing game situation, less conditioned by subjective factors that can influence a single fan. In this work, we exploit the collective intelligence of the audience of a robot soccer match to improve the performance of the robot players. In particular, audio features extracted from the crowd noise are used in a Reinforcement Learning process to possibly modify the game strategy. The effectiveness of the proposed approach is demonstrated by experiments on registered crowd noise samples from several past RoboCup SPL matches.

Keywords: Crowd noise interpretation · RoboCup SPL · Sound recognition

1 Introduction

Crowd noise is a crucial factor in sport competitions. The team designated as "home team", which enjoys a largely sympathetic crowd, is more likely to win with respect to the "away team". There is even evidence that, under certain conditions, the entire home advantage between the two teams is attributable to the crowd effect [3].

Sports psychology has highlighted the influence of the fans in the behavior of athletes in competition. The "hometeam effect" is the psychological advantage offered to a team when it plays in its own field, with its fans' support, which has a significant positive impact on the team's performance [13]. Athletes in

---

E. Antonioni and V. Suriani—These two authors contributed equally.

R. Alami et al. (Eds.): RoboCup 2021, LNAI 13132, pp. 153–164, 2022.
https://doi.org/10.1007/978-3-030-98682-7_13

Fig. 1. Crowd sound wave for the second Maradona's goal in 1986 World Cup Argentina vs. England.

different sports (i.e., basketball, baseball, and golf) show the same behaviour: Positive cheering can improve their performance, while a negative cheering can instead decrease their results and increase the possibility of error [6].

Crowd Noise in Human Soccer. Audience sentiment is an extremely powerful index to infer the current context and the future evolution of a soccer game. This is particularly clear in the case of the famous second Diego Armando Maradona's goal during the match Argentina vs. England of the 1986 soccer World Cup (see Fig. 1). The audio signal presents an increasing average peak-to-peak amplitude that can be interpreted as proportional to the probability of watching a goal scored.

Since the COVID-19 lockdown, however, stadiums around the World have gone silent due to the lack of fans. At the reopening of the major competitions, it has been evident that the crowd noise is fundamental in giving matches energy and personality. One example can be found in Germany's top soccer league, the Bundesliga: After the first closed door matches with echoing and sterile atmosphere, carpet audio (from earlier matches) has been added to give viewers at home a more realistic experience. This was a major success as declared by Sky Deutschland [17].

Crowd Noise in RoboCup SPL. The RoboCup 2050 challenge consists in creating a team of fully autonomous humanoid robot soccer players able to win a real soccer game against the winner of the FIFA World Cup. To achieve this ambitious goal, the RoboCup soccer Standard Platform League (SPL) is committed in creating a more and more real-world game environment, e.g., using artificial turf, realistic ball, colored jersey, and avoiding visual landmarks [1]. The 2019 SPL Rule Book [10] states that "the robots must play without human control. Communication is only allowed among robots on the field and between the robots and the GameController". Moreover, "there are no restrictions on

(a) Large crowd around the field.

(b) Crowd sound when the ball was on the goal line without being kicked even if the robots where about to score.

Fig. 2. Moments of the RoboCup SPL 2016 final.

communication between robots in play on the field using visual signalling (e.g., gestures) or the robot's built-in microphones, speakers, and infrared transceivers". An example of gesture-based robot-to-robot communication between robots in play is presented in [5].

The 2019 SPL Rule Book states also that "if acoustic communication is used by both teams, they shall negotiate before the match how they can reduce interference. If only one team uses acoustic communication, the robots of the other team shall avoid producing any sound. In addition, both the teams and the audience shall avoid intentionally confusing the robots by producing similar sounds to those used for communication".

Our speculation is that the crowd noise is not a form of direct communication, but instead it is part of the playing environment. Figure 2 shows a moment of the

RoboCup SPL 2016 final with a large crowd around the field (see Fig. 2a). During that match, the involvement of the crowd was particularly intense, because the ball lied on the goal line for more than two minutes without being kicked even if the robots where about to score (see Fig. 2b).

Contributions. In this work, we present a method to integrate the external collective intelligence of the audience (made explicit in the form of the crowd sound) in the robot cognition process, thus increasing the robot's set of perceptions. The contribution of this paper is twofold. First, we present a strategy for improving the decision making process in robot soccer by conveniently interpreting the crowd noise. Second, we have created a dataset of sound samples extracted from different RoboCup SPL matches.

The rest of the paper is organized as follows. Section 2 provides a brief overview of the literature on the use of sound signals in robotics. Section 3 presents the Reinforcement Learning theory used in this work. Section 4 describes our approach and how to integrate the interpretation of the crowd noise in the robots' behaviours. Experimental results are shown in Sect. 5. Finally, conclusions and future directions are given in Sect. 6.

2   Related Work

Due to the effect that the crowd noise has on the game result, its analysis is useful to understand the evolution of the game. In 2018, Wimbledon used IBM Watson to assist production teams in selecting highlights automatically. By considering player emotion, movement, and crowd noise, Watson was able to determine the must-see moments to include faster than human operators [7]. In the case of IBM Watson at Wimbledon, the goal was to select which game situations might be interesting to a TV audience. In the general case of an autonomous agent (e.g., a robot) instead, we can use the semantic information inferred from the crowd noise to reinforce the internal knowledge of the agent.

Use of Sound in Robotics. Speech recognition techniques are part of the core functionalities of Human-Robot interaction systems. However, the audio source is usually filtered and the noise discarded. In the so-called cocktail party problems [8], mixtures of sounds coming from different sources are processed to recognize and track multiple talkers [9]. The problem of interpreting ambiguous auditory data has been tackled using a generative probabilistic model and an active binaural hearing system, allowing a robot to robustly perform sound-source separation and localization by achieving a robust sound-source separation and localization [4].

Apart from understanding the semantic content of the sound stream (e.g., natural language), sound processing has been also exploited to recognize recurring sound patterns that provide context about the environment. For example, in [18], a household robot has been used to detect abnormal events by utilizing video and audio information. Mel frequency cepstral coefficients (MFCC) is used to extract features from audio information and these features have been

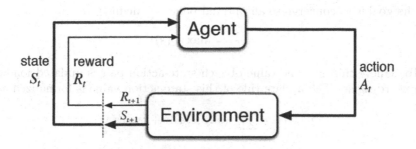

Fig. 3. Reinforcement learning general concept diagram.

used as input to a support vector machine classifier for analysis. MFCCs have been also used in [2] to identify sounds relevant to a fire-fighter mobile robot, such as people in distress, structural failure, fire, fire trucks, and crowds. The outputs of the classifier are then used as alerts for the fire-fighter or to modify the configuration of a robot capable of navigating unstructured terrain.

In this work, we rely on MFCCs to extract information from the audience noise during RoboCup SPL soccer matches.

3   Reinforcement Learning Background

Robot soccer is an excellent environment for testing the generalization capability of the robot players, since the playing scenario presents high perception noise, adversarial multi-robot problems, unexpected events, and interventions by external agents (e.g., the referee). Given the environment's similarities to real-world soccer, the algorithmic solution used on soccer robots could imitate the processes that affect human players.

In particular, crowd noise can be modelled as a stimulus for the agent. The fans can punish a wrong action with a negative roar or can reward a correct action that could lead to a positive result with cheers and ovations. This behavior is very similar to that commonly associated with reward signals in decision processes such as Markov Decision Processes [16] or the Option Framework [12]. For this reason, the use of reward signals for behavior development leads intuitively to the idea of Reinforcement Learning (RL) [14].

Through the use of RL algorithms, in fact, an agent can build an optimal policy using the rewards obtained from the interaction with the environment (see Fig. 3). Following a policy π defined as

$$\pi = S \times A \tag{1}$$

the agent can collect the rewards obtained and update its policy to maximize the expected value of its cumulative reward. This can be formalized as

$$v_\pi(s) = E_\pi[\sum_{k=0}^{\infty} \gamma^k r_k] \tag{2}$$

The goal is to converge to an optimal policy π^* defined as

$$v_{\pi^*}(s) = \max_{\pi} v_{\pi}(s) \tag{3}$$

To achieve this goal the value of each state-action pair is updated following the reward signal. The update rule of this state-action value is formalized as

$$q_{\pi}(s, a) = \sum_{s'} p(s', r|s, a)[r + \gamma v_{\pi}(s')] \tag{4}$$

At this point, after the collection of new rewards from the environment, the policy π can be updated to a new policy π'

$$\pi'(s) = \operatorname*{argmax}_{a} q(s, a) \tag{5}$$

After each update the policy will converge a little bit more towards the optimal policy.

Using the crowd roars as sparse reinforcement learning signals is possible to improve the robot policy, giving the agent a feedback about the effects of its actions. As an athlete can obtain positive improvements listening to the reaction of the crowd to its movements on the field, a robotic agent can store such information in the form of a value function that will guide its policy both in the present game and in the future ones.

4   Material and Methods

The audience sound in human soccer matches is characterized by time intervals (aka segments) with different levels of noise. For example, in a goal move, the audience tends to cheer up the ball carrier to encourage him to kick when he/she is near the goal, while the crowd is almost silent when the ball is far from the goal. To confirm that even in the RoboCup environment we have the same pattern, we have created an annotated dataset containing video of recent RoboCup matches, which have been manipulated to extract audio segments. In particular, the audio tracks have been extracted on wav format and qualitatively analyzed on their waveforms. Then, the audio have been classified and analized by using the Librosa[1] library.

RoboCup SPL Crowd Sound Dataset. Due to lack of recordings from NAO robot microphones, the online available videos of the RoboCup finals have been used to gather the audio from the crowd. To this end, we collected the video of the SPL finals of RoboCup competitions from 2016 to 2019 and GermanOpen 2019. These videos have been analyzed to find out intervals of interest. In this analysis, considering the moves of the robots in the videos, we labeled the intervals with three values, i.e., **Highlights**, **Potential goal moves**, and **Goal moves**. All

---

[1] https://librosa.org/.

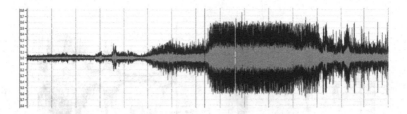

Fig. 4. The waveform of a SPL goal move. It is possible to observe an increment of the audience cheering while the robot in kicking toward the goal.

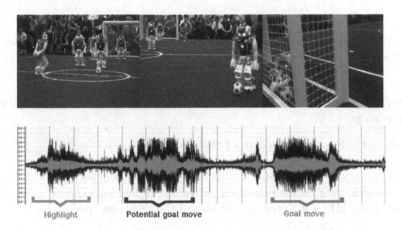

Fig. 5. The waveform and the corresponding pictures of a SPL goal move taken from the final match of the Robocup 2019.

these labeled situations are publicly released and can be found at: https://sites. google.com/unibas.it/crowdsounddataset

The inspection of the file audio allowed to recognize the audience cheering before a goal. As can be seen in Fig. 4, the waveform in a goal move has a substantial increment of the audience cheering.

The morphology of the waveforms have been mapped to the respective game moves in order to show how the audio from the audience evolve during particular game situations. One of these situations is shown in Fig. 5.

Analysing and labelling all the noise increasing situations on the final match of the last SPL RoboCup competitions, it has been noted how the increment of the noise in the waveforms has a similar pattern in corresponding situations. In Fig. 6, the waveforms of two kicks situations are shown. It is possible to establish some similarities even though they belong to different RoboCup matches.

Audio Feature Extraction. In order to extract the audio features from the audio segments mapped to the chosen game moves, we rely on the *MFCCs* (Mel-frequency cepstral coefficients). These coefficients are the amplitudes of the

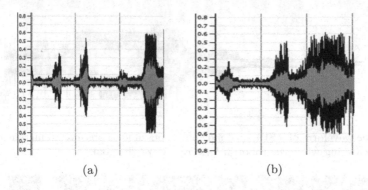

(a)   (b)

Fig. 6. Waveforms of two kicks situations from different matches. a) RoboCup 2019 SPL final match. b) RoboCup 2019 SPL semi-final match.

mel-frequency cepstrum (MFC). As in [11], these coefficients are derived following these steps:

1. Perform the Fourier transform of the signal;
2. Map the powers of the spectrum obtained onto the mel scale;
3. Take the logs of the powers at each of the mel frequencies;
4. Take the discrete cosine transform of the list of mel log powers;
5. Extract the MFCCs as the amplitudes of the resulting spectrum.

The obtained MFC is a compact representation of the short-term power spectrum of a sound, based on a linear cosine transform of a log power spectrum on a nonlinear *Mel scale* of frequency. This scale relates the perceived frequency of a tone to the actual measured frequency. Hence, it is used to scale the frequency in order to match more closely what the human ear can hear.

Humans are capable to identify more precisely small changes in sound or speech at lower frequencies, but it is much harder to differentiate between sounds at higher frequencies. By adopting this transformation, sounds of equal distance on the Mel Scale are perceived to be of equal distance to humans. The transformation from the Hertz scale to the Mel Scale is:

$$m = 1127 \cdot \ln\left(1 + \frac{f}{700}\right) \tag{6}$$

With this change of scale, the distance that a human perceives between two sets of sounds can be measured and used to our audio analysis, mimicking our own perception of sound.

To conduct this analysis we rely on the Librosa library and we analyse all the set of sounds, classifying them in the three categories (Highlights, Potential goal moves, Goal moves) of audience noise. More in detail, we perform the feature extraction by using 3 MFCC components using the *librosa.feature.mfcc* tool. On these 3 components, we set up thresholds to identify the three categories. MFCC allowed to be more robust in the identification of patterns in the audience noise.

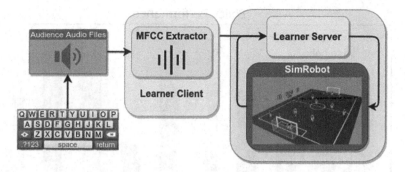

Fig. 7. The system architecture with the keyboard that can be used to generate the audience noise, the feature extractor of the audio files, and the learner's client and server.

5   Experimental Evaluation

Given the constraint imposed by the global COVID-19 pandemic, it has been impossible for us to perform experiments with a real crowd in a real-world scenario. To simulate the crowd behavior, we used an external software client and a set of pre-registered audio signals from the recording of past RoboCup competitions, the system diagram can be seen in Fig. 7. We have obtained the base policy used in these experiments using a DDQN algorithm [15]. In this section, we will compare the results obtained by the base policy with the ones obtained by the new policy improved using the audio signals from the crowd.

5.1   Experimental Setup

The scenario considered for the experiment is the one of a robot soccer player which has to carry the ball to the goal in the presence of three static opponents randomly placed on the field. The robot receives a positive reward for moving the ball towards the opponent's goal and a negative reward for moving the ball towards one of the opponent's robots.

The DDQN algorithm used for obtaining the base policy relies on two networks consisting of 4 hidden layers of 256 neurons each, $\gamma = 0.99$, and $\epsilon = 0.05$.

The source code with the audio parser and the learner can be found at the following public repository https://github.com/SPQRTeam/PolicyImprovementWithAudienceNoise.

5.2   Policy Improvement

After completing the learning phase to generate the basic policy through the use of the DDQN algorithm, we further change the robot's policy by using an external software client capable of playing and simulating crowd audio signals. A human operator (chosen among the members of the SPQR Team) selects,

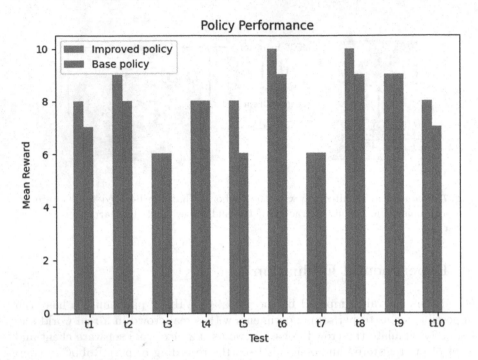

Fig. 8. Policy rollout results on ten games after training.

according to the situations in the field, which audio signals to play, dividing them into three categories: (1) Low signal, (2) Medium signal, (3) High signal. In cases where the robot switches from a lower to a higher signal, we assign a positive reward; otherwise, we assign no reward. Figure 8 shows the results obtained by the two different policies on ten games. It is possible to see that the intervention of a new reward signal, controlled by a human operator through the use of audio signals, has improved the overall policy performance, leading to better average results of the improved policy with respect to the base one.

5.3   Discussion

In this section, we have evaluated how audio signals from the crowd contribute to improve the policy efficiency of a RoboCup SPL player. The experimental evaluation focused on the ability of the player to dribble a set of obstacles and place itself and the ball in an advantageous position. The experiments show how the crowd's reactions improved the overall policy performance, with a better average result with respect to the original policy.

This result implies that often human response could be complicated to model and that, even if a standard reward signal is accurately crafted, there could still be some situations that are not completely embedded inside the reward function. In fact, crowd signals can help the agent learn from the collective intelligence behaviors that are not formalized inside the original policy developed by an expert.

Nowadays, robots are way more present in environments that also involve a large set of human operators. The idea of learning from the collective intelligence of the humans involved in the robot scenario could lead to future development in several robotics fields such as social assistive robots or industrial ones.

6 Conclusions and Future Directions

The goal of playing a soccer match in 2050 between the best robot team in RoboCup and the FIFA world champion team can be achieved by making robot players more and more similar to human ones. A key aspect of this process is to make robots able to perceive and understand the environment around them. Crowd noise and audience reactions represent a significant aspect of the environment and should be considered as part of the knowledge base of a humanoid soccer robot, due to their strong influence in the game result.

This paper is a first step in this direction. We provide a policy improvement system based on Reinforcement Learning to take into account audio signals from the RoboCup audience. Experimental results, conducted on a dataset of different SPL matches, show that robots can benefit from interpreting the fans' collective intelligence, and consequently, this can lead them to improve their capabilities to accomplish their task.

As future directions, we intend to test the proposed approach during future open door SPL matches with a real audience. Furthermore, we want to differentiate the audience signals into multiple subclasses to employ a wider set of reward signals.

References

1. Albani, D., Youssef, A., Suriani, V., Nardi, D., Bloisi, D.D.: A deep learning approach for object recognition with NAO soccer robots. In: Behnke, S., Sheh, R., Sariel, S., Lee, D.D. (eds.) RoboCup 2016. LNCS (LNAI), vol. 9776, pp. 392–403. Springer, Cham (2017). https://doi.org/10.1007/978-3-319-68792-6_33
2. Baum, E., Harper, M., Alicea, R., Ordonez, C.: Sound identification for fire-fighting mobile robots. In: 2018 Second IEEE International Conference on Robotic Computing (IRC), pp. 79–86. IEEE (2018)
3. Boudreaux, C.J., Sanders, S.D., Walia, B.: A natural experiment to determine the crowd effect upon home court advantage. J. Sports Econ. 18(7), 737–749 (2017). https://doi.org/10.1177/1527002515595842
4. Deleforge, A., Horaud, R.: The cocktail party robot: sound source separation and localisation with an active binaural head. In: 2012 7th ACM/IEEE International Conference on Human-Robot Interaction (HRI), pp. 431–438. IEEE (2012)
5. Di Giambattista, V., Fawakherji, M., Suriani, V., Bloisi, D.D., Nardi, D.: On field gesture-based robot-to-robot communication with NAO soccer players. In: Chalup, S., Niemueller, T., Suthakorn, J., Williams, M.-A. (eds.) RoboCup 2019. LNCS (LNAI), vol. 11531, pp. 367–375. Springer, Cham (2019). https://doi.org/10.1007/978-3-030-35699-6_28

6. Epting, L.K., Riggs, K.N., Knowles, J.D., Hanky, J.J.: Cheers vs. jeers: effects of audience feedback on individual athletic performance. North Am. J. Psychol. **13**(2) (2011)
7. Gilliland, N.: How wimbledon is using AI to enhance the fan experience (2018). https://econsultancy.com/how-wimbledon-is-using-ai-to-enhance-the-fan-experience/. Accessed 25 Mar 2021
8. Haykin, S., Chen, Z.: The cocktail party problem. Neural Comput. **17**(9), 1875–1902 (2005)
9. Okuno, H.G., Nakadai, K., Hidai, K.I., Mizoguchi, H., Kitano, H.: Human-robot interaction through real-time auditory and visual multiple-talker tracking. In: Proceedings 2001 IEEE/RSJ International Conference on Intelligent Robots and Systems. Expanding the Societal Role of Robotics in the the Next Millennium (Cat. No. 01CH37180), vol. 3, pp. 1402–1409. IEEE (2001)
10. RoboCup SPL Technical Committee: RoboCup Standard Platform League (NAO) Rule Book (2019). https://spl.robocup.org/wp-content/uploads/downloads/Rules2019.pdf. Accessed 26 Mar 2021
11. Sahidullah, M., Saha, G.: Design, analysis and experimental evaluation of block based transformation in MFCC computation for speaker recognition. Speech Commun. **54**(4), 543–565 (2012). https://doi.org/10.1016/j.specom.2011.11.004, https://www.sciencedirect.com/science/article/pii/S0167639311001622
12. Stolle, M., Precup, D.: Learning options in reinforcement learning. In: Koenig, S., Holte, R.C. (eds.) SARA 2002. LNCS (LNAI), vol. 2371, pp. 212–223. Springer, Heidelberg (2002). https://doi.org/10.1007/3-540-45622-8_16
13. Strauss, B., MacMahon, C.: Audience influences on athlete performances. In: Routledge Companion to Sport and Exercise Psychology. Global Perspectives and Fundamental Concepts, pp. 213–216. Routledge (2014)
14. Sutton, R.S., Barto, A.G.: Reinforcement Learning: An Introduction. MIT Press, Cambridge (2018)
15. Van Hasselt, H., Guez, A., Silver, D.: Deep reinforcement learning with double Q-learning. In: Proceedings of the AAAI Conference on Artificial Intelligence, vol. 30 (2016)
16. Van Otterlo, M., Wiering, M.: Reinforcement learning and Markov decision processes. In: Wiering, M., van Otterlo, M. (eds.) Reinforcement Learning. Adaptation, Learning, and Optimization, vol. 12, pp. 3–42. Springer, Heidelberg (2012). https://doi.org/10.1007/978-3-642-27645-3_1
17. Whiting, K.: This app lets sports fans cheer out loud in the stadium when watching remotely (2020). https://www.weforum.org/agenda/2020/06/sport-app-cheer-technology-japan-soccer-watch-remote-cheerer/. Accessed 25 Mar 2021
18. Wu, X., Gong, H., Chen, P., Zhong, Z., Xu, Y.: Surveillance robot utilizing video and audio information. J. Intell. Rob. Syst. **55**(4), 403–421 (2009)

rSoccer: A Framework for Studying Reinforcement Learning in Small and Very Small Size Robot Soccer

Felipe B. Martins[✉], Mateus G. Machado, Hansenclever F. Bassani,
Pedro H. M. Braga, and Edna S. Barros

Centro de Informática - Universidade Federal de Pernambuco,
Av. Jornalista Anibal Fernandes, s/n - CDU 50.740-560, Recife, PE, Brazil
{fbm2,mgm4,hfb,phmb4,ensb}@cin.ufpe.br

Abstract. Reinforcement learning is an active research area with a vast number of applications in robotics, and the RoboCup competition is an interesting environment for studying and evaluating reinforcement learning methods. A known difficulty in applying reinforcement learning to robotics is the high number of experience samples required, being the use of simulated environments for training the agents followed by transfer learning to real-world (sim-to-real) a viable path. This article introduces an open-source simulator for the IEEE Very Small Size Soccer and the Small Size League optimized for reinforcement learning experiments. We also propose a framework for creating OpenAI Gym environments with a set of benchmarks tasks for evaluating single-agent and multi-agent robot soccer skills. We then demonstrate the learning capabilities of two state-of-the-art reinforcement learning methods as well as their limitations in certain scenarios introduced in this framework. We believe this will make it easier for more teams to compete in these categories using end-to-end reinforcement learning approaches and further develop this research area.

Keywords: Reinforcement learning · OpenAI Gym · Continuous control · Robot soccer · Simulation

1 Introduction

Reinforcement Learning (RL) [22], in conjunction with the machine learning field, has obtained interesting results in progressively more complex decision-making competitive scenarios, such as learning how to play Atari games [25], Go [21], and Starcraft 2 [24], achieving or even surpassing human-level performance. In robotics, RL showed promising results in simulated and real-world environments, including approaches for motion planning, optimization, grasping, manipulation, and control [1,5,11].

Robot soccer competitions are an exciting field for researching and validating RL usage, as it involves robotic systems capable of tackling challenging sequential decision-making problems in a cooperative and competitive scenario [8].

© Springer Nature Switzerland AG 2022
R. Alami et al. (Eds.): RoboCup 2021, LNAI 13132, pp. 165–176, 2022.
https://doi.org/10.1007/978-3-030-98682-7_14

Developing those systems can be very hard using traditional methods in which hard-coded behaviors need to foresee a multitude of possibilities in an unpredictable game such as soccer.

In the RoboCup *Small Size League* (SSL) competition, Fig. 1(a), teams with up to eleven omnidirectional mobile robots compete against each other to score goals within a set of complex rules, such as limiting how far a robot can move with the ball, therefore requiring explicit cooperation. Previous works in this setting have successfully learned specific skills, such as moving to the ball, kicking, and defending penalties by using RL control approaches [26–28]. However, those works did not make the learning environment available, which can hinder reproducibility.

On the other hand, achieving an end-to-end control policy capable of cooperating on a robot soccer match is still an open problem, requiring even further research and development as the league evolves. Similarly, training a single policy capable of controlling a complete SSL team is also challenging, as the total number of control actions increases with the number of robots.

The *IEEE Very Small Size Soccer* (VSSS) competition, Fig. 1(b), compared to the SSL, establishes teams with three robots each, with a smaller field and robot sizes. The robot hardware does not have ball dribbling and kicking capabilities, and a match does not require explicit cooperation, by the rules. Although the differential drive robots used pose a more challenging path planning, the league can be seen as a simplified version of the SSL. In this domain, earlier work applied RL for learning specific skills [6]. And more recently, Bassani et al. [3] achieved 4th place in an international VSSS competition, using an end-to-end learned control without explicit cooperation and made the learning environments publicly available. Still, they do not support the SSL setting and are not easily adaptable for different scenarios.

(a) SSL   (b) IEEE VSSS

Fig. 1. Competition environments of SSL and IEEE VSS.

We consider that by supplying a simpler path towards creating and using RL SSL environments, the results achieved by Bassani et al. [3] can be replicated on the SSL competition and be further used to encourage RL approaches in the SSL context. In summary, the contributions of the present work are the following:

1. An open-source framework following the OpenAI Gym [4] standards for developing robot soccer RL environments, modeling multi-agent tasks in competitive and cooperative scenarios;
2. An open-source SSL and VSSS robot soccer simulator, adapted from the grSim Simulator [16], focused on RL use;
3. A set of eight benchmark learning environments with a focus on reproducibility, for evaluating RL algorithms in robot soccer tasks, including four tasks based on the RoboCup SSL 2021 hardware challenges.

The rest of this article is organized as follows: Sect. 2 presents related work on robot soccer simulators and environments. Section 3 describes the proposed framework. Section 4 introduces a set of benchmark environments created using the proposed framework. Section 5 presents the results, and finally, Sect. 6 draws the conclusions and suggests future work.

2   Related Works

There is a large variety of RL environments and frameworks on the literature which aim at allowing the easy reproduction of state-of-the-art RL algorithms results, such as the OpenAI Gym [4]. However, the existing robot soccer environments lack the needed characteristics, such as extensibility to different scenarios, proper real-world robot simulation, and hard to reproduce results. Therefore, they do not apply to the RoboCup categories. These issues are discussed as follows.

Suitable Frameworks. There are frameworks for simulating soccer matches such as the RoboCup's Soccer 2D [9] and The Google Research Football Environment [10]. However, the actions defined are too high level. The DeepMind MuJoCo Multi-Agent Soccer Environment [13] define low-level actions such as accelerating and rotating the body, but it is not related to a real robot soccer league. Bassani et al. [3] proposed an framework for the VSSS setting, but it does not enable the creation of new scenarios. Although Robocup's Soccer 3D provides a low-level action and believable environment, there is no framework that enables the creation of scenarios.

Simulator's Purpose. There are well known simulators for robot soccer competitions such as SSL [16] and VSSS [15,19]. They provide a real-time simulated environment with a rich graphical interface for developing robot soccer algorithms. However, the preferences for RL are simulation speed and synchronous communication.

Reproducibility Issues. Previous work achieved interesting results using RL in robot soccer competition settings [6,20,26]. But they do not describe the environments and simulators used nor made them openly available, coupled with a lack of clearly defined tasks and availability of stable baseline implementations of robot soccer agents, poses several issues to the advancement of research in this field.

3   rSoccer Gym Framework

The proposed framework[1] is a tool for creating robot soccer environments ranging from simple single-agent tasks to complex multi-robot competitive cooperative scenarios.

It is defined by three modules: **simulator**, **environment**, and **render**. The
simulator module describes the physics simulation. The environment module is
designed to receive the agent action, communicate with the other modules, and
return the new observations and rewards. The render module does the environment visualization. Figure 2 illustrates the modules architecture. A set of
data structures labeled **entities** are defined to enable a common communication between modules for every environment. The following subsections describe
these modules and *entities*.

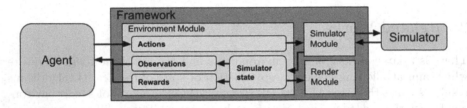

Fig. 2. Framework modules architecture

3.1   Entities

The *entities* structures are standardized for consistency by defining positional
values using the field center as a reference point. The units conform to the
International System of Units (SI), except for robot angular position and speed
values which are in degrees. The following *entities* are defined:

- *Ball*: Contains the ball position and velocity values and is used both to read
  the current state or to set the initial position;
- *Robot*: Contains a robot identification, flags, position, velocity, and wheel
  desired speed values. Used to read the current state, to set the initial position,
  or to send control commands;
- *Frame*: Contains a *Ball entity* and *Robot entities* for each robot in the environment, structured in a way that each robot is easily indexable by team
  color and id. Used to store the complete state of the simulation;
- *Field*: Contains specifications of the simulation values, such as the field and
  robot geometry and parameters.

---

[1] Code available at https://github.com/robocin/rSoccer.

3.2   Simulator Module

The simulator module carries out the environment physics calculations. It communicates directly with the environment module, receiving actions and returning the simulation state.

For physics calculations, we developed the rSim[2] simulator specially for RL. It was based on the grSim simulator [16], due to its reliable physical simulation, with the following modifications:

- Removal of graphical interfaces to increase performance, reduce memory usage, and ease server deployment on headless servers;
- Synchronous operation for more consistent training results as in an asynchronous setting the synchronization between agents and simulator may depend on hardware performance;
- Support for a different number of robots in each team, to enable more environment possibilities;
- Split simulated objects collision spaces to create separate collision groups;
- Added motor speed constraints matching real-world observations;
- Enable cylinder collision, removing the dummy collision object to reduce the total number of simulated bodies;
- Defined direct simulator calls in Python for fast communication. Enabling the instantiation of multiple simulators without the need to manage network communication ports.

Although the simulator is external to the framework, the simulator module abstracts its interface. Table 1 presents the rSim simulator performance in comparison with the grSim simulator in headless mode for a different number of robots on field. The grSim used in the comparison had slight modifications for removing frequency limits, and it also includes a modified version with synchronous operations for comparison.

Table 1. Simulation performance in average and standart deviation of steps per second, for 1, 6 and 11 SSL robots in each team.

Simulator	1 vs 1	6 vs 6	11 vs 11
grSim (asynchronous)	2167.9 (8.4)	408.7 (0.3)	228.3 (0.1)
grSim (synchronous)	1894.0 (8.4)	390.0 (0.5)	219.0 (0.7)
rSim (proposed, synchronous)	**2408.8 (9.3)**	**510.8 (1.8)**	**288.0 (0.4)**

3.3   Environment Module

The environment module is where the environment task itself is defined. It implements the interface with the agent and communication with the other framework

---

[2] Code available at https://github.com/robocin/rSim.

modules. The interface with the agent complies with the OpenAI Gym [4] framework, and it communicates with the other modules using the *entities* structures.

The use of common interfaces enables the definition of base environments, which handle the communications with the other modules and the compliance with Gym. The framework provides benchmark environments of important tasks related to the RoboCup challenges [9], serving as examples and making it easier for other researchers to develop and evaluate new RL methods in these benchmark scenarios. The work needed for defining a new environment consists of the implementation of only four methods:

- **get_commands:** Returns a list of *Robot entities* containing the commands which are sent to the simulator;
- **frame_to_observations:** Returns an observation array which will be forwarded to the agent as defined by the environment;
- **calculate_reward_and_done:** Returns both the calculated step reward and a boolean value indicating if the current state is terminal;
- **get_initial_positions_frame:** Returns a *Frame entity* used to define the initial positions of the ball and robots.

3.4 Render Module

Although we explicitly removed the graphical interface from the simulator for performance, the render module enables visualization without previous drawbacks. It renders on-demand a 2D image of the field and has no performance reduction when not in use. Its implementation is independent of the simulator and enables it to be used at training time for monitoring purposes since it is based on the Gym base environment solution.

4   Proposed Robot Soccer Environments

Due to the differences of the leagues mentioned in Sect. 1, we propose a complete soccer game environment based on Latin American Robotics Competition competition for the VSSS and simple skills learning environments for the SSL.

A *state* is defined as the complete set of data returned by the simulator after a performed action and an *observation* as a subset or transformation of this state. On the following proposed environments, we described the state by positions (x, y), angles (θ), and velocity $(vx, vy, v\theta)$ of each object (ball, teammate, and opponent) in reference to the field center. On the SSL environments there is an additional *Infrared sensor* (IR) signal of each robot, indicating if the ball is in contact with the kicking device.

4.1   IEEE Very Small Size League Environments

Based on Bassani et al. [3], we developed a single and a multi-agent benchmark for the VSSS league. The observation is the complete state defined above. We describe the actions of each robot as the power percentage for each wheel that the robot will apply in the next step. For the non-controlled agents, we use a random policy based on Ornstein-Uhlenbeck process (OU) [2]. The OU process creates a more continuous motion trend for a few steps, which allows the agents to follow a more structured random trajectory instead of just oscillating around the initial point. An episode finishes if the agent received/scored a goal or if the timer reaches 30 s of simulation. In the **IEEE VSSS Single-Agent** environment, only one robot learns a policy, and the other five (two teammates and three opponents) follow a random policy that consists of executing actions sampled according to the OU process. In the **IEEE VSSS Multi-Agent** environment, the controlled robots share the learning policy. See on Fig. 3(a) the rendered Frame entity of the IEEE VSSS environments.

4.2   Small Size League Environments

The first environment developed is the basic GoToBall. The other environments were based on RoboCup's 2021 hardware challenge [17].

The actions of the SSL environments are the global frame velocities on each axis, kick power, and dribbler state (on/off). For all environments, we defined rewards based on energy spent by the robot, its distance to the ball, and for reaching the objective.

The **GoToBall** environment is the most straightforward skill to be learned. In this environment, the controlled agent must reach the ball and position its IR sensor on it, i.e., arriving at the ball at a certain angle. The episode ends when the robot completes the objective, if the agent exits the field limits, or if the simulation timer reaches 30 s. See on Fig. 3(b) an example of rendered Frame of the environment.

The **Hardware Challenges** environments consist of four environments based on RoboCup's 2021 hardware challenges. We made certain simplifications to the original environments to make them learnable by the currently available methods in a reasonable amount of time [17]. They are:

1. **Static Defenders:** the episode begins with the controlled agent in the field center and 6 opponents and the ball randomly positioned in opponent's field. The episode ends if the agent scores a goal, the ball or the agent exits the opponent's field, the agent collides with an opponent, or the timer reaches 30 simulated seconds. See on Fig. 3(c) an example of initial Frame.
2. **Contested Possession:** the episode begins with the controlled agent in the field center and an opponent is randomly positioned in the opponent's field, with the ball on its dribbler. The objective of this challenge is to sneak the ball from the opponent and score a goal. The episode ends with the same conditions of the Static Denfenders environment. See on Fig. 3(d) an example of initial Frame.
3. **Dribbling:** the episode begins with the controlled agent in the field center with the ball on its dribbler and four opponent robots positioned in a sparse row, leaving "gates" between each of them. The objective of this challenge is

to dribble the ball while the agent moves through these gates. The episode ends if the agent collides with any robot or exits the field. See on Fig. 3(e) an example of the initial Frame.

4. **Pass Endurance (single and multi-agent):** the episode begins with the two robots at random positions, with the ball on the dribbler of one of them. There are no opponents in this environment. In the single-agent environment, the objective is to perform a pass in three seconds. For the multi-agent, they have to perform as many passes as possible in 30 s. The episode ends if a pass does not reach the teammate or if the time is out. See on Fig. 3(f) an example of initial Frame.

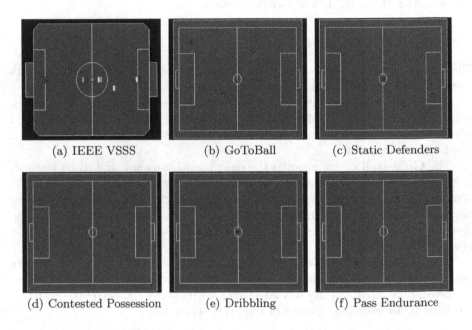

(a) IEEE VSSS   (b) GoToBall   (c) Static Defenders

(d) Contested Possession   (e) Dribbling   (f) Pass Endurance

Fig. 3. Initial states of the proposed benchmark environments.

5   Experimental Results

This section presents and discusses the results obtained on our framework with two state-of-the-art deep reinforcement learning methods for continuous control.

We chose Deep Deterministic Policy Gradient (DDPG) [12] and Soft Actor Critic (SAC) [7] because both are known for presenting great performance in robot control environments such as Deepmind Control Suite [23]. We have also tested Proximal Policy Approximation (PPO) [18], however, despite all our efforts in parameter tuning, it was not able to learn even in the easiest environments. Therefore, we concentrated our efforts on DDPG and SAC. On the

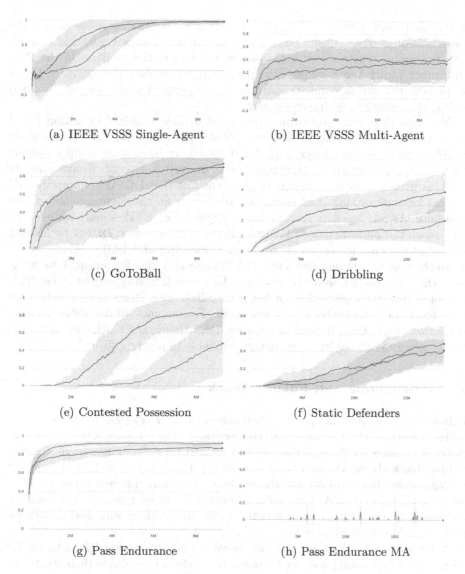

(a) IEEE VSSS Single-Agent

(b) IEEE VSSS Multi-Agent

(c) GoToBall

(d) Dribbling

(e) Contested Possession

(f) Static Defenders

(g) Pass Endurance

(h) Pass Endurance MA

Fig. 4. Mean (lines) and standard deviation (shades) of the results obtained for each environment (DDPG in blue and SAC in orange). The Y axis represents: Goal Score for a, b, e, and f; Ball Reached for c; Number of gates transversed for d; Inverse Distance to Receiver for g; and Pass Score for h. (Color figure online)

multi-agent environments, we used a shared policy to control all agents. For each environment, we executed five runs of each method. We ran 10 million steps for each experiment, except for the Dribbling and Static Defenders environments, in which we ran 20 million steps. For the IEEE VSSS environments, Contested Possession and Static Defenders we use the goal score to evaluate the agents.

In the GoToBall, and Dribbling we evaluate if the agents complete or not the respective objective. In the Pass Endurance Single-Agent we used $1/d$ to evaluate the agent, where d is the distance of the ball to the receiver. In the Pass Endurance Multi-Agent we used the pass score to evaluate the agent. In Fig. 4 we present the average and standard deviation of the learning curves obtained with each method in each environment.

We note that both algorithms presented a high standard deviation in all environments, except Pass Endurance. We also point out that DDPG was more sample efficient in most tasks (Fig. 4(a) to 4(e)), an interesting result considering SAC usually performs better than DDPG in continuous control environments [7]. This performance may be explained by the fact that DDPG employs the OU process for exploration, which seems to suite better for the environments considered here. As SAC uses an entropy-based exploration, it takes more samples for it to reach the performance of DDPG, although it surpassed DDPG by a small margin at the end, in certain environments (Fig. 4(c) and 4(f)).

In the multi-agent environments (IEEE VSSS and Pass Endurance), we highlight that the results were worse than the respective single-agent ones. This indicates that the agents did not learn to collaborate, since more agents were expected to perform better than a single one. For instance, in the VSSS, a visual inspection revels that, instead of collaborating, the agents block each other, as can be observed in the frame sequences available in our repository[3].

6   Conclusions and Future Work

This article presented an open-source framework for developing robot soccer RL environments for the VSSS and SSL competitions. The framework includes a simulator optimized for RL experiments and an API for defining new environments compatible with the OpenAI Gym standards. It also provides eight benchmark environments that can evaluate RL methods regarding different types of robot soccer challenges. The API is easily extensible for other types of environments and tasks. The simulator can be replaced by an interface with real robots for evaluating Sim-to-Real as in [3].

With this, we aim to put forward research and application RL methods for robot soccer by making it easier for other researchers to evaluate their strategies and compare the results in standardized scenarios, therefore improving reproducibility.

Although our results are promising in certain tasks, achieving better results than we would be able to achieve with traditional handcrafted methods, it also makes it clear that much research is needed to achieve an effective robot soccer team trained end-to-end by reinforcement learning. Studying why PPO performed so poorly is essential for our future works, once it achieved interesting results on other studies. The multi-agent (Fig. 4(b), 4(f)) and the Static Defenders Fig. 4(h) environments show that certain benchmarks are too difficult for the

---

[3] https://github.com/robocin/rSoccer.

currently available methods, indicating an open area of research. In the Static Defenders environment, the best reward function we developed seems inadequate when the dimensionality of the observations increases, hence the poor results. In multi-agent environments, the methods could not learn to cooperate using a shared policy. However, we believe that multi-agent specific algorithms focusing on collaboration such as MADDPG [14] would improve the results.

Acknowledgments. The authors would like to thank RoboCIn - UFPE Team and Mila - Quebec Artificial Intelligence Institute for the collaboration and resources provided; Conselho Nacional de Desenvolvimento Científico e Tecnológico (CNPq), and Coordenação de Aperfeiçoamento de Pessoal de Nível Superior (CAPES) for financial support. Moreover, the authors also gratefully acknowledge the support of NVIDIA Corporation with the donation of the RTX 2080 Ti GPU used for this research.

References

1. Andrychowicz, M., et al.: Learning dexterous in-hand manipulation. arXiv preprint arXiv:1808.00177 (2018)
2. Arnold, L.: Stochastic Differential Equations. New York (1974)
3. Bassani, H.F., et al.: A framework for studying reinforcement learning and sim-to-real in robot soccer (2020)
4. Brockman, G., et al.: OpenAI gym (2016)
5. Christiano, P., et al.: Transfer from simulation to real world through learning deep inverse dynamics model. arXiv preprint arXiv:1610.03518 (2016)
6. Duan, Y., Liu, Q., Xu, X.: Application of reinforcement learning in robot soccer. Eng. Appl. Artif. Intell. **20**(7), 936–950 (2007)
7. Haarnoja, T., et al.: Soft actor-critic algorithms and applications. arXiv preprint arXiv:1812.05905 (2018)
8. Kim, J.H., Kim, D.H., Kim, Y.J., Seow, K.T.: Soccer Robotics, vol. 11. Springer, Heidelberg (2004). https://doi.org/10.1007/b95999
9. Kitano, H., Asada, M., Kuniyoshi, Y., Noda, I., Osawa, E.: RoboCup: the robot world cup initiative. In: Proceedings of the First International Conference on Autonomous Agents, AGENTS 1997, pp. 340–347. Association for Computing Machinery, New York (1997). https://doi.org/10.1145/267658.267738
10. Kurach, K., et al.: Google research football: a novel reinforcement learning environment. arXiv preprint arXiv:1907.11180 (2019)
11. Levine, S., Finn, C., Darrell, T., Abbeel, P.: End-to-end training of deep visuomotor policies. J. Mach. Learn. Res. **17**(1), 1334–1373 (2016)
12. Lillicrap, T.P., et al.: Continuous control with deep reinforcement learning. arXiv preprint arXiv:1509.02971 (2015)
13. Liu, S., Lever, G., Merel, J., Tunyasuvunakool, S., Heess, N., Graepel, T.: Emergent coordination through competition (2019)
14. Lowe, R., Wu, Y., Tamar, A., Harb, J., Abbeel, O.P., Mordatch, I.: Multi-agent actor-critic for mixed cooperative-competitive environments. In: Advances in Neural Information Processing Systems, pp. 6379–6390 (2017)
15. Monajjemi, V., Koochakzadeh, A.: FIRASim (2020). https://github.com/fira-simurosot/FIRASim. Accessed 28 Apr 2021

16. Monajjemi, V., Koochakzadeh, A., Ghidary, S.S.: grSim – RoboCup small size robot soccer simulator. In: Röfer, T., Mayer, N.M., Savage, J., Saranlı, U. (eds.) RoboCup 2011. LNCS (LNAI), vol. 7416, pp. 450–460. Springer, Heidelberg (2012). https://doi.org/10.1007/978-3-642-32060-6_38

17. RoboCup: Robocup small size league (SSL) hardware challenges 2021. https://robocup-ssl.github.io/ssl-hardware-challenge-rules/rules.html. Accessed 04 Aug 2021

18. Schulman, J., Wolski, F., Dhariwal, P., Radford, A., Klimov, O.: Proximal policy optimization algorithms. arXiv preprint arXiv:1707.06347 (2017)

19. SDK, V.: VSS SDK (2019). https://vss-sdk.github.io/book/general.html. Accessed 5 Apr 2021

20. Shi, H., Lin, Z., Hwang, K.S., Yang, S., Chen, J.: An adaptive strategy selection method with reinforcement learning for robotic soccer games. IEEE Access **6**, 8376–8386 (2018)

21. Silver, D., et al.: Mastering the game of go without human knowledge. Nature **550**(7676), 354–359 (2017)

22. Sutton, R.S., Barto, A.G.: Reinforcement Learning: An Introduction. MIT Press, Cambridge (2018)

23. Tassa, Y., et al.: DeepMind control suite (2018)

24. Vinyals, O., et al.: AlphaStar: mastering the real-time strategy game starcraft ii. DeepMind Blog (2019)

25. Volodymyr, M., Kavukcuoglu, K., Silver, D., Graves, A., Antonoglou, I.: Playing atari with deep reinforcement learning. In: NIPS Deep Learning Workshop (2013)

26. Yoon, M.: Developing basic soccer skills using reinforcement learning for the RoboCup small size league. Ph.D. thesis, Stellenbosch: Stellenbosch University (2015)

27. Zhu, Y., Schwab, D., Veloso, M.: Learning primitive skills for mobile robots. In: 2019 International Conference on Robotics and Automation (ICRA), pp. 7597–7603 (2019)

28. Zolanvari, A., Shirazi, M., Menhaj, M.: A Q-learning approach for controlling a robotic goalkeeper during penalty procedure. In: 2019 II International Congress on Science and Engineering, Hamburg-Germany, pp. 1–12 (2019)

Optimized Wireless Control and Telemetry Network for Mobile Soccer Robots

Lucas Cavalcanti$^{(\boxtimes)}$, Riei Joaquim$^{(\boxtimes)}$, and Edna Barros$^{(\boxtimes)}$

Centro de Informática, Universidade Federal de Pernambuco, Av. Prof. Moraes Rego, 1235 - Cidade Universitária, Recife, Pernambuco, Brazil
{lhcs,rjmr,ensb}@cin.ufpe.br

Abstract. In a diverse set of robotics applications, including RoboCup categories, mobile robots require control commands to interact with surrounding environment correctly. These control commands should come wirelessly to not interfere in robots' movement; also, the communication has a set of requirements, including low latency and consistent delivery. This paper presents a complete communication architecture consisting of computer communication with a base station, which transmits the data to robots and returns robots telemetry to the computer. With the proposed communication, it is possible to send messages in less than 4.5 ms for six robots with telemetry enables in all of them.

Keywords: Wireless · Communication · Base-station · Mobile robots · RoboCup ssl

1 Introduction

Competitions like RoboCup, the most significant autonomous robotics competition, creates high dynamic environments where robots should play soccer autonomously against another team [3]. The soccer competition is perfect for developing interdisciplinary technologies, as it has obstacles and target positions are moving, similar to industries and warehouses. That dynamic requires accurate sensing of the field situation, combined with fast decision algorithms and real-time control.

With the evolution of wireless technologies, it became present in diverse solutions, including Industry 4.0 and smart houses. Moreover, in soccer categories, like Small Size Soccer (SSL) [12], where a team of multiples robots plays soccer autonomously against another team, each team needs to communicate wirelessly with its robots. This communication is responsible for sending movements that the robot should follow on the field.

At the Small Size Soccer (SSL), motion control is considered a system output where a complex robotic system is required. Furthermore, for wireless control

Supported by RobôCIn, FACEPE and Centro de Informática - UFPE.

R. Alami et al. (Eds.): RoboCup 2021, LNAI 13132, pp. 177–188, 2022.
https://doi.org/10.1007/978-3-030-98682-7_15

robots, high accuracy and speed are needed. Then, communication is a critical factor to move the robots precisely. In the 2019 RoboCup, some SSL teams had communication failures, which delayed its game. Also, there were teams with special requirements to avoid failures that affects the control of robots.

Besides the soccer robots, other applications, like industrial robots, require reliable wireless communication. Then, the main goal of this work is to propose an efficient wireless network for mobile robots. This work analyzes the network qualities through the application in SSL competition, using RobôCIn's robots. For bringing the needed efficiency, the proposed network aims to reduce latency when sending control packets. It is achieved with a communication technology analysis, together with the embedded system design. This work goes more in-depth, building and analyzing peripherals connections, configurations, and proposing a protocol that minimizes data usage.

Considering that robots should be monitored, this work also brings a telemetry network without affecting the control latency to a point where control is compromised. Telemetry consists of sending information from robots, to the computer, giving the team's software the robot status. The telemetry network leverages the challenge because multiple robots should receive and send messages from one base station.

This work is divided as follows: Sect. 2 is a short introduction to wireless technologies and other team networks. In Sect. 3, the proposed system is described, together with the SSL application description. In Sect. 4, the test method alongside the results is shown and discussed. Finally, in Sect. 5, the conclusion of this work is presented.

2   Background and Related Work

This section goes through the technologies and characteristics necessary to build a radio frequency control network capable of controlling a mobile robot in real-time.

2.1   Requirements of Wireless Communication

Wireless networks increase their usage, getting cheaper and better year over year. It is possible to see these technologies applied in Internet of Things (IoT) and Industry 4.0. Another application field affected by wireless technology is the Wireless Networked Control Systems (WNCS) [10]. It requires flexibility in wireless communication; however, the main focus is on controlling a remote system.

The system model with a WNCS has a higher risk because wireless may have bits failures, data loss, delay, and other problems due to environmental uncertainty and technologies. These problems increase the misbehaviors rate.

Besides the communication reliability, WNCS also requires low energy consumption to increase the system autonomy and high transference bandwidth to exchange the information needed [10].

2.2   Transmission Technology

The technology for a wireless communication system needs to match the application requirements. The requirements matching reduces the risk of failure or malfunctioning. Several wireless technologies and protocols have been developed in the last years, and concepts like ubiquitous computing appeared.

There are several technologies and transmission protocols, and for building an optimized wireless control network, it is vital to analyze them and define which technology best matches the requirements.

In robot soccer, like SSL, one concern is related to energy consumption since other components such as motors already generate great demand. Another factor is the time to deliver messages, which is essential to reduce errors in the control process. In addition, lower exposure to interference in the competition environment and a high data transmission rate are desired.

The nRF24l01 is a low energy consumption transmitter and developed, focusing on low latency communication, being advantageous concerning Wi-Fi [7]. In addition, Wi-Fi and Bluetooth networks are standard in every environment due to computers and smartphones. So, if one of these is adopted, we would have high interference. With the nRF24l01, the communication may operate at a frequency above Wi-Fi, Bluetooth, and ZigBee, reducing your exposure to interference [9].

As for ZigBee [14], its main disadvantage is its transmission rate, which is lower than the nRF24l01. Also, it has high exposure to interference because it uses the same frequency as Wi-Fi and Bluetooth. However, ZigBee has a lower transmission power than Wi-Fi, and Bluetooth [2].

Modules like ZigBee and nRF24l01 were designed for embedded system. Then it is necessary to interface the cognition software that remains in a computer with an embedded system that transmits the data wirelessly. This embedded system is known as a radio base station, and the communication technology between computer and base station is also important to avoid bottlenecks.

A comparison of the main parameters of each technology is shown Table 1, and, after analyzing the advantages and disadvantages of each technology, we chose the nRF24l01 developed by Nordic in 2008 [9].

Table 1. The specifications of Bluetooth, ZigBee, WiFi and nRF24l01 modules [5, 9, 11]

Characteristics	Bluetooth	ZigBee	WiFi	nRF24l01
Frequency	2.4 GHz	0.86/0.91/2.4 GHz	2.4, 5–6 GHz	2.4–2.48 GHz
Chanels	79	1/10/16	14	126
Speed rate	3 Mbit/s	20–250 Kb/s	11 Mb/s–10 Gb/s	2 Mbps
Devices	8	65000	2007	N/A
Radius	10 m	10–100 m	100 m	350 m
Power	0 to 30 dBm	0 to 10 dBm	15 to 20 dBm	−18 to 0 dBm
Current (TX, Stb)	40 mA, 0.2 mA	30 mA, 1 μA	400 mA, 20 mA	13.5 mA, 26 μA

With that in mind, we chose to use an Ethernet connection, a standard available in some embedded systems and most computers. It is a standard that is easy to integrate and has data transmission that can reach up to 10Gbps. Different from Ethernet, the USB serial connection is common to debug and transfer the program between computers and boards, but is a slow protocol. And, due to the serial nature, it does not have support to continuous send and receive data at the same bus.

2.3 Related Work

Most wireless networks are modeled to IoT applications, where the main goal is to monitor. However, this work focuses on controlling mobile robots by using wireless networks. Then, the communication solution should minimize latency and provide reliability, which is fundamental for real-time applications, like mobile robots control.

There are studies developing robots that work with wireless networks [5]. The system's communication was built using nRF24l01 modules and analyzed the power consumption of each component. Although it succeeds in controlling an autonomous robot, it does not report any data from the communication efficiency and is tested in a single robot application.

Additional theoretical studies also gain relevance in network optimization, being essential to support the design decisions. In [8], the author does not consider the nRF24l01 technology, but it concludes that radio configurations have a significant impact on the control network of soccer robots.

For narrowing the scope, some works report the impacts of nRF24l01 adoption in a wireless control network [4]. The author discussed parameters, like data size and communication speed, to increase efficiency. Besides the parameters, the work reported tests with broadcast messages and multi-channel communication, but, in the end, did not report the latency of the whole wireless control network, crucial to the design of a robotic system.

Tigers Mannheim robotics team proposed a communication architecture for controlling its robots using the Ethernet protocol between the central unit and the base-station [13]. The same work suggests using two nRF24l01 modules, one for sending messages and another for receiving messages. The Tigers team developed communication with real robots, but the team uses semi-autonomous navigation in their robots, which reduces the dependence on real-time communication to control the robots. Also, the Tigers' works did not perform communication or reliability tests.

3   System Architecture

In this section, the wireless network is presented. It consists of a network that controls and monitors multiples mobile robots. It starts with commands from a computer connected to a base station, an embedded system that transmits and receives data through a wireless module. Each robot also has wireless modules responsible for receiving packets sent from the base station. For monitoring the robots, additional transceivers create a second channel of data exchange without interfering in the control messages transmissions.

There are two data exchange points to build the communication system: the first between the computer and the base station and the latter between the base station and robots. Both connections need to be optimized to achieve the lowest delay.

3.1 Network Architecture

The network implementation started by choosing the best modules that fit the system requirements. With that in mind, the technology that best fits is nRF24l01 [9]. In the proposed system, two modules in each embedded system are used to create the control and the telemetry communication. The nRF24l01 configuration and control interface is the Serial Peripheral Interface (SPI) [6], which provides synchronized transmission and operates at a 10 Mbit/s transfer rate.

For the robot's microcontroller, the RobôCIn uses the NUCLEO-F767ZI [15] development board with an ARM Cortex M7 operating at 216 MHz, in the base-station, we chose the NUCLEO-H743ZI2 [16], an ARM Cortex M7 that operates at 400 MHz. This processor speed is essential to the base station since one of them communicates with multiple robots on the network.

For delivering a reliable communication system, it is necessary to develop robust software. For this, we use the environment of the mbed Operating System (mbedOS) [1], which is a real-time operating system for ARM micro-controllers that supports ARM peripherals and emulates virtual thread.

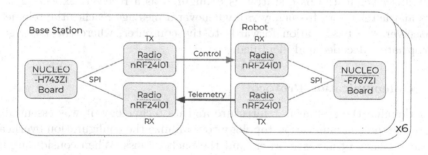

Fig. 1. Diagram of radios used for control and telemetry network on the Base Station and Robot, together with its way of communication.

The base-station, together with the proposed architecture, is shown in Fig. 1. The flow of control packets is made with one transceiver at the base station and another at the robot. This transceiver is configured as a sender radio to the robot's address in the base station, as shown in Table 2. In the robots, it is in receiver mode with the same address.

Table 2. Project modules and configuration in base station and robots

	Base station	Robots
Transceiver	nRF24l01	nRF24l01
Embedded board	Nucleo F767ZI	Nucleo H743ZI
CPU frequency	400 MHz	216 MHz
Operating system	mbedOS	mbedOS
Radio frequency (control)	2504 MHz	2504 MHz
Radio frequency (telemetry)	2529 MHz	2529 MHz
Radio address	0x753FAD299ALL	0x753FBD299ALL

The base station allows communication between the computer and the robots through Gigabit Ethernet. In the data connection, we use the User Datagram Protocol (UDP) protocol to minimize the protocol overhead. As discussed previously, the Ethernet transfer delay is lower than Serial and the nRF24l01 transmissions, so the bottleneck stands in the wireless connection.

Finally, to build the telemetry in the network, an additional transceiver is used in the robot and the base station, as illustrated in Fig. 1. To report the robot's status to the computer, it checks how long it has sent telemetry; when it is longer than the configured value, it measures the robot's status and sends the telemetry encoded back to the base station. The transceivers in the robot are configured in sender mode and address the base station (Table 2).

For receiving a telemetry packet, the base station has a virtual thread, parallel to the control code, to deal with the incoming messages. The second transceiver in the base station is configured as a receiver, expecting messages at the telemetry frequency. So, whenever a message reaches the telemetry transceiver, the base station forwards to the computer, where the message is appropriately decoded and identified.

3.2 Communication Protocol

After defining the system's architecture and its technology, it was essential to determine the communication topology to minimize the configuration overhead, the dependency of message order, and the packets' loss. When considering the control and telemetry messages, there is no need to recover old packets. So, the topology chosen was the star network, in which the base station sends and receives messages of all robots. There is no overhead of dynamic configuring the parameters of the transceiver with this topology, and no acknowledge packet is necessary. On the other hand, the message should include a robot identification so that each robot can identify its message.

Finally, with the chosen communication architecture and topology, a message protocol has been developed for control messages. It aims to minimize the payload size to optimize the delivery time. So, in the first half byte, there is the message type identification, at the second half, there is the robot identifier.

These initial bytes enable the robot to recognize different messages and filters the ones addressed to them. Additional bytes define the robot's movements, like linear and angular speed, and its peripheral's actions.

For telemetry, another messaging protocol has been created, but equally to the control protocol, the telemetry message has the message and robot identification in the first byte. But, differently from the control protocol, the telemetry protocol has each motor speed, measured by the robot's sensors, battery level, and peripherals state.

No matter the message, the base station only needs to re-transmit messages. Then, the protocol encodes and decodes messages for computers and robots only. The data exchange goes by Ethernet, between computer and base-station, and nRF24l01, base-station, and robot.

3.3 Applying to Small Size League (SSL)

This section presents how the proposed communication has been used in the SSL competition. So, it was necessary to build the control packet protocol, including the information required to control the robot, and monitor it, create the telemetry packet. In the following, the control and telemetry packets defined are presented.

SSL Control Packet: Message Type (4 bits), Robot ID (4 bits), Vx - Linear Speed (20 bits), Vy - Linear Speed (20 bits), ω - Angular Speed (20 bits), θ - Robot Angle (20 bits), Kick Front (1 bits), Kick Chip (1 bits), Charge the Kick (1 bits), Strength of the Kick (8 bits), Turn on the Dribbler (1 bits), Speed of the Dribbler (8 bits), Additional Command (4 bits). With a total of 14 bytes of payload.

SSL Telemetry Packet: Message Type (4 bits), Robot ID (4 bits), m1 - Motor 1 Speed (16 bits), m2 - Motor 2 Speed (16 bits), m3 - Motor 3 Speed (16 bits), m4 - Motor 4 Speed (16 bits), Dribbler's Motor Speed (15 bits), Kick's Capacitor Load (8 bits), Ball on the Robot (1 bits), Robot's Battery (8 bits). With a total of 13 bytes of payload.

Once both communication packets were defined, the robot and computer can understand each other the messages. The next step is configuring the base station and robot transceivers. One address and frequency channel for a pair of transceivers are necessary, one in the base station and another in the robot.

4   Validation and Results

In this section, the proposed base-station is analyzed in the SSL environment. Based on these results, the parameters that optimize the communication were found.

4.1   Time Analyses

The interval between each message transmission is essential and different for each communication system. It is necessary because computers are normally faster than embedded systems. Then, an uninterrupted flow of messages may increase the overhead of the base station. Moreover, this work searches the ideal interval period based on the delivery delay at the robots.

The delivery time test measures the interval between messages that should arrive at a robot. The interval between messages varies because the network works asynchronously and may lose packages. So, here, the delivery time between messages means the average interval between 500 messages received. Due to the reception variation between messages, the standard deviation is also calculated.

The test flow begins with the computer sending messages to robots via the base station, with some send interval. The robot measures the interval between 500 messages separately. After the measurements, the robot reports each interval to a computer, where the data is analyzed. With the results analyzed, another interval is configured at the computer to search for the optimal one.

Although the telemetry impacts the communication delivery performance, the test uses the same flow to test the telemetry. So, the optimal interval for control packets is configured in the computer. Another interval is configured at the robots for the telemetry. The results reveal the impact of telemetry in the control network.

Control Message Interval Time. Analyzing the results in Fig. 2(a), the base-station using serial interface has a fast and reliable throughput at 1900 μs of an interval between each message sent. Smaller intervals caused a bit flip in communication, which causes undesired robot behavior.

The Fig. 2(b) shows the test result with an optimum interval time for Ethernet interface is 500 us. Almost four times smaller than the Serial, the Ethernet approach does not corrupt the bits with a shorter interval time than 500 us but increases the delivery time.

Telemetry Message Interval Time. Finally, the telemetry impact in the control network is analyzed. The control messages interval was measured in a scenario with no telemetry and an unknown telemetry interval. Again, the tests were applied to find an optimal interval for sending telemetry packets. The test analyzes the delivery time of control packets, as it is essential to robots even with telemetry.

The disadvantages of the serial interface and the results above lead to discarding the serial interface to control communication with telemetry. After all, the tests initially used the interval of 200 ms between telemetry messages because of RobôCIn's requirement. The tests decreased the telemetry interval to find a balance that guarantees quickly sampling without damaging the control network.

Table 3 shows the network time performance of an Ethernet base station, sending control packets with 500 ms of interval. The test applied different telemetry intervals, so, Table 3 presents an impact of 0.39% with a 200 ms telemetry

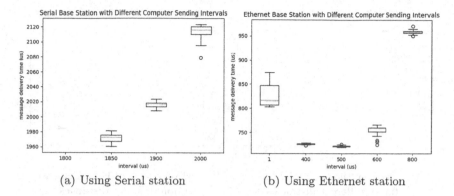

(a) Using Serial station　　　　　(b) Using Ethernet station

Fig. 2. Reception delay for 25 tests at each different sending interval, using Serial (a) or Ethernet (b) base station transmitting computer messages at the configured sending intervals

interval; at 50 ms of sampling, the reception interval increases 1.23%. Furthermore, the 10 ms sampling increases 6.48% of average delivery time. Then, the Ethernet base station receiving telemetry packets at every 50 ms guarantees a control update every 730.89 ms.

4.2 System Validation

The network efficiency was tested and validated by changing the number of robots, its distances to the base station, and enabling the telemetry. These tests were performed in the RobôCIn field, focusing on the Ethernet configuration and serial interface.

Different Distances. An important characteristic is a robustness in different distances. For simulating that environment, the robot was, first, positioned 0.4 m from the transceiver, after it was 2.5 m of distance, and finally at the opposite side of the field, 5 m of distance.

In Fig. 3 shows a consistent delivery time in robots with previous results; the differences appear only in the communication interface.

Multiple Robots. Today, the SSL there are six robots from each team in Division B and 11 in Division A. So, the network needs to communicate with multiple robots.

After testing with 1, 2, and 6 robots using the Ethernet interface, the results, available in Fig. 4(a), revealed that the delivery time is proportional with the number of robots. Outcome expected because the base station sends six messages to control six robots, one for each robot.

Therefore, to test consistency, tests were realized at two different robots separately. The test result, presented in Fig. 4(b), confirms the expectation that

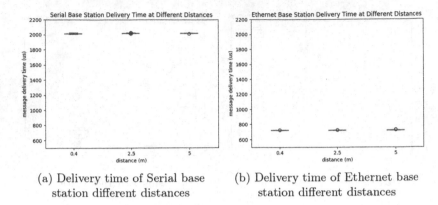

(a) Delivery time of Serial base station different distances

(b) Delivery time of Ethernet base station different distances

Fig. 3. Delivery time of base station with different distance between transceivers

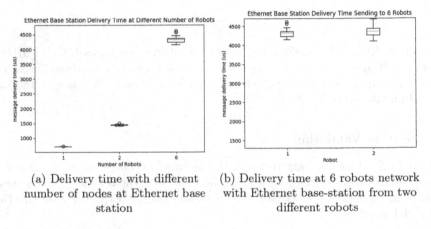

(a) Delivery time with different number of nodes at Ethernet base station

(b) Delivery time at 6 robots network with Ethernet base-station from two different robots

Fig. 4. Delivery time analysis between network size (1, 2 and 6 robots)

a network with six robots has a delivery time similar for two different robots. Even though each robot receives all messages, the test considers only the packets addressed to the given robot.

Telemetry. To safely use telemetry in games, the control network was tested with telemetry enabled for six robots. The telemetry interferes in base-station flow; then, it may interfere with the control delay. After testing, the results, presented in Table 3, show an increase of tens of microseconds. And, using a telemetry sampling time of 50 ms, for each robot, the delay increase is less than 2%. This result does not compromise the control efficiency.

Table 3. Ethernet base station with telemetry different sampling interval

Test condition	Delivery time		Increase	
	Average	Standard deviation	Average	Standard deviation
Without telemetry	721.98 µs	140.12		
200 ms sampling	724.78 µs	159.44	0.39%	13.79%
50 ms sampling	730.89 µs	196.07	1.23%	39.93%
10 ms sampling	768.80 µs	217.69	6.48%	55.36%

5 Conclusion

This paper presented a wireless network architecture to control mobile robots. The communication built was applied and validated in RobôCIn SSL robots, using the competition environment as the system requirement. The soccer competition simulates a dynamic environment, where all the obstacles and goals are moving. Then, the control system needs a quick reaction and good reliability to change robots' movements.

Usually, communication is not the focus of the control system or soccer teams in RoboCup; however, it is essential to accomplish a high rate of delivered messages. Then, this work brings a simple communication system that leverages the control and monitor capabilities of teams and wireless systems. The work presents the modules, their connections, and required configuration to work inside the proposed architecture.

In the paper, the communication validation uses the delivery time of messages in the robots, as it is the main objective of a wireless control system. The results show an average delivery time smaller than one millisecond, for one robot, even with robots telemetry. Moreover, although the delivery time increases with the number of robots, the proposed communication achieves a SSL team, a delivery time smaller than 16 ms, a typical specification of competition cameras. Future works will analyze energy consumption and bandwidth in each component to evaluate possible optimization opportunities. Moreover, future work will introduce inter robots communication and analyze new communication modules with different technologies.

Acknowledgements. The authors would like to acknowledge the RoboCIn's team and Centro de Informática - UFPE for all the support in this research. The authors would like to thanks the founding provided by FACEPE (Fundaçäo de Amparo a Ciëncia e Tecnologia de Pernambuco).

References

1. Arm: Mbed operating system - open-source RTOS (2019). https://os.mbed.com/. Accessed 05 Feb 2019

2. Karia, D., Baviskar, J., Makwana, R., Panchal, N.: Performance analysis of ZigBee based load control and power monitoring system. In: 2013 International Conference on Advances in Computing, Communications and Informatics (ICACCI), pp. 1479–1484. IEEE (2013)
3. Kitano, H., Asada, M., Kuniyoshi, Y., Noda, I., Osawa, E.: RoboCup: the robot world cup initiative. In: Proceedings of the First International Conference on Autonomous Agents, AGENTS 1997, pp. 340–347. ACM, New York (1997). https://doi.org/10.1145/267658.267738, http://doi.acm.org/10.1145/267658.267738
4. Kordas, J., Wagner, P., Kotzian, J.: Wireless transceiver for control of mobile embedded devices. In: Proceedings of the International Multiconference on Computer Science and Information Technology, pp. 869–872 (2010)
5. Kulasekara, V., Balasooriya, S., Chandran, J., Kavalchuk, I.: Novel low-power NRF24L01 based wireless network design for autonomous robots. In: 2019 25th Asia-Pacific Conference on Communications (APCC), pp. 342–346. IEEE (2019)
6. Leens, F.: An introduction to I2C and SPI protocols. IEEE Instrum. Meas. Mag. **12**(1), 8–13 (2009)
7. Ma, X., Chen, X.: Performance analysis of IEEE 802.11 broadcast scheme in ad hoc wireless LANs. IEEE Trans. Veh. Technol. **57**(6), 3757–3768 (2008)
8. Nadarajah, S., Sundaraj, K.: Wireless communication in robot soccer: a case study of existing technologies. In: 2012 IEEE Conference on Sustainable Utilization and Development in Engineering and Technology (STUDENT), pp. 33–38 (2012)
9. Nordic: NRF24L01+ single chip 2.4GHz transceiver (2008). https://www.sparkfun.com/datasheets/Components/SMD/nRF24L01Pluss_Preliminary_Product_Specification_v1_0.pdf. Accessed 15 Mar 2021
10. Park, P., Coleri Ergen, S., Fischione, C., Lu, C., Johansson, K.H.: Wireless network design for control systems: a survey. IEEE Commun. Surv. Tutor. **20**(2), 978–1013 (2018)
11. Proskochylo, A., Vorobyov, A., Zriakhov, M., Kravchuk, A., Akulynichev, A., Lukin, V.: Overview of wireless technologies for organizing sensor networks. In: 2015 Second International Scientific-Practical Conference Problems of Infocommunications Science and Technology (PIC S T), pp. 39–41. IEEE (2015)
12. RoboCup: Laws of the RoboCup Small Size League. Small Size League Technical Committee, December 2021. https://robocup-ssl.github.io/ssl-rules/sslrules.pdf
13. Ryll, A., Geiger, M., Ommer, N., Sachtler, A., Magel, L.: Extended team description for RoboCup 2016 (2016). https://ssl.robocup.org/wp-content/uploads/2019/01/2016_ETDP_TIGERs_Mannheim.pdf. Accessed 01 Sept 2019
14. Saha, H., Mandal, S., Mitra, S., Banerjee, S., Saha, U.: Comparative performance analysis between nRF24L01+ and XBEE ZB module based wireless ad-hoc networks. Int. J. Comput. Netw. Inf. Secur. **9**, 36–44 (2017)
15. ST: NUCLEO-F767ZI (2021). https://www.st.com/en/evaluation-tools/nucleo-f767zi.html. Accessed 01 Sept 2020
16. ST: NUCLEO-H743ZI (2021). https://www.st.com/en/evaluation-tools/nucleo-h743zi.html. Accessed 12 Sept 2020

A Telemetry-Based PI Tuning Strategy
for Low-Level Control
of an Omnidirectional Mobile Robot

Victor Araújo[✉], Felipe Martins, Roberto Fernandes, and Edna Barros

Centro de Informática, Universidade Federal de Pernambuco,
Av. Prof. Moraes Rego, 1235 - Cidade Universitária,
Recife, Pernambuco, Brazil
{vhssa,fbm2,rcf6,ensb}@cin.ufpe.br

Abstract. Mobile robot control requires precision and accuracy to react
to unpredictable situations. However, it is non-trivial to design a low-
level controller for each wheel that combines fast response and stability in the presence of disturbances. The Proportional-Integral (PI) controller algorithm is the most used technique for DC motors; however,
tuning these controllers can become a time-consuming task depending
on the number of robots and tuning methodology. We propose a novel
telemetry-based strategy to find suitable PI controller parameters more
quickly using accurate motor models of the omnidirectional mobile robots
obtained from an on-site data sampling mechanism. We evaluate our approach on an omnidirectional robot designed within the RoboCup Small
Size League (SSL) competition rules. The results compare the proposed
method with a based on Quantitative Feedback Theory (QFT) approach.
Our strategy improved on average the robot's performance by 17.95%
when using Integral Absolute Error (IAE) and by 12.75% when using
Integral Squared Error (ISE) criteria.

Keywords: Low-level control · PI tuning · Omnidirectional mobile
robot

1 Introduction

An Omnidirectional Mobile Robot (OMR) is a type of holonomic robot widely
used in dynamic environments with the ability to translate and rotate independently in a two-dimensional plane. The RoboCup Small Size League (SSL) competition is a highly dynamic environment where two teams with up to eleven
OMRs each compete within rules adapted from FIFA soccer. Currently, the
teams use a shared vision system [22]. However, the league is moving towards an
onboard vision for each robot. All groups are encouraged to develop their systems through technical challenges. This perspective change requires the teams

Supported by Centro de Informática (CIn - UFPE), Fundação de Amparo a Ciência e
Tecnologia do Estado de Pernambuco (FACEPE), and RobôCIn Robotics Team.

to design a very reliable low-level control for their robots without external feedback. In the context of robot competitions such as robot soccer, a robot must act fast and precisely because defenders of the opposing team quickly block the opportunities to score a goal.

A significant number of works have investigated the control of OMRs [1,7, 10]. The leading causes of trajectory tracking errors are nonlinearities due to slippage between wheel and ground, friction, vibrations, and disturbances [16]. To reduce these errors, we have to design an accurate motor control system for each OMR wheel. One of the most used approaches in the literature to design, analyze, verify, and validate dynamic systems is the model-based design [15]. Model-based design techniques use approximate mathematical models of the system to estimate unknown parameters, such as Proportional, Integral, and Derivative (PID) controller parameters for DC motor control [12]. Linearization and discretization techniques can simplify dynamic models and satisfy real-time constraints [10].

Works dealing with the motor model acquisition and PID tuning generally use robots connected to embedded computers communicating through serial communication [1,6]. The methodology used to identify the motor model differs among existing approaches [6,12,21]. The use of data acquired only in simulation for tuning and validation of controllers is widespread in works in the area [4,16]. When working in a multi-robot environment with robot size restrictions, it can be very time-consuming to tune a PID controller for each robot's motors in a new environment. It usually requires a lot of human effort [9]. It is also essential to establish wireless communication so that the robot can move freely in an environment of data acquisition and real validation.

This work presents a novel telemetry-based PI tuning strategy for low-level control of omnidirectional mobile robot motors. We propose a data-collecting mechanism that allows the PI tuning of the motors using data sampled on-site in a real multi-robot environment with low latency. The proposed strategy includes a technique based on Multi-level Pseudo-Random Sequence (MPRS) of signals for motor model acquisition. The use of this signal improves the linearized motor model estimation accuracy compared to traditional techniques based on Pseudo-Random Binary Sequence (PRBS). The telemetry-based strategy allows a fast tuning of the PI constants for multiple robots without changing the embedded code. The proposed strategy is implemented and validated with a robot built under the RoboCup SSL rules and compared with an approach based on the QFT technique. Our main contributions are:

1. A data sampling engine based on wireless communication supporting on-site data sampling from multiple robots with low latency,
2. A method for system identification using MPRS signals to identify linearized model based on specific motor parameters, and
3. A novel strategy for fast tuning of a PI controller for low-level control in an OMR.

The rest of this paper is organized as follows: Sect. 2 presents the related works. Section 3 details the system architecture, model acquisition, and PI tuning strategy. Section 4 presents the experimental results. Finally, Sect. 5 concludes the work and presents further works.

2   Related Works

System identification is the process of constructing mathematical models of the system under study from prior knowledge [17]. In mobile robots, different system identification methods have been applied to derive a DC motor model. The most common is to apply Random Binary Sequences to the motor to collect motor response information and use this data to obtain a transfer function of the motor [13]. Sahputro et al. [20] used Pseudo-Random Binary Sequence (PRBS) to get the estimated transfer function of a DC motor to control a mobile robot using the Recursive Least Square (RLS) method. Hat et al. [12] also applied PRBS signal for determining a brushless DC motor model using MATLAB software. Braun et al. [5] presented an identification methodology using Multi-level Pseudo-Random Sequence (MPRS) applied to a Rapid Thermal Processing (RTP) reactor plant as one of its case studies. Although the MPRS approach was applied primarily with process systems, systems with different model structures can also use this method. One advantage of the MPRS approach is that it can use different values within the motor operating range, while the PRBS uses only two values to perform the identification.

Data sampling and acquisition are crucial steps to perform reasonable control of mobile robots. Recent works present embedded computers using serial communication to read motor data [6,21]. When working with mobile robots with tight constraints such as size or cost limitations, there is a need to use lower-cost embedded development boards. An alternative is to use wireless communication to send and receive information from a desktop that can compute complex algorithms without those restrictions.

Different approaches have been proposed to address the low-level control for four-wheeled OMRs. The approach described in [11] used a discrete-time Linear Quadratic Tracking approach (LQT) as a low-level controller for the trajectory tracking of an OMR. Al et al. [1] improved the work in [11] presenting an embedded system for motion control. The system controls an OMR using Linear Quadratic Regulator (LQR) as a low-level controller. A fuzzy-PI controller controls the position of the OMR as a high-level controller for solving the problem of trajectory tracking. Comasolivas et al. [6] presented a control technique called Quantitative Feedback Theory (QFT) for low-level control for an OMR. The QFT technique is a frequency domain technique based on the Nichols chart, offering a robust design over specified frequency domain tolerances. The QFT approach identifies multiple linear models to design a PI controller in a standard platform called iSRob, comparing its experimental results with a gain-scheduling PI-controller based on pole assignment.

Most of the works that address the problem of trajectory tracking require an external source such as a vision system to be used as position feedback instead of robot odometry due to the use of a high-level controller [1,11]. When working in a dynamic multi-robot environment, the approach proposed by [6] can be time-consuming because it estimates multiple linear models, and the loop shaping controller stage requires manual adjustments for each controller.

3   Telemetry-Based PI Tuning Strategy

The proposed strategy for designing the low-level controller has four main stages: motor parameters acquisition, motor model estimation, PI tuning, and validation. For the motor parameters acquisition stage, we defined the encoder sampling rate for the motors. We also developed a data sampling engine for finding the motor's rise time and settling time using data sampled from the motors attached to a real SSL robot moving with all loads acting on it in a competition field.

In the motor model estimation stage, we propose using a Multi-level Pseudo-Random Sequence (MPRS) as the signal input of the motors. The generated MPRS signals are sent to the robot through wireless communication using the mentioned data sampling engine. For each signal received, the robot returns a message containing the four motors' speed (in rad/s). Then, this collected data is used to find the linearized motor model estimation following the methodology proposed by [12].

The PI controller's tuning stage can find suitable control constants for the application using the motor's approximate model for instant validation. We use the identified model from the model estimation stage as input to tuning a PI controller based on the design requirements. The control constants found are sent to the robot through telemetry for validation in the next step.

The validation stage consists of implementing the discrete-time PI controller with tuned parameters as a low-level controller in a real robot. We validate by sending 20 different signal levels during a specific time and receive the robot's speed through telemetry. Finally, we use Integral Absolute Error (IAE) and Integral Squared Error (ISE) performance metrics to evaluate the validation results.

3.1   Data Capturing Mechanism

This section will present the proposed strategy for capturing and sampling data from the motors in a robot. Figure 1 shows an overview of the proposed system architecture. The control of each robot includes high-level control and low-level control. The high-level control is implemented in the external computer connected to a base station through Ethernet protocol. This control sends different control messages such as the desired robot's speed, selected motor's PWM, or control constants. The base station includes a NUCLEO-H743ZI2 development board responsible for communicating with the robot using radio modules (nRF24L01+).

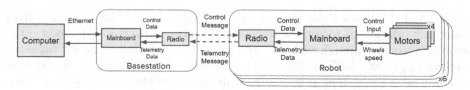

Fig. 1. System architecture overview.

The low-level control is implemented in the robot using a NUCLEO-F767ZI development board and communicates with the base station using radio modules (nRF24L01+). The robot decodes the control message received and acts accordingly for each wheel.

This proposed data acquisition engine includes different types of messages that use the presented system architecture to communicate with each robot for sampling motor data to perform the model estimation, send the PI controller parameters after tuning, and validate the low-level control.

The proposed data collecting mechanism based on wireless communication allows the sample more precise motor data in the real-world environment (onsite). Another advantage of this mechanism is the possibility of configuring tuning parameters online by sending configuration messages to adjust the PI controller constants without changing the embedded code.

3.2   Motor Parameters and System Identification

The encoder sampling rate is one of the key parameters in a discrete controller. It determines the measurement frequency of the number of pulses read by the sensor, both clockwise and counterclockwise. Therefore, the higher the sampling rate, the faster the motor speed updates. However, there is a trade-off between the sampling rate and the uncertainty of the encoder. The faster the encoder update frequency, the greater the associated uncertainty. Equation 1 shows how to obtain the uncertainty (Δ) for one encoder pulse:

$$\Delta = 2\pi \cdot \frac{1}{EncoderMode \cdot PPR \cdot t_{sample}} \tag{1}$$

The *EncoderMode* refers to the quadrature encoding type, which can be 1, 2, or 4. *PPR* refers to the number of pulses per revolution, and T_{sample} refers to the time between each encoder update.

This work uses Maxon's Inductive Little Encoder (MILE), designed for the EC-45 flat motors from Maxon Global. When choosing the encoder sampling rate, it is necessary to consider the hardware's ability to process the inner closed-loop control in real-time. To control the motor efficiently, the time between the encoder samples must be at least 5 to 10 times lower than the motor rise time to a step input [8].

To find the motor's rise time and settling time, we use the mentioned data sampling mechanism to send a step signal control message and to receive the motors' response through telemetry messages. The rise time is when it takes the system to go from 10% to 90% of the specified value [19]. The settling time is when it takes the system to be stable at around 2% of the final value [19]. These parameters are essential for determining the design requirements.

The complexity of the driver and motor system makes the formal definition of the motor model mathematically very difficult due to the high number of electrical components involved. To solve that, we can approximate the motor model using its response when applying a signal as input. This work proposes using MPRS signal for system identification as it has an amplitude varied and fixed frequency. A larger range of inputs allows a better estimation of the system's dynamic behavior as it covers a more significant number of input possibilities. One of the main advantages of the MPRS signal is that it can afford more nonlinearities as it does not vary its frequency pulses depending on the application environment. Table 1 shows the parameters for the MPRS signal generation MPRS signals.

Table 1. Parameters used for MPRS signal generation.

Signal	Parameter	Value
MPRS	Number of samples	511
	Sampling period	0.3 (sec)
	Input range	−100 to 100

Figure 2 shows a fragment of the MPRS signal applied to one of the robot motors with its response. The MPRS signals are applied to the motors remotely through specific messages. The motor's responses also received by messages are used to estimate a first-order discrete-time transfer function using an Output-Error (OE) model with the aid of MATLAB's System Identification Toolbox [18]. The OE algorithm relates data measured inputs to outputs. It returns the estimated values of the model parameters with a percentage of how well the model's response fits the input data. The nonlinear least squares with an automatically chosen line search algorithm are used to estimate the percentage of fitting of the identified function. The transfer function estimated allows the design of an initial PI controller to control the motor safely, reducing the risks of damaging the equipment [2].

3.3   Motor Control and PI Tuning

A PI controller is the best controller for this type of the first-order system. Previous works in the literature show that the derivative term does not bring many advantages in this control system by performing a root-locus analysis, and

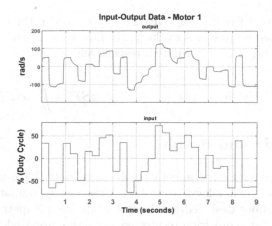

Fig. 2. Fragment with nine seconds of the motor response (in rad/s) to an MPRS input signal (in % Duty Cycle).

has the drawback of amplifying noise [3,6]. The method used to discretize the PI controller was the backward difference method [3]. The digital PI controller implemented is described in Eq. (2):

$$u(t) = K_p \cdot e(t) + K_i \cdot T_s \cdot \min \left(\sum_{i=0}^{t} e(t), error_{threshold} \right) + u_0 \qquad (2)$$

The u_0 term is the controller's initial output value. The integral term is the integral constant (K_i) multiplied by the sampling time (T_s) and the sum of all errors during the control execution time. The proportional term is the proportional constant (K_p) multiplied by the actual error ($e(t)$). The backward difference method converts the integral and derivative terms to their corresponding discrete parts over time. An integral anti-windup was implemented to avoid saturation of the integrator term, considering the minimum between the sum of errors and the maximum error threshold ($error_{threshold}$).

The PI tuning step uses the fitted models of the motors to adjust the discrete controller using MATLAB's interactive tool *PID Tuner*. The designer must specify predefined parameters in the tool based on the OMR application: response time and transient behavior. The response time impacts the maximum rise time and maximum settling time of the system, and the transient behavior influences maximum overshoot.

The validation step consists of using the telemetry to measure the response of the robot's motors with the tuned controller. In this validation we sent 20 different speed values during 0.5 s each. We evaluate these responses measuring the error of each experiment with two metrics: Integral Absolute Error (IAE) and Integral Squared Error (ISE). Given $e(t)$ the error in the time t. We choose these metrics, based on previous works [6,14]. Equation (3) and (4) presents how the IAE and ISE criteria is calculated, respectively:

$$IAE = \int_0^\infty |e(t)| dt \quad (3) \qquad\qquad ISE = \int_0^\infty e(t)^2 dt \quad (4)$$

4   Case Study and Results

This section presents the experimental results to validate the proposed telemetry-based strategy for the low-level controller. A case study validates the proposed approach with a robot designed for the RoboCup SSL competition. We present the motor parameter acquisition results, compare the proposed MPRS signal for system identification to a PRBS signal, and the proposed PI tuning approach to a robust QFT controller implemented in an SSL robot under the same conditions.

4.1   Motor Parameters

First, to acquire the motor parameters, we need to determine the encoder sampling rate, which needs to be large enough to detect the motor's transient response and identify external noise's influence. Table 2 shows some uncertainty values for each interval between samples based on Eq. 1 using a 1024 PPR MILE encoder.

Table 2. Relationship between the time between samples (T_{sample}) in seconds and associated uncertainty (Δ) in RPM and rad/s.

$[T_{sample}](s)$	$[\Delta](RPM)$	$[\Delta](rad/s)$
0.001	14.6484	1.534
0.002	7.3242	0.767
0.005	2.9297	0.307
0.01	1.4648	0.153

As mentioned in Sect. 3.2, the time between samples must be at least 5 to 10 times lower than the motor rise time to a step input. We applied a step using the telemetry system to measure the motor response, and Table 3 shows the results with 30 repetitions and their respective standard deviation.

Table 3. Step response characteristics for a Maxon EC-45 flat 50W motor with 30 repetitions, the rising time mean $(\overline{T_r})$ and settling time mean $\overline{T_s}$ are in seconds and $\sigma(T_r)$ and $\sigma(T_s)$ represent their standard deviations.

Rising	Time	Settling	Time
$[\overline{T_r}](s)$	$[\sigma(T_r)]$	$[\overline{T_s}](s)$	$[\sigma(T_s)]$
0.049	0.006	0.125	0.064

With the results in Table 2 and Table 3 we can conclude that the T_{sample} should be lower than 0.01 s, depending on the maximum uncertainty defined by the designer in the system requirements.

4.2 System Identification for the Motors

The motor model identification process provides a transfer function of the system. This transfer function is the motor's digital representation as it simulates its response to signal inputs accurately. In this work, we proposed using an MPRS signal to identify the motor model with high accuracy.

Since the MPRS signal has not been used before to identify DC motors, we compare the identification results using the proposed MPRS signal and a PRBS signal implemented by [20]. MATLAB's System Identification toolbox processes the collected data through the robot telemetry messages from the base station to identify both transfer functions. Table 4 show experimental results representing the percentage of fitting for the identified discrete-time transfer function for the PRBS signal and proposed MPRS signal.

Table 4. Percentage of fitting for the identified discrete-time transfer function with classic PRBS and proposed MPRS signal inputs for each robot's motor.

Motor (#)	PRBS fitting (%) [20]	MPRS fitting (%)
1	65.76	91.09
2	65.44	91.22
3	64.9	91.38
4	65.54	91.08

The proposed MPRS identification method improved the PRBS method by an average of 39.41%. This improvement makes the constants obtained in the tuning stage more reliable and directly impacts the experimental results of the low-level controller.

4.3 Motor Control and PI Tuning

The proposed strategy is compared with the control approach called Quantitative Feedback Theory (QFT) using the performance specifications presented by

[6]. Figure 3a shows the motor response for one motor in an SSL environment, and Fig. 3b presents a detailed view of the motor response for a better transient behavior understanding. The proposed strategy demonstrated a significant reduction in the overshoot, which reduces the error in performance evaluations, avoids current peaks during acceleration, and collaborates for a smoother movement in a global aspect.

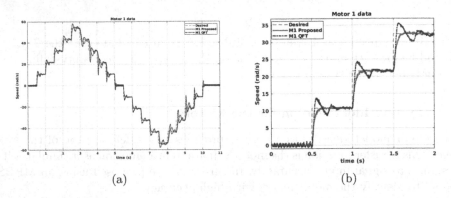

(a)   (b)

Fig. 3. Results for the proposed approach and QFT in one robot motor: (a) comparison between reference speed (dashed line) and angular speed with proposed strategy (solid line) and QFT approach (dash-dot line); (b) detailed view of the first two seconds.

Figure 4 presents the error (in rad/s) during time of the proposed strategy and QFT approach for the inputs applied in Fig. 3a. The error analysis shows how overshoot impacts performance metrics as the area under the curve for the QFT approach is significantly higher than the area in the proposed strategy.

To compare the proposed approach with the QFT technique, we executed the validation experiments 30 times for each motor due to the non-deterministic aspect. Table 5 shows the average of the IAE and ISE metrics for each technique. The results show that the proposed approach reduced on average the IAE by 17.95% and the ISE by 12.75% when compared to the QFT approach.

Table 5. Average results in a real scenario with the proposed strategy and the QFT approach using IAE and ISE criteria for each motor.

Criteria	Motor	Proposed	QFT [6]
IAE	1	15.92	19.19
	2	16.64	20.29
	3	16.96	20.86
	4	16.84	20.56
ISE	1	92.86	104.40
	2	96.94	111.82
	3	95.84	111.31
	4	97.07	111.26

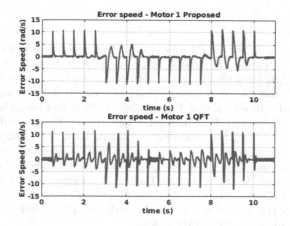

Fig. 4. Comparison of the error speed for the proposed strategy (up) and QFT approach (down).

5   Conclusion and Further Works

This work presented a telemetry-based PI tuning strategy for low-level control of an OMR. We proposed the use of the MPRS method instead of PRBS to obtain the discrete-time transfer function that best reproduces each motors' behavior. It accurately represented the motor response with the real-world experiments with fitting above 90% for all tested motors while the PRBS only reached around 65% of the fitting.

The mechanism for data sampling based on wireless communication presented in this work allows on-site fast PI tuning to deliver suitable constants that meet the requirements of SSL competition robots. Finally, the PI controller validated in the case study had its performance compared to the QFT approach. The QFT approach's main drawbacks were the time consumed to estimate the constants, the need for manually adjusting the open-loop frequency response, and the presence of overshoot during the validation. In contrast, the proposed PI tuning strategy supports finding suitable control constants by configuring response time and transient response following motor restrictions and design requirements, reducing the testing time significantly.

The proposed strategy supports the tuning of a PI controller and tests different control constants multiple times without changing the embedded code, reducing the implementation time significantly. We can also use this strategy in a multi-robot scenario for tuning each robot's motor. Further works include validating this strategy in other types of mobile robots and implementing the telemetry-based strategy with multi-objective optimizations using the obtained control constants as initial input for evolutionary algorithms or neural networks.

References

1. Al Mamun, M.A., Nasir, M.T., Khayyat, A.: Embedded system for motion control of an omnidirectional mobile robot. IEEE Access **6**, 6722–6739 (2018)
2. Araújo, V.H.S.S.: Uma abordagem para tuning de um controlador PI para motores brushless DC: um estudo de caso aplicado ao controle de movimento de um robô omnidirecional. Master's thesis, Universidade Federal de Pernambuco (2020)
3. Åström, K.J., Hägglund, T.: PID Controllers: Theory, Design, and Tuning, vol. 2. Instrument society of America Research Triangle Park, NC (1995)
4. Azizi, M.R., Rastegarpanah, A., Stolkin, R.: Motion planning and control of an omnidirectional mobile robot in dynamic environments. Robotics **10**(1), 48 (2021)
5. Braun, M., Rivera, D., Stenman, A., Foslien, W., Hrenya, C.: Multi-level pseudo-random signal design and model-on-demand estimation applied to nonlinear identification of a rtp wafer reactor. In: Proceedings of the 1999 American Control Conference, vol. 3, pp. 1573–1577 (1999)
6. Comasolivas, R., Quevedo, J., Escobet, T., Escobet, A., Romera, J.: Modeling and robust low level control of an omnidirectional mobile robot. J. Dyn. Syst. Meas. Control **139**(4) (2017)
7. Conceição, A.S., Oliveira, H.P., e Silva, A.S., Oliveira, D., Moreira, A.P.: A nonlinear model predictive control of an omni-directional mobile robot. In: 2007 IEEE International Symposium on Industrial Electronics, pp. 2161–2166. IEEE (2007)
8. Haidekker, M.A.: Linear Feedback Controls: The Esentials. Elsevier, Amsterdam (2020)
9. Han, J., Wang, P., Yang, X.: Tuning of pid controller based on fruit fly optimization algorithm. In: 2012 IEEE International Conference on Mechatronics and Automation, pp. 409–413. IEEE (2012)
10. Han, Y., Zhu, Q.: Robust optimal control of omni-directional mobile robot using model predictive control method. In: 2019 Chinese Control Conference (CCC), pp. 4679–4684. IEEE (2019)
11. Hashemi, E., Jadidi, M.G., Jadidi, N.G.: Model-based pi-fuzzy control of four-wheeled omni-directional mobile robots. Robot. Auton. Syst. **59**(11), 930–942 (2011)
12. Hat, M., et al.: Model based design of pid controller for bldc motor with implementation of embedded arduino mega controller. J. Eng. Appl. Sci. **10**, 8588–8594 (2015)
13. Hussin, M.S., Azuwir, M.N., Zaiazmin, Y.N.: Modeling and validation of brushless dc motor. In: 2011 Fourth International Conference on Modeling, Simulation and Applied Optimization, pp. 1–4 (2011)
14. Ibrahim, M.A., Mahmood, A.K., Sultan, N.S.: Optimal pid controller of a brushless dc motor using genetic algorithm. Int. J. Power Electron. Drive Syst. **2088**, 8694 (2019)
15. Jensen, J.C., Chang, D.H., Lee, E.A.: A model-based design methodology for cyber-physical systems. In: 2011 7th International Wireless Communications and Mobile Computing Conference, pp. 1666–1671 (2011)
16. Jianbin, W., Jianping, C.: An adaptive sliding mode controller for four-wheeled omnidirectional mobile robot with input constraints. In: 2019 Chinese Control And Decision Conference (CCDC), pp. 5591–5596. IEEE (2019)
17. Keesman, K.J.: System Identification: An Introduction. Springer Science & Business Media, Heidelberg (2011)

18. Ljung, L.: System Identification Toolbox: User's Guide, 4th edn. MathWorks, Natick (2012)
19. Nise, N.S.: Control Systems Engineering. John Wiley & Sons, Hoboken (2020)
20. Sahputro, S.D., Fadilah, F., Wicaksono, N.A., Yusivar, F.: Design and implementation of adaptive pid controller for speed control of dc motor. In: 2017 15th International Conference on Quality in Research (QiR) : International Symposium on Electrical and Computer Engineering, pp. 179–183 (2017)
21. Tang, W.J., Liu, Z.T., Wang, Q.: Dc motor speed control based on system identification and pid auto tuning. In: 2017 36th Chinese Control Conference (CCC), pp. 6420–6423. IEEE (2017)
22. Zickler, S., Laue, T., Birbach, O., Wongphati, M., Veloso, M.: SSL-Vision: the shared vision system for the robocup small size league. In: Baltes, J., Lagoudakis, M.G., Naruse, T., Ghidary, S.S. (eds.) RoboCup 2009. LNCS (LNAI), vol. 5949, pp. 425–436. Springer, Heidelberg (2010). https://doi.org/10.1007/978-3-642-11876-0_37

Soccer Field Boundary Detection Using Convolutional Neural Networks

Arne Hasselbring[1]([✉])(iD) and Andreas Baude[2]

[1] Deutsches Forschungszentrum für Künstliche Intelligenz, Cyber-Physical Systems,
Enrique-Schmidt-Str. 5, 28359 Bremen, Germany
`arne.hasselbring@dfki.de`
[2] Fachbereich 3 – Mathematik und Informatik, Universität Bremen,
Postfach 330 440, 28334 Bremen, Germany
`an_ba@uni-bremen.de`

Abstract. Detecting the field boundary is often one of the first steps in the vision pipeline of soccer robots. Conventional methods make use of a (possibly adaptive) green classifier, selection of boundary points and possibly model fitting. We present an approach to predict the coordinates of the field boundary column-wise in the image using a convolutional neural network. This is combined with a method to let the network predict the uncertainty of its output, which allows to fit a line model in which columns are weighted according to the network's confidence. Experiments show that the resulting models are accurate enough in different lighting conditions as well as real-time capable. Code and data are available online (https://github.com/bhuman/DeepFieldBoundary, https://sibylle.informatik.uni-bremen.de/public/datasets/fieldboundary).

1 Introduction

When playing soccer, the field boundary is a prominent visual feature. It allows to separate the environment into important and unimportant areas. For a computer vision pipeline, this means that it can be used to exclude false positive detections outside the field of play and reduce the amount of computations because only a certain part of the camera image needs to be included in further processing. The field boundary can furthermore be used as an observation for localization algorithms [8].

Most approaches in the past have been based on some kind of green classifier which is either completely static (like a pre-calibrated color lookup table) or determined online. However, this often causes difficulties with changing lighting conditions, hard shadows, or spotlights, which make different parts of the field appear in different colors. A deep neural network has the potential to utilize spatial context within an image in addition to per-pixel colors.

In RoboCup leagues with less restricted computational resources, fully convolutional neural networks have become popular for object detection [11,12]. They operate with no preprocessing and only little post processing. In principle, they do not need a separate field boundary detection because they already have

R. Alami et al. (Eds.): RoboCup 2021, LNAI 13132, pp. 202–213, 2022.
https://doi.org/10.1007/978-3-030-98682-7_17

access to image context that should prevent them from detecting objects outside the field. If the field boundary is desired as a specific feature, either the method of this paper can be integrated into the FCNN or a conventional method based on the output of semantic field segmentation can be employed. However, if most objects are detected using analytical methods anyway, the input image size can be chosen much smaller and the upscaling part of a segmentation network is not necessary, in order to reduce computational cost.

This paper contributes (a) a full description, code and data of a convolutional neural network approach to detect the field boundary which was previously mentioned without details in a team report [15], and (b) the combination with the prediction of confidence scores which can act as weighting factors in line model fitting. The paper continues as follows: Sect. 2 reviews related work on the topic of field boundary detection in robot soccer, Sect. 3 describes our methods in detail, Sect. 4 evaluates the approach and presents the results, and Sect. 5 concludes this paper.

2 Related Work

A classic approach to detect the field boundary consists of three steps: Firstly, a classifier for pixel colors is established. Secondly, spots on the field boundary are determined. Thirdly, a model of line segments is fitted through these spots. There have been many implementations of this pattern, each differing in details.

Reinhardt [9] first estimates the field color from channel-wise histograms over the entire subsampled image. Then, the image is split into segments along scan lines at edges in the luminance channel. Segments are classified into the categories field, line or unknown. An unknown segment above a field segment creates a candidate spot (i.e. there can be multiple spots per scan line). In order to reject outliers, e.g. from a neighboring field, an iterative convex hull algorithm evaluates multiple hypotheses and the one supported by most spots is chosen.

Qian and Lee [8] start by sampling a guess of the field color near the robot's own feet, assuming that the majority of pixels there always belongs to the field. Candidate boundary spots are generated by scanning downwards from the horizon and choosing the spot where the difference in the number of visited green and non-green pixels reaches its minimum. Finally, a model of one or two perpendicular lines is fitted using RANSAC.

Fiedler et al. [4] include a field boundary detection in their vision pipeline. Green pixels are masked based on a pre-calibrated seed that is dynamically adjusted using a field boundary that is calculated from the previous field color estimate, creating feedback loop. Depending on the camera angle, either the topmost green pixel or the bottommost non green pixel (applying a low pass filter in order to skip field lines) is chosen as candidate spot per vertical scan line. Over these spots, the convex hull is computed to remove gaps caused by occlusion of the field boundary by other players.

However, CNN-based approaches have also been proposed: Mahmoudi et al. [7] describe a network that predicts five vertices of a polygon which bounds the field. They use a 128×128 HSV image as input, followed by three pairs of convolutional and pooling layers, and two fully connected layers in the end. However, no quantitative results are given.

Finally, Tilgner *et al.* [15] shortly mention in their team report that they detect the field boundary using a deep neural network. The properties mentioned there are 40×30 YCbCr images as input, a CNN architecture based on four Inception-v2 blocks, and an output size matching the width of the input. Apparently, they have successfully used the results at RoboCup 2019. This paper started as an attempt to reproduce their approach.

3   Approach

In this section, the details of our approach are given. In general, like in [15] the network takes a 40×30 image (downsampled from the full camera resolution) as input and predicts 40 outputs, one per image column. Each output is the ratio of the image height at which the field ends in the column that it represents, i.e. 0 means that the field boundary is at or above the image and 1 means that the field boundary is at or below image (i.e. the column does not contain any field). In contrast to Mahmoudi *et al.* [7], who predict the vertices of a polygon in the image, this is potentially less sensitive to small errors in the predictions and allows for later regression (cf. Sect. 3.5) to attenuate errors even more.

3.1   Dataset

Our dataset consists of images taken by the upper camera of NAO V6s. They come from green RoboCup Standard Platform League fields in ten different locations, including dark indoor environments (which also means that the images are blurred due to high exposure times) as well as outdoor environments with uneven natural lighting. The images have been JPEG-compressed and logged by our robots during actual games, so there is occlusion by robots and all other real-world effects. In order to reduce redundancy in the data, only about one image per second has been kept.

The resulting set of 36399 images, some of which are shown in Fig. 1, has been manually labeled with a custom tool. The annotation tool allows to mark the field boundary as up to two lines by selecting two boundary points per line. The labels are represented by the vertical coordinates at the left and right image border as well as the location of the intersection of both lines, if it exists. This means that we do not handle the case of two or more field corners in the image, which only happens very rarely on a NAO due to the relation of the field size and the camera's horizontal field of view.

For this work, the set is split into three parts: a training set of 28641 real images and 4219 computer-generated images with ground-truth labels using a derivative of *UERoboCup* [5], a validation set of 3449 real images and a test set of 4309 images. The images in the validation set come from a location that is

Fig. 1. Examples from the set of labeled real images

not present the training set, and the test set includes yet more locations. The complete dataset is publicly available.[1]

3.2   Model Architecture

As in [15], the architecture is based on four Inception-v2 [13] blocks. Each block is divided into three N-filter branches which are concatenated in the end to $3N$ channels. The first branch starts by quartering the number of channels in a pointwise Conv+BN+ReLU block. The following 3×3 Conv+BN+ReLU each double the number of channels back to N and aggregate information from the neighborhood. The second branch is similar to the first one, but with only one 3×3 Conv+BN+ReLU block. The third branch consists of a 3×3 max pooling, followed by a pointwise Conv+BN+ReLU block. All blocks divide the vertical resolution by two via strides, while keeping the number of columns.

When the vertical size has been reduced to two rows after four blocks, a final convolution layer aggregates all $2 \cdot 3N$ channels within a column to O output channels, i.e. it can also be seen as a fully connected layer with identical weights per column. In each block, the horizontal receptive area is increased by 2 from the two successive 3×3 convolutions in the first branch. This means that in the end, each column output can contain information from 8 neighboring input columns to both sides and is not restricted to data from its own column. The architecture is depicted in Fig. 2.

---

[1] https://sibylle.informatik.uni-bremen.de/public/datasets/fieldboundary.

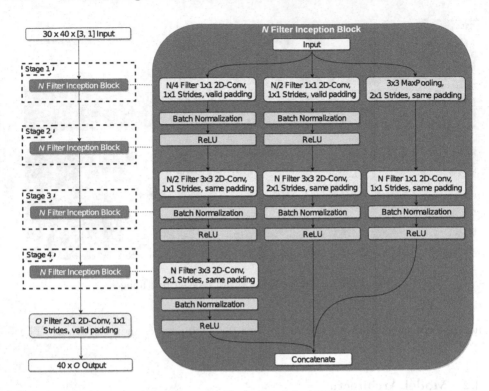

Fig. 2. Architecture of the CNN

3.3 Training

The network is trained in batches of 16 elements using the Adam algorithm with Nesterov momentum [3] for up to 50 epochs. Training is stopped early when the validation loss has not improved for five epochs. In the basic configuration without predicting uncertainty (see Sect. 3.4), the loss is defined as the mean absolute difference between predicted and true vertical coordinate per column. The learning rate starts at 0.001 and is quartered when there is no significant improvement in validation loss for three epochs.

Each batch of training data is augmented online before being fed into the network. For this, we use *imgaug* [6] with several global and point-wise operators, including flipping and cropping the image, adding noise and a constant brightness offset, as well as motion blur. In addition, a custom augmentation that randomly selects polygonal regions of the image and randomly scales their brightness in order to model hard shadows [1] is applied.

3.4 Predicting Uncertainty

In some cases, it is impossible to determine the location of the field boundary at a specific column in the image. For example, if the field boundary is occluded at one of the image borders, there could be a corner behind it or not. However, the network could actually *see* in the image that the predictions in those columns are uncertain. Therefore, we employ the approach as in Richter-Klug and Frese [10] to let the network predict its own uncertainty without needing additional labels. Instead of predicting just a vertical coordinate, the network predicts the parameters of a one-dimensional Gaussian distribution for each column.

This can be achieved by using as loss function the negative log-likelihood of a Gaussian parameterized by mean $\hat{\mu}$ and variance $\hat{\sigma}^2$ as predicted by the network, evaluated at the true y-coordinate for a given column:

$$L(y, (\hat{\mu}, \hat{\sigma})) = -\log p(y|\hat{\mu}, \hat{\sigma}^2)$$

$$= -\log \frac{1}{\sqrt{2\pi\hat{\sigma}^2}} e^{-\frac{(y-\hat{\mu})^2}{2\hat{\sigma}^2}}$$

$$= \frac{\log 2\pi}{2} + \log \hat{\sigma} + \frac{(y-\hat{\mu})^2}{2\hat{\sigma}^2}$$

Rewriting in terms of the reciprocal of the variance, the information $\hat{\omega}^2 = \frac{1}{\hat{\sigma}^2}$ (which our network actually predicts) yields

$$L(y, (\hat{\mu}, \hat{\omega})) = \frac{\log 2\pi}{2} - \log \hat{\omega} + \frac{(y-\hat{\mu})^2 \cdot \hat{\omega}^2}{2}.$$

This loss function can be interpreted in the following way: In order to minimize the $-\log\hat{\omega}$ term, the information must be maximized. At the same time, the error of the predicted mean $(y - \hat{\mu})^2$ is scaled by this number, so in order to simultaneously reduce that term, the mean prediction $\hat{\mu}$ must be moved closer to the true label y. This way, $\hat{\omega}$ is guided to neither over-nor underestimate the error of $\hat{\mu}$.

In fact, the raw output of the network is $\sqrt{\hat{\omega}}$ in order to ensure that $\hat{\omega}$ is always nonnegative. Furthermore, we add a small value ϵ to the argument of the $-\log\hat{\omega}$ term to shift it away from the singularity at 0. Also, the log-likelihood loss is used *in addition to* the absolute coordinate difference $|y - \hat{\mu}|$, which should put a bit more emphasis on actual accuracy.

3.5   Post Processing

In the simplest case, the coordinates predicted by the neural network can be used directly as a polygonal chain. However, we can enhance the prediction by fitting a model to the predicted values. Algorithm 1 describes a possible procedure to fit up to two lines, which is enough for typical images taken by a NAO on a standard platform league field. It takes advantage of the predicted $\hat{\omega}$ by using it as weighting factor in the regression objective. This way, columns in which the network is uncertain about its $\hat{\mu}$ prediction (i.e. $\hat{\omega}$ is low) do not contribute much to the overall cost to be minimized.

On a real robot, instead of selecting the model with lowest line fitting residual c, one could also use the deviation of the angle between the two lines projected

Algorithm 1. Fitting a model through predicted boundary spots using weighted linear regression and exhaustive search for the apex.

1: **function** FITLINE($\mathbf{X} = (x_{1..k}, \hat{\mu}_{1..k}, \hat{\omega}_{1..k})$)
2:     $C := (m, b) \mapsto \sum_{i=1}^{k} \hat{\omega}_i^2 \cdot (mx_i + b - \hat{\mu}_i)^2$
3:     $L \leftarrow \arg\min_{m,b} C(m, b)$
4:     **return** $(L, C(L))$
5: **end function**
6:
7: **function** FITMODEL($\mathbf{X} = (x_{1..N}, \hat{\mu}_{1..N}, \hat{\omega}_{1..N})$)
8:     $M^*, c^* \leftarrow$ FITLINE($\mathbf{X}$)
9:     **for** $i = 2$ to $N - 2$ **do**
10:         $L_A, c_A \leftarrow$ FITLINE($\mathbf{X}_{1..i}$)
11:         $L_B, c_B \leftarrow$ FITLINE($\mathbf{X}_{i+1..N}$)
12:         **if** $c_A + c_B < c^*$ **then**
13:             $c^* \leftarrow c_A + c_B$
14:             $M^* \leftarrow (L_A, L_B)$
15:         **end if**
16:     **end for**
17:     **return** M^*
18: **end function**

---

on the ground (using the camera pose) from 90°. If no two lines have an angle close to 90° the single line through all points is accepted.

In principle, this method can be extended to cameras with wide-angle lenses with distortion by choosing an appropriate model function. However, as soon as it frequently happens that more than one field corner is in the image, searching for them becomes more complex, e.g. quadratic for two corners.

In addition, if $\hat{\omega}$ is low for most columns, i.e. the network is overall uncertain, it can be assumed that the field boundary is not in the image at all (e.g. because another robot is standing directly in front of the camera).

4   Evaluation

This section describes the experiments done to evaluate the approach and their results. We have created 12 different versions of the CNN: combinations of three different filter numbers $N \in 8, 16, 24$, grayscale or color input, and with or without uncertainty prediction. The networks without uncertainty prediction differ in that they have only one output channel which is the target coordinate, and that this output is only trained on the mean absolute error as described in Sect. 3.3.

4.1   Accuracy

The first experiment for evaluating the accuracy of the method is to calculate the mean absolute difference between predicted and true vertical field boundary location over all columns in the test set. For interpreting these numbers, recall that the network operates on an input that is 30 pixels high, so an error of one pixel corresponds to 0.03333. The results are given in Table 1. It is noticeable that all color networks are consistently better than their grayscale counterpart. This is not surprising, as the green color is the main feature of the field. Also, for each column in Table 1, the performance improves with the number of filters per branch N. Increasing N even further, e.g. to 32, also increases the number of parameters in the network, e.g. to about 60000 for $N = 32$, and is therefore not desirable. Using different filter numbers per block is possible too, but expands the design space a lot. The counterparts with uncertainty prediction are, with one exception[2], significantly worse than the networks which have been trained to predict the coordinate only. This is understandable in the way that they actually have been trained for a different objective.

Table 1. Mean absolute error of raw network output on the test set

	Without Uncertainty		With Uncertainty	
	Grayscale	Color	Grayscale	Color
$N = 8$	0.05708	0.03108	0.06061	0.03800
$N = 16$	0.05412	0.02357	0.05110	0.03168
$N = 24$	0.03998	**0.02355**	0.04734	**0.02781**

Next, we evaluate the performance after model fitting according to Sect. 3.5. Here, the mean absolute error is determined after discretizing the fitted model in the same way as the labels are, so the numbers in Table 2 are comparable to Table 1. The fitting for the networks without uncertainty prediction assigns a unit weight to all columns. For comparison, results in which unit weights are used are also included for the color networks with uncertainty. In all 12 configurations, the error has been reduced by line fitting with respect to the raw outputs from Table 1. However, the errors of the models fitted with weighting factors predicted by the network are still worse than those fitted through the outputs of a network that has been trained to predict the coordinate only. On the other hand, there is an improvement in the uncertainty models when using the predicted instead of unit weights (i.e. from the rightmost column of Table 2 to the one next to it), indicating that the predicted uncertainty actually correlates with the positional accuracy of the network in a specific image column.

For a visual evaluation of the networks with uncertainty prediction, $N = 24$ and line fitting, refer to Fig. 3. All nine images are neither in the training nor in

---

[2] The optimization for the combination *without uncertainty, grayscale*, $N = 16$ stopped after only 9 epochs.

Table 2. Mean absolute error of fitted models on the test set

	Without Uncertainty		With Uncertainty		
	Grayscale	Color	Grayscale	Color	Color Unweighted
$N = 8$	0.05271	0.02907	0.05293	0.03374	0.03665
$N = 16$	0.05060	**0.02226**	0.04431	0.02727	0.03037
$N = 24$	0.03718	**0.02226**	0.04123	**0.02436**	0.02668

the validation set. While the neural network using colors looks quite accurate, the performance on grayscale images is significantly worse. Occlusion of the field boundary from robots often causes the mean prediction to deviate, but the uncertainty reflects this well, as can be seen, e.g., in the leftmost image in the fourth row.

A frequent artifact are arcs at the borders of the image, i.e. the left-/rightmost few columns deviate increasingly from the actual field boundary. We hypothesize that this is due to the zero padding which causes the outer columns to receive less activation. However, the uncertainty also correctly increases there. A column-specific bias could help with this.

4.2 Inference Time

In order to run our networks on a NAO V6, we use *CompiledNN* [14]. The numbers in Table 3 have been obtained using the included benchmark tool with 10000 iterations. The inference times are mainly influenced by the number of filters N. The usage of color in the input adds $20\,\mu s$ on average, while the additional output channel for predicting uncertainty has no significant impact. Anyway, all networks are fast enough to be used as a preprocessing step of a real-time 30 Hz vision pipeline.

Table 3. Inference times of the CNNs on a NAO V6 in milliseconds

	Without Uncertainty		With Uncertainty	
	Grayscale	Color	Grayscale	Color
$N = 8$	0.555	0.573	0.558	0.572
$N = 16$	1.539	1.557	1.533	1.562
$N = 24$	3.198	3.223	3.204	3.218

Fig. 3. Grayscale/color image pairs with the output of the respective networks with uncertainty and $N = 24$. The solid red line is the predicted mean, the dotted lines are $\pm\hat{\sigma}$ intervals, and the blue line is the fitted model. (Color figure online)

5   Conclusion

In this paper, we expanded on [15] and showed that a convolutional neural network is able to detect the field boundary in an image from raw pixels to column-wise vertical coordinates. Color information is important for this to work properly. The overall accuracy is reasonably good also in difficult conditions, as can be seen in Fig. 3. Results about uncertainty prediction are inconclusive: Numerical results even after weighted line fitting are not as good as the plain coordinate predictions of networks which do not predict uncertainty, but at least for the networks with uncertainty output, the weighted line fitting is more accurate than with unit weights. To combine the advantages of both variants, it can be examined to pretrain a network without the uncertainty output and then introduce the additional output while freezing some of the layers. The inference times of all presented networks are low enough to be used in a real-time vision pipeline.

Some of the presented networks are used by the SPL team B-Human. They apply different postprocessing that also transfers information between the two cameras of the NAO, but uses the uncertainty prediction only for determining whether the field boundary is in the image at all. It has already been used in test games and the German Open Replacement Event 2021 and will be used at RoboCup 2021.

For future investigation, we have started experiments to replace the CNN by a transformer, similar to [2]. The prototype treats each column of the image as an element in a sequence, such that in the end, the results can be read from a regression head for each element. The idea is that the transformer is more able to combine global features while retaining the column-wise structure of the problem, but without being restricted to the receptive field of convolutions. However, we cannot report results yet.

The code as well as the dataset that have been used for this paper are available online: https://github.com/bhuman/DeepFieldBoundary

Acknowledgements. This work is partially funded by the German BMBF - Bundesministerium für Bildung und Forschung project Fast&Slow (FKZ 01IS19072). Furthermore, the authors would like to thank the past and current members of the team B-Human for developing the software base for this work.

References

1. Blumenkamp, J., Baude, A., Laue, T.: Closing the reality gap with unsupervised sim-to-real image translation for semantic segmentation in robot soccer (2019). https://arxiv.org/abs/1911.01529
2. Dosovitskiy, A., et al.: An image is worth 16×16 words: transformers for image recognition at scale (2020). https://arxiv.org/abs/2010.11929
3. Dozat, T.: Incorporating Nesterov momentum into Adam. In: ICLR Workshop (2016)

4. Fiedler, N., Brandt, H., Gutsche, J., Vahl, F., Hagge, J., Bestmann, M.: An open source vision pipeline approach for RoboCup humanoid soccer. In: Chalup, S., Niemueller, T., Suthakorn, J., Williams, M.-A. (eds.) RoboCup 2019. LNCS (LNAI), vol. 11531, pp. 376–386. Springer, Cham (2019). https://doi.org/10.1007/978-3-030-35699-6_29
5. Hess, T., Mundt, M., Weis, T., Ramesh, V.: Large-scale stochastic scene generation and semantic annotation for deep convolutional neural network training in the RoboCup SPL. In: Akiyama, H., Obst, O., Sammut, C., Tonidandel, F. (eds.) RoboCup 2017. LNCS (LNAI), vol. 11175, pp. 33–44. Springer, Cham (2018). https://doi.org/10.1007/978-3-030-00308-1_3
6. Jung, A.B., et al.: imgaug (2020). https://github.com/aleju/imgaug
7. Mahmoudi, H., et al.: MRL team description paper for humanoid KidSize league of RoboCup 2019. Technical report, Mechatronics Research Lab, Qazvin Islamic Azad University (2019)
8. Qian, Y., Lee, D.D.: Adaptive field detection and localization in robot soccer. In: Behnke, S., Sheh, R., Sariel, S., Lee, D.D. (eds.) RoboCup 2016. LNCS (LNAI), vol. 9776, pp. 218–229. Springer, Cham (2017). https://doi.org/10.1007/978-3-319-68792-6_18
9. Reinhardt, T.: Kalibrierungsfreie Bildverarbeitungsalgorithmen zur echtzeitfähigen Objekterkennung im Roboterfußball. Master's thesis, Hochschule für Technik, Wirtschaft und Kultur Leipzig (2011)
10. Richter-Klug, J., Frese, U.: Towards Meaningful uncertainty information for CNN based 6d pose estimates. In: Tzovaras, D., Giakoumis, D., Vincze, M., Argyros, A. (eds.) ICVS 2019. LNCS, vol. 11754, pp. 408–422. Springer, Cham (2019). https://doi.org/10.1007/978-3-030-34995-0_37
11. Rodriguez, D., et al.: RoboCup 2019 AdultSize winner NimbRo: deep learning perception, in-walk kick, push recovery, and team play capabilities. In: Chalup, S., Niemueller, T., Suthakorn, J., Williams, M.-A. (eds.) RoboCup 2019. LNCS (LNAI), vol. 11531, pp. 631–645. Springer, Cham (2019). https://doi.org/10.1007/978-3-030-35699-6_51
12. Schnekenburger, F., Scharffenberg, M., Wülker, M., Hochberg, U., Dorer, K.: Detection and localization of features on a soccer field with feedforward fully convolutional neural networks (FCNN) for the adult-size humanoid robot Sweaty. In: Proceedings of the 12th Workshop on Humanoid Soccer Robots, IEEE-RAS International Conference on Humanoid Robots. Birmingham (2017)
13. Szegedy, C., Vanhoucke, V., Ioffe, S., Shlens, J., Wojna, Z.: Rethinking the Inception architecture for computer vision (2015). https://arxiv.org/abs/1512.00567v3
14. Thielke, F., Hasselbring, A.: A JIT compiler for neural network inference. In: Chalup, S., Niemueller, T., Suthakorn, J., Williams, M.-A. (eds.) RoboCup 2019. LNCS (LNAI), vol. 11531, pp. 448–456. Springer, Cham (2019). https://doi.org/10.1007/978-3-030-35699-6_36
15. Tilgner, R., et al.: Nao-Team HTWK team research report. Technical report, Hochschule für Technik, Wirtschaft und Kultur Leipzig (2020)

Towards Building Rapport with a Human Support Robot

Katarzyna Pasternak[1]($\boxtimes$), Zishi Wu[1], Ubbo Visser[1], and Christine Lisetti[2]

[1] Department of Computer Science, University of Miami,
Coral Gables, FL 33146, USA
{kwp,zishi,visser}@cs.miami.edu
[2] Knights Foundation School of Computing and Information Sciences,
Florida International University, 11200 SW 8th Street, Miami, FL 33199, USA
lisetti@cis.fiu.edu

Abstract. Human support robots (mobile robots able to perform useful domestic manipulative tasks) might be better accepted by people if they can communicate in ways they naturally understand: e.g. speech, but also facial expressions, postures, among others. Subtle (unconscious) mirroring of nonverbal cues during conversations promotes rapport building, essential for good communication. We investigate whether, as in human-human communication, the ability of a robot to mirror its user's head movements and facial expressions in real time can improve the user's experience with it. We describe the technical integration of a Toyota Human Support Robot (HSR) with a facially expressive 3D embodied conversational agent (ECA) (named ECA-HSR). The HSR and the ECA are aware of the user's head movements and facial emotions, and can mirror them, in real time. We then discuss a user study we designed in which participants interacted with ECA-HSR in a simple social dialog task with three conditions: mirroring of user's head movements, mirroring of user's facial emotions, and mirroring of both user's head movements and facial emotions. Our results suggest that interacting with an ECA-HSR that mirrors both the user's head movements and the facial expressions is preferred over the other conditions. Among other insights, the study revealed that the accuracy of open source, real-time recognition of facial expressions of emotion needs improvement for the best user's acceptance.

Keywords: Human robot interaction · 3d embodied conversational agents · Autonomous support robots · Nonverbal communication

1 Introduction

Forthcoming human-support robots are anticipated to assist people in a variety of contexts [3,22] involving socio-emotional personal information (e.g. helping an elderly person live safely independently) best communicated to humans via their innate communication modalities (e.g. speech, facial expressions, gestures), and ideally with established rapport between interlocutors. We aim to continue

© Springer Nature Switzerland AG 2022
R. Alami et al. (Eds.): RoboCup 2021, LNAI 13132, pp. 214–225, 2022.
https://doi.org/10.1007/978-3-030-98682-7_18

investigating the introduction of ECAs on social and service robots as a natural user interface metaphor for Human Robot Interaction (HRI) [10,17].

Establishing and maintaining rapport between humans is a proven determinant of positive communication outcomes, and is the result of a combination of highly socio-cultural-emotional complex processes, some of which are unconscious: *mutual attentiveness* (e.g., mutual gaze, mutual interest, and focus during interaction), *positivity* (e.g., head nods, smiles, friendliness, and warmth) and unconscious *coordination* (e.g., postural mirroring, synchronized movements, balance, and harmony) [11,26].

In this article, we focus on one of these processes, *coordination*. Specifically, we examine the coordination/mirroring of (1) head movements and (2) facial emotions [2,8,14]. Mirroring has been studied extensively in interactions between robots and humans, as well as in interactions between ECAs and humans. However, there are only a few studies [1,5] that examine interactions between humans and ECAs that are integrated with robots, and none of them examine the effect of mirroring nonverbal behaviors in such interactions.

Our aim is to answer the question of whether integrating an ECA capable of mirroring its interlocutor's head movements and facial emotions (continuously or intermittently) with a support robot will improve the user's experience with that robot, which is capable of performing useful mobile manipulative tasks in a home environment. We review the latest research on our topic and propose to model rapport for human-robot interaction. We discuss the integration of our speaking, expressive, and realistic ECA with a robotic platform, Toyota's Human-Support Robot (HSR, shown in Fig. 1). For the sake of brevity, we will use the term "ECA-HSR" throughout this paper to refer to the integrated ECA and HSR. Furthermore, we discuss how we enabled the ECA-HSR to subtly track its interlocutor's face, and to mirror their head movements and facial emotions in real time. Lastly, we describe a user study we conducted towards answering our research question.

2 Related Work

In human-robot interaction, research on robots establishing rapport is under way, with some research groups investigating verbal [4,12,23] and non-verbal [13,20,21] social cues. Previous work has examined how mimicry affects human-ECA interaction and human-robot interaction, but not human interaction with an ECA running on a robot. Hasumoto et al. [13] studied the effects of body movement mimicry in human-robot interaction by designing the Reactive Chameleon, a method of generating robot body movements that subtly mimics human body swaying during interactions. They found that subtle mimicry can positively impact the establishment of rapport, while noticeable mimicry can negatively impact it. However, this method was limited to mimicking movements of the torso and did not consider movement of other parts of the robot such as the head.

In the experiment by Riek et al. [20], participants interacted with a robotic chimpanzee named Virgil that exhibited three different types of behavior: full mimicry of head gestures, partial mimicry of nodding gestures only, and no mimicry accompanied by periodic blinks. Afterwards, participants filled out a survey that measured the social attraction toward and emotional credibility of conversation partners. No significant differences were found between participant ratings of the different mimic conditions. However, this might have been due to technical issues, as a few participants "said that the head movements were too erratic or jerky." Other participants wished for the robot to make "non-speech

sounds" (backchannel cues) to indicate understanding in conjunction with head gestures. This suggests that robot mimicry of nonverbal behavior by itself might not be enough to create rapport during an interaction with a human.

Niewiadomski et al. [16] studied how mimicry of smiles influenced interactions between ECAs and humans by testing three different types of ECA smiling behavior when providing backchannel cues: mimicking the smiles of a participant (MS), randomly smiling (RS), and no smiling (NS). They found that participants felt less engaged and more frustrated in condition NS than in condition MS, and "felt more at ease and more listened to" while telling a story

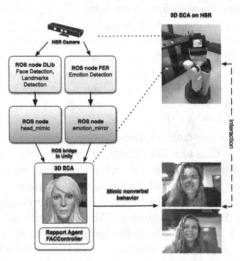

Fig. 1. Data flow in our rapport-building ROS nodes.

to the ECA in condition MS than in RS. These results suggest that mimicry in the smiling behavior of an ECA influences "the quality, ease, and warmth, of the user-agent interaction."

In the first experiment of the case study by Stevens et al. [24], participants read some sentences and then listened to an ECA speak some of those sentences incorrectly. They were then asked to say the correct version of the sentence to the ECA. Afterwards, when interacting with the experimental group, the ECA repeated what the subject said while mirroring the eyebrow raises and head nods that were observed during the subject's reading and correcting of potentially erroneous sentences, whereas in the control group no mimicry occurred when the sentence was repeated. The results showed that more prominent cues lead to higher ratings of ECA lifelikeness in the mimic condition, which supports the use of mimicry for building rapport in human-ECA interaction.

Although there exists previous work that integrates an avatar on a robot, to the best of our knowledge no study examines how the mimicry of nonverbal behavior by an ECA running on a robot influences interactions with humans. For example, Domingo et al. [5] projected an avatar on a robotic head and designed a gaze control system that enabled the robotic head to reorient its position based on the location of people that it interacted with. However, the study did not investigate mimicry of nonverbal behavior by the avatar or by the robot.

3   Technical Approach

We integrated the HSR [28] with a fully autonomous ECA. HSR is a social robot designed to assist people with disabilities and the elderly with household tasks such as cleaning or bringing objects. The software empowering the behavior of the HSR runs on top of the Robot Operating System (ROS), a middle-ware for robotic platforms where running programs called *nodes* communicate with each other by subscribing and publishing to data channels called *topics*. The hardware of the HSR includes a wide array of sensors that provide rich data on its surrounding environment, which can be accessed through pre-defined ROS topics. For example, the image data from the robot head camera can be accessed via a ROS topic called */hsrb/head_rgbd_sensor/rgb/image_raw/compressed*.

Our system consists of four ROS nodes and an ECA from a modular framework called eEVA [19], which enables the creation of ECA dialogs suitable for a wide range of scenarios. Two of the nodes run Dlib and the Facial Emotion Recognition (FER) toolkit [25], which are third-party libraries that we adapted for the purpose of analyzing images of faces. The other two nodes, named *head_mimic* and *emotion_mirror*, were created by our group to drive the nonverbal behavior of the ECA-HSR based on the analysis of face images. Below we describe in detail the functionality of each of these ROS nodes.

3.1   Face Detection and Posture Mimicking

To detect the face of a participant interacting with the HSR, we use an adapted version of Dlib [15] that runs on a ROS node and gets images from HSR's Asus Xtion Pro RGB-D camera at approx. 30fps. When the node running Dlib detects a face in the image, it draws a box around the face and marks the face with 68 landmarks as seen in Fig. 1. Then, the node gets the central position of the user's face and publishes that information to a ROS topic. Our *head_mimic* node subscribes to this topic and uses the information to drive the posture mimicry behavior of the ECA-HSR.

To move the HSR's head such that it mirrors the user's head movements, we calculate the delta values of the (x, y) coordinates of the center of the user's face from image to image. Then we scale the delta values (under the assumption that the user is approximately 60 cm away from the robot) and use the scaled values to move the HSR's head, which can move left-right-up-down (all 4 directions and their mixtures). Specifically, it can tilt up or tilt down up to $\pm 23°$, and rotate left or rotate right up to $\pm 35°$. This allows for following the position of the user in the real space and the head movements such as "nodding" and "shaking". To move the ECA, which runs on as a stand-alone Unity application, we use the Rosbridge 2[1] library to facilitate communication between the *head_mimic* node

---

[1] http://wiki.ros.org/rosbridge_suite.

and the ECA, and utilize the scaled delta values to move the ECA in the same way as was done for the HSR's head.

3.2 Facial Emotion Mirroring

In addition to mimicking posture, the ability to mirror the emotions from facial expressions, or at least the most universal of such emotions, helps to build rapport in human-human communication. According to Ekman [7], there are seven basic emotions that can be expressed by the human face. Our eEVA agent [19] (cf. Fig. 4) is an ECA capable of portraying any of these emotions in real time through movements of all the individual facial action units described in Ekman's Facial Action Coding System (FACs) [6].

To enable our system to recognize emotions, we adapted the FER toolkit to run on a ROS node. FER leverages deep learning with Linear Support Vector Machines to classify Ekman's seven basic emotions from facial expressions (see Fig. 1). We also considered another toolkit for emotion classification called EmoPy [18], but ultimately we chose FER because it classified emotions more accurately than EmoPy did. The node running FER publishes the classified emotion to another ROS topic, which is then subscribed to and used by our *emotion_mirror* node to drive the ECA's facial emotion mirroring (which we will refer to as "emotion mirroring" for short) behavior during its interaction with a participant.

3.3 Technical Considerations

Prior to our study, we tested our system and found that the ECA-HSR was performing well under three conditions: (1) the face of a participant was unobstructed, (2) the participant was inside of the maximal scope of sight of the robot's camera, and (3) the participant was facing towards the robot. Dlib excels at detecting faces in a frontal profile but when a participant turns away, it cannot properly detect their face. The same conditions apply when using FER for detecting emotions on facial expressions. Furthermore, we discovered some latency issues when the posture mimicking behavior was enabled, which was likely due to latency issues in the WiFi connection.

4   Experiments and Discussion

Overview. We designed three within-subjects experiments, which are described in the following sections, to assess the impact of various nonverbal behavior skills on the user's sense of comfort and naturalness during their interaction with the robot: *experiment 1* assesses the impact of posture mimicking; *experiment 2* assesses the impact of emotion mirroring; and *experiment 3* assesses the impact of combining posture mimicking with emotion mirroring. With a prior Institutional Review Board (IRB) approval for the study (no. 20210324), we conducted these experiments and discussed the results below.

Material. All three experiments were performed under the following setup: FER and Dlib run on an HP Spectre laptop with 16 GB RAM and four CPUs (Intel Core i7-6500U @ 2.50 GHz). The ECA was created using Unity and runs on HSR, which has an Intel Core i7-4700EQ and a NVIDIA Jetson GPU. Communication between the laptop and HSR was facilitated using a 5G WiFi network with an average package return time of 5 ms.

Participants. All three experiments were conducted with 32 participants recruited from the university campus with ages ranging from 17 to 67 years. Participants were 57.6% male and 42.4% female. The participants reported their age-ranges as under 18 (3.0%), 18–24 (45.5%), 25–50 (33.3%), 51–64 (12.1%), and 65 or above (6.1%). They reported their race as White (49%), Asian (24%), African Descent (15%), Indo-Caribbean (3%), Middle-Eastern (3%), and preferred not to identify (6%). The participants reported their ethnicity as Not Hispanic/Latino (69.7%), Hispanic/Latino (27.3%), and 3% preferred not to answer. Their education level was High School (3%), some College (27.3%), Bachelor's Degree (30.3%), some Graduate School (9.1%), Master's Degree (21.2%), Doctoral Degree (6.1%), and Not Specified (3%).

Participants also answered questions, on a 5-point Likert scale, about their previous technical experience: 6.1% claimed little experience, 36.4% had some experience, and 57.6% had a lot or a professional level experience with computers. Then, when asked about their experience with digital avatars and robots, the majority (over 70%) of participants claimed to have little or no previous experience. Thus, while most of the participants had at least some experience with computers, most had little to no experience with virtual agents or robots.

Procedure. Participants were recruited on campus by staff members who verbally asked if they would like to participate in a study where they would interact with a robot. Prior to the experiments, participants were asked to complete consent forms, demographics questionnaire and the pre-experiment questionnaire relating to their previous experience with computers, robots and virtual agents. They were also briefed about the conversational and nonverbal behavior skills of the ECA-HSR. All three experiments were conducted with the ECA running on the HSR as shown in Fig. 1. The HSR was set up in one spot and lighting conditions remained unchanged. For each experiment, participants were asked to stand in front of the robot (at a distance of approximately 60 cm) and were told they could move around within a marked area while the robot's head camera tracked their face. Furthermore, an additional ROS node controlling the speech component of the interaction was enabled, and initiated a conversation with the participant regarding the weather.

Each experiment was introduced by the ECA to differentiate where each condition of nonverbal interaction was present. For example, at the start of first condition of experiment 1, the ECA would announce, "I will first follow your head movements with the character on the screen." As the condition of the nonverbal interaction was announced by the ECA, a staff member would manually activate the appropriate ROS nodes for that mode of interaction. For each condition, participants were allowed to take two turns to ask the ECA-HSR questions related to the weather.

For each experiment, after interacting with the ECA-HSR, participants filled a questionnaire – their choice of either a form on paper or on a computer – to evaluate the ECA-HSR's performance, all without staff supervision. After completing all three experiments, participants completed an additional questionnaire about their experience and the ECA-HSR's overall performance. They were also given the option to provide suggestions for tasks they would like the robot to do in the future and for changes in the physical appearance of the robot.

EXPERIMENT 1: Assessing Skills in Posture Mimicking. We tested the effect on the user of the posture mimicking skills of the ECA alone, of the robot head alone, and of both the ECA and robot head in synchrony. The ROS node running Dlib was used to control the posture mimicking behavior, specifically mirroring of user head movements (Fig. 1). Our independent variable was posture mimicking, with three possible conditions:

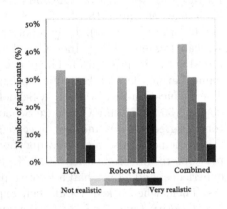

Fig. 2. How realistic were head movements.

1. the ECA mirrors the user's head movements, while the robot head stays immobile;
2. the robot head mirrors the user's head movements, while the ECA stays immobile in the center of the robot screen;
3. both the ECA and the robot head mirror the user's head movements.

Results. A majority of participants (63.6%) identified the interaction with the ECA-HSR to be the most natural in the case where both the robot head and the ECA were mirroring their head movements; furthermore, 38% of those participants commented that they felt as if the ECA-HSR agent was listening to them and that the combined movement gave it more "dimension".

Participants were then asked follow-up questions regarding how realistic the movements of each condition were. The movements were rated on a 5-point Likert scale (1 – not realistic to 5 – very realistic). The realism of the movements by the ECA alone was rated at 4 or 5 points by 36.4% participants, at 3 by 30.3%, and at 2 by 33.3% participants. The realism of the movements by the robot's head alone was rated at 4 or 5 points by 51.5% of participants, at 3 by 18.2% of participants and at 2 by 30.3% of participants. The realism of the combined movements of the ECA and the robot head was rated at 4 or 5 points by 27.3% participants, at 3 by 30.3% of participants and at 2 by 42.4% of participants. None of the movements were rated at 1 – not realistic. Overall, as shown in Fig. 2 the participants rated the movements of the robot's head as being more realistic than that of the ECA alone, or that of the ECA and robot head combined.

EXPERIMENT 2: Assessing Skills in Mirroring Facial Expressions of Emotion. In this experiment, only the performance of the ECA's emotion mirroring skills was evaluated. The ROS node running FER was used to control the mirroring of facial expressions of emotion (Fig. 1, bottom-right). Our independent variable was emotion mirroring, with two possible conditions:

1. mirroring of facial expressions of emotion enabled on ECA;
2. mirroring of facial expressions of emotion disabled on ECA.

Results. After the interaction, the participants were asked which mode of the interaction they found more engaging. 51.5% of participants said the ECA's mirroring of facial expressions made the robot more engaging, while 48.5% said the mirroring did not make the robot more engaging. Participants were then asked two follow-up questions that were rated on a 5-point scale (1 – not realistic/accurate to 5 – very realistic/accurate). The realism of the facial expressions (cf. Fig. 4) of the ECA was rated at 4 or 5 points by 21.3% participants, at 3 by 27.3%, and at 2 or 1 by 51.5%, and at 1 by 24.2% participants.

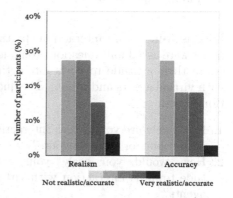

Fig. 3. Realism and accuracy of facial emotion mirroring.

The realism of the movements by the mirrored emotions portrayed by the ECA was rated at 4 or 5 points by 21.2% of participants, at 3 by 18.2% of participants, and at 2 or 1 by 60.6% of participants, as shown in Fig. 3. When given an option to explain their choice, participants who favored the ECA's emotion mirroring behavior wrote that it was *nice* or *amusing* although sometimes inaccurate. Those who did not favor described it as *grotesque* and inaccurate, but suggested they would be more receptive to a version that mirrored facial expressions precisely. The responses to those questions confirmed earlier comments regarding the realism and accuracy of portrayed emotions. For both questions, about half of the participants gave a rating of 1 or 2 points. This lead us to conclude that a better performing emotion mirroring module would be beneficial, whereas if this issue is not addressed, it would hinder our efforts to introduce an emotive ECA on a robotic platform.

EXPERIMENT 3: Assessing Skills Combining Emotion Mirroring with Posture Mimicking. In this experiment, we tested whether posture mimicking *in conjunction with* emotion mirroring, improves the user's comfort level during human-robot interaction. Our independent variable was combined posture mimicking and emotion mirroring. Both posture mimicking and emotion mirroring were engaged – the ECA mirrored facial emotions, while both the ECA and the robot's head mirrored the movements of the participant's face – for a single turn of conversation.

Results. A majority of participants (66.7%) preferred the condition where both posture mimicking and emotive mirroring were enabled. They explained in their questionnaire answers that the two behaviors made the ECA-HSR more engaging, but wished for the emotion mirroring to be more accurate and suffer less latency. Among the remaining participants (33.3%), 73% said they did not prefer this condition because the emotion mirroring was not accurate, but would like it if it was more accurate. Finally, there were two participants (6.2%) who deemed the avatar with its emotion mirroring to be scary and would prefer to not interact with it at all.

Discussion. Before interaction, participants were asked four questions to understand their attitude towards interacting with virtual agents and robots. The questions were:

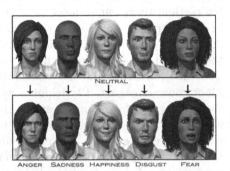

Fig. 4. Examples of eEVA facial expressions.

1. How likely are you to seek interaction with robots or virtual agents?
2. How would you scale your attitude towards interaction with virtual agents?
3. How would you scale your attitude towards interaction with robots?
4. How frustrating do you find interaction with virtual agents or robots?

For the first three questions, on a scale from 1 (never/I dislike it) to 5 (very likely/I love it), the percentage of participants that rated it 4 or 5 points was 42.5%, 39.4%, 36.4% respectively, while the percentage that rated it 3 points (neutral stance) was 27.3%, 39.4%, and 39.4% respectively.

For the fourth question, on a scale from 1 (not frustrating) to 5 (very frustrating), 33.4% rated it 1 or 2 points and 42.4% rated it 3 points. In each of these questions, at least 70% of the participants had a neutral or positive attitude towards interacting with robots or virtual agents.

Based on the evaluation of the participants' answers, the inclusion of the ECA on the HSR was favored. As previously mentioned, the majority of participants chose the interaction with both posture mimicking and emotion mirroring. When asked, on a scale of 1 to 5, of their preference to have the ECA on the robot or not, 72.7% of participants chose the two highest scores (4 and 5) meaning *I would prefer a robot with an ECA character*, 6.1% chose a neutral option (3), and 21.2% leaned towards a robot without an ECA (scores 1 and 2).

When participants were asked (on a 5-point Likert scale where 1 meant *very hard* and 5 meant *very easy*) if the interaction with the ECA-HSR was easy, 54.5% rated it with 4 or 5 points while 15.1% rated it with 1 or 2 points. A majority of the participants liked the robot, with 54.5% rating it 4 or 5 points, on a 5-point scale where 1 meant *not at all* and 5 meant *very much*. Overall,

Table 1. Participant and selected ECA's gender comparison

Participant's gender	Selected gender before Seeing images of ECAs			Selected gender after Seeing images of ECAs		
	Same	Different	No preference	Same	Different	No preference
Female	9 (64.3%)	5 (35.7%)	0	8 (57.1%)	6 (42.9%)	0
Male	4 (22.2%)	7 (38.9%)	7 (38.9%)	3 (16.7%)	13 (72.2%)	2 (11.1%)

we noticed the following patterns: participants with previous experience with robots and/or virtual agents were more critical and had higher expectations of the overall ECA-HSR performance. Furthermore, these participants almost always preferred the integrated of the ECA with the robot.

Another phenomena we investigated was whether participants, given the choice, prefer to interact with an ECA of the same gender as themselves, in the context of a social interaction at home with the ECA-HSR. Table 1 details participants' answers to the preference of an ECA's gender, from both selecting gender before seeing images of (25 different) ECAs and from selecting gender after seeing images of ECAs. In regards to the selected gender (of the ECA) before seeing images of ECAs, we found that 9 out of the 14 female participants (64.3%) expressed a preference to interact with an ECA of the same gender while only 4 out of the 18 male participants (22.2%) expressed a preference to interact with an ECA of the same gender. In regards to the selected gender (of the ECA) after seeing images of ECAs, we found that 8 out of the 14 female participants (57.1%) expressed a preference to interact with an ECA of the same gender while only 3 out of the 18 male participants (16.7%) expressed a preference to interact with an ECA of the same gender. Overall, the participants had a slight preference for interacting with a female ECA, as 16 out of the 32 participants (50%) expressed a preference to interact with a female ECA before seeing images of ECAs and 19 out of the 32 participants (59.4%) expressed a preference to interact with a female ECA after seeing images of ECAs. As an additional finding for further investigation, when asked an open-ended questions for suggestions on "any other ideas for robot tasks", all participants, regardless of their prior experience with robots and/or virtual agents, mentioned they would like the robot to clean for them.

The video demonstration of selected fragments of the study experiments can be found at https://tinyurl.com/pyrrmxft.

5   Conclusion

We studied the effects of integrating an ECA capable of mirroring the interlocutor's head movements and facial emotions (continuously or intermittently) with a human-service robot. We found that the integration of the ECA and its nonverbal behaviors has the potential to improve the overall interaction between human and robot. Specifically, users preferred the integrated ECA-HSR over the HSR alone, even though they rated the mirroring of their head movements by the HSR's head alone as being more accurate than that of the mirroring by both the ECA and the HSR. However, occasional inaccurate portrayals of nonverbal behavior, as exemplified by the facial emotion mirroring behavior of the ECA in our study, can contradict user expectations of how the system should behave and thus leave a negative impression of the interaction. One potential explanation for the ECA's inaccurate facial emotion mirroring behavior is that the seven emotions the ECA mirrored were too broad of categories that prevented the mirroring of more nuanced facial expressions. For future work, we plan to have the ECA mirror the individual facial action units of a user's facial expressions and see if this improves the users' perception of the accuracy of the ECA's facial emotion mirroring skills. We also plan to improve upon our methods for measuring the rapport-building capabilities of the ECA-HSR by incorporating validated questionnaires for HRI [27] and ECAs [9]. Finally, we acknowledge the need to improve our experimental methodology for future studies by randomizing stimuli to account for a potential learning effect among participants.

One novel finding is that the participants, regardless of their gender, responded with a slight preference for interacting with a female ECA in the context of a social interaction in a home environment. Another interesting finding is that when asked for "any other ideas about robot tasks", all the participants mentioned they would like the robot to clean for them. While they are not the main focus of this study on rapport-building, these findings point to a future research direction to investigate user preferences regarding the ECA-HSR.

References

1. Cavedon, L., et al.: C'Mon dude!: users adapt their behaviour to a robotic agent with an attention model. Int. J. Hum. Comput. Stud. **80**, 14–23 (2015)
2. Chartrand, T.L., Maddux, W.W., Lakin, J.L.: Beyond the perception-behavior link: the ubiquitous utility and motivational moderators oi nonconscious mimicry. The new unconscious, pp. 334–361 (2005)
3. Dahl, T.S., Boulos, M.N.K.: Robots in health and social care: a complementary technology to home care and telehealthcare? Robotics **3**(1), 1–21 (2014)
4. Dieter, J., Wang, T., Chaganty, A.T., Angeli, G., Chang, A.: Mimic and rephrase: reflective listening in open-ended dialogue. In: Proceedings of the 23rd Conference on Computational Natural Language Learning (CoNLL), pp. 393–403 (2019)
5. Duque-Domingo, J., Gómez-García-Bermejo, J., Zalama, E.: Gaze control of a robotic head for realistic interaction with humans. Front. Neurorobot. **14**, 34 (2020)
6. Ekman, P.: Facial action coding system (FACS). In: A Human Face (2002). nII Article ID (NAID): 10025007347
7. Ekman, P.: An argument for basic emotions. Cogn. Emot. **6**(3/4), 169–200 (1992)
8. Fischer, A., Hess, U.: Mimicking emotions. Curr. Opin. Psychol. **17**, 151–155 (2017)
9. Fitrianie, S., Bruijnes, M., Bönsch, A., Brinkman, W.P.: The 19 unifying questionnaire constructs of artificial social agents: an IVA community analysis, pp. 1–8 (10 2020). https://doi.org/10.1145/3383652.3423873
10. Goodrich, M.A., Schultz, A.C.: Human-robot interaction: a survey. Hum. Comput. Interact. **1**(3), 203–275 (2007)
11. Grahe, J.: The importance of nonverbal cues in judging rapport. J. Nonverbal Behav. **23**(4), 253–269 (1999)

12. Grigore, E.C., Pereira, A., Zhou, I., Wang, D., Scassellati, B.: Talk to me: verbal communication improves perceptions of friendship and social presence in human-robot interaction. In: Traum, D., Swartout, W., Khooshabeh, P., Kopp, S., Scherer, S., Leuski, A. (eds.) IVA 2016. LNCS (LNAI), vol. 10011, pp. 51–63. Springer, Cham (2016). https://doi.org/10.1007/978-3-319-47665-0_5
13. Hasumoto, R., Nakadai, K., Imai, M.: Reactive chameleon: a method to mimic conversation partner's body sway for a robot. Int. J. Soc. Robot. 12(1), 239–258 (2020)
14. Hess, U., Fischer, A.: Emotional mimicry: why and when we mimic emotions. Soc. Pers. Psychol. Compass 8(2), 45–57 (2014)
15. King, D.E.: Dlib-ml: a machine learning toolkit. J. Mach. Learn. Res. 10, 1755–1758 (2009)
16. Niewiadomski, R., Prepin, K., Bevacqua, E., Ochs, M., Pelachaud, C.: Towards a smiling ECA: studies on mimicry, timing and types of smiles. In: Proceedings of the 2nd International Workshop on Social Signal Processing, pp. 65–70. SSPW 2010, Association for Computing Machinery, New York, NY, USA (2010)
17. Peña, P., Polceanu, M., Lisetti, C., Visser, U.: eEVA as a real-time multimodal agent human-robot interface. In: Holz, D., Genter, K., Saad, M., von Stryk, O. (eds.) RoboCup 2018. LNCS (LNAI), vol. 11374, pp. 262–274. Springer, Cham (2019). https://doi.org/10.1007/978-3-030-27544-0_22
18. Perez, A.: EmoPy: a machine learning toolkit for emotional expression (2018). https://tinyurl.com/y6uwnet3
19. Polceanu, M., Lisetti, C.: Time to go ONLINE! a modular framework for building internet-based socially interactive agents. In: Proceedings of the 19th ACM International Conference on Intelligent Virtual Agents, pp. 227–229. IVA 2019, Association for Computing Machinery, New York, NY, USA (2019)
20. Riek, L.D., Paul, P.C., Robinson, P.: When my robot smiles at me: enabling human-robot rapport via real-time head gesture mimicry. J. Multimodal User Interfaces 3(1), 99–108 (2010)
21. Ritschel, H., Aslan, I., Mertes, S., Seiderer, A., André, E.: Personalized synthesis of intentional and emotional non-verbal sounds for social robots. In: 2019 8th International Conference on Affective Computing and Intelligent Interaction (ACII), pp. 1–7. IEEE (2019)
22. Šabanović, S.: Robots in society, society in robots. Int. J. Soc. Robot. 2(4), 439–450 (2010)
23. Seo, S.H., Griffin, K., Young, J.E., Bunt, A., Prentice, S., Loureiro-Rodríguez, V.: Investigating people's rapport building and hindering behaviors when working with a collaborative robot. IJSR 10(1), 147–161 (2018)
24. Stevens, C.J., et al.: Mimicry and expressiveness of an ECA in human-agent interaction: familiarity breeds content! Comput. Cogn. Sci. 2(1), 1–14 (2016). https://doi.org/10.1186/s40469-016-0008-2
25. Tang, Y.: Deep learning using linear support vector machines. arXiv preprint arXiv:1306.0239 (2013)
26. Tickle-Degnen, L., Rosenthal, R.: The nature of rapport and its nonverbal correlates. Psychol. Inq. 1(4), 285–293 (1990)
27. Yagoda, R., Gillan, D.: You want me to trust a ROBOT? The development of a human-robot interaction trust scale. IJSR 4, 235–248 (2012)
28. Yamamoto, T., Terada, K., Ochiai, A., Saito, F., Asahara, Y., Murase, K.: Development of Human Support Robot as the research platform of a domestic mobile manipulator. ROBOMECH J. 6(1), 1–15 (2019). https://doi.org/10.1186/s40648-019-0132-3

Faster YOLO-LITE: Faster Object Detection on Robot and Edge Devices

ZhengBai Yao⬤, Will Douglas⬤, Simon O'Keeffe⬤, and Rudi Villing(✉)⬤

Department of Electronic Engineering, Maynooth University, Maynooth, Ireland
rudi.villing@mu.ie

Abstract. Mobile robots and many edge AI devices have a need to trade off computational power against power consumption, battery size, and time between charges. Consequently, it is common for such devices to have significantly less computational power than the powerful GPU-based systems typically used to train and evaluate deep neural networks. Object detection is a key aspect of visual perception for robots and edge devices but popular object detection architectures that run fastest on GPU based systems or that are designed to maximize mAP with large input image sizes may not scale well to edge devices. In this work we evaluate the latency and mAP of several model architectures from the YOLO and SSD families on a range of devices representative of robot and edge device capabilities. We also evaluate the effect of runtime framework and show that some unexpected large differences can be found. Based on our evaluations we propose new variations of the YOLO-LITE architecture which we show can provide increased mAP at reduced latency.

Keywords: Deep learning · Object detection · Convolutional neural network · Embedded system · Real-time performance · Edge AI

1 Introduction

Essentially all training and a large majority of the inference and evaluation of deep-learning models reported in the literature is based on powerful GPU-based systems deployed locally or in the cloud. However, mobile robots and many edge AI devices need to trade off computational power against power consumption, battery size, and time between charges. For this reason, such devices are usually much less computationally powerful than those used to train and test deep neural networks and frequently they might not have a GPU. One solution to this problem might be for the edge device to do minimal processing and instead offload data for processing to the cloud [1]. However, this solution has its own issues which include data privacy, the cost of communication, and processing latency, among others. Therefore, there has recently been a trend towards deploying more sophisticated AI functionality in edge devices, including mobile robots.

In this work, we are particularly focused on object detection, a branch of computer vision AI focused on identifying and locating objects within an image. In mobile robotic applications, object detection may be used to identify and locate semantically meaningful

© Springer Nature Switzerland AG 2022
R. Alami et al. (Eds.): RoboCup 2021, LNAI 13132, pp. 226–237, 2022.
https://doi.org/10.1007/978-3-030-98682-7_19

features of the scene including objects to be grasped or manipulated, objects whose location within the map should be remembered, people and obstacles to be approached or avoided, etc. For a review of object detection in general, see [2].

A review of the literature indicates that most new developments in object detection and consequent comparative evaluations focus on increasing the mean average precision (mAP) metric for the COCO [3] or VOC 2007 and 2012 datasets [4, 5]. To achieve small percentage gains the size of neural network models has increased dramatically and real time performance is almost always quoted for GPU based systems only. There has been relatively less attention paid to object detection models that perform well on less powerful hardware using only the CPU. Additionally, most evaluations use general datasets with many object classes, but edge AI applications are often specialized and may only require a small number of classes leading to wasted representational capability (and power consumption) if large models are applied to the problem.

Therefore, this work focuses on deep neural network architectures for object detection using CPU only processing that can potentially achieve real-time video capability for which we have chosen a guideline threshold at 50 ms (or 20 FPS). The main contributions of this paper are as follows:

- We release our SPL Object Detection Dataset V2 as described in Sect. 4.1.
- We evaluate mAP and inference latency for several object detection models on a variety of representative hardware platforms.
- We also examine the effect of inference engine selection on latency and any interactions with the underlying hardware.
- Finally, we propose and evaluate two modified YOLO-LITE architectures [6].

The remainder of this paper is organized as follows. Section 2 presents some related work, particularly focusing on the model architectures. Section 3 introduces the modified YOLO-LITE architectures. Section 4 details the experimental setup used to conduct the evaluations while Sect. 5 presents the results and related discussion. Our conclusions and future work may be found in Sect. 6.

2 Related Work

The two most well known families of object detection models available today are those based on the Single Shot Multi-box Detector (SSD) architecture [7] and those derived from YOLO [8–11]. In their default configurations both these models are rather heavy-weight and real-time performance is usually reported for high-end hardware such as a Titan X GPU.

SSD has been primarily optimized for speed using the MobileNetV1 and MobileNetV2 backbones [12, 13] and generally there are relatively few variations of this model available, though some exist (e.g. [14]). YOLO, on the other hand, has attracted a lot of interest and resulted in many variations (e.g. [6, 15]), perhaps because of its simpler architecture (at least up to YOLOv2). Additionally, a number of studies find that YOLO models outperform SSD in terms of latency and mAP. Such comparisons tend not to use the MobileNet V1 or V2 versions of SSD (giving a latency disadvantage) and such comparisons normally use GPU based systems. Therefore there is a need to compare these model families in an edge device or embedded system environment. In this work we are particularly interested to evaluate lightweight or faster variants of YOLO and SSD, including YOLO-LITE [6] and YOLO with a MobileNet family backbone (e.g. [16]).

Many embedded systems require an inference framework optimized for CPU based operation and that is our focus here. The most well known inference frameworks include TensorFlow Lite [17], OpenVINO [18], and ONNX runtime. ONNX runtime uses some of the same components as OpenVINO so was not considered for evaluation here. In the RoboCup community there are two other inference frameworks of relevance. CompileNN [19] is a JIT compiler which compiles neural network models at runtime into machine code that performs inference. DCG, is an unreleased code generator from the Nao Devils Dortmund RoboCup SPL team which generates a cpp file from a keras model. The cpp file has no dependencies outside the standard libraries. Both CompileNN and DCG make it particularly easy to integrate neural network implementation with custom embedded applications.

The Coral Edge TPU [20] is a USB based accelerator that has been purpose built to run machine learning models on the edge. It operates as a coprocessor to the system it is connected to and can greatly speed up inference on slower devices.

3   New YOLO-LITE Based Models

YOLO-LITE is a simple architecture (with just seven convolutional layers) that is relatively easy to modify but preliminary results indicated it was not the fastest, despite its small size. We observed that MobileNetV1-YOLOv4 offered the best trade-off between mAP and latency while MobileNetV2-SSD had the highest overall mAP. We identified several design decisions in YOLO-LITE which differed from the two better performing models: (1) the use of standard convolutions throughout; (2) the use of Max Pooling layers only after each convolution has been performed at full resolution; (3) the exclusion of Batch Normalization layers; and (4) use of the Leaky ReLU activation function.

Based on this analysis we developed two scalable modifications of the YOLO-LITE architecture for inclusion in our experimental evaluations. Figure 1 shows the key blocks used in the original YOLO-LITE and our modified versions.

3.1   YOLO-LITE-M1

The first variant of YOLO-LITE modifies the backbone of the model inspired by MobileNetV1. The number of channels per layer is based on YOLO-LITE. All convolution layers are replaced by mobile convolution (MConv) layers in which the convolution is replaced by a depthwise convolution followed by a pointwise 1×1 convolution (see Fig. 1). LeakyReLU activations are replaced by ReLU6. Max pooling layers are removed and instead the relevant convolutions are performed with a stride of 2. Finally, in contrast to YOLO-LITE, Batch Normalization layers are re-introduced.

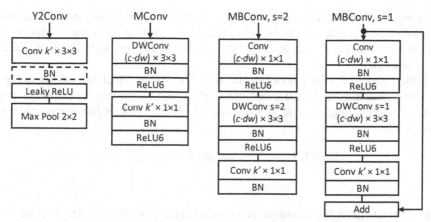

Fig. 1. Main convolutional stages used in TinyYOLOv2 and YOLO-LITE (Y2Conv, no BN in YOLO-LITE), YOLO-LITE-M1 (MConv), and YOLO-LITE-M2 (MBConv). The number of input channels, c, is expanded by the depthwise multiplier, dw. The number of output channels, k', is modified by the channel multiplier in accordance with (1).

Like MobileNetV1 we include a channel multiplier (they call it the width multiplier) which scales the number of kernels or output channels generated at every convolutional layer. A factor of 1 has the same number of output channels at each layer as the original YOLO-LITE architecture. Factors smaller than one reduce the number of channels (and consequently the number of parameters and the computation load) while factors larger than 1 increase them. To facilitate efficient SIMD processing, we constrain the channels at each layer to be the nearest multiple of a tiling parameter that matches the requested channel multiplication factor. The tiling parameter defaults to 8 in this work. In other words the actual output channels, k', is calculated as:

$$k' = \text{round}(k \cdot cm, tile) \tag{1}$$

MobileNetV2 bottleneck layers introduce the concept of an expansion factor such that the number of channels in an input layer is first expanded before applying a depthwise separable convolution. The MobileNetV2 authors found that this increased the expressiveness of the network. In YOLO-LITE-M1 we use a simplification of this idea, controlled by a depthwise multiplier which determines the number of output channels for each input channel. When the depthwise multiplier is 1, this is a standard depthwise separable convolution. When it is greater than 1, the depthwise output is expanded relative to the input and each input layer is convolved depthwise with multiple independent filter kernels, giving the expanded output more representative capability. In this simplified scheme, each expanded channel is a function of one kernel convolved with one input channel whereas in the MobileNetV2 scheme, each expanded channel is a weighted sum of all the input channels.

As a final modification from the original YOLO-LITE architecture, we modify the overall depth of the network in a rather simple manner depending on the input image size. This modification is inspired both by the need to maintain a certain minimum spatial resolution in the object detection head layers and by the development of EfficientNet, whose authors found that network depth (that is the number of layers) should be adjusted alongside other factors such as the input image size. Consequently the 5th convolution layer in the model is optional and is included only if the input image size is of size 224 × 224 or larger.

Table 1 depicts the final model architecture. The MConv block is as shown in Fig. 1. The Conv block is a standard 2D convolutional layer whose number of outputs are scaled by the channel multiplier, cm, in accordance with (1). YOLOChannels is calculated according to:

$$YOLOChannels = anchors \times (classes + 5) \tag{2}$$

Table 1. YOLO-LITE-M1 architecture (for nominal 224 × 224 × 3 input) where s is the stride, cm is the channel multiplier and dw is the depthwise expansion multiplier which is scalable for most stages but fixed at 1 for stage 2 of the architecture. Stage 5 is excluded for inputs smaller than 224 × 224.

Stage	Input size (for $cm = 1$)	Operator(s)
1	224 × 224 × 3	Conv(16, 3 × 3, $s = 2$), BN, ReLU6
2	112 × 112 × 16	MConv(32, $s = 2$, cm, $dw = 1$)
3	56 × 56 × 32	MConv(64, $s = 2$, cm, dw)
4	28 × 28 × 64	MConv(128, $s = 2$, cm, dw)
5 (optional)	14 × 14 × 128	MConv(128, $s = 2$, cm, dw)
6	7 × 7 × 128	Conv(256, 3 × 3, cm), BN, ReLU6
7	7 × 7 × 256	Conv($YOLOChannels$, 1 × 1)

3.2 YOLO-LITE-M2

The second variant of YOLO-LITE modifies the backbone of the model based on MobileNetV2 instead of MobileNetV1. Unlike YOLO-LITE-M1, the number of output channels per stage is based more closely on the MobileNetV2 architecture than YOLO-LITE. The resulting model is much deeper than YOLO-LITE but with fewer output channels per stage. Our expectation was that a deeper but narrower model, with more expressive bottleneck layers would yield higher mAP, possibly at the expense of increased inference latency.

Similar to MobileNetV2, mobile bottleneck (MBConv) blocks are the principal elements of the design. As shown in Fig. 1, these include an extra 1 × 1 convolution that implements the expansion of input channels within the block in a more sophisticated manner than the MConv block. Additionally, when MBConv blocks are repeated in a cascade within a stage, the first block in the cascade implements the specified stride. Subsequent blocks in the cascade use a stride of 1 and in this case include a so-called inverted residual connection (between bottlenecks) as shown in Fig. 1.

Table 2 depicts the final model architecture. The MBConv block is as shown in Fig. 1. Again, the Conv block is a standard 2D convolutional layer whose number of outputs may be scaled by the channel multiplier, cm, in accordance with (1).

Table 2. YOLO-LITE-M2 architecture (for nominal $224 \times 224 \times 3$ input) where s is the stride (only applied to the first block in a cascade), cm is the channel multiplier, dw is the bottleneck expansion multiplier, and n is the number of times the operation is cascaded in that stage. Stage 5 is excluded for inputs smaller than 224×224.

Stage	Input size (for $cm = 1$)	Operator(s)	n
1	$224 \times 224 \times 3$	Conv(32, 3×3, $s = 2$), BN, ReLU6	1
2	$112 \times 112 \times 32$	MBConv(16, $s = 2$, cm, dw)	1
3	$56 \times 56 \times 16$	MBConv(24, $s = 2$, cm, dw)	2
4	$28 \times 28 \times 24$	MBConv(32, $s = 2$, cm, dw)	2
5 (optional)	$14 \times 14 \times 32$	MBConv(64, $s = 2$, cm, dw)	3
6	$7 \times 7 \times 64$	Conv(256, 3×3, cm), BN, ReLU6	1
7	$7 \times 7 \times 256$	Conv($YOLOChannels$, 1×1)	1

4   Experimental Setup

4.1   Dataset and Training

Unlike traditional evaluations which utilize VOC (20 classes) or COCO (80 classes) datasets, the dataset used here was based on RoboCup robot soccer (4 classes) and is available for download[1]. This dataset may be more representative of application specific datasets in embedded or edge AI applications which feature relatively few classes. The dataset comprised 4416 training images and 492 test images with 13178 and 1486 object instances respectively divided into four object classes: robot (5412), ball (4452), goal post (2912), and penalty spot (1888). Objects are present in a variety of sizes and can overlap. The goal post and penalty spot classes are relatively challenging for most object detectors.

For reasons not directly related to this evaluation, two different training regimes were used. MobileNetV2-SSD (at full width) and TinyYOLOv3 were both trained on a Dell XPS 8930 with an Intel i7-9700 CPU and an NVIDIA RTX2060 GPU. Both models were trained using weights that had been pre-trained on the COCO dataset. MobileNetV2-SSD was trained in TensorFlow 1.15 for 40000 iterations with a batch size of 6, resulting in 240000 images being processed in total. TinyYOLOv3 was trained in the DarkNet framework using the same batch size and number of iterations.

All other models were trained on a Dell Precision 3630 workstation with an Intel i7-8700K CPU and an NVIDIA P2000 GPU. These models did not use pre-trained weights

---

[1] https://roboeireann.maynoothuniversity.ie/research/SPLObjDetectDatasetV2.zip.

and were trained from scratch on the evaluation data set. Models were trained for up to 200 epochs with a batch size of 32 and 10% of the training data used for validation. Therefore, 793600 images were processed during training.

The dataset images are 640×480 RGB. We standardized on three input sizes for training and subsequent evaluation: $128 \times 128, 224 \times 224$, and 416×416. The standard training and data augmentation procedures were followed for SSD and YOLO based models.

4.2 Models

We selected models that were specifically designed to be less computationally intensive for evaluation. Two variants of MobileNetV2-SSD were evaluated. The first (using transfer learning from pre-trained weights) utilised the default MobileNetV2 width (width $= 1$). Preliminary investigation indicated this might be very slow, so the second variant used width $= 0.25$ so that it might run with lower latency.

Two variations of TinyYOLO were also included in the evaluation: TinyYOLOv4 and TinyYOLOv3. TinyYOLOv3 used transfer learning from pre-trained weights so its mAP may not be directly comparable to that of TinyYOLOv3. The implementation of TinyYOLOv4 was based on TensorFlow and Keras [16]. The learning rate was set to 1e−4 and the only modifications involved were setting the number of classes, the class names, and the anchors to use.

MobileNetV1-YOLOv4 used width $= 0.25$ for the MobileNetV1 backbone. Again, preliminary work indicated that the full width backbone would run too slowly. The implementation is based on [21]. Other than the width, remaining modifications were the same as for TinyYOLOv4.

YOLO LITE was originally developed for the DarkNet/DarkFlow framework. We ported this to Keras using the general structure of the TinyYOLOv4 implementation. Learning rate, classes, and anchors were set to match the other YOLO family models.

YOLO-LITE-M1 was evaluated in two configurations: (1) cm $= 1$, dw $= 1$; (2) cm $= 0.5$, dw $= 4$ which might have higher mAP. Similarly YOLO-LITE-M2 was evaluated using two configurations: (1) cm $= 1$, dw $= 4$ and (2) cm $= 0.5$, dw $= 4$. MobileNetV2 originally set the expansion to 6 but we used 4 to reduce the size and maintain a number of outputs that was a multiple of 4 and should tile well.

4.3 Inference Configurations

We evaluated the models on the following hardware platforms:

- Raspberry Pi 3B with quad core Broadcom BCM2837 CPU @ 1.2 GHz running Raspian Linux 10 (Buster).
- Acer Aspire One netbook with an Intel Atom N270 CPU @ 1.6 GHz running Lubuntu 18.04.5. This is a very similar vintage and capability to the Atom Z530 CPU in the Softbank Nao V5 robot, but more convenient to use for this evaluation. Notably, unlike other systems in this list, this is a 32-bit processor.

- Softbank Nao V6 with a quad core Intel Atom E3485 CPU @ 1.9 GHz
- Latitude 7400 notebook with an Intel i7-8665U CPU @ 1.9 GHz running Ubuntu 18.04.5 (potentially representative of higher end or more modern robotic systems).

Including the i7-8665U gives some insight into differences that may appear due to more modern instruction sets (for example the inclusion of AVX2 and FMA) and also gives insight into the difference between machines used for development (even those without a GPU) and less powerful CPUs often used in edge and mobile robot devices.

Inference was evaluated using (1) TensorFlow Lite version 2.5.0 or built from source (as of 8 April 2021); (2) CompileNN, built from source (as of 6 April 2021); (3) Nao Devils DCG code generator (unreleased version as of 14 April 2021); (4) Intel Open-VINO developer package, version 2021.3.394; and (5) the Coral Edge TPU Accelerator version 1.0. Table 3 lists the configurations evaluated.

Table 3. Hardware and inference framework combinations evaluated. Note: fp = floating point, q8 = quantized 8-bit integer, NT = not tested, NC = not compatible, NR = tested but not reported as times were worse than floating point

Hardware	tflite-fp	tflite-q8	tflite + Coral	OpenVINO	CompileNN	DCG
RPi3B	Y	Y	Y	NT	NC	NC
Atom N270	Y	NR	NC	NC	Y	Y
NaoV6	Y	NR	Y	Y	Y	Y
i7-8665U	Y	NR	Y	Y	Y	Y

Common benchmarking parameters were used on all systems as follows: a batch size of 1; just 1 thread for inference; at least 5 warm-up runs; and 100 inference runs averaged for latency measurement. Each framework was benchmarked using its own benchmark tool, namely benchmark_model for TensorFlow Lite, Benchmark for CompileNN, benchmark_app.py for OpenVino, and the embedded benchmarking code in DCG generated cpp files.

Perhaps surprisingly, when applied to DCG cpp files, we found that clang (6.0.0) produced a binary that ran 20% faster than code compiled with g++ (7.5.0) using the same optimisation settings.

5   Results and Discussion

5.1   Model Architecture and Input Image Size

The effect of model architecture and input image size was evaluated using all models with the one inference framework (TensorFlow Lite) available on all hardware platforms. On the NaoV6, Fig. 2 shows that just two of the models attain our real-time target and both have an mAP which is much lower than the maximum achieved. MobileNetV2-YOLOv4 and YOLO-LITE both demonstrate significant mAP gains for moderate increase in latency, suggesting that these models are the most promising for further development and tuning. MobileNetV2-SSD-0.25 has the best overall mAP with input size 224 and 416 and is only beaten by MobileNetV2-SSD at size 128.

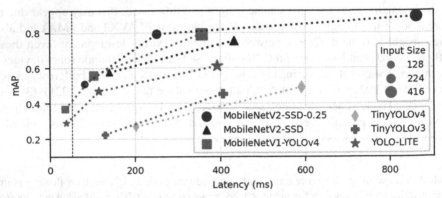

Fig. 2. Latency and mAP in relation to object detection model and input image size evaluated on the NaoV6 (Atom E3845) using the TensorFlow Lite runtime. Very long latencies associated with input size 416 are not shown for presentation reasons.

Latencies for the i7 platform follow a similar pattern to the NaoV6, but are between 6 and 14 times shorter, and are therefore not shown. The situation was broadly similar on the older Atom N270 and the Raspberry Pi, but the latencies are longer as shown in Fig. 3. The latency lead of MobileNetV1-YOLOv4 over YOLO-LITE is more pronounced here. This would suggest that the speedup advantage of the MobileNet family of architectures is even more important on these platforms.

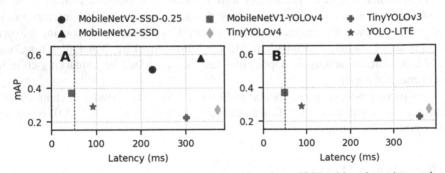

Fig. 3. Object detection latency on Atom N270 and Raspberry Pi 3B with an input image size of 128 × 128. Larger input sizes yielded much longer latencies and are consequently not shown.

5.2 Choice of Inference Framework, Quantization, and Accelerator Support

To compare inference frameworks, we selected two unrelated models that were suitable for quantization: an SSD model and a YOLO based model. Figure 4 shows the latency results for YOLO-LITE (second fastest overall and easy to quantize) and MobileNetV2-SSD (well supported for quantization) across the range of hardware and inference framework combinations presented in Table 3.

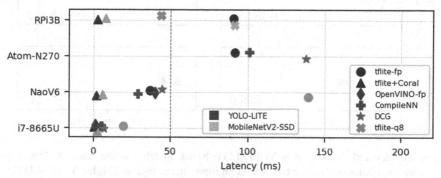

Fig. 4. Object detection latency on multiple hardware platform and inference runtime combinations for two different network architectures. Latencies longer than 200 ms excluded for presentation reasons.

Considering speedup relative to the TensorFlow Lite floating point on each platform we can make some observations. For floating point inference, OpenVINO is fastest on the i7 (1.78×), CompileNN is fastest on the NaoV6 (1.28×), and TensorFlow Lite is fastest on the Atom N270 and Raspberry Pi. OpenVINO likely makes better use of the more powerful SIMD instructions of the i7. DCG yielded latencies that were longer than TensorFlow Lite on the Atom N270 (0.66×) and the NaoV6 (0.83×). However it has the advantage of being very easy to integrate with an application having essentially no non-standard dependencies.

On the Raspberry Pi, quantized models demonstrated a useful speed up (2–2.9×). However, this was not replicated on Intel CPUs where quantized models had larger latency than floating point models. TensorFlow Lite is better optimized for the ARM NEON instruction set and it appears that the XNNPACK delegate does not (yet) sufficiently optimize quantized models. OpenVINO does provide support for quantized models but the process of creating them is much more involved than with TensorFlow Lite and was not completed for this evaluation.

The Coral Edge TPU accelerator demonstrated dramatic latency improvements on the Raspberry Pi (33×), NaoV6 (19–23×), and i7 (5–8×), but required the replacement of LeakyReLU layers with ReLU in the YOLO-LITE model. The edge TPU could not be used with the Atom N270.

5.3   YOLO LITE-M1 and YOLO-LITE-M2

Figure 5 summarizes the performance of the new models (named as model-channel multiplier-depthwise multiplier). YOLO-LITE-M2-1-4 has the best mAP and is always faster than MobileNetV1-YOLOv4 (for the same image size), while YOLO-LITE-M2-0.5-4 is always fastest overall and may have the best tradeoff between mAP and latency. The results also show that it is easy to tune the new models or speed or mAP.

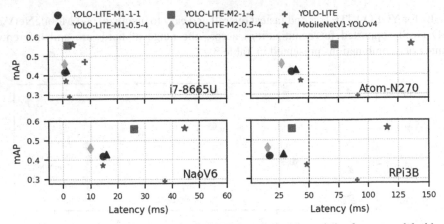

Fig. 5. Latency and mAP for new YOLO-LITE based models and the fastest models identified previously. All models were tested with an input image size of 224, but YOLO-LITE, and MobileNetV1-YOLOv4 were also tested at size 128 (shown with smaller markers).

6   Conclusions

In this work we evaluated several object detection models in the YOLO and SSD families to identify which could provide the best performance (mAP vs latency) on a variety of hardware platforms and inference frameworks. We also proposed two new models based on YOLO-LITE and included these in our evaluations.

Our results showed that our new models offer the best performance amongst the evaluation set and are easy to tune for maximizing speed or maximizing mAP. Our results also suggest that there are additional gains to be made on Intel CPUs if quantization was well supported, but current frameworks all have issues in this regard. We also observe that the Coral Edge TPU facilitates dramatic speed-ups if the model to be used can be easily quantized and only uses operations supported by the TPU. Future work may include evaluation of other accelerators and more recent model architectures.

Finally, to support further building upon this work and development of better object detectors, we have also released the RoboCup SPL object detection data set (V2) used for this evaluation.

Acknowledgements. The authors would like to acknowledge the assistance of Arne Moos and Nao Devils TU Dortmund who kindly generated C++ implementations of object detection networks using their as yet unreleased DCG code generator. We are also grateful for the assistance of Tobias Kalbitz and Nao Team HTWK who provided us with an early build of TensorFlow Lite for the Nao V6 (eventually superseded for the final evaluation).

References

1. Saha, O., Dasgupta, P.: A comprehensive survey of recent trends in cloud robotics architectures and applications. Robotics **7**, 47 (2018)

2. Zhao, Z., et al.: Object detection with deep learning: a review. IEEE Trans. Neural Netw. Learn. Syst. **30**(11), 3212–3232 (2019)
3. Lin, T.-Y., et al.: Microsoft COCO: common objects in context. In: Fleet, D., Pajdla, T., Schiele, B., Tuytelaars, T. (eds.) ECCV 2014. LNCS, vol. 8693, pp. 740–755. Springer, Cham (2014). https://doi.org/10.1007/978-3-319-10602-1_48
4. Everingham, M., Van Gool, L., Williams, C.K.I., Winn, J., Zisserman, A.: The PASCAL visual object classes challenge 2007 (VOC2007) results (2007)
5. Everingham, M., Van Gool, L., Williams, C.K.I., Winn, J., Zisserman, A.: The PASCAL visual object classes challenge 2012 (VOC2012) results (2012)
6. Huang, R., Pedoeem, J., Chen, C.: YOLO-LITE: a real-time object detection algorithm optimized for non-GPU computers. In: 2018 IEEE International Conference on Big Data (Big Data) (2018)
7. Liu, W., et al.: SSD: single shot multibox detector. In: Leibe, B., Matas, J., Sebe, N., Welling, M. (eds.) ECCV 2016. LNCS, vol. 9905, pp. 21–37. Springer, Cham (2016). https://doi.org/10.1007/978-3-319-46448-0_2
8. Redmon, J., et al.: You only look once: unified, real-time object detection. In: 2016 IEEE Conference on Computer Vision and Pattern Recognition (CVPR) (2016)
9. Redmon, J., Farhadi, A.: YOLOv3: an incremental improvement. arXiv e-prints arXiv:1804.02767 (2018)
10. Redmon, J., Farhadi, A.: YOLO9000: better, faster, stronger. In: 2017 IEEE Conference on Computer Vision and Pattern Recognition (CVPR) (2017)
11. Bochkovskiy, A., Wang, C.-Y., Liao, H.-Y.M.: YOLOv4: optimal speed and accuracy of object detection. arXiv e-prints arXiv:2004.10934 (2020)
12. Howard, A.G., et al.: MobileNets: efficient convolutional neural networks for mobile vision applications. arXiv e-prints arXiv:1704.04861 (2017)
13. Sandler, M., et al.: MobileNetV2: inverted residuals and linear bottlenecks. In: 2018 IEEE/CVF Conference on Computer Vision and Pattern Recognition (2018)
14. Zhang, X., et al.: A fast SSD model based on parameter reduction and dilated convolution. J. Real-Time Image Proc. **18**(6), 2211–2224 (2021). https://doi.org/10.1007/s11554-021-01108-9
15. Zhao, H., et al.: Mixed YOLOv3-LITE: a lightweight real-time object detection method. Sensors (Basel Switz.) **20**(7), 1861 (2020)
16. Bubbliiiing: YOLOV4-tiny: the realization of you only look once-tiny target detection model in Keras (2021)
17. Authors, T.: TensorFLow for Mobile & IoT. https://www.tensorflow.org/lite. Accessed 2021
18. Authors, O. OpenVINO Toolkit Overview. https://docs.openvinotoolkit.org/latest/index.html. Accessed 2021
19. Thielke, F., Hasselbring, A.: A JIT compiler for neural network inference. In: Chalup, S., Niemueller, T., Suthakorn, J., Williams, M.A. (eds.) RoboCup 2019. LNCS, vol. 11531, pp. 448–456. Springer, Cham (2019). https://doi.org/10.1007/978-3-030-35699-6_36
20. coral.ai. USB Accelerator datasheet. https://coral.ai/docs/accelerator/datasheet/. Accessed 2021
21. Bubbliiiing: YOLOV4: you only look once object detection model - modified mobilenet series backbone network - realization in Keras (2021)

Invited Champion Track Papers

RoboCup 2021 SSL Champion TIGERs Mannheim - A Decade of Open-Source Robot Evolution

Andre Ryll$^{(\boxtimes)}$, Nicolai Ommer, and Mark Geiger

Department of Information Technology, Baden-Württemberg Cooperative State University, Coblitzallee 1-9, 68163 Mannheim, Germany
management@tigers-mannheim.de
https://tigers-mannheim.de

Abstract. In 2021, TIGERs Mannheim won the RoboCup Small Size League competition with individual success in the virtual tournament, the hardware challenges, and the technical challenge. This paper focuses on our open-source robot hardware which has evolved over the past decade to a highly integrated system. Previous robot generations are outlined and the mechanical and electrical design of generations v2019 and v2020 is explained in-depth.

1 Five Generations of TIGERs Mannheim SSL Robots

Since our first appearance in a world championship in 2011 we designed and manufactured five generations of SSL robots. In our early days we benefited a lot from open-source designs, although they were rare and usually not complete. To give something back to the research community and help other teams to join the league faster we decided to open-source all our designs from day one on. The design files including mechanics, electronics, firmware, as well as our complete central AI software is available for download on our website[1].

Fig. 1. Past and current robot generations. Named after the year of first appearance from left to right: v2011, v2013, v2016, v2019, v2020

The rest of this section outlines most important changes between previous generations and their motivation. Section 2 provides an in-depth explanation of

---

[1] Open source/hardware: https://tigers-mannheim.de/publications.

© Springer Nature Switzerland AG 2022
R. Alami et al. (Eds.): RoboCup 2021, LNAI 13132, pp. 241–257, 2022.
https://doi.org/10.1007/978-3-030-98682-7_20

the mechanics of the latest v2020 generation. Section 3 focuses on the electrical design of the various subsystems and the onboard computer.

1.1 Overview of Past Robot Generations

Figure 1 shows all our robot generations of the past decade. The first generation v2011 was heavily influenced from the Skuba 2009 design [1]. Especially the motor type, the wheel arrangement, and the size and number of subwheels have been taken over. This version used an external spur gear and the encoders were attached to the wheels, not to the motors. This left little space in the top part for electronics. They consisted only of two boards: the mainboard and a kicker board. The robot was powered by two lithium-polymer batteries connected in series. They are mounted standing on the sides of the robot. Wireless communication was done over a 1.9 GHz DECT link. All the onboard control was done with a 72 MHz STM32F1 and two ATMega microcontrollers [2].

Generation v2013 significantly reduced the required space for the drive train by using internal spur gears. Encoders are now attached directly to the motors. The dribbling bar has been made bigger as the v2011 bar tend to bend after a few skirmishes. The split battery was replaced by a single one centrally located in the robot. The additional space for the electronics is used for a bigger PCB stack, including a touchscreen on top as a reconfigurable configuration and debug interface. The main microcontroller was replaced by an 168 MHz STM32F4 together with three ATmegas. The radio link was replaced by off-the-shelf nRF24L01+ modules to decrease command latency [3].

Generation v2016 is our oldest generation still in use. Major changes are stronger drive motors (50 W instead of 30 W) and a new dribbling motor. The electronics arrangement has been mostly unchanged but the PCBs have been updated. All microcontrollers were replaced by a single 216 MHz STM32F7. This greatly reduced embedded programming effort and made the system more robust. The motors are driven by integrated brushless controllers from Allegro Microsystems (A3931) [4]. The radio modules have been extended with a power amplifier to improve connection quality. The touchscreen is still present, but its size has been reduced. This generation represents our recommended design for new teams because it has proven to be robust and the electronics complexity is at a minimum, only two boards are required [5].

Generation v2019 was an attempt to arrange wheels evenly spaced at 90° to reduce non-linear friction effects of the omni-wheel drive. The drawbacks of this design and improvements are explained in detail below. The electronics have undergone a major update. The main microcontroller is now an 400 MHz STM32H7 accompanied by five STSPIN32F0A microcontrollers. Each of them controlling an individual motor. The radio link has been replaced by the SX1280 [6] chip with an additional front-end module to increase signal strength. Furthermore, this robot generation has space for an Raspberry Pi or a nVidia Jetson TX2 onboard computer and a forward looking camera [7].

1.2   Details of v2020 Generation

The v2020 generation presents our fifth iteration of robots for the RoboCup Small Size League. With 10 years of experience in designing such robots many mistakes were made and many lessons learned. In the following sections, we focus on the previous generation (v2019), its strength and weaknesses, and how they are mitigated. The outcome of all fixes is a major overhaul of the powertrain, the dribbler, and kicker. Most of the work went into the powertrain to ensure robust and smooth operation in a competitive environment. More details on the powertrain can be found in Sect. 2.1. The specifications for v2019 and v2020 can be found in Table 1. The most prominent change can be seen on the wheel size and powertrain. A comparison of the older v2016 generation with v2019 exists in our previous year TDP [7].

Table 1. Robot specifications

Robot version	v2019	v2020
Dimension	Ø178 × 146 mm	Ø178 × 148 mm
Total weight	2.5 kg	2.62 kg
Max. ball coverage	19.3%	19.8%
Driving motors	Nanotec DF45L024048-A2, 65 W[a]	
Gear	30: 50	none
Gear type	External Spur	Direct Drive
Wheel diameter	33 mm	62 mm
Encoder	RLS RLC2HD, 36864 ppr [8]	iC-PX2604, 23040 ppr [9]
Dribbling motor	Maxon EXC Speed 13L HP	Moons ECU22048H18, 55 W
Dribbling gear	12: 32 + 14: 18	1: 1: 1
ØDribbling bar	12 mm	11.5 mm
Kicker charge	4400 μF @ 230 V (116.38 J)	3600 μF @ 240 V (103.68 J)
Chip kick distance	approx. 3 m	approx. 3.6 m
Straight kick speed	max. 8.5 m/s	max. 8.5 m/s
Microcontroller	STM32H743 [10]	
Sensors	Encoders, Gyroscope, Accelerometer, Compass, Camera	
Communication link	Semtech SX1280 + FEM @1.3 MBit/s, 2.300–2.555 GHz [6, 11]	
Compute module	Raspberry Pi 3 with forward oriented camera	
Power Supply	Li-Po Battery, 22.2 V nominal (6S1P), 1300 mAh	

[a] Alternative option: Maxon EC-45 flat 70 W

While mechanics have experienced a large update, electronics remain mostly unchanged from v2019 to v2020. They have proven to work well and reliably. The details of the different boards, their purpose, and interconnections are outlined in Sect. 3.

2   Mechanical Design

Modularity Concept. Since v2016 our robots are very modular. This concept has been proven to be very benificial for development and during assembly as well as repair. Each robot has six major modules which can be replaced as a whole. Figure 2 shows an exploded view of these components.

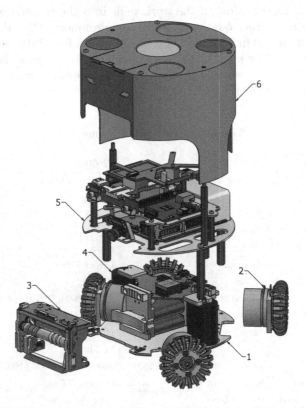

Fig. 2. Exploded view of major robot modules. Each interchangeable individually. 1) Base plate. 2) Powertrain. 3) Dribbler. 4) Kicking device. 5) Electronics stack. 6) Cover.

Module #1 is the base plate. Most of the modules (except for the cover) are mounted directly on the base plate and fixed by screws at the bottom. An important detail here is to use screws with countersunk heads. They allow for an alignment of parts on the base plate. Moreover, they ensure that the bottom surface of the robot is as flat as possible, minimizing friction effects. Module #2 is a powertrain with wheel. In the current configuration four wheels are used with a front angle between the robot's X axis (parallel to the front) and wheel shaft of 31° and a rear angle of 45°.

Module #3 is a dribbler module. It includes the dribbling motor, the dribbling bar, a gear connection between them and electronics for the front break beam to detect the ball. Furthermore, it includes a shovel to translate a linear kick impulse to a rotational impulse for chip kicks. Module #4 is a kicker module. It consists of two rectangular plungers, one for flat kicks and one for chip kicks, two coils, and a capacitor charge PCB with two capacitors.

Module #5 contains the primary electronics stack. That includes a battery, a power board for motor drivers, a mainboard for control, a Raspberry Pi for computer vision algorithms, and a set of auxiliary boards. This module makes extensive use of standard distance bolts to stack the different layers. No custom parts are used here, thus reducing overall cost. Module #6 is a 3D printed cover with standard SSL Vision pattern.

The modules listed above are usually replaced as a whole during a competition to keep time for repairs as low as possible. This allows the team to repair robots not only after a game but already during a game. Experienced team members can replace a dribbler or powertrain unit in less than two minutes. This design allowed us to mostly have the maximum permitted number of robots on the field and have them fully functional.

Manufacturing Methods. Some SSL robots have evolved to a highly-intergrated and compact platform for a special purpose. This is only possible with custom parts and their optimization. Commercial Off-The-Shelf (COTS) components usually do not fullfil the strict size requirements of the SSL.

Most components in our robots are manufactured by *milling* 7075 high-strength aluminum. It offers a low weight and high stiffness at a reasonable price. Some parts without pockets are manufactured via *laser cutting*. An alternative to laser cutting is using a waterjet, as it is done by other teams [12,13]. Two parts of our robots are produced by *turning*, which is the core of the dribbling bar and the subwheel bodies. The previous robot versions v2011, v2013, and v2016 contained custom parts only made by milling and turning.

With v2019 we introduced *3D printing* and *molding*. 3D printing is a common and cheap manufacturing method nowadays. It is well suited for components which would otherwise be difficult to machine (e.g., small dimensions, complex structure, large volumes). However, 3D printed parts are not suited for components experiencing high stress (e.g., impacts). In the v2020 robot design only a few connecting elements and the cover are 3D printed. In contrast to that, other teams have already built most of their robot parts via 3D printing only [14].

Molding was used in the v2019 design for the first time in our robots. It was used to manufacture the dribbling bar with its helix shape. The v2020 design added some molded dampers for the dribbler.

2.1 Powertrain and Wheels

v2019 - 3D Printed Wheels. The v2019 wheels were mostly 3D printed with standard PLA material and had a diameter of 33 mm. 3D printing is cheap and the small wheels allowed them to be arranged in even 90° spacing between all wheels. This is the optimal configuration for an omni-directional robot as most of the non-linear friction effects linearize themselves.

Although the wheels worked on our test field, they suffered heavy damage on the RoboCup 2019 field in Sydney. The top cover was fixed to the wheel base by three screws which directly went into holes in the PLA, without an extra thread. Due to constant repairs these holes were overused and no longer able to retain the cover. Occasionally, the cover was then lost and all subwheels were dropped at once. Furthermore, the white silicon O-rings were regularly broken and had to be replaced. As soon as a wheel started to degrade this was a self-amplifying process. A lost subwheel or O-ring led to direct contact of PLA to the carpet. Heat generated from friction led to melting PLA (PLA gets soft around 60 °C) and rendered the wheel non-repairable.

v2020 - Solid Aluminum Wheels. To obtain a more robust solution the 3D printed wheels are replaced by aluminum ones. However, milling wheels with the dimensions of the v2019 wheels is extremely difficult and expensive. Hence, the wheel size was increased. This implies that the ideal 90° spacing cannot be retained. Overall, wheel size was almost doubled compared to v2019 to a total diameter of 62 mm.

The optimal wheel size for an SSL robot is always a compromise between multiple factors. Some key factors are: robot top speed, gear ratio, energy consumption, and available space. Most of the time an SSL robot is accelerating, it almost never moves with constant velocity. Hence, it makes sense to optimize the motor operating point for acceleration. This can best be achieved with a reduction gear. It decreases speed, but increases torque at the same energy consumption. This is done in the v2019 powertrain. This robot version can run for approximately two full games with one battery. For the exact endurance of v2020 robots no data is available yet.

To reduce the overall powertrain complexity v2020 robots now use a direct drive, i.e. no gears at all. The wheel is directly attached to the motor shaft. Main drawback of this change is the increased energy consumption. Given the v2019 endurance, this is an acceptable minus. Benefit is more precise control as there is no backlash due to gears. Furthermore, it theoretically allows higher top speeds.

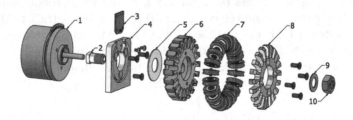

Fig. 3. v2020 powertrain. 1) Motor. 2) Shaft adapter. 3) Encoder PCB. 4) Mounting block. 5) Optical encoder disk. 6) Wheel base. 7) Subwheels. 8) Wheel cover. 9) Spring washer. 10) Hex nut.

Figure 3 shows an exploded view of a complete v2020 powertrain. The shaft adapter (item #2) is glued to the motor (item #1) shaft with Loctite 648. It is very important not to machine the motor shaft. Steel dust or chips are attracted by the motor magnets. If they enter the motor its lifetime is significantly reduced. A small PCB for an optical encoder IC (item #3) is inserted into the mounting block (item #4) which connects to the base plate. On the counterside, a reflective optical encoder disk (item #5) is inserted into the back of the wheel base (item #6).

The integration of the optical encoder directly into the mounting block and wheel make this solution very compact compared to older versions. v2019 robots had magnetic encoders above the wheels, v2016 had optical encoders behind the motors. Both solutions took significantly more space.

Subwheel Design. Inserted into the wheel base are 20 subwheels (item #7). A wheel cover (item #8) secured with four screws tightens it to the wheel base. Items #5 to #8 form a wheel. The wheel can be removed from the shaft adapter by removing a hex nut (item #10), allowing for fast wheel changes. To ensure the hex nut does not loosen itself from vibrations a spring washer is inserted (item #9).

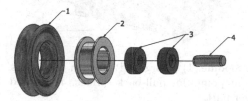

Fig. 4. Exploded view of v2020 subwheel. 1) X-Ring. 2) Roller body. 3) Friction bearings. 4) Dowel pin.

The v2020 subwheels are optimized based on experience with previous generations and publications of other teams [15]. Figure 4 shows an exploded view of the subwheels, they consist of four different parts. Item #2 is the subwheel body. Inserted into the body are two friction bearings (item #3) and a dowel pin (item #4) as shaft. Friction bearings are available off-the-shelf from igus[2]. The bearings are pressed into the body and offer a bearing with very low clearance. The bearing material is shock absorbing and has excellent dry-run capabilities.

An X-Ring is put on the roller body as a connecting element to the carpet to increase friction. X-Rings are superior to O-Rings when it comes to traction, but they have a slightly higher wear. As X-Rings offer two contact points to ground instead of just one like an O-Ring the circular wheel is approximated by 40 contact points, which results in a smooth movement (low vibration, low noise).

---

[2] www.igus.de, type number MSM-0205-02.

These subwheels are similar to v2016 design. However, v2016 did not use a friction bearing, which resulted in higher vibrations and also more wear around the axis. Hence, the center hole was becoming bigger over time, increasing clearance and leading to imprecise control.

2.2 Kicker

The kicker module integrates two coils, two plungers, and a capacitor charge PCB. An overview is shown in Fig. 5. Item #1 is the capacitor charge PCB. One capacitor is hidden for a better view. Details on the charge circuit can be found in Sect. 3.2.

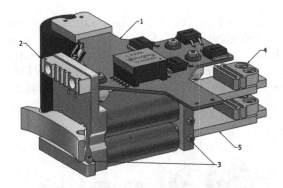

Fig. 5. v2020 kicker module. 1) Charging PCB with capacitors. 2) Damper for dribbling device. 3) Mount points for pull-back springs. 4) Printed plunger dampers. 5) Ferromagnetic plunger part.

Item #2 is the rear damper of the dribbling device. It has to absorb the impact energy of received balls. It is made of a polyurethane rubber with a shore hardness of $30A^3$, manufactured using a 3D printed mold. Item #3 indicates location for a pull spring. The spring itself is not shown in the image. The spring is required to pull back the plunger after a kick.

Item #4 is a damper for the plunger. It is 3D printed and made of TPU98. Despite being a relatively hard rubber, it is still flexible enough and robust. Cutouts in the shape allow the dampers to be compressed upon impact on the rear mounting block. A method of damping the plungers is strictly required. Usually, the kick impulse is transferred to the ball and little energy remains to be absorbed. Nevertheless, if the ball is not present during a kick, the complete energy needs to be absorbed by the structure itself. Without a damper the energy would be transferred during a short time frame, resulting in a severe impact. By using a damper, the energy is transferred over a longer time frame. This mitigates structural damage to the rest of the robot.

---

[3] Smooth-On VytaFlex 30.

Item #5 shows the rear part of a plunger, made of ferromagnetic steel[4]. The steel alloy must be ferromagnetic. This part of the plunger is attracted by a coil made of enameled copper wire with a diameter of 0.63 mm. Approximately 380–450 turns are used on 6–7 layers. A high-voltage, high-current pulse through the coil generates a magnetic field which attracts the plunger. The current flow direction does not matter, the plunger is attracted in all cases.

Half of the plunger is made of steel. The other half is made of aluminum which is not ferromagnetic. The steel part of the plunger is accelerated until it is centered in the coil. After it passes this point, the magnetic field will decelerate it. Hence, a plunger made of steel only would not work. Finding the optimal composition of coil parameters and plunger size as well as position is very difficult and either requires complex simulations or empirical data.

The v2020 kicker design uses a rectangular shaped plunger. It has only one degree of freedom left (moving forward and backward). v2019 used a round bar as plunger. It had one additional (undesired) degree of freedom since it could additionally rotate in place. To prevent this guiding blocks are usually required, which increases mechanical complexity. No deviation in kick strength was noticable when the shape is changed while the coil cross-section area and number of turns is kept equal.

2.3 Dribbler

The dribbler module interacts with the ball and has infrared sensors to detect its presence and position. Figure 6 shows the main components of the dribbler.

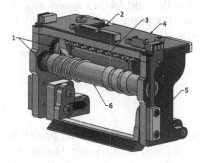

Fig. 6. v2020 dribbler. 1) Gear. 2) Temperature sensor. 3) Infrared (IR) scan array. 4) IR controller PCB. 5) IR barrier PCB and cover. 6) Roller with helix shape.

v2020 uses three gears (item #1) to transfer motor speed to the dribbling bar. All gears are of the same size. Hence, motor speed equals dribbling bar speed. The gear on the motor shaft and on the dribbling bar are made of brass and glued onto the respective components. The middle gear is made of polyketone and is just pushed on two small ball bearings. It is very important to have different

---

[4] Usually St37 or C45 low carbon steel.

materials on mating gears to reduce wear as one part can always yield in such combinations.

The dribbling bar is mounted into a ball bearing on each side. The helix shaped roller (item #6) is molded from polyurethane rubber with a hardness of shore 60A[5].

The dribbling motor in v2020 is a brushless motor with 55 W and a rated speed of 17000 rpm. The dribbling motor is used in short-term overload mode. That implies it is off most of the time but when it is used the rated power is exceeded, leading to heat build up. The winding temperature must not exceed 155 °C, otherwise the motor is permanently damaged. To monitor heat of the motor a temperature sensor (item #2) has been added to the IR controller PCB (item #4).

Apart from dribbling, the module also has sensing capabilities consisting of infrared diodes (receivers) and emitters. On the sides of the dribbler an emitter and receiver are paired to form a break beam. This is mandatory for a precise kick mechanism. Relying on vision data for this purpose is not precise enough due to the visions capture and transfer delay. The components of the break beam are protected by 3D printed PLA covers (item #5) to prevent damage in skirmish situations. Item #3 is an IR scan array, consisting of five receivers and four emitters. An evaluation whether the array can be used to compute a more precise location of the ball in close vicinity is still ongoing.

As illustrated in Fig. 5 (item #2) the dribbler module is damped at the rear to absorb ball impact energy. To improve dribbling behaviour there is another shore 30A damper between the base plate and the dribbler module. This should reduce oscillations of the dribbler module while dribbling a ball [16].

v2019 robots used a smaller and higher speed motor (up to 60000 rpm) with a double reduction gear to 20000 rpm on the dribbling bar. Overall this gear was very loud, had a lot of vibrations, and high wear on the gear teeth. Due to size constrains ball bearings could not be used. All these problems are fixed with v2020.

2.4   Cover

The v2019 as well as v2020 cover is made by 3D printing. Different materials and thicknesses have been evaluated. Empirically the best combination was PETG with a thickness of 1.2 mm. The cover must not be too thick, otherwise it looses flexibility which is required to efficiently absorb contact energy and distribute it over a larger area. During the print of a cover (which takes up to 10 h) layer adhesion is the most critical factor. Tests showed that the cover never broke within a layer but always at the connection of two layers. PETG offered the best layer adhesion as it is usually printed at slightly higher temperatures than PLA. Flexible materials like TPU98 were also tested but they are much too soft given the above thickness.

---

[5] Smooth-On VytaFlex 60.

The key to a robust cover is a combination of the printed PETG cover with an adhesive film over the complete area. PETG and adhesive film form a compound material. Tests showed that the PETG cover can still break during heavy impacts but the design tolerates and expects this. Even if the PETG breaks the cover holds together by the adhesive film without loosing functionality. As 3D printing is cheap, it was accepted to print new covers when needed. After RoboCup 2019 only very few cracks were found on our covers, less than predicted. Covers for v2020 need a cutout for the wheels. Hence, new covers are printed.

3 Electrical Design

The electrical design of v2019 and v2020 robots is more complex than all previous generations. It consists of six different custom boards and one Raspberry Pi 3A+. Figure 7 shows an overview of all major components and their allocation to physical boards. The most important parts are the mainboard (green) and the powerboard (light blue). They are connected via a fine-pitch flex cable.

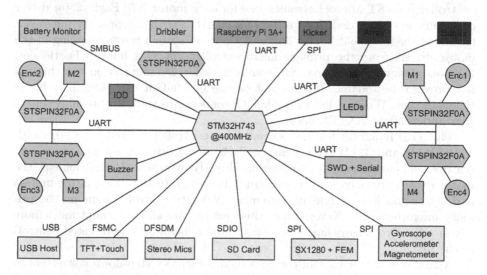

Fig. 7. Overview of main electronic components and interconnections. Color indicates on which physical board the component is located. Light Blue: powerboard. Green: mainboard. Yellow: IR controller. Orange: kicker board. Blue, pink, gray: auxiliary boards. (Color figure online)

In contrast to the mechanical part, the electronics remain mostly unchanged from v2019 to v2020. Only the IR controller and the pattern identification board have experienced minor updates (see Sects. 3.4 and 3.5). All components have proven to work reliably. Furthermore, due to multiple progammable microcontrollers this architecture offers potential for further improvements by software changes only. Without the need to respin a new electronics design.

Especially for new teams such a complex design can be overkill. Our v2016 robots demonstrate that a much simpler design can also work very reliably. Some v2016 robots are still in active use. They use only two custom boards. One mainboard including power electronics for motors and one board for capacitor charging and kicking (kicker board). This is also a more convenient solution.

v2019 and v2020 electronics have been extended especially for more autonomy and onboard processing. They are always running a state estimation, trajectory generation and position control loop onboard. The new design additionally allows more autonomous ball handling via a camera attached to the Raspberry Pi and the improved IR controller. If needed, the Raspberry Pi can be exchanged for a nVidia Jetson TX2 compute module. As technical challenges of the SSL are trending towards more autonomy this design is ready for it.

3.1 Power Electronics

The powerboard contains all components which have to handle high currents. It incorporates five brushless motor drivers based on the STSPIN32F0A microcontroller from ST Microelectronics, one for each motor [17]. Each motor driver communicates via a dedicated serial link (UART) with the primary microcontroller on the mainboard. This link also allows in-system reprogramming of the motor drivers from the primary microcontroller via ST's built-in bootloader. Previous designs used shared SPI connections for communication but this did not prove to be reliable. If one client on the bus fails it can potentially break the whole bus. Whereas individual UART connections work very reliably due to their independant RX/TX lines.

The STSPIN32F0A features a small microcontroller clocked at 48 MHz with 4 kB SRAM and 32 kB flash memory. Each motor driver has a motor, its hall sensors, and encoder signals (if present) directly attached. At the moment, the motor drivers are only doing the commutation logic (6-step) to spin the motors and a common link current measurement. Velocity control is done on the primary microcontroller. Nevertheless, this architecture allows to implement more advanced control algorithms (e.g., sinousoidal control or field-oriented control) in the future.

Apart from motor control the powerboard includes step-down converters to transform the battery voltage to 3.3 V, 5 V, and 12 V. A battery current and voltage monitor and over-current protection are also included. The Lithium-Polymer battery has a nominal voltage of 22.2 V, i.e. six cells in series and a capacity of 1300 mAh.

The powerboard offers a single micro-USB connection for programming of the primary microcontroller. Via this connection, the 5 V and 3.3 V rails are powered as well. Hence, the robot can be programmed and most subsystems tested without a battery. If a battery is attached at the same time a load switch seamlessly switches to the battery to power all systems. This simplifies development and testing of our robots, as no extra equipment is needed.

3.2 Kicker Circuit

The kicker circuit is responsible for charging a set of capacitors to a high voltage and discharging them through the kicker coils to kick the ball. The kick strength is directly proportional to the current flowing through the coil. The current depends on resistance of the coil and supplied voltage. To achieve kick speeds up to the league limit of 6.5 m/s, a high voltage is required. The v2020 design uses a software-controlled soft-limit of 240 V and a hardware-enforced hard-limit of 250 V. A pair of capacitors with 250 V rating and 1800 μF are used, yielding a total of 3600 μF and a stored energy of 112.5 J. The capacitors are used together for a coil, not one capacitor per coil.

The charge circuit uses a flyback converter topology based on the Analog Devices[6] LT3751 capacitor charge IC [18]. This circuit can charge the capacitors form 0 V to 250 V in two seconds. Recharging after a strong kick takes half a second. An advantage of the flyback topology is the isolation of high voltage areas from the rest of the electronics.

The kicker board does not have its own microcontroller. It is intentionally designed to be very simple to reduce the risk of fatal mistakes. It only has a SPI interface to an ADC, used to monitor capacitor voltage and two input lines to trigger a flat or chip kick. These trigger lines are digitally isolated from the high-voltage area. The primary microcontroller monitors the capacitor voltage and stops charging at 240 V. This is the normal operating mode. If this fails for any reason, the LT3751 is configured for a hard-limit of 250 V to ensure capacitors are never overcharged.

It is absolutely vital to design the kicker circuit *as safe as possible* and to do a proper failure analysis and mitigation plan. Failure to do so can result in serious injuries. As an additional safety measure, our robots always discharge themselves upon shutdown. This way we can be relatively sure that a turned-off robot is also safe to touch and work on.

3.3 Mainboard

The mainboard is the primary sensor hub and communication link to our AI software running next to the field. All sensors and motor drivers are connected to the primary microcontroller. Consequently, a powerful STM32H7 with 400 MHz has been chosen for data processing. Previous designs until v2016 used multiple powerful microcontrollers. That required a complex data exchange between them to ensure functionality. This led to an unstable communication.

Hence, we moved from multiple equally powerful microcontrollers to one very powerful primary one and multiple very small sub-microcontrollers with a simple interface. For example, the communication protocol between motor drivers and primary microcontroller consists of only a single defined message for each direction, exchanged at a fixed rate of 1 kHz. With this approach corrupted messages are of minor importance as the message will be transmitted again during the next cycle.

---

[6] formerly Linear Technology.

The mainboard has a full inertial measurement unit (IMU) consisting of a gyroscope, accelerometer, and magnetometer. Gyroscope and accelerometer data is actively used in onboard sensor fusion for state estimation. Furthermore, position input from SSL-Vision is directly used on the robots. It is transmitted over a wireless link with a SX1280 chip from Semtech[7]. To improve link quality an additional front-end module (FEM) is used.

Apart from vital functions the mainboard also offers a user interface and mass storage interfaces. The user interface is a touch display with a resolution of 320×240 pixels. It is used to display system status information and to edit wireless settings or execute self-tests. A touch display has the great advantage of being reconfigurable compared to fixed hardware switches. For example, a recent change extended the selection of the robot ID from a maximum of 12 robots to 16 robots without any hardware modification. Only a change on the graphical user interface was necessary.

Mass storage interfaces are a full-size SD card slot and a USB host interface. The SD card is used to log state estimation and control data at real-time with 1 kHz. That helps to debug and visualize controller performance problems which is mainly done with MATLAB. The USB interface can be used to update the firmware on all microcontrollers.

3.4   IR Controller

The IR controller board is shown in Fig. 6. Its primary function is the detection of a ball close enough to kick via a horizontal break beam. It consists of one infrared emitter and one infrared receiving diode followed by a transimpedance amplifier which converts the IR diode's current to a voltage [19]. This voltage is then measured by an ADC in the IR controller's microcontroller (a STM32F031). The main challenge of the break beam is it's sensitivity to environmental lighting conditions as the infrared diode receives infrared light from the environment and the infrared emitter. The key here is to work with a pulsed emitter. In the current design the emitter is on for $500\,\mu s$ and then off for another $500\,\mu s$. During each phase the resulting voltage is measured and stored. Afterwards the difference of both values is calculated to determine if the beam is interrupted. This efficiently eliminates all effects of environmental lighting. So far we never encountered any issues or interference with this detection method.

The v2019 design also introduced a infrared scan array mounted above the dribbling bar, slightly looking down. In the v2020 design this is also present. Five receiver diodes and four emitters are interleaved as it can be seen in Fig. 6 (item #3). The aim of this scan array is to determine a more precise position of the ball in front of the robot with a high update rate (300 Hz or more). This shall then be used for more efficient dribbling or ball stealing capabilities.

Lastly, a temperature sensor is connected to the IR controller's microcontroller to monitor the dribbling motor. Previously, the motor temperature has

---

[7] www.semtech.com.

been estimated by its consumed energy but it is more convenient and robust to measure it directly.

3.5   Auxiliary Systems

Auxiliary systems include a set of smaller boards. First of all, a Raspberry Pi 3A+ is mounted to all robots with a Raspberry Pi Camera Module v1 and a 140° lens (diagonal field of view). It communicates with the primary microcontroller via a UART and takes 5 V power from the power board. Its purpose is to do image processing for ball detection. This information can then be used to improve pass reception accuracy.

Secondly, the front LED board contains two high-power RGBW (red, green, blue, white) LEDs. For a nice appearance they are mounted behind the *eyes* of our front cover. They also have a practical purpose. We use them for *live debugging* during a game. Depending on the role of the robot (attacker, defender, keeper, supporter) the colors change. This allows us to quickly identify issues during role assignment (especially toggling issues where assignments oscillate). It is also a useful indicator for the audience during ball placement as it had its own color. Consequently, it was immediately visible if the game is in a normal state or in a stop state.

Lastly, a pattern identification system is installed on each robot. Its purpose is to detect which cover is placed on a robot such that it can automatically adjust its internal ID. The system uses RGB sensors with a white illumination LED next to it to detect the blob color from below the cover. The system has been tested under various lighting conditions and proven to work well. We no longer need to look for a cover with a pattern specific to a robot ID but can put any cover on any robot and it will adjust.

4   Results

Apart from a virtual tournament, the 2021 world championship consisted of a series of hardware challenges[8] where each team had to demonstrate special movement and ball handling capabilities. Overall four challenges had to be completed, consisting of multiple scenarios each. Challenge 1 and 2 consisted of scoring a goal from different static scenarios. Challenge 3 required a robot with a ball to dribble through six gates as fast as possible without loosing the ball. Challenge 4 required at least three robots to pass as often as possible within 5 min. Recovering the ball was allowed if a pass was missed.

Furthermore, technical challenges in 2021 and 2019 focused on using computer vision directly on the robots. The camera system above the field was disabled for this challenge. Hence, the robots had no global position information. The challenges required the robot to detect a (moving) ball and the goal. Afterwards it had to touch it, intercept it, or shoot it on a goal.[9]

---

[8] Detailed rules at: ssl.robocup.org/hwc-2021.

[9] Detailed rules at: ssl.robocup.org/tc-2021-blackout and ssl.robocup.org/tc-2019-blackout.

Table 2 shows the result of each hardware and technical challenge. The time is computed by selecting the best attempt per scenario and then averaging it over all scenarios of a challenge. The second value indicates the number of successful attempts.

Table 2. 2021 and 2019 challenge results

	TIGERs Mannheim	Second-Best Team
HW Challenge 1: Static Defenders	3.54 s/24	6.91 s/10
HW Challenge 2: Contested Possession	2.94 s/15	4.63 s/5
HW Challenge 3: Dribbling	13.71 s/3	15.15 s/1
HW Challenge 4: Pass Endurance	288 passes	225 passes
TC 2021: Grab a stationary ball	7.37 s/9	49 s/7
TC 2021: Scoring on an empty goal	10.93 s/12	18.4 s/7
TC 2021: Scoring on a defended goal	11.0 s/10	-/0
TC 2019: Grab a stationary ball	4.42 s/9	9.6 s/6
TC 2019: Intercept a moving ball	2.68 s/8	-/0

5   Conclusion

When we founded the team in 2009 there was little material available on how to build SSL robots. It took two full years to develop the first version of our robots. Since 2014 the *Open Source/Hardware Award* is given to the team with the most comprehensive publication to speed up progression of the league. We have won this award seven times in a row and noticed afterwards that new teams appear more frequently and it takes them less than a year to build their first robots. We hope this paper can act as a quick start for more new teams and further improve the open source mentality in the league.

Over the past years we also noticed that robot reliability is getting more important as the number of robots in a game is constantly increased. Since 2021 each team has to provide 11 robots. We identified two key factors to maintain a high number of operational robots during a game. Ideally, the robots are so robust that they never break. Our v2020 robots are designed with that rational in mind: large aluminum wheels, solid kicker system, and multiple damping points to absorb impact energy. Nevertheless, even the best robot might break. This leads to our second point: Due to our modularity concept we are able to swap broken components very fast. Most components can be exchanged in under a minute. Hence, we can repair a robot even during a game. Broken components are repaired after a game when there is more time for a detailed analysis.

In the future, we plan to further extend our onboard processing capabilities. A notable difference and unique feature of our v2020 robots compared to other teams is the full integration of a camera and Raspberry Pi. All our robots are equipped with this combination, not only a single robot for technical challenges. The robot is already able to detect the ball and goal. This can be used to autonomously shoot on the goal if there is a gap in the opponent's defense. If the onboard processing is faster than the primary control loop (SSL-Vision, AI computer, wireless command transmission), it can give a competitive edge. Furthermore, it could also be used to improve dribbling or ball reception. The exact skill set will be determined after further testing and evaluation.

References

1. Srisabye, J., et al.: Skuba 2009 Extended Team Description (2009)
2. Perun, B., et al.: TIGERs Mannheim–Team Description for RoboCup 2011 (2011)
3. Ryll, A., Ommer, N., Andres, D., Klostermann, D., Nickel, S., Pistorius, F.: TIGERS Mannheim–Team Description for RoboCup 2013 (2013)
4. LLC Allegro MicroSystems: Automotive 3-Phase BLDC Controller and MOSFET Driver (2013). http://www.allegromicro.com/~/media/Files/Datasheets/A3930-1-Datasheet.ashx?la=en
5. Ryll, A., Geiger, M., Ommer, N., Sachtler, A., Magel, L.: TIGERs Mannheim–Extended Team Description for RoboCup 2016 (2016)
6. Semtech Corporation. SX1280 Datasheet, May 2017. http://www.semtech.com/images/datasheet/sx1280_81.pdf
7. Ommer, N., Ryll, A., Geiger, M.: TIGERs Mannheim–Extended Team Description for RoboCup 2019 (2019)
8. RLS: A Renishaw associate company. RLC2HD Datasheet, September 2017. https://www.rls.si/en/fileuploader/download/download/?d=0&file=custom
9. iC-Haus GmbH. iC-PX Series (2016). https://www.ichaus.de/PX_datasheet_en
10. STmicroelectronics: STM32H743xI Datasheet, July 2018. https://www.st.com/resource/en/datasheet/stm32h743bi.pdf
11. Skyworks Solutions, Inc.: SKY66112 Datasheet, March 2017. http://www.skyworksinc.com/uploads/documents/SKY66112_11_203225L.pdf
12. De Iacoc, R., et al.: 2016 Team Description Paper: UBC Thunderbots (2016)
13. MacDougallc, M., et al.: 2018 Team Description Paper: UBC Thunderbots (2018)
14. Koopai, O.N., Ghasemieh, M.A., Khanloghi, M.: Immortals 2018Team DescriptionPaper (2018)
15. Ohno, S., et al.: KIKS Extended Team Description for RoboCup2019 (2019)
16. Huang, Z., et al.: ZJUNlict Extended Team Description Paper forRoboCup 2019 (2019)
17. STmicroelectronics: STSPIN32F0A Datasheet, September 2017. https://www.st.com/resource/en/datasheet/stspin32f0a.pdf
18. Analog Devices: LT3751 Datasheet, July 2017. https://www.analog.com/media/en/technical-documentation/data-sheets/LT3751.pdf
19. Tran, V., Hernandez, J.: Transimpedance Amplifier Design, September 2015. http://www.cel.com/pdf/appnotes/an3025.pdf

Starkit: RoboCup Humanoid KidSize 2021 Worldwide Champion Team Paper

Egor Davydenko, Ivan Khokhlov$^{(\boxtimes)}$, Vladimir Litvinenko, Ilya Ryakin, Ilya Osokin, and Azer Babaev

Team Starkit, Moscow Institute of Physics and Technology, Moscow, Russia
robocup.mipt@gmail.com

Abstract. In 2021, Team Starkit reached the first place of the Robocup Humanoid KidSize 2021 Worldwide competition, using the codebase that was in develop by the team between *RoboCup 2019 Sydney* and *RoboCup 2021 Worldwide*. This article is devoted to the software and hardware features introduced by our team to upgrade the performance of the open source Rhoban Football Club 2019 code release used as the base of our software and hardware framework. These features include vision-related matters, such as detection and localization, electronics, and mechanical and algorithmic novelties. The competition was held virtually for the first time, and despite the fact that our software was developed for the real-life robot, we were able to successfully run it in a simulation environment. The simulation-specific features are also considered in the article.

Keywords: Robotics · Simulation · Computer vision · RoboCup

1 Introduction

The core structure of our software and hardware originates from the highly successful open source code and CAD drawings release of the multiple world champion Rhoban Football Club. This article gives an overview of the approaches that were tried out to further improve its performance, along with the analysis of their preconditions, perspectives and the evaluation of their effect in a real competition.

The competition in 2021 took place in a virtual environment (*Webots* simulator) for the first time, which was a great challenge for all the competitors. We have devoted a lot of time and effort to create a simulation model of our robot that will be similar enough to the real-world one allowing us to use almost all approaches developed for the real robot in the simulation environment. We believe that simulated games with automatic referee will intensify the code development for the competitors. We are glad to announce the publication of our model[1] and docker image[2] to provide the ability to other team to compete with our robots in simulation.

---

[1] Google Drive.
[2] Docker Hub.

© Springer Nature Switzerland AG 2022
R. Alami et al. (Eds.): RoboCup 2021, LNAI 13132, pp. 258–274, 2022.
https://doi.org/10.1007/978-3-030-98682-7_21

The strategy chosen by our team in 2019 to create the high-performance robosoccer platform consists of several aspects:

- Structural integrity robustness
- Onboard electronics robustness
- Onboard vision system performance
- Localisation framework performance
- Game strategy improvements
- Motion performance and stability

The structure of the paper is as follows: Sect. 2 briefly introduces the hardware improvements of the robot, and aspects of precise modeling of this hardware in the simulation environment. Section 3 presents the improvements in the vision subsystem, including the novel wide-angle stereoscopic setup, and the problems which we encountered while transferring this wide-angle setup to the simulation environment. Details of our implementation of the lane-based localisation approach is presented in Sect. 4. Our work in game strategy improvement is described in Sect. 5, and finally efforts to improve the quality of robot motions are described in Sect. 6.

2   Model
(See Figs. 1 and 2).

Fig. 1. Real robot   **Fig. 2.** Robot model in *Webots*

2.1   Model and Electronics Changes

The initial robot structure at the beginning of 2019 was fully inherited from *Rhoban team*, the world champion at that time. This model as a product of several years of development in the *University of Bordeaux* had great robustness, and it gave us an invaluable amount of knowledge about building a good robot for KidSize league competitions.

Its main construction element is the flat milled aluminum plates. Real game tests demonstrated that this structure is prone to small irreversible deformations, often leading the damaged robot to look intact but performing worse.

Thus, we decided to switch to a milled carbon structure, which is both stiffer and lighter, redesigning some parts to better fit the carbon milling process. Also, we installed support bearings at each limb, including head, to mitigate the servo output shaft damage, often occurring when the falling robot hits other objects.

Also, we developed and installed a novel on-board power "hot swap" controller, allowing us to change the battery of the robot without restarting it or pressing any buttons. This controller relies on LTC4228 IC based on "ideal diode" emulation, and we are happy to share it via our GitHub.

2.2   Real2sim

The robot model was exported from *SolidWorks* to URDF[3] and then to PROTO format. We ensured that all the parameters, e.g. masses, inertia tensors, are close to the real values. This approach along with the use of the same material appearances where possible, helped us to get the model not only physically but also visually close to the real robot. Only the minor changes in motion configurations were required to be successfully executed in a virtual environment.

Fig. 3. Head: from real to simplified

As our goal was chosen to model the robot as close as possible to the real world one, the most difficult for us was the simplification according to the Model Specifications document[4]. An example of the head simplification is given in

---

[3] http://wiki.ros.org/sw_urdf_exporter.

[4] https://cdn.robocup.org/hl/wp/2021/06/v-hsc_model_specification_v1.05.pdf.

Fig. 3. Since there is no need for heat dissipation in the simulator, all the ventilation holes were removed. Wires, screws and their landing nests were also considered redundant for the simulation.

Fig. 4. Bounding objects for legs (left), neck (middle) and arms (right)

Another problem was to fit the parts with complex shapes in the simple bounding objects allowing the simulation to run with appropriate performance. Lots of time was spent to ensure that they are close enough to the original details, that there are not too many of them, and that it is possible to turn on the *selfCollision* in the model as required by the rules without ruining the motion because of the self-intersecting rough shapes Fig. 4. As the result this robot model won the *2021 Best Humanoid Model Award*.

3   Vision

3.1   Wide-Angle Lens

Prior to 2020, our robot was equipped with a regular lens with approximately 45° Field of View (FoV). This relatively narrow FoV forced the robot to constantly move the head with moderate velocity to scan the surroundings trying to find a ball or opponent robots, inherently emulating a large-FoV camera with constantly moving narrow-FoV camera. This leads to the drawbacks, causing game quality degradation:

- inability to rapidly detect the ball
- inability to perceive large structures on the field (prolonged goal lane/border lane/central circle)

At the end of 2019 we decided to switch to a wide-angle setup, and started to test it directly after the *RoboCup Asia-Pacific 2019* event. We tested various lens setups and picked up the *Beward BL0220M23* lens model, giving approximately 135° FoV on our FLIR camera. This FoV allows the robot to see the ball in almost all required view angles using only the small panning motion of the camera, allowing the robot to react to the ball movements more rapidly.

But the wide-angle lens setup immediately leads to resolution and rectification problems. The first is the smaller pixel size of objects compared to a narrow FoV imaging. For an "classic" narrow FoV imaging, we use a 720 × 540 resolution of a captured image with a 2 × 2 binning on a camera (which is capable of 1440 × 1080 raw image capturing). This binning allows us to lower the exposure time and to move a camera relatively fast with a little motion blur. At this binned resolution, the ball at the center of a robot's sight has the pixel size of approximately 40 × 40 pixels. This size is enough to robustly detect the ball with our current convolutional neural network-based pipeline. But with 135° FoV at the same 720 × 540 input image resolution the pixel size of a ball is less than 20 × 20, which is below the robust detection threshold. To mitigate this problem, we switched to full 1440 × 1080 capturing with a lower camera panning speed. This resolution can still provide the reasonable pixel size of a ball in the center of a FoV of wide-angle lens, but with a cost of slightly higher motion blur and noise and larger exposure times.

3.2   Vision Pipeline Parallelization and Optimization

Our "classic" vision pipeline prior to the end of 2019 was a slightly modified version of a highly successful vision pipeline of the *Rhoban team*, used by them to win the *RoboCup 2019* competition. This pipeline uses the 640 × 480 or 720 × 540 captured image size and is capable of processing it at 30 frames per second using a strictly "series" processing architecture. The series architecture means that each vision processing step can be performed only after the previous processing step is finished. For example, it's possible to perform the goal post detection only after the ball detection step is done. According to Rhoban's naming, each pipeline processing step is called a "filter", and thus the "classic" vision pipeline is the series connection of different vision filters that runs strictly one after another connected by the corresponding inputs and outputs. Almost none of the vision filters we used at that time were capable of being parallelized, and ran mostly in single-core mode with some minor exceptions to truly OpenCV-based well-parallelized filters like color space conversion.

After switching from 720 × 540 to 1440 × 1080 capturing with a wide-angle setup, the throughput of this "series" vision pipeline degraded to less than 7 frames per second, not allowing us to play a normal dynamic game. In order to optimize the vision pipeline performance, we rewrote it using a hybrid "series-parallel" architecture with an automatic filters parallelization.

At the robot's software boot time, the vision pipeline governor loads its structure from a JSON file and automatically parses it to estimate which vision processing steps (filters) can be done in parallel way (i.e. ball detection and goal posts detection). Here we are exploiting the fact that if all their inputs are already available then filters can safely be run in parallel not depending on each other. This parallel group of filters has a name of "filter's batch". The formal criterion of the possibility of the parallel processing for the group of vision filters is the fact that all their input dependencies are satisfied before the time of filter execution. We use the $C++$ $std::async$ multi-threading framework to run all the filters in a batch in separate threads and wait for all the filters in a batch to finish. This pipeline structure allowed us to better utilize the multi-core architecture of an on-board PC, giving approximately 10–12 frames per second processing.

Despite the fact that similar parallel architecture is already available in other modern vision frameworks like ROS, we are not using it, relying on a current fast and compact architecture initially developed by Rhoban team, allowing us to exploit its simplicity to do a precise fine-tuning and optimisations.

To further upgrade the vision pipeline performance, we divided processing steps that required a full-sized input image and filters that can work on down-sampled input image with small robustness degradation. An example of such filter is the goal posts detector: they are significantly larger than the ball and can be detected well enough on a downsampled 720×540 image. In addition we parallelized all the possible filters internally with the OpenCV "parallel for" approach.

The second major drawback of a wide-angle lens setup we faced is the necessity to undistort the input image. The raw wide-angle image has a heavy radial distortion, causing straight lines to be bent significantly, especially at the borders of an image. At first sight, OpenCV library has a mature set of tools to perform the distortion correction, widely used by the robotics community. But the resultant undistorted image will be significantly larger than the captured image to fit all the pixels present in it, causing the throughput of a vision pipeline to degrade twice: because of the undistortion time and because of the larger image size that will be processed in all the subsequent filters. For example, for the 135 degrees FoV lens with a 1440×1080 capture, the rectified image will have a size bigger than 2880×2160 to cover all the pixels present in the captured image with the same resolution at the center of an undistorted image (assuming we are still using pinhole camera model with a flat imaging plane).

To mitigate this, we modified the underlying math of the vision filters for most of them to perform directly on the raw wide-angle distorted image. For example, our ball detection routine performs its job on a distorted image, and only undistort the final position of several ball candidates, not the full image. So there is no classical undistortion filter at the beginning of our vision pipeline.

After all of these optimization steps, our wide-angle vision pipeline throughput is brought back to 20 frames per second which (at least for us) is enough for a moderate dynamic gameplay, and only a small panning of a head is needed to detect the ball at all the required positions.

3.3 Stereoscopic Camera Setup

The classic approach to detect the opponents at the KidSize league is to use some CNN/DNN processing or semantic segmentation to find the robots on the captured image, and then estimate their field positions from monocular image position utilizing the fact that the opponent robot is standing on a flat ground.

As an attempt to efficiently use this DNN-based approach in a monocular setup on our 2019 robot configuration, we tried to exploit the knowledge of the known flat game field geometry by fusing the monocular vision data with geometrical data estimated from the robot versus field surface orientation. We have implemented a new vision pipeline setup that adds the predicted depth from the flat field hypothesis as an additional channel to the TinyYOLO v3 NN detector, which resulted in a paper [2].

After some testing, we were not satisfied with this approach. Most of the robots in the league use some sort of lightened legs and thin feet, so only the body of a robot can be detected robustly enough but not the legs (at least with our detection approaches), especially when the robot is in front of the observer causing some parts of the legs to be almost indistinguishable from the surroundings. This leads to the large ambiguity of a robot's feet position estimation on a monocular image. But the ability to robustly estimate the opponent's field position is mandatory for obstacle avoidance and ball kick direction calculation for better strategy. Also, to detect the goal posts, goal net, legs of a referee and other obstacles the multi-class segmentation or detection DNN is needed with heavy processing time requirements, requiring to use some hardware neural networks accelerators like *Intel Neural Compute Stick* or its analogues.

After that we decided to use a different approach and install a stereoscopic wide-angle vision system, being the first to do so in the KidSize league to our knowledge.

This stereoscopic setup allowed us to robustly detect all the possible obstacles by their shape and size, not appearance or color, and estimate the distance to them with sufficient precision. This approach forced us to put large effort into solving camera synchronization issues and stereoscopic processing issues to keep the vision pipeline throughput fast enough.

Currently, on our 2021 robot setup we use a pair of *FLIR BFS-PGE-16S2C* cameras with 62 mm baseline. We use a hardware synchronization feature of these cameras, making one of it act as a master, generating the sync signal during the exposure time, and the other camera acts as a slave using the sync signal as a trigger input. Both frames are being augmented with a hardware timestamp. The vision pipeline input routine was modified to support two capture inputs, and the special synchronization governor was implemented to estimate the difference between timestamps of input frames and re-sync the capturing if one of the captured frames was missing due to high CPU load or other issues. Utilizing the fact that the FLIR camera used has a global shutter feature, this setup allows us to get a good quality stereo pair even in the case of a fast-moving robot.

This real-world stereoscopic setup was carefully modeled in a simulation environment (requiring some patches to the Webots camera synchronisation routines) and was intensively used by us in the 2021 competition.

As a small drawback the weight of a large head with a dual camera setup causes our robot to be a little less stable during walk and kick. We are mitigating this with the "active falling" move and other walk stabilization techniques.

3.4 Fast Stereoscopic Vision Processing

To keep the vision pipeline fast enough, we use downsampled 720×540 images as an input to the stereoscopic processing filter. The stereoscopic processing filter used is an optimized custom-written routine doing all the stereoscopic processing steps in one filter. Currently, we use classic OpenCV rectification and disparity estimation, followed by custom disparity to point cloud processing combined with voxelization via binning and filtering. Then we use a ground plane estimation using RANSAC algorithm, and a combination of 2D connected components analysis and Point Cloud Library KD-Tree based EuclideanClusterExtraction [6] to detect obstacles as objects which are protruded by some threshold from a detected ground plane.

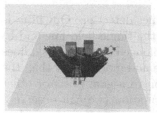

Fig. 5. Three different views of a in-game 3D scene with two opponent robots being detected as obstacles in a 3D point cloud constructed from stereoscopic image using algorithms described above. Pictures are taken from a real-time feed of a point cloud from the real robot. Green points: voxels from stereoscopic processing. Light-green box: estimated field surface by RANSAC. Red boxes: detected obstacles (Color figure online)

Our on-board PC (currently the *Intel NUC i7 gen9*) is capable of performing this stereo pair processing at 10–12 frames per second, which is enough to robustly detect obstacles in a real game taking into account the possible walking speeds of the participating robots. As a comparison, classic Robot Operating System (ROS) stereo processing, being integrated in our vision pipeline for test purposes, gives about 2–3 FPS under the same conditions. So we abandoned it and used our less precise, but faster solution. Currently, we use ROS only for visualization of the resultant point cloud and obstacles for debugging purposes, sample of which is given on Fig. 5.

To integrate these relatively slow 10 frames per second stereoscopic processing in our project, we once again modified the vision pipeline to support filters that operate at the frequency that is a divider of the capturing frequency. Currently, the main pipeline is done at 20 FPS, and stereoscopic processing at 10 FPS.

Our tests show that it is not necessary to detect the obstacles faster than 10 times per second because none of the current robots at the league move so fast that the detection does not work properly. But this holds true only in the case of a wide-angle stereoscopic vision setup that we have. If the robot needs to rapidly pan and tilt its head to cover all the required large field of view with a relatively narrow field of view stereoscopic camera, we assume that the stereo pair processing should be faster in order to not to miss the important data.

4   Localization

4.1   Line-Based Localization on Narrow FoV

The goal post detection based localization (picked from Rhoban 2018 code release) that we used in the beginning of 2019 was not robust enough for our robot to play the high-quality game. To find an alternative we switched to a field lane detection based approach. The main idea was to use some prolonged "global" features like field lanes instead of small "local" ones like goal post bases to make the detection more robust.

We implemented a custom vision filter for field lines detection. Our filter is capable of detecting two major types of features: a) the single field line and b) the corner of two field lines. As said before, due to prolonged structure field lines can be detected more reliably in the presence of noise and motion blur than the goal posts or other local features. Also in comparison to a goal posts or other point-like features with no distinct orientation information (we can observe a goal post from any angle as it will looks the same), the lines and corners embed additional orientation information allowing the particle filter to converge faster due to less potential orientation ambiguity (see Fig. 6).

At the first step, our filter tries to find any local features on the image that can be treated as the part of a straight line. Similar to the classic Sobel edge detection approach, we do two passes of a sliding window convolution - one in the horizontal, and one in the vertical direction. Our sliding window consists of three regions. The horizontal pass sliding window consists of three rectangles - left, middle and right. The middle rectangle corresponds to the line being detected, its size is picked up at each image location according to the expected line width at this field position. Left and right rectangles correspond to the regions to the left and right of a line being detected. The middle rectangle should be white and bright, and the left and right rectangles should be dark and green. To speed up the processing, the estimation of how this current image position fits this criterion is done not via direct convolution, but with a score function using integral image processing similar to ball detection sliding window routine. After this sliding window step, we get two images that we call a horizontal and vertical "heatmaps" for a horizontal and vertical pass separately.

At the second step, we perform a Non-Maximum Suppression (NMS) [5] algorithm to detect the local maximums of these heatmaps. This local maximums

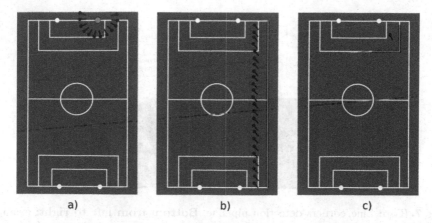

a)   b)   c)

Fig. 6. Possible positions of a robot (blue) to see the observation detected (red). Goal post (a): high orientation ambiguity/moderate position ambiguity. Line (b): very low orientation ambiguity/high position ambiguity. Corner (c): very low orientation ambiguity/very low position ambiguity. The corner is the most valuable observation among listed ones (Color figure online)

correspond to the middle pixels of a line being detected. To speed up the processing, the sliding window and NMS algorithms are performed not on each image row/column, but with decimation.

At the third step, these local maximums act as the inputs to the classic OpenCV Probabilistic Hough Transform [4] algorithm to detect the candidates of the line segments. Its result is then filtered to join the separate short segments into prolonged straight lines and to remove the duplicated lines if there are any. If the length of a line is above the threshold, it will be reported to the particle filter as a "line" observation.

At the fourth step, the resulting array of detected prolonged lines is checked for 90-degrees intersections. The basic type of intersection is the L-corner, and this is the type of observation that will be reported to the particle filter as a single "corner" observation. The T- and X-cross of field lines will be reported to the particle filter as two or four "corner" observations respectively.

As the result, each field line detected on the image is reported to particle filter twice: as an endless line observation, and as the part of a corner if this line intersected by another at the appropriate angle close to 90°. This gives a sufficient number of observations for the particle filter to quickly converge and keep track of the robot's position, even in the narrow-angle FoV vision setup. The overall structure of our localization pipeline is given at the Fig. 7.

4.2   Lane-Based Localization in Wide-Angle Lens Setup

The lane-based localisation in a narrow FoV setup mentioned above was used by us at Robocup Asia-Pacific 2019 competition on a previous generation of our robots, allowing us to win this competition.

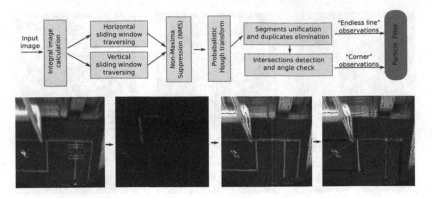

Fig. 7. Top: Line/corners detection pipeline. **Bottom from left to right:** example of a horizontal sliding window applied to the birdview image, example of the horizontal heatmap, example of the NMS result, example of the segment unification and corner extraction

After switching to wide-angle lens setup on the next generation of our robots which we used in Robocup 2021 Worldwide, we extended our line-based localization approach to the large FoV imaging taking into account the heavy lens distortion. Line detection algorithms mentioned above require the lines on the image to be straight to be properly detected. This is not the case in the wide-angle camera setup, thus proper image rectification is needed. The straightforward wide-angle image rectification is too time-consuming and gives a large of the resultant image.

So for a wide-angle setup, we switched to the so-called "birdview" approach. Using camera position and orientation from IMU and forward kinematics, with assumption that the field is flat, we can calculate such a perspective transform that maps image pixels from the current robot's point of view to a point of view of a new virtual camera, observing the field from the top and orthogonal to the field surface. This approach becomes especially efficient with the large field of view of a wide-angle camera setup, giving a good overview of the robot's surrounding. After this transform, all non-planar objects (other robots, goal posts, etc.) are heavily deformed, losing their shape, but the field lines have constant width and proper geometry.

Due to the relatively large, "global" scale of field lines compared to the small size of other "local" features like ball or goal posts, the field lines can be robustly detected on a birdview image using a relatively low-resolution image. Also lowering the resolution acts as an additional "low-pass" image filtering to remove noise and small field line discontinuities due to paint defects and other factors. Using the fact that the amount of pixels to be processed by undistortion routine depends on the undistorted image size and is almost independent from the input image size, a fast undistortion of a large input image to a low-resolution undistorted one could be performed, followed by a perspective transform on the same low resolution. We use a 640×480 output image for a birdview, and this processing can still be performed at more than 30 frames per second on the board CPU.

Using this technique, thanks to the large FoV of a wide-angle setup, the robot could localize itself robustly in approximately 2 s after a complete localization loss.

4.3   Modeling of a Wide-Angle Lens in Webots Simulator

As RoboCup 2021 Worldwide took place in simulation, we had to model our wide-angle camera setup in a simulated environment. The default camera model that Webots 2021b provides can have a planar (rectilinear) and spherical projections, and theoretically speaking only the spherical projection is suitable to simulate the camera with a wide field of view. But at the time of the competition our test have shown that the projection mode of a simulated camera in "spherical mode" is actually a cylindrical projection, and this problem was not solved during the competition by the community[5]. So we were forced to emulate our wide-angle lens setup with a large field of view camera with a planar (rectilinear) projection followed by a simulated heavy radial distortion. This approach limits the actual field of view of a simulated camera and introduces some noise at the borders of the resulting image. Thus, our simulated camera image has a lower field of view than a real-world one (100° instead of 135°), and with a bigger inactive area (we use a procedural-calculated mask to cover this area with a solid black color to not to confuse our vision algorithms, see Fig. 3). So the vision system in Webots simulator was modelled with worse characteristics than the real-world one (Fig. 8).

Fig. 8. Left: example of an input wide-angle image from a real robot with marked detected ball (red circle) and field lanes (green lines). **Middle:** corresponding image after "birdview" transform with marked detected lanes (yellow) and detected corner (orange/red/green triangle) constructed from NMS processing output (blue/red dots). **Right:**example of a simulated image from Webots simulator with a rectilinear projection followed by a radial distortion to mimic the real-world wide-angle image. The radial distortion is notable but less than in a real-world image (Color figure online)

---

[5] forum.robocup.org thread.

5   Strategy

5.1   Ball Path Planning

Improvements in localization and vision systems allow us to construct more complex scoring strategy. We decided to work on the approach to choosing the current kick direction by doing some path planning of the ball entity trying to reach the opponent's goal with the help of robots in multiple steps. The algorithm that we used is described in [3]. We introduce a graph Fig. 9 by discretizing the field. Each cell is a square of 10×10 cm, so there are $90 \times 60 = 5400$ cells overall. Then, given the ball position, the cell with a center that is the closest to the ball position is identified, and it is considered as the first vertex of the graph. Then the edges of the graph are generated with the length of the possible kicks and the shortest path is calculated with the A^* [1] algorithm with the cost (Algorithm 1) and heuristic functions (Algorithm 2). With this algorithm the robot prefers to play a pass and to move the ball to the zones not occupied by opponent.

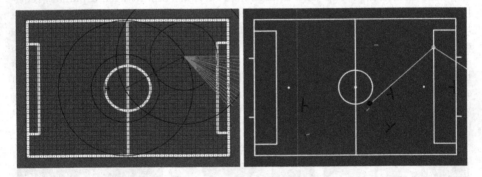

Fig. 9. Left: Graph used for path planning. The centers of the grid cells define the vertices. Edges are defined implicitly by each pair of the vertices that (approximately) lie within the predefined kick distance from each other. **Right:** Example of the algorithm output.

We have used this algorithm for live games prior to the 2021 competition, and at the first half of the competition. But after running local simulated games we decided to abandon this approach and by the time of the final games switch to more simple and straightforward algorithms like kicking directly to the goal even when the goal is too far away to be reached by a single kick.

The main problem with the new more complex strategy is that the planner is highly sensitive to the noise in the relative ball position estimation, mainly because of the underlying discrete structure used. When the ball rapidly changes the occupied discretized cell due to the minor position estimation errors, this often causes the goal attack plan to change rapidly leading to the abrupt jumps in the preferred walk direction of the robot trying to follow the chosen attack plan, causing the walk speed degradation and stability issues. We believe that at

Algorithm 1. Cost function

---

function COMPUTECOST(robotPos, opponentsPositions, ballFromPos, ballToPos, firstKick)

    $ballTravelTime \leftarrow getLength(toPos, fromPos)/ballSpeed$

    if firstKick **then**

        $timeToReachBall \leftarrow calcTimeToApproachBall(fromPos, robotPos)$

        if intersectOpponent(fromPos, toPos, opponentsField) **then**

            return $timeToReachBall + ballTravelTime * 2$

        else

            return $timeToReachBall + ballTravelTime$

        end if

    else

        return $ballTravelTime$

    end if

end function

Algorithm 2. Heuristic function

---

function HFUNC(teamMatesField, toPos, firstKick)

    $timeToReachGoal \leftarrow distToGoal(toPos)/ballSpeed$

    if firstKick **then**

        $timeToApproachBall \leftarrow calcTimeToApproachBall(toPos, teamMatesField)$

        return $timeToApproachBall + timeToReachGoal$

    else

        return $timeToReachGoal$

    end if

end function

---

some point we will be able to improve the algorithm to give satisfactory results by introducing some smoothing or hysteresis.

It's worth mentioning that is the new virtual format of the tournament that allowed us to rapidly run the required amount of virtual test games during the competition to encounter the issues with this new algorithm and make conclusions about its in-game performance.

6 Motions

6.1 Active Falling

We have noticed that our robots spend much time recovering from falls, especially when standing up from the back. Thus, in the 2019 Asia-Pacific competition we introduced the so-called "active falling" movement, which is activated when the robot's center of mass (CoM) ground projection leaves the estimated support polygon (Fig. 10). During this motion the robot bends its knees and throws out its arms in the direction of the fall[6] to catch itself in mid-air. After this, the

---

[6] https://youtu.be/ZZ7lhSuwT2o.

Fig. 10. Example of the "active falling" movement in a real-world game in 2019 performed by the robot at the center

robot starts the shortened stand-up motion directly from this pose. For back stand up the recovery time decreased by the factor of 1.6 and for the front one by the factor of 1.4. To mitigate the impact when hands hitting the ground, we have developed a flexible arms structure consisting of the multi-layer cocentrical leaf springs made by 3D printing it from the PETG material, and also installed support bearings to strengthen the robot's shoulders.

However, real world tests showed that this motion was unstable and potentially harmful to the robot's hardware, so we were not using it during the 2021 competition and are planning to improve it with better falling detection and processing.

6.2   Kick Tuning

Despite the fact that the new virtual setup of the competition allowed participants to do some automated motions tuning using the sample-intense methods like Genetic algorithms or Reinforcement Learning approach, we didn't use these approaches during the competition. We decided to focus on the precise hand-tuning of the kick and walk motions to better suit the virtual competition environment in terms of the game strategy. After many hours of hand tuning we managed to greatly improve the stability of the kick motion resulting in the consistent and predictable final ball position sacrificing the kick length, allowing us to play the good pass game.

7   Conclusion

As said in the introduction, the new format of a virtual competition in a simulation environment with automatic referee allows the participants to greatly intensify their code development, as the full games can be run locally by the teams giving the ability to rapidly test the new features and game configurations without the risk of damaging the robot's hardware. At least it was like that for our team, and we have significantly improved our game quality during the competition by connecting the real robots in the lab to the local network and directly launching the competition docker images on their onboard PCs to run a full test game with all six robots allowed by the rules in action.

In the beginning of the competition alongside with other teams we have had severe problems with the communication setup of *Webots* and docker image using the *protobuf* protocol, but with rapid and valuable support from the technical team we have managed to solve them. As an example of the effect of technical problems in the simulation setup, in one of the playoff games we achieved the world-record score of 23 goals in one game vs *EDROM* team which has some technical problems leading to the inability of its robots to play the full-featured game. And the challenge to rapidly overcome all of these problems by the time of the game schedule was the hard but important part of the competition.

It's worth to say that the most exciting of our games was the final one[7] with the *MRL-HSL* team from Iran. It was a real challenge because the opponent robots were significantly faster in walking speed and able to kick the ball almost twice further than ours. We suppose that changing the strategy to more defensive one and using precise localisation and robust stereoscopic-based opponent avoidance gave us a slight advantage.

Summarizing, we could highlight the following technical and algorithmic features behind the performance of our robots in the 2021 tournament:

- Due to the wide field of view of the cameras of our robots they were capable of fast ball detection in a large variety of viewing angles. So it was possible to instantly start the movement towards the ball when it was necessary, without spending a valuable amount of time scanning the surroundings.
- Fast and robust lane-based localization framework made it possible to walk precisely to the necessary position required by the current strategy. Moreover, the robots were rapidly recovering after falling to the active game, meaning effectively no time to localize from scratch.
- The kick movement was fine-tuned to be robust and stable, leading to predictable final ball position. So the effective strategy of a pass game was possible, being combined with the good localisation leading one of the teammates to be "in the right place and in the right time" to pick up the ball after the mate's kick and continue the attack to the opponent's goal.
- Due to the stereo vision-based obstacle avoidance, our robots were able to prevent collisions with teammates and opponents, thus significantly lowering the amount of collisions which usually leads to the fall ruining the attack plan or unwanted penalisation.

---

[7] YouTube Final Game.

References

1. Hart, P.E., Nilsson, N.J., Raphael, B.: A formal basis for the heuristic determination of minimum cost paths. IEEE Trans. Syst. Sci. Cybern. 4(2), 100–107 (1968)
2. Khokhlov, I., et al.: Tiny-YOLO object detection supplemented with geometrical data. In: 2020 IEEE 91st Vehicular Technology Conference (VTC2020-Spring), pp. 1–5. IEEE (2020)
3. Khokhlov, I., Litvinenko, V., Ryakin, I., Yakovlev, K.: Planning to score a goal in robotic football with heuristic search. In: Ronzhin, A., Rigoll, G., Meshcheryakov, R. (eds.) ICR 2020. LNCS (LNAI), vol. 12336, pp. 148–159. Springer, Cham (2020). https://doi.org/10.1007/978-3-030-60337-3_15
4. Matas, J., Galambos, C., Kittler, J.: Progressive probabilistic Hough transform. In: BMVC (1998)
5. Neubeck, A., Van Gool, L.: Efficient non-maximum suppression. In: 18th International Conference on Pattern Recognition (ICPR 2006), vol. 3, pp. 850–855 (2006). https://doi.org/10.1109/ICPR.2006.479
6. Rusu, R.B.: Semantic 3D object maps for everyday manipulation in human living environments. Ph.D. thesis, Computer Science Department, Technische Universitaet Muenchen, Germany, October 2009

Robocup@Home 2021 Champion Team Paper: SSPL Winner Uchile Peppers

Rodrigo Salas[2]([✉])[iD], Juan Pablo Cáceres[2][iD], Eduardo Loayza[2],
Fernando Feliú[2][iD], Felipe Valenzuela[2][iD], and Javier Ruiz del Solar[1,2][iD]

[1] Advanced Mining Technology Center, Department of Electrical Engineering,
Universidad de Chile, Santiago, Chile
[2] Robotics Laboratory, Department of Electrical Engineering, Universidad de Chile,
Santiago, Chile
rodrigo.salas.o@ug.uchile.cl, rodrigosalaso@gmail.com

Abstract. This paper summarizes the development and strategies used by the Uchile Peppers Team to become champions of the Robocup@Home Social Standard Platform League. First both vision and manipulation skills of the robot are analyzed. Next, the implementation of these modules to create the state machines that solve the tasks given is explained. Finally, a general conclusion about our development experience is given.

Keywords: Robocup · Robocup@Home · Champion Team Paper · Social Standard Platform League · Social robots

1 Introduction

In 2021 the Robocup@Home had to change to a online format due to the world situation. The teams in the Social Standard Platform League (SSPL) chose to compete with the Toyota HSR robot [1] because of the highly advanced robot model and world model used in the available simulation. This simulation was also already tested in another international competition [2] and had a scoring server mounted so it was the best fit. The rules for this year's competition also had to change to ensure fair competition and that it would be feasible because this is not the official robot for all leagues [3].

The Uchile Peppers team has been competing since 2017 with a rising performance, achieving third place in 2018, second place in 2019 and first place in 2021. To prepare for this year, the team focused on learning the new robot and adapting our software to the new tasks at hand.

In this paper we analyze the different approaches that each area of the team took in respect of manipulation and vision capabilities and the states machines to control the robot. For the vision capabilities, the training of a Yolo [6] vision model and its deployment in the robot is explained. For the manipulation capabilities, the implementation of the Grasp Pose Detection (GPD) [7] library to get the grasp poses is described. Finally, the states machines created for the robot behavior are analyzed.

© Springer Nature Switzerland AG 2022
R. Alami et al. (Eds.): RoboCup 2021, LNAI 13132, pp. 275–282, 2022.
https://doi.org/10.1007/978-3-030-98682-7_22

2 Robot Skills

Object recognition and object manipulation are skills required to solve the different tasks in the Robocup@Home 2021. Object recognition enables the robot to analyze its surrounding and find the objects needed. Object manipulation enables the robot to interact with the environment and carry necessary items. This section focuses in describing both skills and their implementation for solving the different tasks.

2.1 Object Recognition and Position Estimation

In a normal situation, the real objects used in the competition belong to the YCB dataset [4] or the most similar available object in the current host country. This year, a big part of the simulated objects available in the YCB dataset were used.

The chosen model for object recognition was YoloV5 [5] due to its speed. The version used is the YoloV5m which has good performance without sacrificing too much accuracy. The algorithm's speed is important in this case because of the limited time available for the tasks. The model was adapted to work with the robot's environment, thus working with *python 2.7* and *torch 1.4.0*. Finally, the team had already defined protocols to easily deploy this type of models in domestic robots.

For the training of the model, the first step is to take pictures of the different objects in the arena. For this, we put multiple random objects in the manipulation areas of the arena and then recorded a video from the robot's point of view (POV). This allows the computer vision model to train with images originating from the robot, thus testing the real scenario. A total of 1700 pictures with all objects manually labeled were used to train the model. Figure 1 is an example of the images used to train the model.

The model returns a bounding box for every object it can see. The position of the object is then defined using the information from the point cloud correlated with the center of the bounding box returned by the model. This can be easily achieved as both RGB and Depth cameras are separated by a negligible distance so no correction was deemed necessary.

2.2 Grasp Pose Definition

The base simulated robot already has available the capability of planning the arm trajectory and moving the arm to the target pose. The definition of pregrasp and graps poses is needed to move the arm and successfully manipulate the desired object.

As previously stated, the GPD library [8,9] is used for defining the grasp poses. GPD needs a segmented point cloud where only the data corresponding to the target object is present. This segmented point cloud is created using a filtering algorithm. First, a binary mask that only contains the object to manipulate is formed. For the mask, everything outside the bounding box is filtered

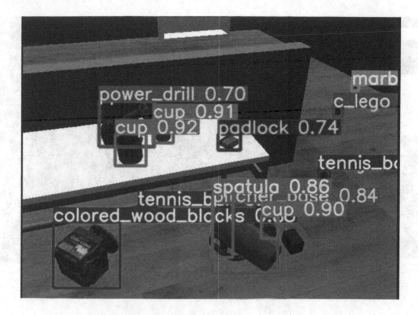

Fig. 1. Example of image for model training.

out because those pixels cannot be part of the object. Then the floor, table and walls are filtered out by using its HSV color space values, which are manually found. Due to the lighting in the simulated space, the colors of the objects and environment do not change no matter the position of the camera, thus filtering by color becomes reliable. Once the object's binary mask was obtained, a clustering process is applied to eliminate all small clusters that are not related to the main object. Finally, the binary mask is projected on the complete point cloud to obtain the segmented point cloud.

This process of segmentation begins to fail when several objects are close together, because the clustering stage cannot differentiate between the target object and other objects nearby. The quality and completeness of this segmented point cloud is a big factor in whether GPD returns a good grasp pose or a bad one.

In Fig. 2 we can see the process applied to a jug. In the middle we can see the binary mask that shows only the points that belong to the jug and some outliers from other objects, which are eliminated using the clustering stage. Finally at the right part of the image is the point cloud filtered and only showing the jug data.

The robot is placed in front of the object at a specific distance so as to maximize the chances for GPD to find an optimum grasp pose. Sometimes, GPD was not capable of finding in the first try a possible grasp position, so several tries were necessary. Using a score point system and a viability filter, GPD ranks all the possible grasp positions for the object and in this case the best one is used.

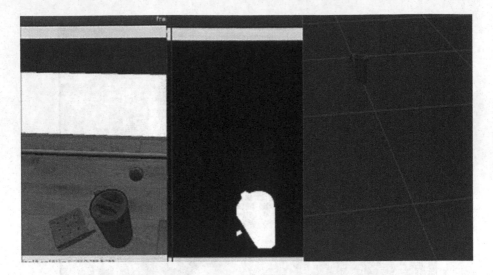

Fig. 2. Color mask filtering for GPD.

For better chances of correctly grasping the object, based on the grasp pose generated by GPD, a pregrasp pose was implemented. The goal of this pose is to take the arm to a point near the object and then try to grasp it. This strategy decreases the chances of the end effector colliding with other objects.

3   Robot Behavior

Both tasks in this competition require a rapid robot execution as to complete more parts of the task thus gaining more points. In this section we analyze the strategies used to speed up task completion and maximize points.

3.1   Clean Up

The first task is Clean Up and consists in clearing a large room with multiple objects scattered in the floor and in the tables, within a pick up zone. The amount of points awarded is determined by the amount of objects the robot can stow. Additionally, objects could be stored in specific containers to gain more points. Figure 3 is a general diagram of the state machine that solves the Clean Up task. The important steps will be reviewed in detail. Several heuristic rules were applied to the search algorithm to speed up the process and protect the machine from getting stuck in a step.

Object Search. Objects placed in the floor are prioritized to avoid collision when approaching the tables. Also, objects under the table were ignored because of the difficulty to manipulate them and thus save time. After clearing the floor, the robot approaches the tables to look for objects.

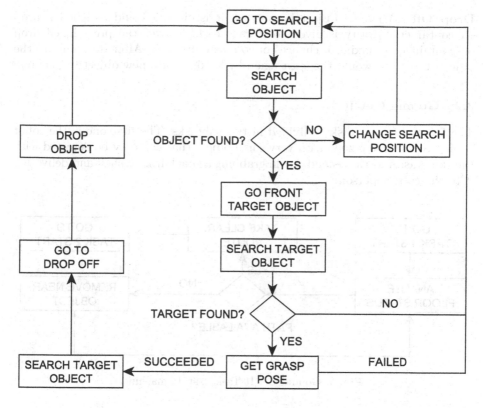

Fig. 3. Clean Up state machine.

When an object was found, the robot positions itself in front of the object and then checks again if the object is there. This check up is done to avoid wrong classification for the drop off part and improve the mask filtering for GPD. If the object is not found, the robot starts looking again.

Grasp Pose. After the robot positions itself in front of the target object it starts looking for the best grasping pose using GPD. Because the result of GPD was not always effective for grasping, two filters were added.

The first filter was based on the score given by GPD. Grasp pose scores needed to be higher than a threshold to be considered viable. This threshold was determined by analyzing the GPD results of all objects in different positions. The second filter is angle of approach. If the grasp pose approached the object from behind, the grasp pose was deemed non viable.

A maximum number of tries was implemented to avoid the robot getting stuck. After 5 tries if there was no viable grasp pose, the object was banned and ignored by the robot which would start to look for a new object.

Drop Off. When an object is grasped, it is classified and assigned a drop off container. Priority is given to storage easiness over the preassigned drop off container to maximize chances of complete drop off. After dropping off the object, the robot would the start again by looking for a new object to pick up.

3.2 Go and Get It

The Go and Get It task is divided in two subtasks. The first one is the robot having to traverse a zone with very small object that can only be detected with the cameras. And the second one in grabbing a snack from a shelf and delivering it to the correct person.

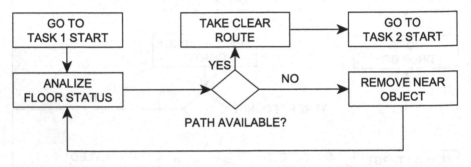

Fig. 4. Go and Get It Task, 1 state machine.

Task 1. Figure 4 shows the state machine diagram for the subtask 1 of the Go and Get It task.

The first step is to analyze the floor status to determine whether the robot can pass without moving any object or which object to move as to pass the fastest possible. For this the hazardous zone is divided in subzones of different sizes. This can be seen in Fig. 5.

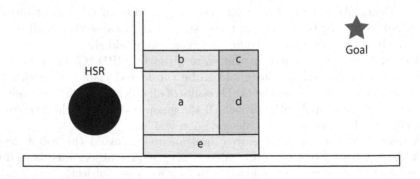

Fig. 5. Task 1 zone division.

First, if the "a" zone is blocked, the robot grasps the object and drops it off behind the starting position. This drop off zone is chosen since the robot only needs to move through the designated area. Once "a" zone is clear, the robot analyzes if "b" zone or "d" zone are clear, then chooses the one that has a clear path to the goal. If both are blocked, then the robots removes the obstacle from "d" zone. Remaining zones "e" and "c" are ignored due to not directly affecting the paths that the robot can take.

For the removal on any object in this subtask, GPD was not used. Instead, objects are always grasped from the top because it is known that they will be on the floor. Object position is obtained using the same algorithm used in the Clean Up task to obtain global position. The drop off zone is the same no matter the zone where the object was found thus clearing the navigation zone.

Task 2. After getting to the first goal zone, the robot receives the command of what snack to fetch and to whom deliver it. The robot then positions itself in front of the shelf and searches for the chosen snack. This snack can be hidden behind other snacks. After a full scan of the shelf if the chosen snack is not found, then the nearest snack is chosen.

For grasping the snack, the gripper is horizontally oriented to allow easier entrance to the shelf space. Due to the forced approach of the hand, GPD is not required and the object position is obtained using the object detection model used in the Clean Up task.

Finally, with the snack in hand, the robot navigates to one of the two previous set points in the map corresponding to the persons. The robot drops the object in front of the target person to finish the test. A summary of this task can be seen in Fig. 6.

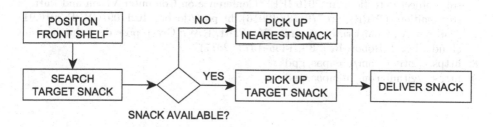

Fig. 6. Go and Get It Task 2 state machine.

4   Conclusion

Several complications appeared with the development of the aforementioned state machines, mainly with manipulation. Due to the robot having to include the movement of the base to be able to freely manipulate, sometimes this would cause it to collide with objects in the arena. GPD is a computer intensive algorithm, so an alternative needs to be chosen as to speed up the grasp process and thus aiming for more points.

The strategies described in this paper take an heuristic approach to solving the majority of the tasks. This was done to lower computational resources and speed up processing. Thus these algorithms can be easily exported to other robots of the Robocup@Home such as the Pepper robot.

Working with a new robot that none of the team members has ever worked with imposed a serious challenge. The team had to start by learning how to use the robot and then how to migrate our previous development and use it.

Acknowledgments. This research work was funded by Chile's FONDECYT Project 1201170 and Chile's ANID/PIA project AFB180004.

References

1. IEEE Robot Description page, HSR details. https://robots.ieee.org/robots/hsr/. Accessed 11 Oct 2021
2. Japan Open 2020 details, RoboCup Japan. https://www.robocup.or.jp/japanopen2020b-en/news/Registration.html. Accessed 11 Oct 2021
3. Robocup@Home Virtual 2021 rules. https://athome.robocup.org/home-virtual-2021/. Accessed 11 Oct 2021
4. Calli, B., Singh, A., Walsman, A., Srinivasa, S., Abbeel, P., Dollar, A.M.: The YCB object and Model set: towards common benchmarks for manipulation research. In: 2015 International Conference on Advanced Robotics (ICAR), pp. 510–517 (2015). https://doi.org/10.1109/ICAR.2015.7251504
5. PyTorch YOLOV5 implementation. https://pytorch.org/hub/ultralytics_yolov5/. Accessed 11 Oct 2021
6. Redmon, J., Divvala, S., Girshick, R., Farhadi, A.: You only look once: unified, real-time object detection. In: 2016 IEEE Conference on Computer Vision and Pattern Recognition (CVPR), pp 779–788 (2016). https://doi.org/10.1109/CVPR.2016.91
7. Ten Pas, A., Gualtieri, M., Saenko, K., Platt, R.W.: Grasp pose detection in point clouds. Int. J. Robot. Res. **36**, 1455–1473 (2017)
8. https://github.com/atenpas/gpd
9. https://github.com/atenpas/gpd_ros

homer@UniKoblenz: Winning Team of the RoboCup Virtual @Home Open Platform League 2021

Daniel Müller[✉], Niklas Yann Wettengel, and Dietrich Paulus

Active Vision Group, Institute for Computational Visualistics,
University of Koblenz-Landau, 56070 Koblenz, Germany
{muellerd,niyawe,paulus}@uni-koblenz.de
http://homer.uni-koblenz.de, http://agas.uni-koblenz.de

Abstract. In this paper we present our approaches for solving this year's virtual RoboCup @Home tasks with special focus on object detection and manipulation in the simulation environment Gazebo, which lead to our successful participation in the Open Platform League. There, we deployed the model of robot *TIAGo Steel Edition*, which is publicly provided by PAL Robotics. For object detection and pose estimation, we use a custom pixel-based clustering approach for segmenting potentially object supporting planes first. Instances of arbitrary and unknown objects can thus be detected and suitable grasping poses can be deduced. We perform object recognition by training our YOLO v3 network on a synthetic dataset of rendered *YCB* object images with *Blender*. A generalized grasping pipeline, which integrates extent and orientation information from our general object detection, performs planning and execution of combined arm and torso trajectory using MoveIt.

Keywords: RoboCup@Home · Open Platform League · Domestic service robotics · homer@UniKoblenz · TIAGo · Gazebo · Simulated robotics

1 Introduction

We are team *homer@UniKoblenz* (short for "home robots"), a mostly student team from the University of Koblenz-Landau in Germany, which is hosted by the Active Vision Group – a research group at campus Koblenz with focus on computer vision and robotics, led by Prof. Dr.-Ing. Dietrich Paulus. Our team for RoboCup 2021 is supervised by research associate Daniel Müller with help from research assistant student Niklas Yann Wettengel and further consists of four students in their Bachelor and Master studies. In the last years, team *homer* has been one of the regularly participating teams in @Home service robot competitions such as RoboCup @Home [12], European Robotics League [6] or its predecessor RoCKIn [5,11].

R. Alami et al. (Eds.): RoboCup 2021, LNAI 13132, pp. 283–290, 2022.
https://doi.org/10.1007/978-3-030-98682-7_23

With the beginning of the COVID-19 pandemic, we switched from working with physical PAL Robotics *TIAGo* [9] in our laboratory to running and developing in the Gazebo [4] simulation environment with the publicly provided robot model of *TIAGo Steel Edition*[1]. We integrated the setup for the *sDSPL* [2] competition arena and the set of standardized *YCB* object models [1] for participating with robot model *TIAGo* in the Open Standard Platform league of RoboCup @Home.

In the years before we gave insights in our contributions and approaches in the fields of mapping and navigation or human interaction [7,8]. As the automatable environment for the competition works without the latter, the tasks' focus strongly shifted to object recognition and manipulation. The teams in the @Home league had to compete in the tasks *Clean Up* and *Go Get It*. In *Clean Up* a large number of objects is scattered across a room, lying on the floor or on and under tables. Goal locations in differently shaped and positioned storage containers are defined for each class of object. In *Go Get It* the robot has to maneuver to a storage cupboard while avoiding small and hard to see obstacles on the floor. A requested item has to be located and grasped out of the narrow cupboard compartments without colliding.

This paper presents the approaches we used for tackling these challenges in the RoboCup 2021 competition. In the following Sect. 2, we introduce our 3D object detection pipeline for segmenting object instances and estimating their pose for grasping. This is extended by recognition of the specific object class using *YOLO v3* weights trained on synthetic data in Sect. 3. Our generalized object grasping pipeline is described in Sect. 4 before we show the extension of our map layers for navigation in Sect. 5. This paper concludes with an outlook on subsequent research and development, our experiences from the competition and the future of domestic service robotics having gone virtual.

2   Plane Segmentation and Object Detection

For general object detection and segmentation, we rely on a self developed pixel-based clustering approach for identifying support planes first and arbitrary objects standing on them afterwards. Based on a previously computed normal image, pixel neighbors are labeled equally if a set of geometric constraints holds for them and the currently processed cluster. Expecting a surface to be flat, the estimated surface normal direction in each neighboring pixel must not exceed a fixed threshold. Furthermore, the position of surface points is only allowed to differ in distance to the estimated plane within the bounds of a sensor's measurement noise, assuming flatness up to a defined degree. Searching for possibly object supporting planes, a majority of points can be filtered out beforehand as their surface normal deviates from an idealized up-vector. A similar task is the identification of doors or drawer fronts, which can be determined by constraining plane surface normals to vectors perpendicular to the up-vector.

---

[1] ROS wiki entry of robot *TIAGo*: http://wiki.ros.org/Robots/TIAGo.

Having identified separate plane instances, their clustered 3D points are down-projected onto a plane texture and contours of the (partial) plane view are determined. Pixel positions which are not marked as plane points can then be checked if they are within the volume above and inside of the plane instance contours in order to form a set of potential object points.

The segmentation of object points is performed in a similar manner as before, but with a relaxation of the object surface normal direction constraint. Partial clusters are merged based on their distances to other clusters within their 2D coordinates on the supporting surface's plane. This yields clusters of 3D points, which can be fitted to eigen vector aligned bounding boxes using *Principle Component Analysis*. This method works for both, known and unknown objects, and does not rely on previous training.

Our implementations work highly in parallel with threads processing disjunctive areas of the input image data without the need for synchronization mechanisms. A post processing step checks the last few open connections on thread working area borders for further merging of clusters (Fig. 1).

Fig. 1. *Left:* objects placed on a table in *Gazebo*. *Right:* segmentation result of the support plane (gray with blue-green contours) and the object instances' oriented bounding boxes (red). (Color figure online)

3   Object Recognition with Synthetic Training Data

For object recognition of known objects, we synthesize virtual image data with *Blender*[2] using the *YCB* [1] models and train *YOLO v3* [10] on this synthetic dataset. Each object is rendered in a manifold of poses relative to the camera, thus also directly yielding labeling information such as their bounding box in

---

[2] *Blender* website: https://www.blender.org/.

image space or a pixel-wise mask of the object image location. We augment the blank object images by randomly positioning them on top of cluttered background images. With the automatically computed label information, we then start training the network with our generated image database.

We perform *Principle Component Analysis* on the contained 3D points in the detection image patch and filter surrounding points along the eigen vector directions to form oriented 3D bounding boxes for each instance of a recognized object. In order to find correspondences between general object detections and specific recognitions we use 3D bounding box metrics as for example their intersection over union. This way, we build up correspondences between detections from different points in time and place.

4   Object Manipulation

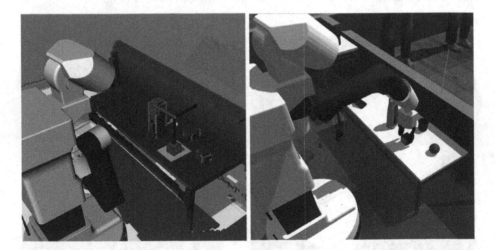

Fig. 2. *Left*: filled *OctoMap* voxels, fitted object bounding boxes (red), end-effector goal pose (coordinate axes). *Right*: execution of planned from top gripping operation before cartesian movement. (Color figure online)

Planning and Control. We are currently working on Ubuntu 18.04 LTS based systems with *ROS Melodic* and the corresponding *MoveIt*[3] version installed which we use for planning and execution of arm and torso trajectories. Our implementations provide ROS services for sending requests for e.g. moving the end-effector to a given target pose or linearly along a cartesian path. This is extended by filling an *OctoMap* [3] from current RGB-D views, which allows for collision aware planning for reaching a target configuration. The direction from where to grip from is estimated based on the relative positioning of the robot and the object's

---

[3] *MoveIt* website: https://moveit.ros.org/.

surroundings (see Fig. 2). Having grasped an object, it is added as attached object to the end-effector, which when planning enables the gripper to be moved safely out of e.g. a cupboard compartment.

Gripping Routine. Using the fitted object bounding boxes, favourable grasping poses are calculated based on the object's extents and relative pose to the robot. If the object is out of reach or end-effector starting poses are blocked, repositioning can take place for approaching the object from a more promising direction. Potential starting poses for moving the end-effector directly towards the object afterwards are calculated on the surface of a semi-sphere centered in the objects centroid. We position the gripper in near proximity in front of the object and use cartesian movement to position the gripper around object and to finally grasp it.

Fig. 3. Using *YOLO* for handle detection and object gripping routine to open drawers. Only the last step (*moving arm back*) was replaced with a combination of cartesian arm movement towards the robot and driving back for pulling the drawer out completely.

For failure detection during gripping, each state provides distinct feedback on the underlying occurring problem. For example if the object to grab fell over or out of the end-effector while moving back. Routines for handling these situations accordingly can easily be deployed afterwards. This routine has proven to be robust and can also be transferred to other tasks as for example opening drawers (Fig. 3) or doors. Handles can be approached in opening direction and the opening routine can be appended after having closed the grippers.

5   Obstacle Avoidance

For navigation and mapping, we build upon our open-sourced ROS packages *homer_navigation* and *homer_mapping*[4]. We extended our mapping component by an additional layer for RGB-D sensor measurements, which is taken into account while navigating (Fig. 4). This layer is updated when driving around with the robot's RGB-D sensor focused on the ground between the next waypoint and itself. Our plane segmentation can further be used to compensate noise in

---

[4] Public *homer* code repositories: https://gitlab.uni-koblenz.de/robbie/homer_navig ation/, https://gitlab.uni-koblenz.de/robbie/homer_mapping.

distance measurements on the floor by estimating an idealized ground plane. The measured points are projected to a grid map and only the visible view area is updated with the latest scan. A heuristic is used based on the times a grid cell is measured as free or blocked in order to update its state.

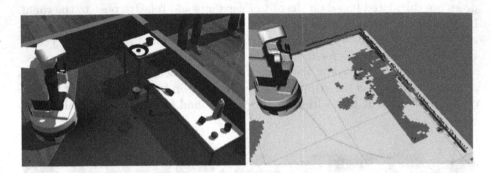

Fig. 4. *Left*: scene in *Gazebo* containing tables and objects lying around. The robot's laser scan beams (blue) do not touch most of the objects. *Right*: internal representation of the robot's occupancy maps for laser (black) and RGB-D (green) obstacles. (Color figure online)

6 Outlook

In this paper we have presented our software structure with the latest improvements in object detection and manipulation routines which enabled our way towards robust and separable execution pipelines for solving the tasks in RoboCup 2021 @Home Open Platform League. Team *homer* is now eager to deploy the new software in the physical world more often again. In the future we hope to refine handling of smaller more delicate or hard to grasp objects building up on the presented routines.

Moving work and development processes completely to the virtual space has caused additional work and new obstacles to overcome for all of us. For the future we hope to see real physical human interaction with domestic service robots get possible again as it adds various currently missing aspects and working fields to the range of service tasks. Simulating and transferring human motion and interaction to the simulated environment is still challenging, but would open up these currently on hold areas for the future of simulated benchmarks and development. As a robotics community we should keep working on extending the possibilities of our shared simulation environments even after the pandemic.

Besides current limitations in the variety of scenarios for domestic service robots, simulation has shown that robotics can be made accessible for potentially even more people spatially separated and even without the need of the real physical hardware being present. Simulation being further developed will become an essential addition in the development and testing process even in a future free of restrictions. When integrated properly, the automatable execution of tasks will speed up detection and avoidance of potential pitfalls and identifying promising approaches.

We hope to see all of you healthy and in good spirits when hosting competitions as RoboCup is possible in presence again.

Acknowledgements. We want to thank the participating students Niklas Yann Wettengel, Robin Bartsch, Janine Buchholz, Maximilian Grothe and Kevin Fischer Rios. Also thanks to everybody in the RoboCup committees who have made RoboCup @Home in this pandemic possible despite all the obstacles and long working hours.

References

1. Calli, B., Singh, A., Walsman, A., Srinivasa, S., Abbeel, P., Dollar, A.M.: The YCB object and model set: towards common benchmarks for manipulation research. In: 2015 International Conference on Advanced Robotics (ICAR), pp. 510–517. IEEE (2015)
2. Contreras, L., Matsusaka, Y., Yamamoto, T., Okada, H.: sDSPL - towards a benchmark for general-purpose task evaluation in domestic service robots. In: The 39th Annual Conference of the Robotics Society of Japan (2021)
3. Hornung, A., Wurm, K.M., Bennewitz, M., Stachniss, C., Burgard, W.: OctoMap: an efficient probabilistic 3D mapping framework based on octrees. Auton. Robot. **34**(3), 189–206 (2013)
4. Koenig, N., Howard, A.: Design and use paradigms for gazebo, an open-source multi-robot simulator. In: 2004 IEEE/RSJ International Conference on Intelligent Robots and Systems (IROS) (IEEE Cat. No. 04CH37566), vol. 3, pp. 2149–2154. IEEE (2014)
5. Lima, P.U., Nardi, D., Kraetzschmar, G., Berghofer, J., Matteucci, M., Buchanan, G.: Rockin innovation through robot competitions [competitions]. IEEE Robot. Autom. Mag. **21**(2), 8–12 (2014)
6. Lima, P.U., Nardi, D., Kraetzschmar, G.K., Bischoff, R., Matteucci, M.: RoCKIn and the European robotics league: building on RoboCup best practices to promote robot competitions in Europe. In: Behnke, S., Sheh, R., Sarıel, S., Lee, D.D. (eds.) RoboCup 2016. LNCS (LNAI), vol. 9776, pp. 181–192. Springer, Cham (2017). https://doi.org/10.1007/978-3-319-68792-6_15
7. Memmesheimer, R., Mykhalchyshyna, I., Seib, V., Evers, T., Paulus, D.: homer@UniKoblenz: winning team of the RoboCup@Home open platform league 2018. In: Holz, D., Genter, K., Saad, M., von Stryk, O. (eds.) RoboCup 2018. LNCS (LNAI), vol. 11374, pp. 512–523. Springer, Cham (2019). https://doi.org/10.1007/978-3-030-27544-0_42
8. Memmesheimer, R., Seib, V., Paulus, D.: homer@UniKoblenz: winning team of the RoboCup@Home open platform league 2017. In: Akiyama, H., Obst, O., Sammut, C., Tonidandel, F. (eds.) RoboCup 2017. LNCS (LNAI), vol. 11175, pp. 509–520. Springer, Cham (2018). https://doi.org/10.1007/978-3-030-00308-1_42
9. Pages, J., Marchionni, L., Ferro, F.: Tiago: the modular robot that adapts to different research needs. In: International Workshop on Robot Modularity, IROS (2016)

10. Redmon, J., Farhadi, A.: Yolov3: an incremental improvement. arXiv preprint arXiv:1804.02767 (2018)
11. Schneider, S., et al.: The rockin@ home challenge. In: ISR/Robotik 2014; 41st International Symposium on Robotics, pp. 1–7. VDE (2014)
12. Wisspeintner, T., Van Der Zant, T., Iocchi, L., Schiffer, S.: Robocup@ home: scientific competition and benchmarking for domestic service robots. Interact. Stud. 10(3), 392–426 (2009)

RoboCup@Home 2021 Domestic Standard Platform League Winner

DongWoon Song[1], Taewoong Kang[1], Jaebong Yi[1], Joonyoung Kim[1],
Taeyang Kim[1], Chung-Yeon Lee[2], Jc-Hwan Ryu[2], Minji Kim[2], HyunJun Jo[3],
Byoung-Tak Zhang[2], Jae-bok Song[3], and Seung-Joon Yi[1(✉)]

[1] Department of Electrical Engineering, Pusan National University, Busan, Korea
seungjoon.yi@pusan.ac.kr
[2] Department of Computer Science, Seoul National University, Seoul, Korea
[3] Department of Mechanical Engineering, Korea University, Seoul, Korea

Abstract. Adoption of the World Robot Summit (WRS) rules and simulated environments for the RoboCup@Home Leagues in 2021 pose significant challenges for perception, manipulation and autonomy of the robot. Especially, the randomized item placement and longer task time highlight the need for a robust long-term autonomy that can recover from various failure cases. In this paper, we present how we have prepared our software for such challenges, which helped us to get the highest score among all the teams participated in RoboCup@Home 2021.

1 Introduction

Team Tidyboy is a joint RoboCup@Home Domestic Standard Platform League (DSPL) team that consists of members from Pusan National University, Seoul National University, and Korea University. We have a strong research experience in state-of-the-art machine learning methods applied to various robotics problems, as well as extensive expertise gained through a number of robotic competitions, including RoboCup soccer leagues, DARPA Robotics Challenges (DRC) and RoboCup@Home Social Standard Platform League (SSPL). Recently, we are focusing on service robots, and we have participated in two major international robotic competitions using the Toyota HSR platform: RoboCup@Home DSPL and World Robot Summit (WRS) Partner Robot Challenge with promising results.

Due to the global pandemic issue, the RoboCup@Home 2021 was held as a virtual event, utilizing the simulated testing environment developed for the WRS 2020. Compared to previous RoboCup@Home leagues which have a wide variety of short manipulation and human-robot interaction tasks, WRS 2020 has only two manipulation tasks, which have to be executed sequentially. In addition, the total duration of the task is much longer at 20 min, and teams are given only a single trial, which makes the robust long-term autonomy of the robot crucial. In this paper, we present the software framework we have used for the RoboCup@Home 2021, and how we have handled various difficulties from the new WRS rule and simulated environments.

© Springer Nature Switzerland AG 2022
R. Alami et al. (Eds.): RoboCup 2021, LNAI 13132, pp. 291–301, 2022.
https://doi.org/10.1007/978-3-030-98682-7_24

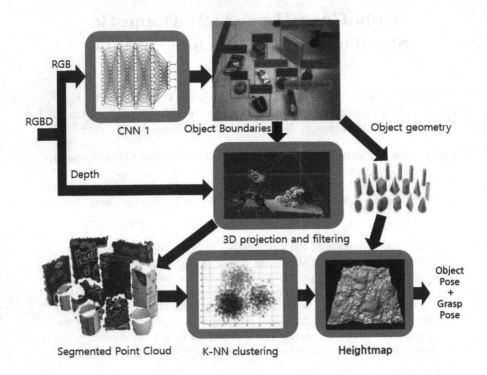

Fig. 1. Object detection pipeline

2   Modular Software Framework

Our software framework has its roots in the RoboCup humanoid league [8]. It is designed to be highly modular to support a variety of robotic hardware and be quickly ported on new robot platforms with minimal effort, as well as supporting various robotic simulators. The framework is extremely flexible, and has been used on tens of different hardware platforms including humanoid robots [12], quadrupeds [4], self driving vehicles [5], stationary robotic manipulators [3] and indoor service robots. It has been used for a wide range of tasks as well, which includes robotic soccer, disaster response, bin picking, robotic assembly, and mobile manipulation. We are periodically releasing cut down versions of the code for specific tasks, which includes our code used for the RoboCup@Home competition. Detailed explanation of our codebase and its application for service robotics can be found in [2,6,7,10,11].

3   Perception

3.1   Detection of Known Objects

We rely on the main RGBD came of the HSR robot to detect the objects and estimate their poses. We first use the YOLOv3 [9] real-time objection

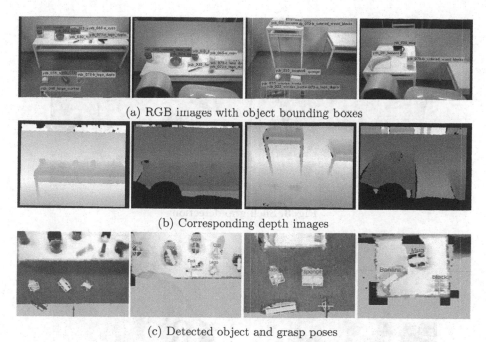

(a) RGB images with object bounding boxes

(b) Corresponding depth images

(c) Detected object and grasp poses

Fig. 2. Object detection results using a physical HSR robot

detection algorithm to detect known objects and their bounding boxes from the RGB image stream. Once the detected objects and their bounding boxes are acquired, the point cloud of each objects are generated using the camera transform and the corresponding depth image. However, such point cloud can contain points from the support surface, wall surrounding the object, or even other objects placed nearby. To filter out points from nearby planar surfaces, we run RANSAC algorithm to detect and track planar surfaces, and use the information to remove points from the surfaces. Previously, we have applied K-nearest neighbor clustering to filter out points from other objects, and finally the PCA algorithm to estimate the pose of the object. Although our previous perception algorithm has worked well for RoboCup@Home objects, WRS rule requires detection and manipulation of big, irregular shaped items that cannot be reliably handled by our previous algorithm. In addition, the rule includes the oriented items, such as forks or markers, the direction of which cannot be determined by point cloud alone.

So we have changed the final stage of the detection pipeline, which is shown in Fig. 1. Once the per-object point cloud is acquired, a colored heightmap is generated. Instead of using the PCA algorithm, we randomly sample a number of grasp positions and orientations, and evaluate them using the heightmap to find out the best grasp pose for the object. The correct direction of orientation items can be reliably estimated by the color statistics of the heightmap, as the fork

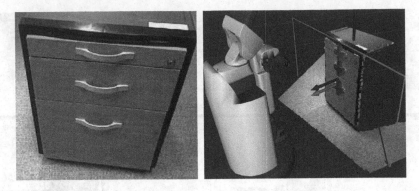

Fig. 3. Shelf grip detection

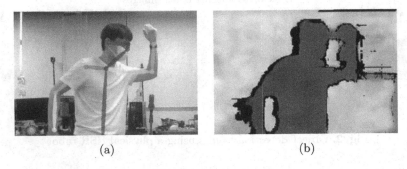

(a)   (b)

Fig. 4. Human gesture detection using OpenPose. (a) RGB image with human keypoints. (b) Matching depth image.

has red handle and marker has black tip. We have found our object detection algorithm to be extremely reliable in simulated environments, and that it works very well even in real environment. Figure 2 shows the object detection results of various WRS 2020 items using the physical HSR robot.

3.2   Detection of Furniture

Many home service tasks include manipulation of various types of furniture such as shelves, closets, and refrigerators. WRS rule also includes opening of three shelves. To reliably detect the grip positions of the shelves, we use the general purpose grip detection algorithm for detecting the grips of the shelves, which are shown in Fig. 3. Vertical surface information is first detected by the RANSAC algorithm, and protruding points from the surface are clustered to detect all possible grip positions.

3.3   Detection of Human Gesture

The second task requires the detection of human gesture to find the delivery target. Although the delivery target is directly provided in the simulated competition, we still have implemented the human gesture recognition module for the physical World Robot Summit competition. First the human and its keypoints are detected by the OpenPose [1] algorithm using the RGB image stream, and then the matching depth image is used to estimate the 3D positions of the keypoints, as shown in Fig. 4, and finally the 3D pose of the human and its limbs are estimated.

4 Manipulation

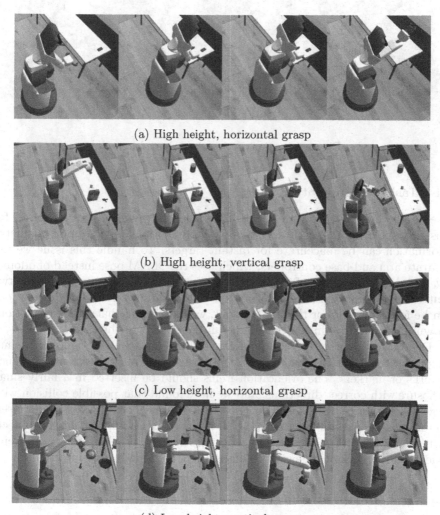

(a) High height, horizontal grasp

(b) High height, vertical grasp

(c) Low height, horizontal grasp

(d) Low height, vertical grasp

Fig. 5. Parameterized pickup motions used for the RoboCup@Home 2021

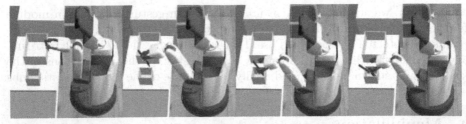

(a) Direct deposit

(b) Flipped deposit

Fig. 6. Insertion motions for oriented items

4.1 Task 1 Manipulation

Due to the low DOF arm of the HSR, whole body motions are required for most manipulation tasks. However, whole body motions relying upon odometry information can be inaccurate for distant targets. To handle this issue we use separate arm and base controllers, which uses the SLAM pose instead of odometry, and design a number of parameterized pickup and release motions using two controllers. A more detailed information of the parameterized pickup motions can be found in [11]. For the WRS task 1, we have found that 4 pickup motions shown in Fig. 5 are sufficient to handle all the objects in the task 1.

Depositing items into containers can be straightforwardly done with similar parameterized release motions, with an exception of orientation items such as forks or markers. The orientation items should be inserted in a fairly small enclosure with correct directions, and we have found that possible collision with previously deposited items can be disastrous. We have designed a special insertion motion for orientation items, which is shown in Fig. 6, that inserts objects with a backward tilt angle. Such a motion makes the previously inserted items to lean on the back of the case, which prevents collision during insertion.

4.2 Task 2 Manipulation

In the task 2, objects are placed in the shelf at three different depths, so in some cases other objects can block the access to the target item. Such a case is shown in Fig. 7(a) and (b), where the chocolate pudding box cannot be picked from either the front or the side without first removing other objects. To handle such

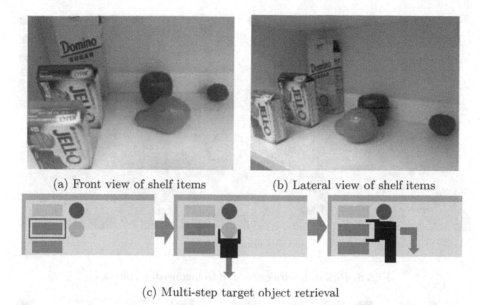

(a) Front view of shelf items   (b) Lateral view of shelf items

(c) Multi-step target object retrieval

Fig. 7. Motion sequence planning for shelf item retrieval

a case, we first design three pickup motions, which includes pickup from left, front and right sides, and develop a recursive planning algorithm that generate a sequence of pickup motions that can lead to the target objects while preventing collision with other objects or walls. Figure 7(c) shows a two-step sequence for picking up the chocolate pudding box.

5   Autonomy and Failure Recovery

As the total task time for two tasks is fairly long at 20 min, a major failure at the beginning of the run can be devastating if the robot cannot recover properly. And the inconsistent physics shown in Subsect. 5.1 and the randomized item positions makes it very hard to completely remove the failure cases. We have developed a number of failsafe and failure recovery methods to keep the robot scoring.

5.1   Pickup Failure Case

We have found that due to the inconsistent physics of the simulator used, the contact behavior between the gripper and manipulation objects can vary greatly between the simulation runs. In some cases, the contact becomes very slippery and the robot is totally unable to pickup some items, as shown in Fig. 8. In such a case, the robot may repeatedly try to pick up the same object in vain, which prevents the robot from scoring additional points. To handle such a case, we have limited the maximum number of trials allowed for each object, so that the robot can try other objects after a number of tries.

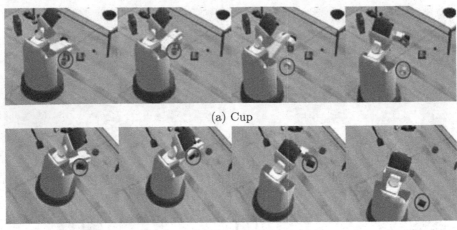

(a) Cup

(b) Foam brick

Fig. 8. Pickup failure cases due to inconsistent physics

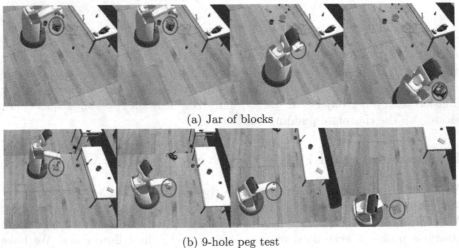

(a) Jar of blocks

(b) 9-hole peg test

Fig. 9. Whole body dragging of non-pickable items

In addition, we have found that some large and heavy items cannot be picked up by the robot at all in the provided simulated environment, and such an object can result in repeated collision penalties or even block the way to other items. To handle such an issue, we have implemented a whole body dragging motion that drags heavy, unpickable objects away, which are shown in Fig. 9.

5.2   Release Failure Case

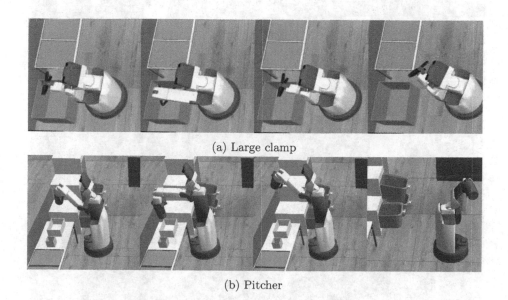

(a) Large clamp

(b) Pitcher

Fig. 10. Release failure cases due to inconsistent physics

In some simulation runs, we have found that the inconsistent physics can sometimes make the contact between the gripper and the object sticky, which makes the robot fail to release the item at the target position, as shown in Fig. 10. We have added multiple failsafe methods to prevent this from happening. We have added a long delay and shake motion after opening the gripper which can help the sticky object to eventually fall down, and scrubbing motion after release to remove stubborn items before next pickup.

5.3   Movement Failure Case

Another failure case we have found is that the robot being incapable of reaching the target pose, mostly due to the collision between the robot and the table legs. Such a collision can happen even with a proper collision check between the robot and the table legs, when multiple large objects lie around the table legs. To handle this issue, we monitor the pose of the robot during the movement phase, and if it fails to reach the target after some duration, we mark the current target object as inaccessible and move back to try another object.

Fig. 11. Technical challenge results

6   Competition Results

We have found out that inconsistency of the physics behavior is largely due to the different real time factors of the simulation runs, so we have used 7 computers with varying computational performance (from Intel i5-8400 CPU to AMD 5950x CPU) to make sure that our code can handle a wide range of different physics behaviors. Total 487 simulation trials have been run using 168 different random seeds. Eventually, at the time of the actual competition, we have found that our code can make the robot handle most setup without any major issues. As a result, our team scored the highest scores in all the tasks, in addition to the technical challenge, among all the teams from three RoboCup@Home leagues. Figure 11 shows the result of our technical challenge run.

7   Conclusions

In this work, we described our software framework for the RoboCup@Home 2021 competition. To overcome the new challenges due to WRS rule, simulated environment and randomized items, we have developed an improved object perception module, recursive motion planner and various failsafe and failure recovery approaches, which helped our team to robustly handle the given tasks and get the highest score among teams from all three RoboCup@Home leagues.

Acknowledgments. This work was supported by a 2-Year Research Grant of Pusan National University.

References

1. Cao, Z., Hidalgo Martinez, G., Simon, T., Wei, S., Sheikh, Y.A.: Openpose: real-time multi-person 2D pose estimation using part affinity fields. IEEE Trans. Pattern Anal. Mach. Intell. (2019)
2. Kang, T., Kim, J., Song, D., Kim, T., Yi, S.J.: Design and control of a service robot with modular cargo spaces. In: 2021 18th International Conference on Ubiquitous Robots (UR), pp. 595–600 (2021). https://doi.org/10.1109/UR52253.2021.9494635
3. Kang, T., Yi, J.B., Song, D., Yi, S.J.: High-speed autonomous robotic assembly using in-hand manipulation and re-grasping. Appl. Sci. **11**(1), 37 (2021)
4. Kim, J., Kang, T., Song, D., Yi, S.J.: Design and control of a open-source, low cost, 3D printed dynamic quadruped robot. Appl. Sci. **11**(9), 3762 (2021)
5. Kim, T., Shin, J., Yi, S.J.: Omnidirectional platform design for TurtleBot3. In: Korean Robotics Conference (2020)
6. Lee, B.J., Choi, J., Baek, C., Zhang, B.T.: Robust human following by deep Bayesian trajectory prediction for home service robots. In: 2018 IEEE International Conference on Robotics and Automation (ICRA), pp. 7189–7195. IEEE (2018)
7. Lee, S.W., Heo, Y.J., Zhang, B.T.: Answerer in questioner's mind: information theoretic approach to goal-oriented visual dialog. In: Advances in Neural Information Processing Systems, pp. 2579–2589 (2018)
8. McGill, S.G., Brindza, J., Yi, S.J., Lee, D.D.: Unified humanoid robotics software platform. In: The 5th Workshop on Humanoid Soccer Robots (2010)
9. Redmon, J., Farhadi, A.: Yolov3: an incremental improvement. arXiv (2018)
10. Yi, J.B., Yi, S.J.: Autonomous mobile manipulation for an intelligent home service robot. In: IEEE/RSJ International Conference on Intelligent Robots and Systems. IEEE (2019)
11. Yi, J.B., Kang, T., Song, D., Yi, S.J.: Unified software platform for intelligent home service robots. Appl. Sci. **10**(17) (2020). https://www.mdpi.com/2076-3417/10/17/5874
12. Yi, S.-J., et al.: RoboCup 2015 humanoid AdultSize league winner. In: Almeida, L., Ji, J., Steinbauer, G., Luke, S. (eds.) RoboCup 2015. LNCS (LNAI), vol. 9513, pp. 132–143. Springer, Cham (2015). https://doi.org/10.1007/978-3-319-29339-4_11

B-Human 2021 – Playing Soccer
Out of the Box

Thomas Röfer[1,2]([✉]), Tim Laue[2], Arne Hasselbring[1],
Lukas Malte Monnerjahn[2], Nele Matschull[2], and Lukas Plecher[2]

[1] Deutsches Forschungszentrum für Künstliche Intelligenz,
Cyber-Physical Systems, Enrique-Schmidt-Str. 5, 28359 Bremen, Germany
{thomas.roefer,arne.hasselbring}@dfki.de
[2] Fachbereich 3 – Mathematik und Informatik, Universität Bremen,
Postfach 330 440, 28334 Bremen, Germany
{tlaue,lumo,ne_ma,plecher}@uni-bremen.de

Abstract. In 2021, our team B-Human participated in two events in the
RoboCup Standard Platform League, namely the German Open Replacement Event and the actual RoboCup. We won both competitions. In both
events, the biggest scientific challenge was to be able to play soccer on
foreign robots in remote locations with the human team members neither
being on site nor having direct access to these robots. We present our
approach to a robot soccer system that only requires a fully automatic
pre-game extrinsic camera calibration, but otherwise works out of the
box. This paper focuses on the automatic calibration and some aspects
of our lighting-independent computer vision system.

1 Introduction

RoboCup is a competition. Thus, teams tune their systems for maximum performance regarding speed and precision. Although overall success depends on
sophisticated algorithms, the actual performance often hinges on a multitude
of suitable parameters. For this reason, during a RoboCup event, one can constantly observe participants on the fields, adapting their software for particular
robots and the current environment. In general, the following robot software
aspects are affected the most:

Vision System: Many efficient robot vision approaches strongly depend on
the current lighting conditions and require a proper preset. However, when
playing next to huge windows, the interplay of sun and clouds might change
these conditions quite quickly and – combined with a fixed vision parameter
preset – cause effects such as overexposure, cast shadows, and changes of
the color saturation.
Camera Parameters: For a precise projection of objects detected in an image
to robot-relative positions on the field plane, a calibration of each individual robot's cameras is necessary. In general, the production tolerance is so
significant that without any calibration, reliable self-localization and object
tracking are not possible.

© Springer Nature Switzerland AG 2022
R. Alami et al. (Eds.): RoboCup 2021, LNAI 13132, pp. 302–313, 2022.
https://doi.org/10.1007/978-3-030-98682-7_25

Joints and Motions: Different robots are in different states of wear. Thus, two robots of the same model often cannot carry out the same motion pattern, such as walking or kicking, in the same way. Furthermore, the structure and state of the field surface is not the same on every field and might strongly affect the reliability of any motion.

In 2021, no regular RoboCup competitions were held at any central place. Instead, most leagues decided to hold virtual and decentralized alternative competitions [8,10]. In the Standard Platform League, two competitions were held: the *German Open Replacement Event (GORE)* as well as the *RoboCup 2021 Virtual.* As all teams use the same robot platform, which is currently the NAO by SoftBank Robotics, for both events a unique setup was possible: Full games as well as different technical challenges were held on real robots but inside labs and on robots that were not directly accessible by the teams playing. Software and (sometimes) robots traveled, but people did not.

Such kind of remote setup poses significant challenges to the aforementioned tuning aspects as time and possibilities for interaction are extremely limited. In this paper, we describe our methods for autonomous calibration and lighting independent vision that we applied successfully at RoboCup 2021 as well as at the German Open Replacement Event. The third aspect – robust motion – has been addressed in a separate paper [5].

The remainder of this paper is organized as follows: Sect. 2 describes the competitions we participated in, along with their particular challenges. Afterwards, our approach for autonomous calibration is presented in Sect. 3. Our developments that allow calibration-free robot vision are described in Sect. 4 and Sect. 5 respectively. Finally, our results in 2021 are summarized in Sect. 6.

2   Challenges of the 2021 Competitions

As mentioned before, in 2021, the Standard Platform League held two competitions that required teams to run their software on robots that were not their own and to let them play on pitches to which the teams did not have direct access to.

As the annual RoboCup German Open was canceled in 2021, the Standard Platform League community organized its own competition, which was called *German Open Replacement Event (GORE)*. The event was held in May 2021 at two places – Technical University of Dortmund and University of Bremen – in parallel. The participating teams sent some of their robots to one of the places to form two robot pools that consisted of 16 robots each. No participants traveled with their robots. To hold full 5 vs 5 games, two hours before each game, every playing team was assigned five random robots from a pool. These could have been some of the own robots, but not necessarily so. Within these two hour time slots, a team had to deploy its software, configure each robot, and perform necessary calibrations and tests. This process had to be fully remote, the actual handling of the robot hardware was executed by local assistants. Given such a short period of time and the large number of robots, any automatisms as well as calibration-free implementations are highly beneficial. A detailed description of the GORE is given by Laue *et al.* [2]. The applied rules, which are mainly based on the standard game rules, featuring some extensions for hardware safety, are described in the GORE rule book [7].

RoboCup 2021 was a virtual event, too. The Standard Platform League competition consisted of four separate challenges, the results of which were combined to determine an overall winner. Two of these challenges were fully local: the Passing Challenge and the Obstacle Avoidance Challenge. Teams performed these challenges on their own robots in their own labs and streamed their attempts. As such a setting allows full control over the robots and their environment, automatic calibration as robust algorithms are less important and can be compensated by hand tuning details. However, the remaining two challenges, namely the Autonomous Calibration Challenge and the 1vs1 Challenge, were held remotely and posed challenges similar to those of the GORE. In both cases, the robot software was run on foreign robots at places that were not accessible by the participants. In the Autonomous Calibration Challenge, a robot calibration had to be performed fully autonomously. Subsequently, the robot had to navigate to multiple targets and detect two balls on the pitch, in all cases as precise and fast as possible, making the quality of the calibration a decisive factor. The 1vs1 Challenge was a minimalistic version of robot soccer, played with one robot per team. For this challenge, the calibration had to be done within 20 min and allowed fully automatic procedures as well as a semi-automatic execution with the help of a local volunteer. A detailed description of all rules is given in the official rule book [9].

3   Autonomous Calibration

One standard step in robot vision is the transformation of a detected object's image coordinates into the robot's world coordinate system. To perform this step, information about the robot's kinematics, the camera's position and orientation with respect to the robot body, as well as certain camera parameters, such as opening angles and the optical center, are needed. Even after careful industrial-scale production, the deviations from the original specifications are often high enough to cause huge transformation errors. Thus, in general, a camera calibration is unavoidable for robust and precise robot perception.

We model the deviation of the camera poses from their specified values by six parameters: a roll and pitch offset in the body and for each of the two cameras. Translational errors are too insignificant to the projection error and the yaw angles cannot be calibrated due to lack of a global reference.

An important feature of the calibration is that it works without exact knowledge of the robot's pose. The parameters are derived from the known relative angles (either parallel or orthogonal) and distances between lines on the field. Specifically, we use the view of the goal area from the side, which gives two right angles and one distance between two lines (see Fig. 1). The goal area is

Fig. 1. The robot's view during the calibration, taken during our attempt in Hamburg.

observed with three different head pan angles with each of the two cameras (this is necessary to distribute the error among the body and camera offsets), which gives 18 samples for 6 parameters in a least-squares optimization. To identify the goal area in the image without needing the yet uncalibrated projection to the field, we search for a short line that connects two long lines in the image, as this relation is true for the goal area only. For improved accuracy, the lines that are returned by our usual detection algorithm are refined by a Hough transform on a Sobel grayscale image before calculating the cost function.

In the autonomous mode required for RoboCup 2021, the robot is initially placed at one of two known positions at the side of the field. The self-localization is running using percepts that are projected using the yet uncalibrated camera pose, but no sensor resetting is performed in order to prevent the robot's pose estimate from jumping due to incorrectly perceived landmarks. The robot walks to a position from which the short line of the goal area can be observed well. It adjusts its head angles and its position if the necessary features are not detected within some time. After each successfully recorded sample, the robot also turns its head and body to observe the goal area from another angle. After all samples have been collected, the optimization process is started. We use a Gauss-Newton optimizer, but since the cost function is quite complex, the Jacobian is approximated by the numerical gradients. The optimization is done once the parameter change is sufficiently low for a number of optimization steps. Figure 2 shows the results of an automatic calibration performed at RoboCup 2021.

4   Preliminary Work on Deep Learning-Based Robot Vision

Due to the increasing complexity of the Standard Platform League's environment – removing color-coded items and enforcing setups with as much natural lighting as possible – we replaced most algorithmic robot vision solutions by Deep

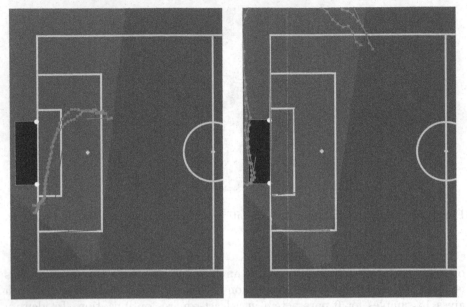

(a) Projected field lines before calibration   (b) Projected field lines after calibration

Fig. 2. Results of the autonomous camera calibration on a robot of the HULKs team during RoboCup 2021. Inside the fields of view of the two cameras, the projected field lines are shown in red, the projected field border in orange. (Color figure online)

Learning based approaches for several years now, as they have been proven to provide the necessary robustness to cope with this level of complexity.

Since 2017, the ball detection is based on the classification of previously determined image patches. The most recent version is described in our 2019 winner paper [11]. It uses an encoder-decoder architecture to determine the pixels belonging to a ball and includes an additional position estimation network to infer the exact ball center within a given patch.

In 2019, we presented and started using JET-Net [4], which is able to perform real-time robot detection. Given a full image and no external preprocessing steps, it is able to determine robot bounding boxes along with an estimate of the distance to a detected robot.

One important step in our vision pipeline is the computation of the field border to exclude most parts outside the field, which are not specified and thus contain random things, from further image processing steps. In the past, the detection of the field border required the calibration of the field's green within the color space. Since this year, we do not require this calibration anymore, as points of the field border are computed by another neural network. Along with their position, an uncertainty of their position is inferred too. This allows a more reliable matching of the field's edges. A full description of this approach is published by Hasselbring and Baude [1].

For fast inference of neural networks on our NAO robots, we use our own implementation, which is available as open source and is described in detail by Thielke and Hasselbring [14].

5 Lighting-Independent Field Line Detection

As described in the previous section, multiple important elements of a robot soccer game can already be detected by neural networks. However, for the field lines as well as for the computation of image patches that are candidates for containing the ball, this is not possible yet. These objects can be quite small or thin in an image and – in case of lines – still span over the whole width of an image. This would require to enter a high resolution image into a neural network and to apply more flexible approaches such as semantic segmentation. As the current computing power of the NAO robot is probably not sufficient for such a task, we developed a lighting-independent algorithmic solution.

The field line detection relies on a grid of horizontal and vertical scan lines along which the image is segmented into the classes *green*, *white*, and a generic class for everything else. In the computation of this segmentation, many thresholding parameters are needed. In past years, these had to be calibrated by hand before the start of the game. Instead, we now calculate all needed parameters per image, allowing the perception to adapt to lighting changes during the game as well as reducing calibration overhead.

5.1 Color-Segmented Scan Lines

Scan lines are a means to analyze only a part of the image while retaining as much useful information as possible. This is especially important now that our color segmentation approach takes significantly more execution time. That makes it impossible to apply the color segmentation to the whole image, so instead we use it only on the scan lines.

A scan line is simply a vertical or horizontal line of pixels in the image, so each scan line position is signified by a single x- or y-coordinate in the image plane. An adaptive grid defines the scan line positions depending on the robot's view angle. We also cut off the scan lines at the field boundary that was computed beforehand.

The color segmentation of the scan lines is done in four steps:

1. Split each scan line into homogeneous regions
2. Classify regions as field
3. Classify regions as white
4. Perform cleanup operations

Currently, this is done for the vertical and horizontal scan lines independently of each other.

For the first step, we draw samples in regular intervals on each scan line. For each sample point, we apply a Gaussian blur filter on the luminance to

(a) Region transition points of vertical scan lines

(b) Region transition points of horizontal scan lines

Fig. 3. The pink dots indicate the positions where two scan line regions are separated. (Color figure online)

smooth out noise. When two consecutive sample points' smoothed luminances differ significantly, a Sobel filter is applied to the interval in between. The highest Sobel value then signifies the exact position that separates two regions of the scan line. In Fig. 3, the resulting region transition points are marked with pink dots. Each region gets a representative YHS2 (see [13, p. 60]) color value by averaging over its pixels.

The field often appears in the image in form of rather big homogeneous patches that are within a certain color range. In order to use this characteristic, we unite neighboring regions with similar YHS2 color values. This is done efficiently using a union-find disjointed tree data structure. All united regions that span enough pixels and are in the expected color range of the field become classified as field and allow to determine the exact color range the field has in this image. Afterwards, all remaining regions are also classified as field, if they are within the ascertained field color range.

The classification of white regions utilizes simple thresholding techniques. The thresholds depend on the previously established field color and the approximated average luminance and saturation of the image. The results can be seen in Fig. 4.

Finally, neighboring regions on the same scan line, which have the same classification, become united into one region. We also noticed that this classification procedure sometimes leaves small gaps in between a field region and a white region. Because this impairs the line detection, we fill small gaps between a field and a white region by dividing them up equally into the neighboring regions, as can be seen in Fig. 5.

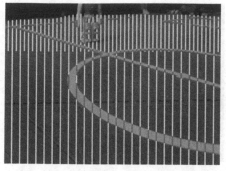

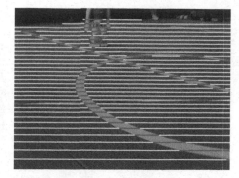

(a) Vertical color segmented scan lines   (b) Horizontal color segmented scan lines

Fig. 4. The color segmented scan lines. For better contrast, the regions classified as white are drawn in red. (Color figure online)

5.2   Line Detection

The perception of field lines relies mostly on the scan line regions. In order to find horizontal lines in the image, adjacent white vertical regions that are not within a perceived obstacle [13, pp. 71–74] are combined to line segments. Correspondingly, vertical line segments are constructed from white horizontal regions. These line segments and the center points of their regions, called *line spots*, are then projected onto the field. Using linear regression of the line spots, the line segments are then merged together and extended to larger line percepts. During this step, line segments are only merged together if at least a given ratio of the resulting line consists of white pixels in the image. Figure 6 shows the process of finding lines and the center circle in the camera image.

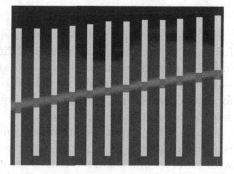

(a) Small wrongly classified regions at the transitions between field and line
(b) Transition between field and line with filled in gaps

Fig. 5. Filling in of small gaps between a field and a white region. Regions classified as white are shown in red. (Color figure online)

(a) Center points of the line spots. The ones found on vertical scan lines are marked in blue and finds on the horizontal scan lines are marked in red.

(b) The line segments built up from the line spots

(c) Circle candidate with points on inner and outer edge marked in yellow and cyan

(d) The final perception of field lines and the center circle

Fig. 6. The process of finding field lines (Color figure online)

We don't compute the color segmentation for the whole image any more. Instead, the pixels on the presumed line are compared to their surroundings in order to find out if the line is actually white. In regular intervals, we draw samples from a presumed line, compute two positions above and below the line for each sample and then use these for individual white tests of each pair of sample and comparison position.

To test the hypothesis that the sample point on a supposed line segment is white on green, we expect it to have a considerably higher luminance paired with lower saturation in relation to the comparison points. Additionally, we then test if the sample point satisfies generic thresholds for luminosity and saturation and if the comparison points are in the field color hue range. That effectively results in testing whether the line is white and embedded in green surroundings. Figure 7 shows the positions of the samples and their comparison positions.

Fig. 7. Sample points (blue) and their corresponding comparison points (orange) for the white test of line segments. (Color figure online)

6 Results

At the GORE, we played three games against the other strongest teams in the competition. Since we provided one of the two competition sites used, all our games took place in the other one, i.e. in Dortmund. We won our games 10:0, 8:0, and 10:0. Thereby, we scored 37% of all goals in this competition of seven teams and achieved the first place. Detailed results of the GORE are provided at the GORE website [3].

At the RoboCup, we won three of the four challenges and became the runner-up in the fourth challenge. In the Obstacle Avoidance Challenge, which required a robot to dribble around obstacles and to score a goal as quickly as possible, two of our three attempts were the fastest ones of all attempts of the fourteen teams that participated in that challenge. In the Passing Challenge, our robots played more passes in all of their three attempts than any other team. In particular, our best attempt with 27 passes in five minutes achieved as many passes as all the other seven teams in all of their attempts combined.

In the Automatic Calibration Challenge, different categories were judged, two time-based and five precision-based. 14 out of 15 times, we achieved the first place in precision-based categories. However, we often only reached the second place in time-based categories, because some teams skipped the calibration phase entirely or finished the main phase very quickly (usually with very low precision results). Overall, we came first place in all remote locations we played at and thereby won the challenge.

In the 1vs1 Challenge, we also used the automatic calibration to prepare for the games. During the games, in contrast to most teams, our robots not only kicked the balls into the opponent half, which was enough to score a point according to the rules. Instead, they actually kicked into the goal, thereby getting the ball back and limiting the opponent's access to balls. Up to the semifinal, this resulted in a point ratio of 57:20 in four games. However, in the final, which was held in the Hamburg arena, our robot always missed the goal, because its support foot had a different grip than usual during a kick, resulting in a slightly different kick direction. The robot then changed its strategy and just kicked the ball into the opponent half, but that way, it could not compensate for the points that were already lost in the beginning of the game. In the end, the robot of the team HTWK Robots scored one point more than ours, i.e. we lost the final with 12:13 points. Detailed results of all four challenges can found at the SPL website [6].

7 Conclusion

In this paper, we described our research that significantly contributed to our success in the 2021 competitions: autonomous camera calibration as well as a set of robust vision approaches. Although future RoboCup events might be held on site and thus allow more manual tuning again, the new capabilities that allow playing soccer out of the box probably have a high impact. It is now possible to play more friendly games against other teams without the need to travel long distances and without any major loss in performance. Furthermore, the required setup time at a RoboCup event is reduced significantly. However, there are still calibrations left that require automation, such as for precisely kicking over long distances. All algorithms presented in this paper are available as open source and are part of our most recent code release [12], giving other teams similar capabilities.

References

1. Hasselbring, A., Baude, A.: Soccer field boundary detection using convolutional neural networks. In: Alami, R., et al. (eds.) RoboCup 2021. LNAI, vol. 13132, pp. 202–213. Springer, Cham (2022). https://doi.org/10.1007/978-3-030-98682-7_17
2. Laue, T., Moos, A., Göttsch, P.: Let your robot go - challenges of a decentralized remote robot competition. In: Proceedings of the 10th European Conference on Mobile Robots (2021)
3. Moos, A., Göttsch, P.: GORE 2021. https://gore2021.netlify.app (2021). (Accessed 15 May 2021)
4. Poppinga, B., Laue, T.: JET-net: real-time object detection for mobile robots. In: Chalup, S., Niemueller, T., Suthakorn, J., Williams, M.-A. (eds.) RoboCup 2019. LNCS (LNAI), vol. 11531, pp. 227–240. Springer, Cham (2019). https://doi.org/10.1007/978-3-030-35699-6_18
5. Reichenberg, P., Röfer, T.: Step adjustment for a robust humanoid walk. In: Alami, R., et al. (eds.) RoboCup 2021. LNAI, vol. 13132, pp. 28–39. Springer, Cham (2022). https://doi.org/10.1007/978-3-030-98682-7_3
6. RoboCup Technical Committee: Standard Platform League history, Website. https://spl.robocup.org/results-2021/
7. RoboCup Technical Committee: GORE Standard Platform League (NAO) Rule Book (2021). Only available online. https://collaborating.tuhh.de/HULKs/gore/-/raw/master/GORe-Rules.pdf

8. RoboCup Technical Committee: RoboCup 2021 virtual tournament (2021), Website. https://ssl.robocup.org/robocup-2021-virtual-tournament/
9. RoboCup Technical Committee: RoboCup Standard Platform League (NAO) Challenges & Rule Book (2021). Only available online. https://cdn.robocup.org/spl/wp/2021/06/SPL-Rules-2021.pdf
10. RoboCup Technical Committee: Virtual RoboCup Soccer Humanoid League laws of the game 2020/2021 (2021). Only available online. https://cdn.robocup.org/hl/wp/2021/06/V-HL21_Rules_v4.pdf
11. Röfer, T., et al.: B-Human 2019 – complex team play under natural lighting conditions. In: Chalup, S., Niemueller, T., Suthakorn, J., Williams, M.-A. (eds.) RoboCup 2019. LNCS (LNAI), vol. 11531, pp. 646–657. Springer, Cham (2019). https://doi.org/10.1007/978-3-030-35699-6_52
12. Röfer, T., et al.: B-Human team report and code release 2021 (2021). https://github.com/bhuman/BHumanCodeRelease/raw/coderelease2021/CodeRelease2021.pdf
13. Röfer, T., et al.: B-Human team report and code release 2019 (2019). https://github.com/bhuman/BHumanCodeRelease/raw/coderelease2019/CodeRelease2019.pdf
14. Thielke, F., Hasselbring, A.: A JIT compiler for neural network inference. In: Chalup, S., Niemueller, T., Suthakorn, J., Williams, M.-A. (eds.) RoboCup 2019. LNCS (LNAI), vol. 11531, pp. 448–456. Springer, Cham (2019). https://doi.org/10.1007/978-3-030-35699-6_36

UT Austin Villa: RoboCup 2021 3D Simulation League Competition Champions

Patrick MacAlpine[1]([✉]), Bo Liu[2], William Macke[2], Caroline Wang[2], and Peter Stone[1,2]

[1] Sony AI, Austin, USA
patrick.macalpine@sony.com
[2] The University of Texas at Austin, Austin, USA
{bliu,wmacke,clw4542,pstone}@cs.utexas.edu

Abstract. The UT Austin Villa team, from the University of Texas at Austin, won the 2021 RoboCup 3D Simulation League, winning all 19 games the team played. During the course of the competition the team scored 108 goals while conceding only 5. Additionally the team finished second in the overall RoboCup 3D Simulation League technical challenge by finishing second in both the fat proxy and scientific challenges. This paper details and analyzes the results of the 2021 competition, and also presents a new deep RL learning framework that was presented during the scientific challenge.

1 Introduction

UT Austin Villa won the 2021 RoboCup 3D Simulation League for the ninth time in the past ten competitions, having also won the competition in 2011 [1], 2012 [2], 2014 [3], 2015 [4], 2016 [5], 2017 [6], 2018 [7], and 2019 [8] while finishing second in 2013 (there was no official competition in 2020, however the team also won the Offenburg Open replacement competition that year). During the course of the competition the team won all 19 games it played and scored a total of 108 goals while conceding only 5. Many of the components of the 2021 UT Austin Villa agent were reused from the team's successful previous years' entries in the competition. This paper is not an attempt at a complete description of the 2021 UT Austin Villa agent, the base foundation of which is the team's 2011 championship agent fully described in a team technical report [9].

In addition to winning the main RoboCup 3D Simulation League competition, UT Austin Villa took second place in the RoboCup 3D Simulation League technical challenge by taking second in each of the two league challenges: fat proxy and scientific challenges. This paper serves to document these challenges as well as the main competition.

The remainder of the paper is organized as follows. In Sect. 2 a description of the 3D simulation domain is given highlighting differences from the previous

© Springer Nature Switzerland AG 2022
R. Alami et al. (Eds.): RoboCup 2021, LNAI 13132, pp. 314–326, 2022.
https://doi.org/10.1007/978-3-030-98682-7_26

year's competition. Section 3 provides an overview of the 2021 UT Austin Villa team and its key components, while Sect. 4 analyzes the overall performance of the team at the competition. Section 5 describes and analyzes the fat proxy challenge, while also documenting the results of the overall league technical challenge consisting of both the fat proxy and scientific challenges. Section 6 provides details about a new deep RL learning framework that was presented during the scientific challenge, and Sect. 7 concludes.

2 Domain Description

The RoboCup 3D simulation environment is based on SimSpark [10,11], a generic physical multiagent system simulator. SimSpark uses the Open Dynamics Engine (ODE) library for its realistic simulation of rigid body dynamics with collision detection and friction. ODE also provides support for the modeling of advanced motorized hinge joints used in the humanoid agents.

Games consist of 11 versus 11 agents playing two 5 min halves of soccer on a 30 × 20 meter field. The robot agents in the simulation are modeled after the Aldebaran Nao robot, which has a height of about 57 cm, and a mass of 4.5 kg. Each robot has 22 degrees of freedom: six in each leg, four in each arm, and two in the neck. In order to monitor and control its hinge joints, an agent is equipped with joint perceptors and effectors. Joint perceptors provide the agent with noise-free angular measurements every simulation cycle (20 ms), while joint effectors allow the agent to specify the speed/direction in which to move a joint.

Visual information about the environment is given to an agent every third simulation cycle (60 ms) through noisy measurements of the distance and angle to objects within a restricted vision cone (120°). Agents are also outfitted with noisy accelerometer and gyroscope perceptors, as well as force resistance perceptors on the sole of each foot. Additionally, agents can communicate with each other every other simulation cycle (40 ms) by sending 20 byte messages.

In addition to the standard Nao robot model, four additional variations of the standard model, known as heterogeneous types, are available for use. These variations from the standard model include changes in leg and arm length, hip width, and also the addition of toes to the robot's foot. Teams must use at least three different robot types, no more than seven agents of any one robot type, and no more than nine agents of any two robot types.

In 2019 a pass play mode was introduced to the RoboCup 3D simulation league to encourage more passing and teamwork. The pass play mode allows players some extra time on the ball to kick and pass it during which time the opponent is prevented from interfering with a kick attempt. A player may initiate the pass play mode as long as the player is within 0.5 m of the ball and no opponents are within a meter of the ball. Once pass play mode for a team has started the players from the opponent team are prevented from getting within a meter of the ball. The pass play mode ends as soon as a player touches the ball or four seconds have passed. After pass mode has ended the team who initiated the pass mode is unable to score for ten seconds—this prevents teams from trying to take a shot on goal directly out of pass mode. However, new for this year's competition, a team may score before 10 s after their pass play mode has ended if multiple players from the team have touched the ball with at least one touch coming after the ball has traveled beyond the area where opponents were not allowed to enter when pass mode was active—this allows a player to take a quick shot on goal and score after receiving a teammate's pass out of pass mode.

One significant change for the 2021 RoboCup 3D Simulation League competition was in how robots are penalized for a couple of types of fouls. Previously, if robots committed touching fouls (a group of three or robots touching at the same time), or illegal defense fouls (more than three robots inside their own goal area), robots were beamed (moved) to the sideline outside of the field of play. Both touching and illegal defense fouls were created to prevent crowding that could inhibit play and potentially make the simulator unstable due to handling a large amount of robots colliding at the same time. While enforcing these fouls is currently necessary for smooth play in RoboCup 3D simulation games, moving robots off the field for having committed the fouls looks very unnatural as they are not part of normal soccer, and could even be exploited by a team committing a foul to their advantage (e.g. a team could purposely commit an illegal defense foul during their own goal kick to have their robot moved to a forward position just outside the field to receive a pass from a goal kick). Now, instead of moving robots all the way off the field after having committed these fouls, robots are only slightly repositioned to have less of an effect on game play: robots are moved to as close a position on the field as possible to their current position where they are not touching other robots, and for illegal defense fouls robots are also moved to a position outside of their own goal area.

Figure 1 shows images of the Nao robot and soccer field during a game.

Fig. 1. A screenshot of the Nao humanoid robot (left), and a view of the soccer field during a 11 versus 11 game (right).

3   2021 UT Austin Villa Team

The UT Austin Villa team was largely unchanged from the previous RoboCup competition in 2019, with many components developed prior to 2021 contributing to the success of the team including dynamic role assignment [12], marking [13], and an optimization framework used to learn low level behaviors for walking and kicking via an overlapping layered learning approach [14].

The primary changes to the team for this year's competition were related to pass mode: a bug was fixed that would sometimes cause an agent to take a shot on goal directly out of pass mode, and logic was added to no longer need to wait 10 s before trying to score after pass mode has ended in order to account for the pass mode rule change in this year's competition. The decision to keep the agent almost the same as that which was used in the previous competition was twofold. First, instead of focusing on the competition, the team decided to dedicate more time and resources to research and development of a deep RL framework detailed in Sect. 6. Second, keeping the team almost the same allows for it to serve as a benchmark for league progress as discussed in Sect. 4.

4   Main Competition Results and Analysis

In winning the 2021 RoboCup competition UT Austin Villa finished with a perfect record of 19 wins.[1] During the course of the competition the team scored 108 goals while conceding only 5. Despite the team's strong performance at the competition, the relatively few number of games played at the competition, coupled with the complex and stochastic environment of the RoboCup 3D simulator, make it difficult to determine UT Austin Villa being better than other teams by a statistically significant margin. At the end of the competition, however, all teams were required to release their binaries used during the competition. Results of UT Austin Villa playing 1000 games against each of the other eleven teams' released binaries from the competition are shown in Table 1.

UT Austin Villa finished with at least an average goal difference greater than 1.6 goals against every opponent. Additionally, UT Austin Villa's win percentage was greater than 94% against all teams except for a 78.1% win percentage against magmaOffenburg. These results show that UT Austin Villa winning the 2021 competition was far from a chance occurrence.

As mentioned in Sect. 3, the UT Austin Villa team was largely unchanged from the previous competition, and can thus serve as a benchmark for the progression of the league by looking at the team's relative performance against opponents between the previous and current competitions. Analysis from the 2019 competition showed that UT Austin Villa had an average goal difference of at least 2.4 goals and a winning percentage greater than 91% against all opponents [8]. Also, among the six common opponents between the 2019 and 2021 competitions (magmaOffenburg, WrightOcean, HfutEngine, FCPortugal,

---

[1] Full tournament results can be found at http://www.cs.utexas.edu/~AustinVilla/?p=competitions/RoboCup21#3D.

Table 1. UT Austin Villa's released binary's performance when playing 1000 games against the released binaries of all other teams at RoboCup 2021. This includes place (the rank a team achieved at the 2021 competition), average goal difference (values in parentheses are the standard error), win-loss-tie record, and goals for/against.

Opponent	Place	Avg. Goal Diff.	Record (W-L-T)	Goals (F/A)
magmaOffenburg	2	1.612 (0.048)	781-68-151	2073/461
WrightOcean	4	2.989 (0.047)	963-4-33	3181/192
Apollo3D	3	3.119 (0.053)	941-16-43	3690/571
HfutEngine	5	3.835 (0.049)	995-1-4	4055/220
FCPortugal	6	4.106 (0.062)	975-8-17	6045/1939
Miracle3D	7	5.819 (0.048)	1000-0-0	5820/1
BahiaRT	9	6.806 (0.060)	1000-0-0	6809/3
KgpKubs	10	7.337 (0.052)	1000-0-0	7337/0
ITAndroids	8	8.031 (0.058)	1000-0-0	8033/2
MIRG	7	12.193 (0.049)	1000-0-0	9193/0
WITS-FC	11	10.552 (0.054)	1000-0-0	10552/0

BahiaRT, and ITAndroids), the opponents improved by an average goal difference of 0.97 when playing against UT Austin Villa during this year's competition. The significant overall relative improvement in performance by teams from the previous competition is a strong sign of the league progressing, and suggests that to repeat again as champions in future competitions UT Austin Villa will likely need to return focus toward improving the team's performance.

4.1   Additional Tournament Competition Analysis

To further analyze the tournament competition, Table 2 shows the average goal difference for each team at RoboCup 2021 when playing 1000 games against all other teams at RoboCup 2021.

It is interesting to note that the ordering of teams in terms of winning (positive goal difference) and losing (negative goal difference) is transitive—every opponent that a team wins against also loses to every opponent that defeats that same team. Relative goal difference does not have this same property, however, as a team that does better against one opponent relative to another team does not always do better against a second opponent relative to that same team (e.g. UTAustinVilla has a higher average goal compared to magmaOffenburg when playing Apollo3D but not MIRG).

Table 2. Average goal difference for each team at RoboCup 2021 (rows) when playing 1000 games against the released binaries of all other teams at RoboCup 2021 (columns). Teams are ordered from most to least dominant in terms of winning (positive goal difference) and losing (negative goal difference).

	UTA	mag	Apo	Wri	Hfu	FCP	Mir	ITA	Bah	Kgp	MIR	WIT
UTAustinVilla	—	1.612	3.119	2.989	3.835	4.106	5.819	8.031	6.806	7.337	9,193	10.552
magmaOffenburg	−1.612	—	1.399	1.407	2.386	4.101	4.481	5.099	6.157	5.771	9.947	8.288
Apollo3D	−3.119	−1.339	—	0.379	0.996	3.321	3.130	4.816	3.201	4.512	6.717	6.483
WrightOcean	−2.989	−1.407	−0.379	—	0.349	1.332	2.961	3.738	2.735	4.237	7.520	6.181
HfutEngine	−3.835	−2.386	−0.996	−0.349	—	0.557	2.113	4.075	1.952	3.661	6.398	6.000
FCPortugal	−4.106	−4.101	−3.321	−1.332	−0.557	—	0.664	0.567	0.544	1.125	3.454	2.772
Miracle3D	−5.819	−4.481	−3.130	−2.961	−2.113	−0.664	—	0.857	0.589	1.712	5.581	3.962
ITAndroids	−8.031	−5.099	−4.816	−3.738	−4.075	−0.567	−0.857	—	0.340	0.819	3.461	3.738
BahiaRT	−6.806	−6.157	−3.201	−2.735	−1.952	−0.544	−0.589	−0.340	—	0.606	2.462	1.387
KpgKubs	−7.337	−5.771	−4.512	−4.237	−3.661	−1.125	−1.712	−0.819	−0.606	—	0.610	0.154
MIRG	−9.193	−9.947	−6.717	−7.520	−6.398	−3.454	−5.581	−3.461	−2.462	−0.610	—	0.161
WITS-FC	−10.552	−8.288	−6.483	−6.181	−6.000	−2.772	−3.962	−2.306	−1.387	−0.154	−0.161	—

5   Technical Challenges

During the competition there was an overall technical challenge consisting of two different league challenges: scientific and fat proxy challenges. For each league challenge a team participated in, points were awarded toward the overall technical challenge based on the following equation:

$$\texttt{points}(rank) = 25 - 20 * (rank - 1)/(numberOfParticipants - 1)$$

Table 3. Overall ranking and points totals for each team participating in the RoboCup 2021 3D Simulation League technical challenge as well as ranks and points awarded for each of the individual league challenges that make up the technical challenge.

	Overall		Scientific		Fat Proxy	
Team	Rank	Points	Rank	Points	Rank	Points
magmaOffenburg	1	50	1	25	1	25
UTAustinVilla	**2**	**40**	**2**	**20**	**2**	**20**
BahiaRT	3	25	4	10	3	15
FCPortugal	4	20	2	20	—	—
WITS-FC	5	10	—	—	5	10

Table 3 shows the ranking and cumulative team point totals for the technical challenge as well as for each individual league challenge. UT Austin Villa finished second in both the scientific challenge and fat proxy challenge resulting in a second place finish in the overall technical challenge. The following subsections detail UT Austin Villa's participation in each league challenge.

5.1 Scientific Challenge

During the scientific challenge, teams give a five minute presentation on a research topic related to their team. Each team in the league then ranks the presentations with the best receiving a score of 4 (based on four teams participating in the challenge), second best a score of 3, etc. Additionally several respected research members of the RoboCup community outside the league rank the presentations, with their scores being counted double. The winner of the scientific challenge is the team that receives the highest score. Table 4 shows the results of the scientific challenge in which UT Austin Villa tied for second place.

Table 4. Results of the scientific challenge.

Team	Score
magmaOffenburg	43
FCPortugal	36
UTAustinVilla	**36**
BahiaRT	25

UT Austin Villa's scientific challenge submission[2] presented research on using a deep RL framework to learn running behaviors which is presented in detail in Sect. 6. The other teams participating in the scientific challenge also presented interesting work:[3] magmaOffenburg talked about learning a multi-directional kick using deep RL, FCPortugal discussed work on 6D localization [15], and BahiaRT presented a custom OpenAI Gym environment for skills optimization in the 3D Soccer Simulation League.

5.2 Fat Proxy Challenge

While strategy and teamwork is important for success in the RoboCup 3D Simulation League [12,13], historically the teams with the best low level skills such as fast and stable walks and long and quick kicks have performed the best. Creating these low level skills serves as a barrier for entry to new teams in the league, however, as the skills can be difficult to develop with teams often employing machine learning techniques to generate them [16].

As a way to make it easier for new teams to join the league, and also to allow teams to focus on high level strategy without needing to worry about low level skills, a fat proxy[4] was created that controls the low level motions of

---

[2] Scientific challenge entry description available at https://www.cs.utexas.edu/~AustinVilla/sim/3dsimulation/AustinVilla3DSimulationFiles/2021/files/UTAustinVillaScientificChallenge2021.pdf.

[3] All participating teams' scientific challenge entry descriptions available at http://archive.robocup.info/Soccer/Simulation/3D/FCPs/RoboCup/2021/.

[4] https://github.com/magmaOffenburg/magmaFatProxy.

the robots for walking, kicking, and getting up after having fallen over. The fat proxy processes all communication between agents and the simulation server, and receives messages from agents that include high level `dash` and `kick` commands for walking and kicking the ball that are similar to the same commands in the RoboCup 2D Simulation League:

```
dash <forward/backward speed> <left/right speed> <turn_angle>
kick <power> <horizontal_angle> <vertical_angle>
```

When the fat proxy receives a `dash` command from an agent, it translates the command to torques to apply to the robot's joints to have the robot walk in the direction specified in the `dash` command using the magmaOffenburg team's walk engine embedded inside the fat proxy. In the case of a `kick` command, the fat proxy sends a message to the simulation server to propel the ball in the direction specified in the command assuming that the agent that sent the `kick` command is close to the ball. By controlling the low level motions of the robots, the fat proxy levels the playing field such that robots from different teams all have the same set of skills.

The only change made to the UT Austin Villa agent to participate in the fat proxy challenge was to map the teams own high level commands used as input for the team's walk engine [17] and kicks [18] to that of the fat proxy's `dash` and `kick` commands. The team used the same strategy and formations for the fat proxy challenge as were used during the main competition.

Four teams participated in the fat proxy challenge which consisted of a round robin tournament where every team played every other team using the fat proxy. Teams were ranked by how many points they received (3 points for a win, 1 point for a tie, and 0 points for a loss), with the tie breaker when teams have the same number of points being the number of goals a team scored minus the number of goals they conceded. Results of the fat proxy challenge are shown in Table 5.

Table 5. Overall rank, goals scored, goals conceded, and points for each team participating in the fat proxy challenge

Team	Rank	Goals scored	Goals conceded	Points
magmaOffenburg	1	27	4	9
UTAustinVilla	**2**	**15**	**8**	**4**
BahaiRT	3	13	12	4
WITS-FC	4	0	31	0

UT Austin Villa took second in the challenge with magmaOffenburg winning the challenge. A noticeable difference during the challenge between UT Austin Villa and magmaOffenburg was that the UT Austin Villa team was not as stable when walking and often fell over. A likely reason for the instability is that the distribution of high level motions normally sent to the UT Austin Villa team's walk engine are different from the distribution of walk trajectories that the magmaOffenburg team's walk engine embedded in the fat proxy is tuned for. For future iterations of the fat proxy challenge the UT Austin Villa team's performance could be improved by attempting to constrain the walk commands to be closer to those normally used by the magmaOffenburg team in the magmaOffenburg team's code release.[5]

6   Deep RL Framework

Previous work from FCPortugal [19,20] and ITAndroids [21] demonstrated that Offline Deep Reinforcement Learning is capable of learning faster walking/running behaviors than previously hand designed policies. Continuing with this line of work, UT Austin Villa has been working on facilitating the use of Deep RL algorithms with the Robocup 3DSim league. As the majority of contemporary deep RL frameworks are written in Python, the UT Austin Villa team developed a custom OpenAI Gym [22] environment in Python that connected to the 3DSim platform via network sockets. The environment follows the same definition of the state and action spaces as FCPortugal [19]. The reward is −1 if the agent falls; else, 10 * forward distance of agent from time t to $t + 1$. The OpenAI Gym environment wraps the 3DSim environment, enabling applying Python deep RL libraries to the existing C++ simulation software.

FCPortugal and ITAndroids used the on-policy RL algorithm, Proximal Policy Optimization (PPO) [23], to learn faster walking/running behaviors. As an on-policy RL algorithm, PPO has relatively high data requirements, which ITAndroids addressed by using parallel actors to gather data. UT Austin Villa instead investigated using the off-policy algorithm, Soft Actor Critic (SAC) [24]. Off-policy RL algorithms have demonstrated better sample-efficiency than on-policy algorithms in a variety of domains. UT Austin Villa used the implementation of SAC provided by Tianshou [25]. All experiments were performed with a single actor.

Fig. 2. The environment APIs.

In preliminary experiments, SAC has been able to learn simple walking behaviors that allow it to move forward small amounts before falling over (See Fig. 3). The preliminary learning curves are also provided in Fig. 4, and the hyperparameters used for SAC are summarized in Table 6. UT Austin is hopeful that with further training SAC will be able to learn a full running behavior that can be integrated into existing play strategies.

---

[5] https://github.com/magmaOffenburg/magmaRelease.

Fig. 3. Preliminary result: the agent learns to take a large step forward.

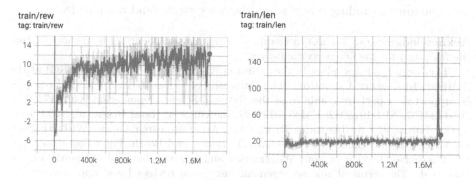

Fig. 4. The average return (**left**) and episode steps (**right**) over training.

Table 6. Hyperparameters of the SAC algorithm for training a fast walk.

Hyperparameters	Value
Time-step per epoch	10 K
Number of epochs	2 K
Learning rate of actor	0.0003
Learning rate of critic	0.0003
Learning rate of the entropy regularizer α	0.0001
Replay buffer size	1 M
Critic update parameter τ	0.005
Initial α in SAC	0.2
Number of hidden layers in the neural network	128
Number of neurons in each hidden layer	2
Learning batch size	256

7   Conclusion

UT Austin Villa won the 2021 RoboCup 3D Simulation League main competition and finished second in the overall league technical challenge.[6] Data taken using released binaries from the competition show that UT Austin Villa winning the competition was statistically significant.

In an effort to make it easier for new teams to join the RoboCup 3D Simulation League, and also provide a resource that can be beneficial to existing teams, the UT Austin Villa team has released their base code [26].[7] This code provides a fully functioning agent and good starting point for new teams (it was used by seven out of the other eleven teams at the 2021 competition: Apollo3D, HfutEngine, KgpKubs, Miracle3D, MIRG, WITS-FC, WrightOcean). Additionally the code release offers a foundational platform for conducting research in multiple areas including robotics, multiagent systems, and machine learning.

Acknowledgments. Thanks to members of the magmaOffenburg teams for creating the fat proxy for the fat proxy challenge.

This work has taken place in the Learning Agents Research Group (LARG) at the Artificial Intelligence Laboratory, The University of Texas at Austin. LARG research is supported in part by grants from the National Science Foundation (CPS-1739964, IIS-1724157, NRI-1925082, FAIN-2019844), the Office of Naval Research (N00014-18-2243), Future of Life Institute (RFP2-000), Army Research Office (W911NF-19-2-0333), DARPA, Lockheed Martin, General Motors, and Bosch. Peter Stone serves as the Executive Director of Sony AI America and receives financial compensation for this work. The terms of this arrangement have been reviewed and approved by the University of Texas at Austin in accordance with its policy on objectivity in research. Patrick MacAlpine is an employee of Sony AI America and is supported by Sony.

References

1. MacAlpine, P., et al.: UT Austin Villa 2011: a champion agent in the RoboCup 3D soccer simulation competition. In: Proceedings of 11th International Conference on Autonomous Agents and Multiagent Systems (AAMAS 2012) (2012)
2. MacAlpine, P., Collins, N., Lopez-Mobilia, A., Stone, P.: UT Austin Villa: RoboCup 2012 3D simulation league champion. In: Chen, X., Stone, P., Sucar, L.E., van der Zant, T. (eds.) RoboCup 2012. LNCS (LNAI), vol. 7500, pp. 77–88. Springer, Heidelberg (2013). https://doi.org/10.1007/978-3-642-39250-4_8
3. MacAlpine, P., Depinet, M., Liang, J., Stone, P.: UT Austin Villa: RoboCup 2014 3D simulation league competition and technical challenge champions. In: Bianchi, R.A.C., Akin, H.L., Ramamoorthy, S., Sugiura, K. (eds.) RoboCup 2014. LNCS (LNAI), vol. 8992, pp. 33–46. Springer, Cham (2015). https://doi.org/10.1007/978-3-319-18615-3_3

---

[6] More information about the UT Austin Villa team, as well as video from the competition, released binaries, and team publications, can be found at the team's website: http://www.cs.utexas.edu/~AustinVilla/sim/3dsimulation/#2021.

[7] Code release at https://github.com/LARG/utaustinvilla3d.

4. MacAlpine, P., Hanna, J., Liang, J., Stone, P.: UT Austin Villa: RoboCup 2015 3D simulation league competition and technical challenges champions. In: Almeida, L., Ji, J., Steinbauer, G., Luke, S. (eds.) RoboCup 2015. LNCS (LNAI), vol. 9513, pp. 118–131. Springer, Cham (2015). https://doi.org/10.1007/978-3-319-29339-4_10

5. MacAlpine, P., Stone, P.: UT Austin Villa: RoboCup 2016 3D simulation league competition and technical challenges champions. In: Behnke, S., Sheh, R., Sariel, S., Lee, D.D. (eds.) RoboCup 2016. LNCS (LNAI), vol. 9776, pp. 515–528. Springer, Cham (2017). https://doi.org/10.1007/978-3-319-68792-6_43

6. MacAlpine, P., Stone, P.: UT Austin Villa: RoboCup 2017 3D simulation league competition and technical challenges champions. In: Akiyama, H., Obst, O., Sammut, C., Tonidandel, F. (eds.) RoboCup 2017. LNCS (LNAI), vol. 11175, pp. 473–485. Springer, Cham (2018). https://doi.org/10.1007/978-3-030-00308-1_39

7. MacAlpine, P., Torabi, F., Pavse, B., Sigmon, J., Stone, P.: UT Austin Villa: RoboCup 2018 3D simulation league champions. In: Holz, D., Genter, K., Saad, M., von Stryk, O. (eds.) RoboCup 2018. LNCS (LNAI), vol. 11374, pp. 462–475. Springer, Cham (2019). https://doi.org/10.1007/978-3-030-27544-0_38

8. MacAlpine, P., Torabi, F., Pavse, B., Stone, P.: UT Austin Villa: RoboCup 2019 3D simulation league competition and technical challenge champions. In: Chalup, S., Niemueller, T., Suthakorn, J., Williams, M.-A. (eds.) RoboCup 2019. LNCS (LNAI), vol. 11531, pp. 540–552. Springer, Cham (2019). https://doi.org/10.1007/978-3-030-35699-6_44

9. MacAlpine, P., et al.: UT Austin Villa 2011 3D simulation team report. Technical report AI11-10, The Univ. of Texas at Austin, Dept. of Computer Science, AI Laboratory (2011)

10. Obst, O., Rollmann, M.: Spark – a generic simulator for physical multi-agent simulations. In: Lindemann, G., Denzinger, J., Timm, I.J., Unland, R. (eds.) MATES 2004. LNCS (LNAI), vol. 3187, pp. 243–257. Springer, Heidelberg (2004). https://doi.org/10.1007/978-3-540-30082-3_18

11. Xu, Y., Vatankhah, H.: SimSpark: an open source robot simulator developed by the RoboCup community. In: Behnke, S., Veloso, M., Visser, A., Xiong, R. (eds.) RoboCup 2013. LNCS (LNAI), vol. 8371, pp. 632–639. Springer, Heidelberg (2014). https://doi.org/10.1007/978-3-662-44468-9_59

12. MacAlpine, P., Price, E., Stone, P.: SCRAM: scalable collision-avoiding role assignment with minimal-Makespan for formational positioning. In: Proceedings of the Twenty-Ninth AAAI Conference on Artificial Intelligence (AAAI-15) (2015)

13. MacAlpine, P., Stone, P.: Prioritized role assignment for marking. In: Behnke, S., Sheh, R., Sariel, S., Lee, D.D. (eds.) RoboCup 2016. LNCS (LNAI), vol. 9776, pp. 306–318. Springer, Cham (2017). https://doi.org/10.1007/978-3-319-68792-6_25

14. MacAlpine, P., Stone, P.: Overlapping layered learning. Artif. Intell. **254**, 21–43 (2018)

15. Abreu, M., Silva, T., Teixeira, H., Reis, L.P., Lau, N.: 6D localization and kicking for humanoid robotic soccer. J. Intell. Robot. Syst. **102**(2), 1–25 (2021). https://doi.org/10.1007/s10846-021-01385-3

16. MacAlpine, P., Depinet, M., Stone, P.: UT Austin Villa 2014: RoboCup 3D simulation league champion via overlapping layered learning. In: Proceedings of the Twenty-Ninth AAAI Conference on Artificial Intelligence (AAAI-15) (2015)

17. MacAlpine, P., Barrett, S., Urieli, D., Vu, V., Stone, P.: Design and optimization of an omnidirectional humanoid walk: a winning approach at the RoboCup 2011 3D simulation competition. In: Proceedings of the Twenty-Sixth AAAI Conference on Artificial Intelligence (AAAI-12) (2012)

18. Depinet, M., MacAlpine, P., Stone, P.: Keyframe sampling, optimization, and behavior integration: towards long-distance kicking in the robocup 3d simulation league. In: Bianchi, R.A.C., Akin, H.L., Ramamoorthy, S., Sugiura, K. (eds.) RoboCup 2014. LNCS (LNAI), vol. 8992, pp. 571–582. Springer, Cham (2015). https://doi.org/10.1007/978-3-319-18615-3_47

19. Abreu, M., Lau, N., Sousa, A., Reis, L.P.: Learning low level skills from scratch for humanoid robot soccer using deep reinforcement learning. In: 2019 IEEE International Conference on Autonomous Robot Systems and Competitions (ICARSC), pp. 1–8. IEEE (2019)

20. Abreu, M., Reis, L.P., Lau, N.: Learning to run faster in a humanoid robot soccer environment through reinforcement learning. In: Chalup, S., Niemueller, T., Suthakorn, J., Williams, M.-A. (eds.) RoboCup 2019. LNCS (LNAI), vol. 11531, pp. 3–15. Springer, Cham (2019). https://doi.org/10.1007/978-3-030-35699-6_1

21. Melo, L.C., Melo, D.C., Maximo, M.R.O.A.: Learning humanoid robot running motions with symmetry incentive through proximal policy optimization. J. Intell. Robot. Syst. **102**(3), 1–15 (2021). https://doi.org/10.1007/s10846-021-01355-9

22. Brockman, G., et al.: Openai gym. arXiv preprint arXiv:1606.01540 (2016)

23. Schulman, J., Wolski, F., Dhariwal, P., Radford, A., Klimov, O.: Proximal policy optimization algorithms. ArXiv abs/1707.06347 (2017)

24. Haarnoja, T., Zhou, A., Abbeel, P., Levine, S.: Soft actor-critic: Off-policy maximum entropy deep reinforcement learning with a stochastic actor. In: Dy, J., Krause, A. (eds.) Proceedings of the 35th International Conference on Machine Learning. Volume 80 of Proceedings of Machine Learning Research, PMLR, pp. 1861–1870 (2018)

25. Weng, J., et al.: A highly modularized deep reinforcement learning library. arXiv preprint arXiv:2107.14171 (2021)

26. MacAlpine, P., Stone, P.: UT Austin Villa RoboCup 3D simulation base code release. In: Behnke, S., Sheh, R., Sarıel, S., Lee, D.D. (eds.) RoboCup 2016. LNCS (LNAI), vol. 9776, pp. 135–143. Springer, Cham (2017). https://doi.org/10.1007/978-3-319-68792-6_11

Vision-Based Machine Learning in Robot Soccer

J. J. Olthuis[1]([✉])[iD], N. B. van der Meer[2][iD], S. T. Kempers[1], C. A. van Hoof[2],
R. M. Beumer[1], W. J. P. Kuijpers[1][iD], A. A. Kokkelmans[1], W. Houtman[1][iD],
J. J. F. J. van Eijck[2], J. J. Kon[1], A. T. A. Peijnenburg[2],
and M. J. G. van de Molengraft[1][iD]

[1] Tech United Eindhoven, De Rondom 70, P.O. Box 513,
5600 MB Eindhoven, The Netherlands
`techunited@tue.nl`, `j.j.olthuis@student.tue.nl`
[2] RobotSports, De Schakel 22, 5651 GH Eindhoven, The Netherlands
`ton.peijnenburg@vdletg.com`
`https://www.techunited.nl/`, `https://www.robotsports.nl/`

Abstract. Robots need to perceive their environment in order to properly interact with it. In the RoboCup Soccer Middle Size League (MSL) this happens primarily through cameras mounted on the robots. Machine Learning can be used to extract relevant features from camera imagery. The real-time analysis of camera data is a challenge for both traditional and Machine Learning algorithms, since all computations in the MSL have to be performed on the robot itself.

This contribution shows that it is possible to process camera imagery in real-time using Machine Learning. It does this by presenting the current state of Machine Learning in MSL and providing two examples that won the Scientific and Technical Challenges at RoboCup 2021. Both examples focus on semantic detection of objects and humans in imagery. The Scientific Challenge winner presents how YOLOv5 can be used for object detection in the MSL. The Technical Challenge winner demonstrates how to improve interaction between robots and humans in soccer using OpenPose. This contributes towards the goal of RoboCup to arrive at robots that can beat the human soccer world champion by 2050.

Keywords: RoboCup soccer · Middle size league · Machine learning · Object detection · People detection · Real-time

---

We would like to thank all members of RobotSports, current and past, for their help and support in making this possible. Moreover, additional thanks goes out to the other team members of Tech United Eindhoven: W. H. T. M. Aangenent, P. E. J. van Brakel, L. L. A. van Bree, M. Briegel, D. J. H. Bruijnen, E. Deniz, Y. G. M. Douven, P. H. E. M. van Lith, H. C. T. van de Loo, K. J. Meessen, F. B. F. Schoenmakers, J. Selten, C. A. M. Steijlen, and P. Teurlings.

R. Alami et al. (Eds.): RoboCup 2021, LNAI 13132, pp. 327–339, 2022.
https://doi.org/10.1007/978-3-030-98682-7_27

1   Introduction

Soccer is a complex game to play for robots. An important aspect is being able to properly respond to and interact with the relevant objects in the environment. According to the rules [17], robots in the RoboCup Middle Size League (MSL) need to have all their sensors on-board. In practice, this means that the soccer robots have, among other sensors, cameras to perceive their surroundings.

So far, image recognition in the MSL is performed mostly by color segmentation, aided by fixed colors for specific elements of the soccer field [9], and pattern recognition algorithms [24]. Recent improvements in Machine Learning – making it more effective and computationally efficient – enable local execution on robots. This paper discusses current and future applications of Machine Learning on robots in the MSL. This is particularly relevant because the evolution of the rules force the robots to be more flexible in their environment (e.g. the ball may no longer always be yellow).

The remainder of this paper is structured as follows: Sect. 2 discusses the current state of Machine Learning in RoboCup MSL. Section 3 describes an example of a low-cost, efficient, and real-time generic object detection by team Robot-Sports. Section 4 describes the use of OpenPose for human gesture detection in robot soccer by team Tech United Eindhoven. These teams were the winners of the Scientific and Technical Challenge at RoboCup 2021, respectively. Finally, Sect. 5 concludes this paper.

2   Machine Learning in Middle Size League Soccer

One of the big challenges towards the RoboCup objective of winning against the human world champion in 2050 [21] is playing proactively. This can be realized by recognizing and predicting opponents' intentions. To understand the complex signals, both verbal and non-verbal, that a human soccer player uses to express their intentions will require vision or speech algorithms that are aided by Machine Learning. It is also the topic of research areas such as object recognition and data processing. Each year, RoboCup teams showcase new Machine Learning applications in their leagues. Machine Learning algorithms could be used to decide which strategy (sequence of future actions) can be best selected for the current configuration of the game. Strategy algorithms aided by Machine Learning are explored mostly in the Simulation League [1,4] and the Small Size League [23]. In the MSL, however, Machine Learning research is mostly focused on object recognition and image processing, as also demonstrated in Sects. 3 and 4 of this paper. The only published research of the combination of Machine Learning and strategy in the MSL has been performed by Lopez et al. [13] by using reinforcement learning for fixed gameplay scenarios.

Other works all focus on object recognition. For example, Luo et al. [14] propose how opponent recognition based on color segmentation can be made more robust and adaptive by making use of Convolutional Neural Networks. In this case the soccer robots combine RGB images with depth information to localize opponent robots. A different way of opponent detection is described by Van Lith et al. [12]. Here, the authors took a minimalistic approach to make the training of the network as quick as possible. Van Lith et al. combined a Fully Convolutional Network with a blob detector, and were able to complete the full training procedure within thirty minutes. This allows the network to be trained at a tournament, as teams may change their look in-between.

This work presents a generalization of object recognition in the MSL. And unlike previous research this work also shows the first steps towards understanding opponent intentions, which is a prerequisite for realizing proactive gameplay.

3   Scientific Challenge

In the past decade, the field of AI has produced a number of ever-improving deep learning algorithms for object detection. One of the most well-known object detection systems is the YOLO (You-Only-Look-Once) framework, originally introduced in 2016 [19]. Over the years, numerous iterations and improvements of the YOLO algorithm have been presented, such as YOLO9000 [20] and more recently YOLOv5[1]. YOLOv5 is aimed at providing accurate, real-time object detection on low-cost mobile devices such as smartphones. These properties can make the YOLOv5 framework suitable for use in the RoboCup MSL.

Fig. 1. Object detection at the RobotSports arena using the YOLOv5 framework.

In the remainder of Sect. 3, the YOLOv5-based AI architecture as used by the RobotSports team is presented. RobotSports currently applies the presented solution on one robot using the Stereolabs Zed2 sensor and NVIDIA Jetson platform, with plans for it to be deployed on more robots in the future. Due to the focus on modularity, interoperability, and maintaining low computing power requirements, this AI architecture is accessible to other teams participating in RoboCup as well. Currently, the AI software used by RobotSports is able to recognize robots, balls, humans, the goal and the goalposts. The result can be seen in Fig. 1.

---

[1] https://github.com/ultralytics/yolov5

3.1   Continuous Digital Feedback Loop

The *continuous digital feedback loop* is a model used by the automobile manufacturer Tesla in its fleet of cars [8]. The goal of the model is to continuously improve the behavior and intelligence of the fleet by continually collecting data, learning from new images and re-deploying the re-trained networks. RobotSports has adapted this architecture for use on their robots in the RoboCup MSL, as shown in Fig. 2. The continuous digital feedback loop consists of the following four steps:

1. **Data collection.** Section 3.2 discusses how data is continuously collected during all matches, capturing a diverse range of interesting situations and serving as valuable training material. After a match, the collected data is transmitted to the cloud, where it can be annotated.
2. **Training in the cloud.** Section 3.3 discusses how the YOLOv5 model is trained in the cloud on the collected data, using high-performance servers.
3. **Model deployment.** Section 3.4 presents how the trained YOLOv5 model is represented using the framework-independent ONNX standard and subsequently distributed to the soccer robots.
4. **Real-time inference on the robot.** Finally, in Sect. 3.5, the YOLOv5 model is optimized for the specific hardware installed on the robot, and used for real-time object detection in the field.

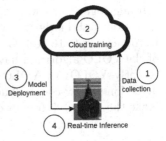

Fig. 2. The continuous digital feedback loop used in the RobotSports AI strategy.

3.2   Data Collection (Step 1)

An essential aspect of the overall AI architecture is data collection. Data is the fuel on which deep learning networks rely for training, directly influencing the performance of the resulting networks.

Acquisition. In order to acquire data and eventually perform object detection, RobotSports has installed the Stereolabs Zed2 sensor on their robots. All soccer matches are structurally recorded by this sensor, providing large amounts of data that can potentially be used for training. These recordings are encoded using the H.265 codec, accelerated by dedicated video encoding circuitry provided by the NVIDIA Jetson platform. This minimizes storage requirements and allows for real-time data collection. After the data has been collected on the soccer robot, it is transmitted to the cloud platform.

Annotation. When the data is available on the cloud platform, it can be annotated by a person, indicating the positions and classes of objects present in images. While there are many advanced annotation platforms available today that can be used for this task, many of these require commercial licenses or have severe limitations (such as a maximum amount of data). To keep the costs of the solution low, the open-source LabelImg software is used instead. LabelImg[2] is free to use and has support for a variety of commonly-used annotation standards.

3.3   Training the Model in the Cloud (Step 2)

When annotated data is available in the cloud, the YOLOv5 network is trained using the online Google Colab platform. Colab provides computing resources to experiment with and use artificial intelligence networks free of charge.

YOLOv5 provides different model variants, from *Small* to *XLarge*, differing mostly in model size (i.e. total number of parameters). In general, the larger models perform better in object detection tasks, but this is accompanied by a significant increase in the computing power required to perform inference with the network. In order to maximize performance on low-cost hardware, the *Small* variant of YOLOv5 is used by the RobotSports team. Due to the modular nature of the architecture, it is also possible to train and use one of the larger variants without impacting any of the other steps.

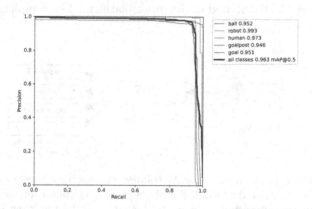

Fig. 3. Recall/precision curve of the resulting YOLOv5 model.

The YOLOv5 models are pre-trained on the widely-used COCO (Common Objects in Context) dataset [11], and using transfer learning the network can re-train the last few layers on an MSL dataset. This construction significantly speeds up training time and still achieves solid performance, even when using only 1000 annotated images[3]. The resulting recall/precision graph, as shown in Fig. 3, shows promising results which have been confirmed by actual image recognition of the various objects on the field.

---

[2] https://github.com/tzutalin/labelImg.

[3] The training data is available at https://github.com/Charelvanhoof/robocup_vdl.

Using this approach, the entire model could be trained on 300 epochs in only 2 h using the cloud platform. This demonstrates that the network can potentially be re-trained during a tournament. During the set-up days, one could collect data on the particular venue used in the tournament, and then the model can be re-trained for the specific scenario. While re-training is not strictly necessary, this approach could still improve performance and deal with unexpected lighting conditions and changing audiences around the field.

3.4   Model Deployment (Step 3)

Once training is complete, the resulting network needs to be distributed to and deployed on the robots. However, the trained network parameters resulting from the process described in Sect. 3.3 are YOLO-specific, and not suitable for deployment yet. For this purpose, the entire network architecture along with the trained weights are first represented using the Open Neural Network Exchange (ONNX) standard[4]. ONNX facilitates interoperability between AI platforms, and is supported by many popular AI frameworks such as TensorFlow, MXNet and PyTorch. This is also necessary for the next step, since training is done in the cloud using the PyTorch-based YOLOv5, while the inference hardware on the robots is running the NVIDIA TensorRT framework [25]. Finally, the resulting ONNX model is distributed to the robot platform. The complete deployment workflow can be seen in Fig. 4.

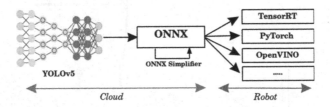

Fig. 4. ONNX is supported by many AI frameworks, such as TensorRT, OpenVINO and PyTorch. In addition, the ONNX-Simplifier (https://github.com/daquexian/onnx-simplifier) software can optimize the model for inference by removing layers that are unnecessary.

3.5   Real-Time Inference on the Robot (Step 4)

A challenge that persists when applying deep learning models in practice is performing real-time inference in a mobile setting. While the model can be trained in the cloud using datacenter-grade hardware, such equipment is typically not suitable for deployment on a mobile and independent platform such as an MSL soccer robot. RobotSports uses the NVIDIA Jetson platform, which has a small form factor, has desirable power characteristics, and is low-cost. For instance,

---

[4] https://github.com/onnx/onnx

the entry-level Jetson Nano can be obtained for as little as $60 and possesses enough computing power to run the YOLOv5 models in real-time.

In order to perform object detection on the Jetson platform, the TensorRT software is used, which is specialized in inference on NVIDIA hardware. The YOLOv5 model is provided to the inference hardware in ONNX format as described in Sect. 3.4, and is then fully optimized for inference on the specific device. This optimization step is performed once, which leads to an engine that can be used repeatedly for inference. Using this approach, inference can be performed within 40 ms on the Jetson Nano, resulting in a processing framerate of 25 fps. For this step, the open-source YOLOv5-TensorRT library[5] is used, which was originally developed for use by RobotSports.

Generic object detection as described in this section could potentially be complemented by the solution described in Sect. 4, which is specifically aimed at recognizing human gestures. The YOLOv5 model could be used to look for a variety of objects at a high frequency, and if any humans are detected, the more computationally intensive OpenPose-based gesture recognition can be applied to recognize and act upon detected gestures.

4   Technical Challenge

In order to win a soccer match against the human world champions in 2050 [21], we can identify two types of required developments. On the one hand, the robots should be able to execute basic technical skills such as detecting and shooting the ball. On the other hand, they should be able to play against and together with humans.

For robots to properly interact with humans, there has to be a mutual understanding of intent. In the first place, the robot has to ensure safety, which can already be obtained by avoiding collisions with humans detected by the work presented in Sect. 3. Enabling more complex interactions such as cooperation requires both to understand the interaction cues. There are many ways for a robot to convey their intent [3,16,18]. The other way around, however, is much more complex. Because humans do not have fixed signals for their intentions (e.g. one can ask for the ball by yelling or raising their hand, but raising a hand or yelling is not always a request for the ball), they can be challenging to interpret for robots.

Recognition of human gestures by robots has been shown to work by augmenting standard RGB video algorithms with OpenPose [22]. Subtle hand gestures can be identified and tracked using a combination of Convolutional Neural Networks and OpenPose [15]. For service robots, interaction with people is especially important. To this end, a RoboCup team has created a combination of OpenFace with OpenPose that can be used recognize and interact with people [5].

Apart from robot-human communication, robot-to-robot gesture recognition in robot soccer has been demonstrated in NAO humanoid robots [7]. Here, the

---

[5] https://github.com/noahmr/yolov5-tensorrt.

Fig. 5. Fifth generation TURTLE robots, with the goalkeeper on the left-hand side. (Photo by Bart van Overbeeke)

humanoid soccer robots are able to signal different strategies to one another with the use of their arms. Similarly, Tech United Eindhoven takes this approach to communicate with humans, instead of with other robots. Their submission won the RoboCup MSL 2021 Technical Challenge by presenting a proof-of-concept system where the soccer robots can detect humans, and act upon their behavior. This is discussed in more detail in the remainder of Sect. 4.

4.1   System Architecture

Current Robot Platform. The Tech United Eindhoven robots are called TURTLEs (acronym for Tech United RoboCup Team: Limited Edition), which are shown in Fig. 5. The current fifth generation TURTLEs have proved to be a very robust and reliable platform at several tournaments[6].

TURTLEs are equipped with an omnivision camera, i.e. a camera looking up into a parabolic mirror, providing a 360° view of the ground around them. Moreover, they carry an Xbox Kinect V2 camera pointing forward. The Kinect camera is currently only used for detecting airborne balls. Other detections are performed on data provided by the omnivision camera, by means of real-time color segmentation for object detection. Anything that is not of an expected color in the field is assumed to be an obstacle. This also means that people are treated no different than a static obstacle, or an opponent robot.

Hardware. In order to obtain more computational power, the NVIDIA Jetson TK1 was replaced by a NVIDIA Jetson Xavier NX for this challenge. The Xbox Kinect V2 3D camera is connected to this board. The Jetson board is connected to the main PC of the robot using ethernet.

---

[6] Hardware designs are available on http://roboticopenplatform.org, open-source source code is available on https://gitlab.tue.nl/tech-united-eindhoven.

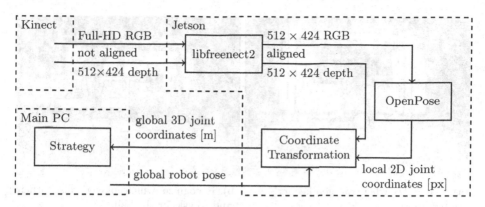

Fig. 6. Schematic overview of the data flow within the system architecture.

Software. A schematic overview of the software architecture for the relevant components in this Technical Challenge is shown in Fig. 6.

Both a 512 × 424 depth map and a Full-HD RGB color image are obtained at 30 Hz from the Kinect by the Jetson using libfreenect2[7]. Due to different lenses, the depth and RGB data are not aligned by default. Alignment of the data is performed by libfreenect2, which unfortunately comes with a significant decrease in resolution as the aligned depth and RGB color images both become 512×424 pixels.

The resulting color image is fed into OpenPose [6], which is a software library that enables the detection of joints of people in a picture or video. It does this using a pre-trained Machine Learning model, constructing people's skeletons bottom-up using Part Affinity Fields. OpenPose offers programmers an interface in C++ and Python to analyze images in real-time. Every joint is not only labeled by its type (e.g. right ankle, left wrist), but also to which person it belongs. An advantage of OpenPose is that the computational time is not affected by the number of people in the frame. Furthermore, it can perform detections with partial occlusion of people. The positions of the detected joints are expressed as pixel coordinates of the 2D color image.

Subsequently, the depth data from the pixels in the aligned depth frame are linked to the pixel coordinates of each of the joints from the color image. These pixel coordinates together with the depth information are transformed to a 3D position on the field. This coordinate transformation is done using the known mounting position of the camera on the robot, the focal length of the camera, and the pose of the robot on the field communicated over ethernet from the main PC to the Jetson Xavier NX using the RTDB communication protocol [2].

The resulting coordinates of all joints are sent to the main PC of the robot using RTDB. Here, the coordinates are handled by the strategy software to determine the intent of the people in frame. In the case of this Technical Challenge, the humans received instructions for their behavior.

---

[7] https://github.com/OpenKinect/libfreenect2.

(a) Recognize when the goalkeeper's legs are far apart.

(b) Recognize which player raises their hand to ask for the ball.

Fig. 7. Images taken by the TURTLE's Kinect camera, showing two different detection scenarios. The detections by OpenPose are visualized by the skeleton drawn on top of the Kinect image.

To enable the robot to react to the information from OpenPose, the STP framework [10], which contains the strategy, is augmented with the desired behavior. New STP preconditions are programmed to trigger their respective plays. When someone raises their left or right hand a minimum distance above the height of their nose, the robot will pass to their corresponding foot. When the precondition determines that there is a minimum distance (i.e. sufficient room for a ball to pass) between a person's feet, a nutmeg[8] is attempted.

4.2 Results

The system was tested in real-time on a robot soccer field. A video[9] was recorded, which Tech United Eindhoven showed during RoboCup 2021. First, it was shown how the robot can take advantage of a human goalkeeper when they have their feet spread apart. The detection by the robot is shown in Fig. 7a. Moreover, an example was given where with multiple people on the field, the robot can distinguish them properly, and detect when one raises their hand as shown in Fig. 7b, and pass the ball towards the correct person. Lastly, two situations were shown in the video where a human player is able to cooperate with a robot and score a goal.

Performance. As mentioned before, the NVIDIA Jetson TK1 was replaced by a Jetson Xavier NX to increase the computational power and analyze frames more quickly. OpenPose v1.7.0 was able to analyze 2 to 3 frames per second in real-time. Preliminary tests with promising results have shown that this frame rate can be increased to at least 7 to 8 frames per second by tuning parameters.

---

[8] In soccer, to kick the ball between the legs of an opponent. Also known as a *panna*.
[9] https://youtu.be/V2flK6joM4s.

Future work. The current proof-of-concept shows several limitations of this approach. Some are very practical and may be easy to resolve such as the limited field of view of the Kinect V2, the low resolution after transformation, and low framerate.

A more fundamental limitation of the proposed approach concerns occlusions in depth measurements leading to incorrect conversions to global coordinates. This can be resolved by combining measurements from multiple robots, which would however introduce more latency (e.g. from communication and measurement fusion) and is a different research topic by itself.

Another challenge is to interact with humans without predefined gestures. It may be possible to ask peers to perform certain movements to convey their intentions, when playing *together with* humans. Playing *against* humans, however, requires the robot to understand how a human body moves, and how it can use that information to predict human actions. Understanding more complex human communications will require additional Machine Learning models to determine the humans' intentions from a set of OpenPose skeletons over time.

5 Conclusion

This work has presented how Machine Learning can be applied in the RoboCup MSL, focused on image processing. An overview was given of the current application of Machine Learning in the MSL. Two examples were covered in detail: the winners of the Scientific and Technical Challenges at RoboCup 2021.

RobotSports, the winner of the Scientific Challenge, presented how YOLOv5 can be used for recognition of objects relevant in the MSL. The proposed solution was shown to run in real-time locally on the robot. New models can be trained in the cloud within two hours, allowing for fast re-training at tournament venues. The proposed solution is mobile and low-cost, making it accessible to other teams participating in RoboCup.

Tech United Eindhoven, the winner of the Technical Challenge, demonstrates how OpenPose can be applied to the MSL for detecting human intentions. Detecting joints of people in camera imagery, allows robots to detect human gestures and use this to interact more safely and cooperate with humans. Future developments may allow for detecting any, rather than only predefined, typical soccer-related poses and gestures.

References

1. Abreu, M., Reis, L.P., Lau, N.: Learning to run faster in a humanoid robot soccer environment through reinforcement learning. In: Chalup, S., Niemueller, T., Suthakorn, J., Williams, M.-A. (eds.) RoboCup 2019. LNCS (LNAI), vol. 11531, pp. 3–15. Springer, Cham (2019). https://doi.org/10.1007/978-3-030-35699-6_1
2. Almeida, L., Santos, F., Facchinetti, T., Pedreiras, P., Silva, V., Lopes, L.S.: Coordinating distributed autonomous agents with a real-time database: the CAMBADA project. In: Aykanat, C., Dayar, T., Körpeoğlu, İ (eds.) ISCIS 2004. LNCS, vol. 3280, pp. 876–886. Springer, Heidelberg (2004). https://doi.org/10.1007/978-3-540-30182-0_88

3. Andersen, R.S., Madsen, O., Moeslund, T.B., Amor, H.B.: Projecting robot intentions into human environments. In: 2016 25th IEEE International Symposium on Robot and Human Interactive Communication (RO-MAN), pp. 294–301 (2016). https://doi.org/10.1109/ROMAN.2016.7745145
4. Asali, E., Valipour, M., Zare, N., Afshar, A., Katebzadeh, M., Dastghaibyfard, G.: Using machine learning approaches to detect opponent formation. In: 2016 Artificial Intelligence and Robotics (IRANOPEN), pp. 140–144 (2016)
5. van der Burgh, M., et al.: Tech United Eindhoven @home 2020 team description paper (2020). https://www.techunited.nl/uploads/Tech_United_At_Home_TDP_2020.pdf
6. Cao, Z., Hidalgo, G., Simon, T., Wei, S.-E., Sheikh, Y.: OpenPose: Realtime multi-person 2D pose estimation using part affinity fields. IEEE Trans. Pattern Anal. Mach. Intell. **43**(1), 172–186 (2021). https://doi.org/10.1109/TPAMI.2019.2929257
7. Di Giambattista, V., Fawakherji, M., Suriani, V., Bloisi, D.D., Nardi, D.: On field gesture-based robot-to-robot communication with NAO soccer players. In: Chalup, S., Niemueller, T., Suthakorn, J., Williams, M.-A. (eds.) RoboCup 2019. LNCS (LNAI), vol. 11531, pp. 367–375. Springer, Cham (2019). https://doi.org/10.1007/978-3-030-35699-6_28
8. Eady, T.: Tesla's deep learning at scale: using billions of miles to train neural networks (2019). https://towardsdatascience.com/teslas-deep-learning-at-scale-7eed85b235d3. Accessed 21 Oct 2021
9. Kitano, H., Asada, M., Kuniyoshi, Y., Noda, I., Osawa, E.: RoboCup: the robot world cup initiative. In: Proceedings of the First International Conference on Autonomous Agents, AGENTS 1997, pp. 340–347. Association for Computing Machinery, New York (1997)
10. de Koning, L., Mendoza, J.P., Veloso, M., van de Molengraft, R.: Skills, tactics and plays for distributed multi-robot control in adversarial environments. In: Akiyama, H., Obst, O., Sammut, C., Tonidandel, F. (eds.) RoboCup 2017. LNCS (LNAI), vol. 11175, pp. 277–289. Springer, Cham (2018). https://doi.org/10.1007/978-3-030-00308-1_23
11. Lin, T.-Y., et al.: Microsoft COCO: common objects in context. In: Fleet, D., Pajdla, T., Schiele, B., Tuytelaars, T. (eds.) ECCV 2014. LNCS, vol. 8693, pp. 740–755. Springer, Cham (2014). https://doi.org/10.1007/978-3-319-10602-1_48
12. van Lith, P., van de Molengraft, M., Dubbelman, G., Plantinga, M.: A minimalistic approach to identify and localize robots in RoboCup MSL soccer competitions in real-time (2019). https://www.techunited.nl/uploads/Minimalist%20MSL%20Robot%20Location%205.0.pdf
13. Lopez Martinez, C., et al.: Tech United Eindhoven team description (2014)
14. Luo, S., Lu, H., Xiao, J., Yu, Q., Zheng, Z.: Robot detection and localization based on deep learning. In: 2017 Chinese Automation Congress, pp. 7091–7095 (2017). https://doi.org/10.1109/CAC.2017.8244056
15. Mazhar, O., Ramdani, S., Navarro, B., Passama, R., Cherubini, A.: Towards realtime physical human-robot interaction using skeleton information and hand gestures. In: 2018 IEEE/RSJ International Conference on Intelligent Robots and Systems (IROS), pp. 1–6 (2018). https://doi.org/10.1109/IROS.2018.8594385
16. Mizuchi, Y., Inamura, T.: Estimation of subjective evaluation of HRI performance based on objective behaviors of human and robots. In: Chalup, S., Niemueller, T., Suthakorn, J., Williams, M.-A. (eds.) RoboCup 2019. LNCS (LNAI), vol. 11531, pp. 201–212. Springer, Cham (2019). https://doi.org/10.1007/978-3-030-35699-6_16

17. MSL Technical Committee 1997–2021: Middle Size Robot League Rules and Regulations for 2021. https://msl.robocup.org/rules
18. Nakata, T., Sato, T., Mori, T.: Expression of emotion and intention by robot body movement (1998)
19. Redmon, J., Divvala, S., Girshick, R., Farhadi, A.: You only look once: unified, real-time object detection. In: Proceeding of CVPR, pp. 779–788. IEEE (2016). https://doi.org/10.1109/CVPR.2016.91
20. Redmon, J., Farhadi, A.: YOLO9000: better, faster, stronger. In: Proceedings of CVPR, pp. 7263–7271. IEEE (2017)
21. RoboCup Federation: RoboCup objective. https://www.robocup.org/objective. Accessed 21 Oct 2021
22. Schneider, P., Memmesheimer, R., Kramer, I., Paulus, D.: Gesture recognition in RGB videos using human body keypoints and dynamic time warping. In: Chalup, S., Niemueller, T., Suthakorn, J., Williams, M.-A. (eds.) RoboCup 2019. LNCS (LNAI), vol. 11531, pp. 281–293. Springer, Cham (2019). https://doi.org/10.1007/978-3-030-35699-6_22
23. Schwab, D., Zhu, Y., Veloso, M.: Learning skills for small size league RoboCup. In: Holz, D., Genter, K., Saad, M., von Stryk, O. (eds.) RoboCup 2018. LNCS (LNAI), vol. 11374, pp. 83–95. Springer, Cham (2019). https://doi.org/10.1007/978-3-030-27544-0_7
24. Trifan, A., Neves, A.J.R., Cunha, B., Azevedo, J.L.: UAVision: a modular time-constrained vision library for soccer robots. In: Bianchi, R.A.C., Akin, H.L., Ramamoorthy, S., Sugiura, K. (eds.) RoboCup 2014. LNCS (LNAI), vol. 8992, pp. 490–501. Springer, Cham (2015). https://doi.org/10.1007/978-3-319-18615-3_40
25. Vanholder, H.: Efficient inference with TensorRT (2016). https://on-demand.gputechconf.com/gtc-eu/2017/presentation/23425-han-vanholder-efficient-inference-with-tensorrt.pdf. Accessed 21 Oct 2021

Improving Dribbling, Passing, and Marking Actions in Soccer Simulation 2D Games Using Machine Learning

Nader Zare[1(✉)], Omid Amini[4], Aref Sayareh[5], Mahtab Sarvmaili[1], Arad Firouzkouhi[6], Stan Matwin[1,2], and Amilcar Soares[3]

[1] Institute for Big Data Analytics, Dalhousie University, Halifax, Canada
{nader.zare,mahtab.sarvmaili}@dal.ca, stan@cs.dal.ca
[2] Institute for Computer Science, Polish Academy of Sciences, Warsaw, Poland
[3] Memorial University of Newfoundland, St. John's, Canada
amilcarsj@mun.ca
[4] Qom University of Technology, Qom, Iran
[5] Shiraz University, Shiraz, Iran
[6] Amirkabir University of Technology, Tehran, Iran
arad.firouzkouhi@aut.ac.ir

Abstract. The RoboCup competition was started in 1997, and is known as the oldest RoboCup league. The RoboCup 2D Soccer Simulation League is a stochastic, partially observable soccer environment in which 24 autonomous agents play on two opposing teams. In this paper, we detail the main strategies and functionalities of CYRUS, the RoboCup 2021 2D Soccer Simulation League champions. The new functionalities presented and discussed in this work are (i) Multi Action Dribble, (ii) Pass Prediction and (iii) Marking Decision. The Multi Action Dribbling strategy enabled CYRUS to succeed more often and to be safer when dribbling actions were performed during a game. The Pass Prediction enhanced our gameplay by predicting our teammate's passing behavior, anticipating and making our agents collaborate better towards scoring goals. Finally, the Marking Decision addressed the multi-agent matching problem to improve CYRUS defensive strategy by finding an optimal solution to mark opponents' players.

Keywords: Feature engineering · RoboCup · Soccer marking · Multi-agent matching · Dribble · 2D soccer simulation

1 Introduction

The idea of robotic soccer games was proposed as a novel research topic in 1992. Since then, the RoboCup has been considered the annual international competition for developing new ideas in A.I. and robotics. This competition is comprised of various leagues such as Rescue, Soccer Simulation, and Standard Platform leagues. Team CYRUS has participated in the annual RoboCup competitions

© Springer Nature Switzerland AG 2022
R. Alami et al. (Eds.): RoboCup 2021, LNAI 13132, pp. 340–351, 2022.
https://doi.org/10.1007/978-3-030-98682-7_28

and placed first, second, third, fourth, and fifth in RoboCup 2021, 2018, 2019, 2017, 2014. In RoboCup 2021, Cyrus played 21 games in total, winning nineteen games, and drawing two times. CYRUS also won first place in the IranOpen in 2021, 2018, and 2014; first place in RoboCup Asia-Pacific 2018; and second place in the Japan Open 2020 competition.

The rest of this paper is organized as follows. In Sect. 2, we present a new dribbling system and opponent behavior prediction. Afterwards, we describe our new Pass Prediction module (Sect. 3) which is used to predict the action of a ball holder teammate. In Sect. 4, we detail the improvements of CYRUS' defensive strategy. Finally, we conclude our work and point to some directions for future works in Sect. 5.

1.1 Previous Works

Sixteen teams qualified for the 2D soccer simulation league in the 2021 RoboCup competition, including teams from Brazil, Canada, China, Germany, Iran, Japan, and Romania. In recent years, most of the teams have employed artificial intelligence algorithms to improve their game performance. For example, Helios has developed an algorithm called Player's MatchUp for exchanging players' positions [6]. FRA-UNIted has released a new 2D soccer simulation Python-based framework for performing reinforcement learning experiments [7]. ITAndroids optimized its field evaluator algorithm using Particle Swarm Optimization (PSO) and improved the goalkeeper performance for penalty kicks [8]. Persepolis proposed an evolutionary algorithm to improve their offensive strategy [9] and YuShan applied Half Field Offense framework to build overall portraits of a team [10]. CYRUS has concentrated its efforts on creating and applying machine learning techniques to improve its gameplay [2–5]. In general terms, the improvements made in CYRUS are on the defensive decision-making method using Reinforcement Learning (RL), the opponents' behavioral analysis and prediction, and players' shooting skills.

1.2 Release

In this subsection we list several of our contributions towards increasing the popularity and improvement of 2D Soccer Simulation league competition.

Cyrus 2014 Source. As a part of our contribution to the development of the 2D Soccer Simulation league, we have released the Cyrus 2014 [2] source code to encourage new teams to participate in the competitions. The source code can be found in github[1].

---

[1] Cyrus 2014 Source https://github.com/naderzare/cyrus2014.

CppDNN. The C++ Deep Neural Network (CppDNN) library was developed by CYRUS team members to facilitate the implementation of Deep Neural Networks in the 2D Soccer Simulation environment. This library stores the weights of a neural network trained using the Keras library. The developed script within CppDNN transforms the trained weights of a deep neural network into a plain text file that is subsequently loaded to recreate the original deep neural network in C++. In CYRUS, we use CppDNN to enhance our goalie performance, to predict opponent's movements against our dribbling agent, and to improve passing prediction between teammates. The library can be found in our github[2].

Pyrus - Python 2D Soccer Simulation Base. Most 2D soccer simulation teams exploit the Helios [1], Gliders2d [11], WrightEagle [12] or Oxsy [13] bases which are all developed in C++. Although those have shown fast processing and execution time, developing machine learning algorithms using C++ would be a time-consuming process. Due to the fast growth and popularity of the Python programming language among students and scientists and its plethora of libraries containing machine learning algorithms, the CYRUS team members have started developing an open-source python base for the 2D soccer simulation league. This base is currently available in the CYRUS github[3] and it will support all features of the current 2D soccer simulation server in the Full-State mode in the near future.

2   Multi-action Dribble

In soccer games, it is usual that the opponent's players tries to block the path of our ball holder, and a dribbling action can be helpful to escape from such situations. Dribbling also helps a player lead the ball forward and/or move it to a safer position. Besides, some teams employ heavy defensive strategies that make the ball's movement extremely challenging. Therefore, dribbling is an essential skill to tackle harsh defensive strategies, and at the same time, to find a good spot for passing or shooting.

Our team implemented an algorithm called Multi-Action Dribble (MAD) for improving our dribbling skills in SS2D games. MAD uses a Deep Neural Network (DNN) for predicting the opponents' movements so that the kickable player can find better positions to dribble. Before detailing MAD, we will first explain the agent 2D offensive algorithm known as *Chain Action* and the *Basic Dribble*. Once this background is given, we will detail how MAD works.

2.1   Chain Action Algorithm

The Chain Action algorithm [1] employs the Breadth First Search (BFS) to make decisions for a kickable player. First, the Chain Action algorithm creates

---

[2] CppDNN Source Code https://github.com/Cyrus2D/CppDNN.

[3] Pyrus Base Source Code https://github.com/Cyrus2D/Pyrus.

a decision tree with the root node of the game's current state. Afterwards, simulated actions (e.g., Shoot, Pass, Dribble, etc.) change the state of each node and create new children for this node. Then, a **Field Evaluator** analyzes every node in the tree by the ball's predicted position. Finally, the best node is the node which has the maximum value of the evaluation and the action that leads the current state to this state is selected.

2.2   Agent 2D Dribble Action Generator

In the Agent2D base [1], dribbling was developed in order to find a safe position for the kickable player to go without losing the ball or having an opponent intercept them. The Agent 2D Dribble Action Generator can only be evaluated on the game's current state (i.e., at the first level of the decision tree). To evaluate the dribbling action, this agent first simulates turning in different directions (-180 to $+180$ with steps of $30°$) and dashing in each direction in order to create candidates for each position. In addition, for each point that the simulated agent has reached, the ball's velocity is calculated based on the cycles needed to reach that position so the agent can kick it before starting to dribble. The cycles required for each candidate position is detailed in Eq. 1 and is equal to the sum of the number of turns and dashes plus one cycle for kicking the ball.

$$dribbleCycle = turnCycle + dashCycle + 1 \qquad (1)$$

Next, for each player's dribbling candidate position, the opponent's players are evaluated to determine if they can reach the position before the agent or intercept the ball in the middle of the dribbling action. If any of these two situations occur, the candidate action is removed; otherwise, a new predicted state is created where the kickable player and the ball are now in the new position. Finally, a list of dribbles and predicted states are returned to the chain action tree. Depending on the neck angle chosen by the agent, it might not have vision access to all of the field; therefore, the agent might not be able to see all opponents in every cycle. The number of cycles that an opponent has not seen is called their **pos-count**. The agent should consider the pos-count and the last position of the opponent and an area is created which will likely contain the opponent. Therefore, a significant number of available candidates may be removed (Fig. 1) since there's always uncertainty in some areas not seen by the agent.

2.3   MAD Generator

Our team created a new dribble generator that inserts a simple action such as Kick, Dash, and Turn before the start of dribbling actions. This generator makes a one-step action before the basic dribble generator, and its goal is to deceive the opponent to a wrong position so that the kickable agent may generate a better dribbling action. Therefore, the MAD generator only creates new child nodes from the current state (root of the tree). As previously mentioned, the basic dribble generator only runs in the first layer. If the action of a parent state

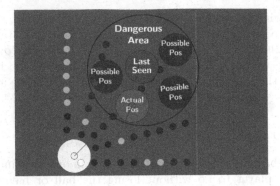

Fig. 1. Effecting pos-count on dribbling. Blue dots are possible candidates, red dots are candidates removed since they are impossible to be reach, and yellow dots are the possible candidates which are removed incorrectly because of the pos-count. (Color figure online)

is generated by MAD, the basic dribble generator runs in the second layers as well.

MAD generates three types of one-step action that are described below (Fig. 2):

- **Two-Step Kick:** the agent kicks the ball so that it remains within the kickable area of the agent to distract opponent's player. This action changes the ball position and velocity.
- **Move Before First Kick:** The agent moves around the ball where the ball stays in the kickable area of the agent. This action changes the position of the player and updates the ball's position according to its velocity.
- **Turn Before First Kick:** The agent turns towards a direction where it causes some previous basic dribble candidates to become available after turning. However, it is important that the ball remains in the kickable area of the agent in next cycle. This action changes the direction of the player's body and updates the ball's position according to its velocity.

2.4   Opponent Movement Prediction

The Chain Action algorithm should predict the result of previous actions in the tree to find possible actions in the next layers after the first one. A predictor module in the Chain Action algorithm is available and is called State Predictor. The State Predictor should forecast the position and velocity of every object in the field after each action, but the implemented predictor in the Agent 2D base simply updates the position and velocity of the ball and the receiver teammate. We added one cycle to the pos-count of opponents because the predictor was not forecasting the position of the closest opponents after MAD. Increasing the pos-count eliminates possible dribbling actions that might be considered difficult to perform. This problem led us to implement a position predictor module that

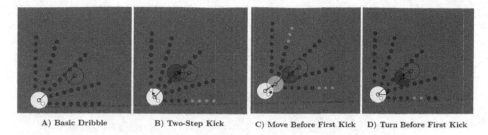

A) Basic Dribble   B) Two-Step Kick   C) Move Before First Kick   D) Turn Before First Kick

Fig. 2. Types of MAD and basic dribble, blue dots stands for possible actions generated by Basic Dribble, red dots show impossible dribbles, and orange dots demonstrate possible actions that have been added after using MAD. (Color figure online)

receives information about an opponent and the ball, and then forecasts the position of the opponent after one cycle using a Deep Neural Network.

We collected data for training our DNN model running games between Cyrus and other teams. Each cycle was collected when a CYRUS player was kickable, and at least one opponent was near the ball (i.e., within 10 m). The data set included the ball's position and the position of each opponent who was near the ball. All the positions are relative to the kickable agent's position and body direction. Next, we implemented a DNN using the position and velocity of the ball and the blocker, and the body direction of the blocker as input variables. The DNN architecture includes four hidden layers with 128, 64, 32, and 16 neurons, respectively. The output of this DNN is the opponent's predicted position, and its accuracy was ±0.01 m.

2.5   Results

We executed some early tests with MAD, and MAD with the DNN predictor and verified their efficiency as follows. First, we trained DNNs to predict the opponent's position by running 1000 games against YuShan and Persepolis. The results are shown in Table 1 where we present CYRUS's winning probability, without MAD and the DNN Predictor, with MAD but without the DNN Predictor, and with both when playing against Yushan and Persepolis. The results show that our winning rate against both teams increases when using both MAD and the DNN predictor when playing against both teams. One interesting result is that using MAD alone actually decreases our winning rate (we believe this is due to the use of the additional pos-count alone) against both teams. Once the DNN predictor is included, we see that the rate increases.

3   Pass Prediction

As in real soccer, passing behavior in a 2D Soccer Simulation (SS2D) game plays a critical role in increasing the chance of winning. A team with excellent passing skills prevents opponents from scoring, may create better chances of scoring

Table 1. Winning rate of CYRUS using MAD and DNN

Experiments	Yushan	Persepolis
CYRUS	77%	88%
CYRUS with MAD	76%	85%
CYRUS with MAD and DNN Predictor	80%	90%

themselves, and may conserve stamina. We believe that strengthening a team's passing decision-making algorithm will lead the team to have better performance and to win games. However, the random noises from the environment in the partial observation of the agents is a major challenge the players face while choosing their actions since it creates uncertainty on the best action to take in a given moment. Many approaches such as Monte Carlo or Kalman Filter were used in the past to address this problem, but in CYRUS we took a different route. In our work, we attempted to predict the action of the ball owner if our agent had pure observation data (i.e., no noise generated by the simulator). We used a full state action predictor from noisy observation that is detailed in [15] and features engineered in [16] to improve the prediction of the behavior of our ball owner player and are detailed below.

In [15], the full state action predictor from noisy observation is trained to receive noisy observations from the server and to forecast the action of a player if it gets an observation without noise. The soccer simulation server has another option known as *full-state mode* which does not apply the random partial noises observations to the agents' vision. When this option is enabled, the server also sends normal observation. We have also developed a module named *Data Extractor* to create training data to feed machine learning models in an SS2D game (more details are available in [15] and [16]). In summary, this module collects the events of the game and transforms these events into training data for machine learning models.

3.1   Experimental Setup

For the purposes of evaluating passing actions we used the data extractor module as follows. The data extractor module generates a new data instance for each cycle that one of our agents is the ball holder and the selected action is a pass. For the early results showed in [15], we generated 794 features from these observations, but for playing in the Robocup 2021, we used the features presented in [16]. In [16], each data instance contains 12 features for the ball, 42 for each one of our players (42×11), and 24 for each of the opponent's players (24×11), totaling 738 features. The list of extracted features is divided into nine feature subgroups that are measured for the ball, our players, or the opponents' players. These nine groups are Position, Kicker, Velocity, Body, Team, Player Type, Top k high-risk opponents, Top k nearest opponents, and Goal. Since at each time step, the ball holder is responsible for generating a data instance, the module creates all of these features for all agents in the field.

We used two labels for each data instance from the sorting module proposed in [16] which are the Index Number and Uniform Number (Unum). The Uniform Number is the unique number of a target agent (who may receive the ball) in the game. Differently from Unum, the Index Number refers to the index of a target agent in the sorted data. The sorting module is an essential component in the data preparation step since it organizes the input features and creates the training data set for our machine learning model. We have also used the *Kicker be First* field which is a binary attribute that pushes the features of the ball holder as the first element of data [16]. After sorting the data, this field assigns a label to them that is based on the index of ball receiver. Therefore, applying two sorting methods and changing the *Kicker be First* attribute (i.e., true or false), we generated four different experiments with a different order of the input data.

3.2   Result

Differently from what was presented in [16], where we showed the effects of the 738 features when forecasting the player's pass action using Agent2D as the base team, we show in this paper the results of using CYRUS as our base team. In Table 2, we compared the features used in [15] and the features used in [16] with (Noisy) and without (Pure) the presence of noise when running matches. We ran over 1000 games for collecting data and testing our methods using CYRUS as the base team and the results are presented in Table 2. When using the data without noise, we see that the features presented in [16] when combined with the proposed strategies produces pass prediction accuracy rates ranging from 76.23 to 80.51. Although these results are very promising, this setup using data without noise is not the one used in the Robocup competitions. Therefore, we tested the differences between the features shown in [15] and [16] using the proposed strategies when noise was present. The results in Table 2 shows that the 738 features of [16] produces generally better accuracy values (e.g., a difference ranging around 8% to 10%) when compared to the 794 features of [15].

Table 2. Accuracy of the two models for six datasets and three feature groups

Strategies		Features		
Sorting	Kicker be first	Features [16] pure	Features [15] noisy	Features [16] noisy
Uniform	False	80.51	57.90	67.86
Uniform	True	79.60	58.74	67.63
X-Sorting	False	76.23	53.64	63.86
X-Sorting	True	77.48	57.60	65.13

4   Improved Marking Decision

In a soccer game, marking is a defensive strategy that helps to prevent an opposing team member from taking control of the ball. Several marking strategies exist
in soccer such as *man-marking* and *zonal-marking*. In the man-marking strategy,
defenders have to mark a specific opponent player, and zonal-marking is a defensive strategy where defenders have to cover an area of the field [14]. Defining a
marking strategy is one of the most challenging actions in defensive algorithms
for soccer 2D games. The challenge is mainly to be able to synchronize the
agents' decisions, despite different and noisy partial observational views.

In this section we will first discuss some marking strategy algorithms that
are based on greedy strategies. Then we will explain how the CYRUS team
strives to minimize the effects of the challenges imposed by greedy strategies by
using strategies called *"Optimized multi-agent matching" (OMAM)* and
Player Grouping method.

4.1   Marking Algorithms

Proximity-Based Marking. Using Proximity-Based Marking, each player
simply selects their nearest opponent to mark. This algorithm is one of the
most rudimentary solutions and has several problems. For example, it is common when using this strategy that more than one player decides to mark a single
opponent, and as a consequence, several opponents are left unmarked.

Danger-Based Marking. A solution to solve the main problem of *Proximity-
Based Marking* which we explored was to rank opponents based on how dangerous they are using various attributes such as distance to our goal and distance
to the ball. After sorting them, we assign the closest player who is not marking
anyone to the most dangerous players. More specifically, the first most dangerous
opponent is marked by the closest teammate, and the second opponent is marked
by the closest teammate, which is not marking the most dangerous opponent, and
so on. This algorithm, while theoretically may avoid multiple players marking
a single opponent fails when each player is computing the dangerous opponents
and distances separately and each player has different and noisy observational
views of the game. An example is shown in Fig. 3, where the greediness of this
algorithm stops it from reaching a solution that is good for the team as a whole.

The Hungarian Method. To find an optimal solution and eradicate the issues
found with acting in a greedy manner such as the one presented in Fig. 3, each
agent must also consider the difficulty of other agents marking each opponent.
The Hungarian Matching algorithm receives as input the number of agents, tasks
which must be completed, and the cost for each agent to do each task as input.
After, it assigns exactly one agent to each task, in a way that minimizes the
total cost of completing all of the tasks.

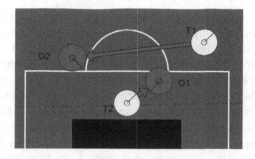

Fig. 3. Improper defense strategy, leaving the leftmost player empty for a longer time, while T1 should mark O1 and T2 should mark O2 for an optimal solution.

We used this method in the 2D soccer simulation league by assigning the distance between agents and their opponents as their costs. The result is the minimal total movement of the team towards covering all of the opponents. However, this method does not improve the synchronization problem that arises from our agents having different observations. In fact, the problem is worsened as our solutions become more dependant on observation and require more information about other players' positions. As there are 10 factorial ways that an entire team can mark their opponents (not including goalkeepers), even a little noise can disrupt the synchronization of the agents. This results in our agents calculating different solutions, which would lead to two or more agents marking a single opponent and leaving some opponents unmarked. The number of agents and the number of opponents that need to be covered are not always the same, as the opposing defense does not need to be covered. Also, our offensive players should not mark any players to be ready for a counter-attack and to avoid wasting stamina.

In summary, using Hungarian method has the following problems: (1) the number of tasks and agents should be equal; (2) the method does not consider the importance of each task; and (3) is very susceptible to observational noise, as the number of candidate solutions is high.

Optimized Multi-Agent Matching (OMAM). The new method we used in Robocup 2021 aims to avoid the first and second problems of the *Hungarian Method* by combining ideas from Danger-Based Marking and Multi-Agent Matching. This method handles synchronization by decreasing the total possible candidate solutions that are considered using K-top tasks.

This algorithm contains multiple steps to find the best solution for assigning agents' tasks. In OMAM, a solution is a collection which includes pairs of agents and tasks to be performed. The number of pairs are less than or equal to the minimum number of tasks or agents. To compare two solutions, we assign two values to each solution. The first value is the summation of the pairs' cost in the solution. To calculate the second value, we sort the tasks by using their importance value, then we generate a string containing 0 and 1 (i.e., if a task has been assigned in the solution we add 1 for the task, otherwise we add 0). A solution A is better than B if its second value is greater than B's. If their second values are the same, the solution with a lower first value is taken. To decrease time complexity to find the best solution, we keep pairs in the best k-tasks for each agent. In CYRUS, the value of k is set to be three, meaning we remove all tasks except the best three ones for each agent. Any solution A with an opponent with a higher value marked will have a higher second score than any other solution such as B. We first process solutions that have the more dangerous opponents covered since it will have a higher second value when compared with any other solutions that only have less dangerous opponents. We use this idea to optimize the time complexity of this algorithm since we do not need to search for any other candidate with a lower score. Keeping k-tasks helps our players to improve the synchronization of the agents and time complexity. To further decrease the number of solutions, we separated our players into three groups: Back, Middle, and Forward players. We also divided opponents players into two groups: Attacker and Normal. In the CYRUS defense algorithm, first, our Back players mark the opponent's Attackers. Then our Middle players mark unmarked Attackers' opponents. Finally, our free players, including Middle and Forwards except for Back players, try to mark other unmarked opponent's players. Therefore, the number of solutions decreases to 6 factorial.

4.2 Results

The effectiveness of OMAM can be seen comparing the average goals our team has conceded in the main round over 28 games in 2019 and 2021. OMAM has improved the Cyrus defense strategy from an average of 0.9 goals taken in main round in 2019 competition to 0.33 in 2021. We do believe that the opponents' offenses have improved as well within these 3 years so the results are interpreted as even better from our perspective.

5 Conclusion

In this paper we detailed the major algorithms and innovations of our team CYRUS that we believe led us to become the RoboCup 2021 champions in the Soccer Simulation League 2D. In the past two years, and in in-between competitions, we improved many algorithms in CYRUS and saw drastic improvements in our positions in competitions. In the future, we will release the first official version of PYRUS 2D base which is written in Python 3 and open several venues to apply machine learning techniques in Soccer Simulation League 2D.

References

1. Akiyama, H., Nakashima, T.: Helios base: an open source package for the RoboCup soccer 2D simulation. In: Behnke, S., Veloso, M., Visser, A., Xiong, R. (eds.) RoboCup 2013. LNCS (LNAI), vol. 8371, pp. 528–535. Springer, Heidelberg (2014). https://doi.org/10.1007/978-3-662-44468-9_46

2. Khayami, R., et al.: CYRUS 2D simulation team description paper 2014. In: RoboCup 2014 Symposium and Competitions: Team Description Papers 2014. Joao Pessoa, Brazil (2014)
3. Zare, N., et al.: CYRUS 2D simulation team description paper 2015. In: The 19th Annual RoboCup International Symposium. China, Hefei (2015)
4. Zare, N., et al.: Cyrus 2D simulation team description paper 2018. In: RoboCup 2018 Symposium and Competitions. Montreal, Canada (2018)
5. Zare, N., et al.: Cyrus 2D simulation 2019. In: RoboCup 2019 Symposium and Competitions. Sydney, Australia (2019)
6. Yamaguchi, M., Kuga, R., Omori, H., Fukushima, T., Nakashima, T., Akiyama, H.: Helios 2021: team description paper. In: RoboCup 2021 Symposium and Competitions, Worldwide (2021)
7. Gabel, G., Kloppner, Pr., Eren, Y., Sommer, F., Breuer, S., Godehardt, E.: FRA-UNIted-team description 2021. In: RoboCup 2021 Symposium and Competitions, Worldwide (2021)
8. Fidalgo, D.T.M., et al.: ITAndroids 2D Soccer simulation team description paper 2021. In: RoboCup 2021 Symposium and Competitions, Worldwide (2021)
9. Noohpisheh, M., Shekarriz, M., Zaremehrjardi, F., Khademi Ardekani F, Khorsand, S.A.: Persepolis soccer 2D simulation team description paper 2021. In: RoboCup 2021 Symposium and Competitions, Worldwide (2021)
10. Cheng, Z., Zhang, F., Guang, B., Wang. L.: YuShan2021 team description paper for RoboCup 2021. In: RoboCup 2021 Symposium and Competitions, Worldwide (2021)
11. Prokopenko, M., Wang, P.: Gliders2d: source code base for RoboCup 2D soccer simulation league. In: Chalup, S., Niemueller, T., Suthakorn, J., Williams, M.-A. (eds.) RoboCup 2019. LNCS (LNAI), vol. 11531, pp. 418–428. Springer, Cham (2019). https://doi.org/10.1007/978-3-030-35699-6_33
12. Bai, A., Lu, G., Zhang, H., Chen, X.: WrightEagle 2D soccer simulation team description 2011. In: RoboCup 2011 Symposium and Competitions: Team Description Papers, Istanbul, Turkey, July 2011
13. Marian, S., Luca, D., Sarac, B., Cotarlea, O.: OXSY 2014 team description. In: RoboCup 2016 Symposium and Competitions: Team Description Papers, Leipzig, Germany, July 2016
14. Catlin, M.G.: The Art of Soccer: A Better Way to Play. Soccer Books, St. Paul (1990)
15. Zare, N., Sayareh, A., Sarvmaili, M., Amini, O., Soares, A., Matwin, S.: CYRUS 2D soccer simulation team description paper 2021. In: RoboCup 2021 Symposium and Competitions, Worldwide (2021)
16. Zare, N., Sayareh, A., Sarvmaili, M., Amini, O., Matwin, S., Soares, A.: Engineering features to improve pass prediction in 2D soccer simulation games. In: Alami, R., et al. (eds.) RoboCup 2021. LNAI, vol. 13132, pp. 140–152. Springer, Cham (2022). https://doi.org/10.1007/978-3-030-98682-7_12

Humanoid Adult Size Champion 2021
Sweaty

Klaus Dorer[✉], Maximilian Giessler, Ulrich Hochberg, Manuel Scharffenberg,
Rico Schillings, and Fabian Schnekenburger

University of Applied Science Offenburg, Offenburg, Germany
{klaus.dorer,maximilian.giessler}@hs-offenburg.de

Abstract. Due to the Covid-19 pandemic, the RoboCup WorldCup 2021 was held completely remotely. For this competition the Webots simulator (https://cyberbotics.com/) was used, so all teams needed to transfer their robot to the simulation. This paper describes our experiences during this process as well as a genetic learning approach to improve our walk engine to allow a more stable and faster movement in the simulation. Therefore we used a docker setup to scale easily. The resulting movement was one of the outstanding features that finally led to the championship title.

Keywords: CMA-ES · Docker · Webots · ROS2

1 Introduction

Due to the Covid-19 pandemic, in early 2021 the decision was taken to run the annual RoboCup competition as a worldwide virtual competition. The technical committee took the decision to partner with Cyberbotics in order to provide a platform (Webots) for a simulated humanoid robot challenge. Tremendous effort was spent to define and implement a specific communication protocol for such a competition as well as an automated referee. Also, the existing Webots simulation has been extended to provide support for joints with backlash and for the special turf. Despite the very narrow timeframe for this, this goal has been achieved an virtual competitions could be run.

Teams were asked to transform their real robots into simulated Webots robot models. In the end, three teams of humanoid adult size league accepted this challenge and successfully qualified for the 2021 RoboCup Worldwide.

2 Sweaty

Sweaty is a 1.70 m tall humanoid robot that first participated in RoboCup 2014 in Brazil. 2019, Sweaty achieved the title of a vice-world champion in the humanoid adult size league. One of the major tasks for 2021 has been to make the robot available in the Webots simulation.

© Springer Nature Switzerland AG 2022
R. Alami et al. (Eds.): RoboCup 2021, LNAI 13132, pp. 352–359, 2022.
https://doi.org/10.1007/978-3-030-98682-7_29

2.1 Robot Model

Sweaty is special in that it uses linear actuation in its legs [3]. So the motors are not sitting in the rotation axes of the joint, but indirectly drive the joints. Apart from other advantages, this provides a considerably lower backlash compared to having e.g. Dynamixel servos sitting in the joint. This is because the force of the robot weight pushes on the mechanical joints.

In a first attempt, this design was transferred into simulation. However, the simulation speed dropped to unacceptable cycle times with only one robot of this kind on the field. Therefore, the technical committee decide to allow to replace the linear actuated motors with servo motors that have a comparable backlash as the linear motors had. This rendered the motor mapper component in our software not needed in the simulated version of Sweaty (see Sect. 2.2). An image of the simulated and the real Sweaty is shown in Fig. 1.

Fig. 1. Real Sweaty (left) and simulated (right).

2.2   Software Architecture

Sweaty uses ROS2 as its software architecture. Figure 2 shows the components. Similar to the previous design, all hardware components are incorporated into the ROS2 ecosystem via their corresponding drivers.

For the simulation, all hardware related nodes like imu/camera/motor joints and force sensors were replaced by an additional Webots-controller-node. We just had to make some minor changes in our walk engine to get the robot moving inside Webots, e.g. handle the divergent update rate from asynchronous hardware sensors to the simulation step size.

For decision making, our software uses an adapted version of our 3d soccer simulation team Magma as has been done in previous years. To perform the communication between our ROS2 ecosystem and the decision component written in java, a ROS bridge was used. This has been the only major change compared to the ROS1 setup used in previous years.

2.3   Vision

Our vision [4], used for the object detection and localization on the real robot, was already able to also detect landmarks and the ball from the rendered camera images of the Webots simulator. To improve the accuracy, we trained our model with the rendered images. Therefore, we have developed a tool for auto-labeling. It moves the camera randomly around the soccer field and extracts the landmark/object position from Webots to label the images automatically. This allowed us to generate 200–300 labeled images per minute on a single Webots instance to retrain our vision model. We used roughly 6000 such images to get a result good enough to localize and play well, but more would have been no problem to generate.

3   Learning

A major building block for our success has been a successful improvement of our walking gait by the use of genetic optimization. It is noteworthy that the gait of our real robot worked with very minor manual changes immediately in the Webots simulation at a speed of about 0.2 m/s. With the availability of having the robot in a simulation, we used the strength of simulations to allow for machine learning.

3.1   Algorithms

Based on our experiences in the RoboCup 3D simulation league [1], we already had a existing solution for the genetic algorithm CMA-ES [2]. CMA-ES is especially powerful when there is already a working solution to start with as it was the case here. Our implementation is based on the commons math implementation[1] but has been extended twofold: first, it allows to calculate the fitness of

---

[1] https://commons.apache.org/proper/commons-math/.

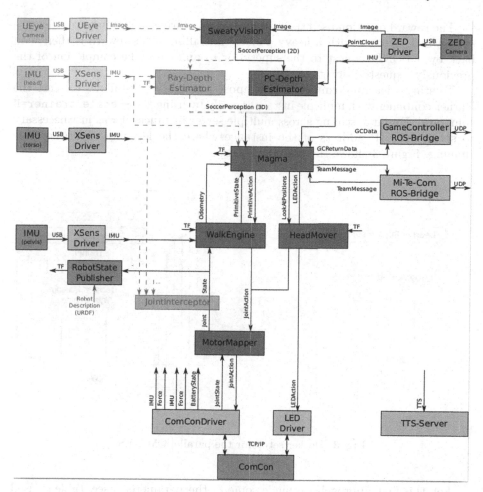

Fig. 2. Nodes and exchanged messages in ROS2.

each individual of a generation in parallel. Second, it allows to run oversampling runs of the same individual in parallel.

The learning architecture uses two separate docker containers in order to spread learning on multiple computers of the university. For the communication between those containers a REST API was implemented. The first container is the learning supervisor and runs the parallel CMA-ES algorithm and provides a ticket system by using the REST API. The other container includes a Webots simulator instance as also our robot specific code. This container then is able to send a GET request for a new ticket to the supervisor. The supervisor then responds with a new parameter set, generated from the CMA-ES. With this new parameter set, the walk engine of the robot is initialized and starts an attempt with those generated values. We specified a fixed duration Δ t to ensure each attempt was executed with the same conditions.

The reward function used the walked distance during the attempt to calculate the reward together with a heavy penalty for falling. This reward is then send back by a POST request to the supervisor to announce the completion of the previously requested ticket.

To start a learning run, docker compose was used. This allows to start the learner container with multiple instances easily by using the `--scale trainer=N` command. For large scaling across multiple server instances it was just necessary to specify the IP address of the instance where the learning supervisor was running. Figure 3 shows the described setup.

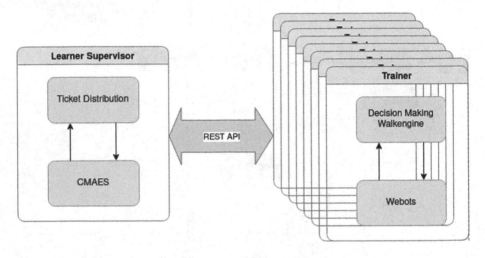

Fig. 3. Docker setup for the parallel CMA-ES

For this first approach we made some of the parameters (see Table 1) used by the walk engine injectable to let CMA-ES optimize them. These parameters were stored in an external file to allow a quick exchange. In a further approach we attached a stability criteria to evaluate the performance of the gait. Therefor we integrated a calculation for the Imaginary Zero-Moment Point (IZMP) [6] and the support polygon. The support polygon is calculated using the geometry, the orientation of the feet and force-/torque-sensors mounted in both feet. We used the force in z-direction and the 3D pose to detect the contact state of the robot. To quantify the stability of the gait cycle we also introduced an algorithm, which evaluates on the one hand if the IZMP coordinates are located within the support polygon. On the other hand it evaluates the distance from the IZMP to each side of the support polygon. The integration into the reward function was realized through penalty for each cycle the IZMP was not located in a desired region of the support polygon.

Table 1. Used walk parameters to learn by CMA-ES.

Name	Description
max-step-size-turn	Maximal stepsize while turning around
max-step-size-x (y)	Maximal stepsize while moving on one axis direction
omni-dir-walk-dis	Maximal destination distance to use omnidirectional walk
rate	Update rate
control.hip (.pitch/.foot)	P/I/D values to control specific joints

3.2 Results

The learning runs were distributed on an increasing number of computers at our university with a peak of 500 docker containers running in parallel. Typical setups have been to use 50 individuals in a population and perform 30 oversampling runs for each individual to average out noise in each try.

Figure 4 shows the improvements over such a learning run. Typically, already the best individual of the first generation outperformed the manual solution used as a starting point. The best fitness of about 8.5 achieved in generation 81 translates into a speed of roughly 0.43 m/s. The speed of the walk gait doubled, while also the stability of the walk was improved by learning.

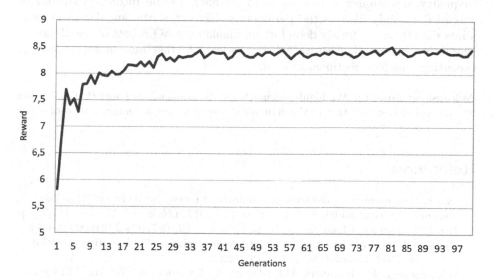

Fig. 4. Fitness of the best individual over the generations.

4 Conclusion

The required transfer of our real robot into the simulation was a profitable challenge. The competition was our first extensive use of ROS2, which runs very stable. The described approach for genetic optimization was also working very well an within a short timeframe of development. By using docker we can easily scale through available servers and take advantage of the resulting acceleration. The learned parameters already show a more stable movement and its speed could be increased by a factor of two.

Sweaty won the final game of the adult size competition 21:0. The overall number of goals was subject to an undesired behavior of the automated referee to extend the game for each goal scored. But the result shows that the Sweaty team succeeded best in transferring the work on the real robots into the Webots simulation. We attribute this to two main factors: first, our team has been the only team that finally had an overall technical system that was running stable enough throughout a game to keep two players on the field up and walking. This is mainly a matter of excellent programming skills in the tight schedule of the league. Second, machine learning turned out to improve the game play considerably. More important than the duplication of our walking speed - in humanoid adult size league, where robots are typically not able to get up after falling - has been the higher stability of the gait learned.

For the future we will try to transfer the learned parameters back to the real sweaty to observe if we also can use CMA-ES to optimize the behavior of our real robot. Furthermore we want to increase the parameter space to learn more parameters. At this time, only high level parameters like step length, step frequency and similar were subject to learning. In the future, this could be extended possibly also to the parameters that define the angular motions of joints directly as is already done for our simulated NAO robots of the 3D soccer simulation league [1]. Also we will try to learn further motion sequences, e.g. executing a multi-directional kick [5].

Acknowledgements. We highly acknowledge the tremendous effort that was taken by the technical committee of the humanoid league to get a competition running in the Webots simulator.

References

1. Dorer, K.: Learning to use toes in a humanoid robot. In: Akiyama, H., Obst, O., Sammut, C., Tonidandel, F. (eds.) RoboCup 2017. LNCS (LNAI), vol. 11175, pp. 168–179. Springer, Cham (2018). https://doi.org/10.1007/978-3-030-00308-1_14
2. Hansen, N., Ostermeier, A.: Completely derandomized self-adaptation in evolution strategies. Evol. Comput. **9**(2), 159–195 (2001)
3. Scharffenberg, M., Hochberg, U.E., Dorer, K., Friedrich, A., Wülker, M.: Improving torque and speed of joints by using rod-and-lever systems for electrically driven humanoid robots. In: 10th Workshop on Humanoid Soccer Robots, IEEE-RAS International Conference on Humanoid Robots (2015)
4. Schnekenburger, F., Scharffenberg, M., Wülker, M., Hochberg, U., Dorer, K.: Detection and localization of features on a soccer field with feedforward fully convolutional neural networks (FCNN) for the adult-size humanoid robot sweaty. In: Proceedings of the 12th Workshop on Humanoid Soccer Robots, 17th IEEE-RAS International

Conference on Humanoid Robots. IEEE, Birmingham (2017). https://nbn-resolving. org/urn:nbn:de:bsz:ofb1-opus4-26557

5. Spitznagel, M., Weiler, D., Dorer, K.: Deep reinforcement multi-directional kick-learning of a simulated robot with toes. In: 2021 IEEE International Conference on Autonomous Robot Systems and Competitions (ICARSC), pp. 104–110 (2021). https://doi.org/10.1109/ICARSC52212.2021.9429811

6. Vukobratovic, M., Borovac, B., Šurdilović, D.: Zero-moment point - proper interpretation and new applications. In: IEEE-RAS International Conference on Humanodi Robots, pp. 237–244. IEEE (2001)

Author Index

Printed in the United States
by Baker & Taylor Publisher Services

Printed in the United States
by Baker & Taylor Publisher Services